THE MAN WHO PUNCHED JEFFERSON DAVIS

SOUTHERN BIOGRAPHY

Andrew Burstein, Series Editor

THE MAN WHO  PUNCHED JEFFERSON DAVIS

THE Political Life OF Henry S. Foote, Southern Unionist

BEN WYNNE

LOUISIANA STATE UNIVERSITY PRESS

BATON ROUGE

Published with the assistance of the V. Ray Cardozier Fund

Published by Louisiana State University Press
Copyright © 2018 by Louisiana State University Press
All rights reserved
Manufactured in the United States of America
First printing

DESIGNER: Michelle A. Neustrom
TYPEFACE: Adobe Caslon Pro
PRINTER AND BINDER: Sheridan Books, Inc.

LIBRARY OF CONGRESS CATALOGING-IN-PUBLICATION DATA
Names: Wynne, Ben, 1961– author.
Title: The man who punched Jefferson Davis : the political life of
    Henry S. Foote, Southern Unionist / Ben Wynne.
Description: Baton Rouge : Louisiana State University Press, [2018] |
    Series: Southern biography | Includes bibliographical references and
    index.
Identifiers: LCCN 2018008653| ISBN 9780807169339 (cloth : alk. paper) |
    ISBN 9780807170144 (pdf) | ISBN 9780807169346 (epub)
Subjects: LCSH: Foote, Henry S. (Henry Stuart), 1804–1880. | Statesmen
    —United States—19th century—Biography. | Legislators—United
    States—Biography. | Unionists (United States Civil War)—
    Mississippi—Biography.
Classification: LCC E415.9.F7 W96 2018 | DDC 328.73/092 [B] —dc23
LC record available at https://lccn.loc.gov/2018008653

To Cotton

CONTENTS

Illustrations follow page 116

⤮⤮⤮ ACKNOWLEDGMENTS ⤮⤮⤮

I COULD NOT HAVE PRODUCED THIS WORK without the assistance of many people. As always, MaryKatherine Callaway, Rand Dotson, and the staff at LSU Press have been extremely helpful and easy to work with and I owe them a great debt. I would also like to thank Andrew Burstein, the Charles P. Manship Professor of History at LSU, whose early enthusiasm for this project is greatly appreciated, and Todd Manza, whose editing skills greatly improved the manuscript. The research for this book could not have been completed without the assistance of the staffs from a number of archives and libraries, including the Mississippi Department of Archives and History; the J. D. Williams Library at the University of Mississippi; the Tennessee State Library and Archives; the Alabama Department of Archives and History; Vanderbilt University Library, Special Collections; the Georgia Department of Archives and History; the Southern Historical Collection at the University of North Carolina; the California State Archives; the Robert W. Woodruff Library at Emory University; the Odum Library at Valdosta State University; the Illinois Historical Society; the John Harrison Hosch Library at the University of North Georgia; the Briscoe Center for American History at the University of Texas; the Beinecke Rare Book and Manuscript Library at Yale University; the Library of Congress and National Archives in Washington, DC; Mitchell Memorial Library at Mississippi State University; the Cook Library at the University of Southern Mississippi; the Millsaps-Wilson Library at Millsaps College; the Delta State University Library; the Eudora Welty Library in Jackson, Mississippi; and the Old Capital Museum in Jackson, Mississippi.

A number of former professors and colleagues from several institutions have, through the years, allowed me to benefit from their counsel and example, and I would like to offer them my thanks as well. They include Charles Sallis at

Millsaps College; Ron Howard and Kirk Ford at Mississippi College; Robert Haws, David Sansing, Ted Ownby, Nancy Bercaw, Charles Reagan Wilson, Sheila Skemp, Michael Namorato, and Charles Eagles at the University of Mississippi; James C. Cobb at the University of Georgia; and W. Scott Poole at the College of Charleston. I would also like to take this opportunity to acknowledge every teacher that I had at Saint Andrew's Episcopal School in Jackson, Mississippi, from the first grade, in 1967, through my senior year, in 1979. They laid the foundation for my life at what I believe is one of the best schools in the entire nation.

I am fortunate to work at the University of North Georgia in Gainesville, Georgia, where the administration at every level is very supportive of my teaching and publishing pursuits. Along with many other members of our university community, I have benefitted from the generosity of our president, Bonita Jacobs, who is always quick to provide encouragement and resources for all types of scholarly activity. I also owe a great debt of gratitude to Chris Jespersen, dean of the College of Arts and Letters; Ric Kabat and Tim May, associate deans of the College of Arts and Letters; and Jeff Pardue, department head for the History, Anthropology, and Philosophy department, all of whom have provided me with great support. I would also like to recognize my colleagues in the History, Anthropology, and Philosophy department who have, throughout my entire tenure at the university, fostered a warm and collegial work atmosphere conducive to academic ventures of all kinds.

On a good many occasions I discussed this project with friends Lee Cheek, dean of the School of Social Sciences at East Georgia State College, and Johnny Greer of Oxford, Mississippi, who is one of my key sources for northeast Mississippi history and lore. I appreciate their input and their good humor. Friends Brant Helvenston, John Leggett, Marty Lester, and Alan Vestal were also instrumental in helping me get this project off the ground. Last but certainly not least, nothing I do is possible without the support, love, and comfort of my family, Carly Wynne, Lily Wynne, Cotton Wynne, Patricia Wynne, and Noelle Wynne. Cotton, as you are the newest member of the family, I dedicate this book to you.

THE MAN WHO PUNCHED JEFFERSON DAVIS

Introduction

Henry Stuart Foote is an interesting man. He was sort of a renegade.
. . . He was a fiery man, something of a blowhard I think,
and a mortal enemy of Jefferson Davis.
—Shelby Foote

ON CHRISTMAS MORNING 1847, six very important men assembled in one of the public rooms of a large boarding house in Washington, DC, ostensibly for casual, after-breakfast conversation. In the parlance of the era, it was a "mixed" group of four southerners and two northerners. Two of the men were United States senators, the other four were members of the House of Representatives, and because of the climate of the times, they all had much to discuss. The end of the Mexican War was close at hand and the future of slavery in vast western territories hung in the balance. As they sat and talked, the men haphazardly raised a number of sectional issues, including the merits of popular sovereignty and the extension of the Missouri Compromise Line to the Pacific Ocean as potential remedies for the slavery "problem."

Though the holiday atmosphere lent itself to informality, their political banter grew heated. Within minutes, two of the men came to physical blows, their colleagues finally pulling them apart as they rolled around on the floor like a pair of angry schoolboys. Despite the topics under discussion, sectionalism had little to do with the encounter. The fight was merely the physical manifestation of an already strained relationship between two politicians who should have had much in common. The combatants were Mississippi's Democratic senators Henry Stuart Foote and Jefferson Davis. Foote resented Davis for his natural aloofness, while the future president of the Confederacy bristled at the venomous personal jibes that more often than not punctuated his fellow Mississippian's political rhetoric. For Davis, the encounter was a rare loss of self-control, a brief but intense drop of his guard. In short, it was a rare, emotional display of barbarism from a man who was accustomed to public formality. For Foote, the fight was business as usual.[1]

Henry Stuart Foote was one of American history's great political contrarians. He loved to fight, be it with words, fists, or dueling pistols. His ego was as vast and turbulent as the open sea, and he always seemed firm in the belief that he was the smartest person in any room that he occupied. Foote was blustery and rash but supremely articulate, with a highly focused intelligence and dry wit that could, in an instant, arouse laughter in his friends or enrage his enemies. He started his professional career as a successful lawyer and newspaper publisher before making a seamless transition into politics. As a United States senator before the Civil War, he deferred to no one unless it suited his needs, and he seemed to take perverse pleasure in provoking his opponents to blind rage. Later, as a Confederate congressman, he never missed an opportunity to criticize the Confederate government or to publicly insult his archnemesis, Confederate president Jefferson Davis. One contemporary noted that Foote was a charming conversationalist but, as a public speaker, "had great powers of satire and ridicule."[2] Part of Foote's popularity with voters stemmed from the fact that, to the masses, an address by Henry Foote was usually an object of great curiosity that could suddenly deteriorate into a shouting match or fistfight, depending on the circumstance. On the stump he was relentless, unpredictable, rude, and very effective, and his enemies hated him accordingly. Although a quick and clever man in every sense, he once joked with a friend that "ignorance and impudence will succeed far better than intellect and modesty."[3]

Probably no man relished the times in which he lived more than Henry Foote. He came of age and honed his political skills during the first half of the nineteenth century as the sectional crisis that would lead to civil war began and escalated. "Foote was," a friend once wrote, "the personal embodiment of the period that embraced the origin, the progress, and the close of the most thrilling drama of modern years."[4] He was an eyewitness to the monumental national events of his era as the United States simultaneously expanded west and, for four years, split in two and made war on itself, and he opined on everything.

Chaos and conflict seemed to empower him, and he could not let an issue, large or small, pass by without commenting on it at length. He wrote, debated, carried out speaking tours, and pontificated in general at a furious pace, apparently believing in all instances that his was the one and only view that mattered, regardless of the subject. Not long after the end of the Texas Revolution, when the annexation of Texas became a key national issue, he traveled to the Lone Star Republic and took it upon himself to produce a massive history of the region, published in 1841.

After moving to Mississippi from Alabama, where he had been disbarred for dueling, Foote's tenacity led to his election as a United States senator, and it was on the floor of the Senate between 1847 and 1850 that he made some of his most memorable and controversial speeches. In a body filled with ferocious egos, Foote was right at home, and he never backed down from a fight, whether he was in the right or in the wrong. He made friends in Washington, but the harsh, sarcastic rhetoric that often was his weapon of choice in a debate also burned many bridges.

In 1851, he left the Senate and defeated Jefferson Davis in an election for governor of Mississippi, running as a pro-Union candidate in a state where secession was already being talked about as a solution to the slavery issue. Later in the decade, as sectional tension increased, Foote left Mississippi and moved to California, staying there long enough to influence politics in the Golden State and to get his children married into some of the country's most prominent western families. On the eve of the Civil War, Foote moved back East, to Tennessee, and eventually won election to the Confederate Congress, where he remained a thorn in the side of the Davis administration.

Later, as the Confederacy was crumbling, Foote launched a wild scheme that took him from the South to Washington, DC, where he tried on his own to broker an unauthorized peace settlement with the Lincoln government. Given the choice by Federal authorities to return to the Confederacy or to leave the country, Foote escaped to Europe and then, for a short time, lived in Canada. After the war's end, he returned to the United States and remained active, writing his own massive history of the sectional conflict as well as a five-hundred-page personal memoir with the ominous title *Casket of Reminiscences*. Shunned by many Democrats who considered him a traitor to the southern cause, he joined the Republican Party and later received an appointment as director of the United States mint in New Orleans, a position he held at the time of his death, in 1880. Few politicians in the nineteenth century had a career with more dramatic twists and turns than Henry Foote.

Of course, like most politicians, especially those who are excessively vocal during trying times, Foote had his critics. His long-winded bravado and general irascibility made him a controversial figure and a target for angry barbs from many of his contemporaries. Some called him nothing more than a demagogue and opportunist looking to feather his own nest and willing to follow any course to do so. As early as 1836, one newspaper reported that Foote's methods for his own advancement were "very devious and very singular."

Foote unquestionably had a talent for bullying his way to the forefront of an argument, and he was not averse to making wild claims in an effort to get people to notice him. Throughout his life, he relocated all over the country, moving from Virginia to Alabama, to Mississippi, to Texas, back to Mississippi, to California, to Tennessee, and finally to Louisiana in search of opportunities to wedge himself into the limelight. He attached himself to men who could help him, and their enemies became his enemies. "He had a sublime conception of the dignity of Henry S. Foote," one of his contemporaries later wrote, tongue in cheek. "His calculations were always made with Foote as the central sun around which satellites revolved."

Foote's memoirs, as well as other books that he authored, created a significant record and interpretation of the major events of his era, but the works were also celebrations of his ego, written under the assumption that his view on any subject was the only relevant view. He used his books to inform but also to promote himself and to tear down his enemies in a sometimes petty manner. Although he promoted states' rights views, he was a staunch unionist who drew the ire of many southern radicals and their sympathizers during the 1850s and the Civil War years. The famous South Carolina diarist Mary Chesnut called Foote a "false-tongued traitor," and Edmund Ruffin, himself an irascible antebellum character, "abhorred and despised" the man.[5]

Foote's critics consistently condemned him as an opportunist, which he was. However, much of their criticism seemed to come not necessarily from the idea that he could read a situation and take advantage of it but from the fact that he did so in such an aggressive manner, and that he was so successful at the practice. In short, he probably was no more of an opportunist than any other shrewd politician, but he was more transparently belligerent in pursuing power than many of his contemporaries. Foote could be rude and obnoxious, and he sometimes tripped over his own personality. "Governor Foote was a thoroughly aggressive politician," one observer wrote, who "possessed a fiery and vehement temper."[6] In politics, especially at the national level, well-placed hypocrisy sometimes is the grease that turns the governing wheel. Overexaggerated niceties among senators and congressmen and flowery public pronouncements of respect passed between colleagues—even colleagues who might privately hate one another—have always been used to smooth over the rough edges of the governing process in Washington. Foote could play this game as well as anyone, but only up to a point. At times he could not temper his anger, could not control himself in an atmosphere where men with titanic egos routinely collided. He was an expert at finding an opponent's weakness during an election campaign and attacking it relentlessly until his rival fell, mortally wounded, but too often he tried to use the same tactic after being elected. He often created irreparable hard feelings during the process of campaigning, which made it more difficult to build governing coalitions with other politicians once he took office.

Critics also charged that Foote was unprincipled, that he was motivated exclusively by personal notoriety and the pursuit of political power. The same could be said about many others in the political field, but in Foote's case the charges were valid though not completely true. He was not that one-dimensional. While his bluster and general theatrics were his most prominent traits as a politician, they sometimes masked the fact that Foote was, throughout most of his career, dedicated to keeping the federal union of states together. Decade in, decade out, Foote remained a preeminent southern unionist. Up until it became a reality, he never wavered in his highly focused belief that secession was madness and that the union of states that made up his country was sacred.

Just a few years before his death, in a moment of overbearing but accurate immodesty, Foote blew his own horn by declaring, "No one, I am sure, can be mentioned who more uniformly condemned the dangerous and absurd principle of secession, in support of which that [civil] war commenced, than myself." At a time when the nation was coming apart at the seams and the section of the country in which he lived was inching closer to open rebellion against the federal government, he took a definitive stand. He argued *for* the Union and *against* secession in the face of enormous political pressure to do otherwise. In so doing, he took a stand on principle that did him irreparable political harm.

The position that he took against the rising tide of secessionism cost him his Senate seat and ultimately drove him out of the state of Mississippi. It also led to his undoing. Once he saw that secession was inevitable, he compromised his principles for political gain, in a move that damaged his credibility and started a personal downhill spiral from which he never recovered. He had positioned himself as a champion of the Union and was admired by many for his convictions, but once he abandoned those principles, he had no ideological foundation on which to stand. Secessionists despised him for his earlier criticisms and unionists felt that he had betrayed them.

He ended up representing Tennessee in the Confederate Congress, but he did little there aside from criticizing Jefferson Davis's every move as Confederate president. After the war, his credibility with the national political community was in tatters, but he joined the Republican Party and continued to agitate for the rest of his life. With the Republicans, he was able to resurrect his career somewhat, at one point being viewed as a leader of the party in Tennessee. However, he was never able to recapture the national attention that he had garnered before the war, when his dramatic pontifications and general antics as a politician routinely made national news.[7]

Henry Foote's career garnered mixed reviews from his peers, and his legacy remains clouded by his own overbearing personality. Upon his death, many obituaries described him with terms such as *pompous*, *arrogant*, *delusional*, and *ignorant*, while others called him *scholarly*, *brilliant*, and a *genius*. In truth, all of those words might be applicable when describing Foote. What he lacked in focus he made up for in tenacity. He was rarely at a loss for words, regardless of the situation, and he never seemed intimidated, even among the most formidable company. His belief in himself seemed boundless, though it was likely the product of some deeply hidden insecurity. Everyone who met Foote had an opinion about him. He was provocative by nature and could be disciplined and uncontrollable all at the same time. He was a complicated man with a complicated personality, and while that did not necessarily make him one of the most influential political characters in nineteenth-century America, it certainly made him one of the more interesting.

1

The Rise of Lawyer Foote

My life, upon the whole, has been more or less tempestuous.
—Henry Stuart Foote

HENRY STUART FOOTE'S LONG AND STORMY LIFE began in Fauquier County, Virginia, on February 28, 1804. According to a nineteenth-century genealogical treatment and Foote's own memory of his family lineage, he was a fifth-generation American on his father's side. At the time of his birth, the Foote family had been in northern Virginia since the 1680s and was among a small group of significant landowning families who had dominated the region for decades.[1] The first Foote to arrive in Virginia was apparently an immigrant from Cardinham, County Cornwall, in southwest England. The progeny of the original immigrant flourished in America and the family was well established by the time the British officially organized Fauquier County, in 1759.

Foote's father, Richard Helm Foote, was born shortly before the American Revolution, and around the turn of the nineteenth century he married Jane Stuart, the daughter and granddaughter of prominent local ministers. Henry Foote's mother had Scottish roots. Her clergyman grandfather, David Stuart, immigrated to Virginia in 1715 and settled on the banks of the Potomac River in what at the time was Stafford County. Her father, William Stuart, was sent to England to study for the ministry and, according to one account, "studied theology in London and was ordained for the priesthood in 1745." Called Parson Stuart by his flock, William married into money and raised his children on the family estate, Cedar Grove, in northern Virginia.[2]

The product of a family of landed gentry and a family of ministers, Henry Foote was educated in local schools and by private tutors, including Eliab Kingman, a man who left a lasting impression on the youth. Kingman came to Fauquier County around 1816 looking for work as a schoolteacher. A native of Rhode Island and a recent graduate of Brown University, he approached Foote's father for assistance and eventually moved into the Foote home. With the help of the Footes, Kingman organized a small school with about fifteen pupils and also tutored Henry in the evenings. The youngster's experience with his new teacher represented a turning point in his life. He was an eager student and later credited Kingman with instilling in him all of the qualities of "a refined and well-bred gentleman, as well as a patriotic and useful citizen." Throughout his life Foote placed a high value on education, and until his death he held an enthusiasm for Latin, Greek, and other classical studies that could be traced back to his early training with his tutor. Kingman also fired the imagination of his pupils with regard to the nature of public discourse and current events, and Foote's time with the teacher was likely the genesis of the young boy's interest in public affairs.

Kingman eventually left Fauquier County and moved to Washington, DC, where he became a prominent newspaper reporter and columnist. During his career, he wrote for a number of major publications, including the *Baltimore Sun,* the *Charleston Courier,* the *New York Journal of Commerce* and the vaunted *National Intelligencer* in the nation's capital. By the start of the Civil War, some called Kingman "the dean of the Washington press corps," and when he died, in 1883, at age eighty-six, one obituary stated that "he may fairly be classed among the most noted and popular newsmen of the last half-century." Unable to break the habit of his youth even after his election to the United States Senate, Foote always referred to the reporter as "Mr. Kingman" and later wrote that his old tutor was "as pure a model as I have ever known of domestic and social excellence."[3]

Whether it was through the direct influence of Eliab Kingman or the product of natural curiosity, Henry Stuart Foote had a keen interest in national affairs by the time he passed through his teenage years. In late 1824, at the age of twenty, he traveled from his home in the Virginia countryside to Washington, DC, a distance of around fifty miles, "attracted thither," he later said, "by the interesting scenes of one kind or another known to be there." Upon his arrival, Foote found the city buzzing over the recent presidential election involving John Quincy Adams, Andrew Jackson, Henry Clay, and William Crawford. Adams's victory over Jackson was perhaps the most controversial in the history of American presidential politics. Because four candidates were involved in the race, no candidate was able to collect a majority of the presidential electoral votes and therefore the contest was decided in the House of Representatives, with the two leading candidates, Adams and Jackson, competing for the seat. Although Jackson had received more popular and electoral votes than Adams, the House declared Adams the winner. Furious at the results, Jackson's supporters claimed that Henry Clay, the Speaker of the House at the time, had manipulated the election's outcome in exchange for Adams agreeing to appoint Clay as secretary of state. The accusation stuck and would haunt Adams's one-term presidency, hurting his bid for reelection four years later.

Foote arrived in Washington as this saga unfolded, and he secured a seat in the House chamber gallery to watch Adams take the oath of office with Chief Justice John Marshall presiding. "I had the honor to witness this ceremony, which to me at the time was full of novelty and interest," Foote remembered. "[Adams] enunciated the oath in a clear and distinct tone, and ascended the Speaker's chair for the purpose of delivering therefrom his inaugural address." When the president concluded his remarks, Foote left the House chamber and assembled with a large crowd on the grounds of the White House to watch outgoing president James Monroe depart for retirement. According to Foote, who was able to elbow his way through the throngs of people to get a good look at the former president, Monroe "wore a kindly and genial smile, and he was evidently rejoicing inwardly at being relieved at last from the toils and cares of office." The young Virginian soon afterward returned home with his patriotic spirit fired and his resolve to enter public life firmly established.[4]

Henry Foote attended both Georgetown University and Washington College (now Washington and Lee University) but never graduated. "I never took a degree of any kind at any college or university," he later wrote, claiming that any knowledge and skills that he might possess were merely "the result of self-culture." He later studied law in the office of John Scott and Francis P. Brooks in Warrenton, Virginia, and it was there that he made his first friend of substance, a fellow student named Noah Haynes Swayne. The two aspiring attorneys began a lifelong friendship as they pored over law texts, and Foote later dedicated two of his own books to Swayne.

On the surface the two men seemed very different. Foote was from a family of slave-owning Virginians, while Swayne came from a family of antislavery Pennsylvania Quakers who had only recently moved to the Old Dominion. Despite these differences, they were drawn to one another from the first day they met, and they would remain, in Swayne's words, "as close as brothers" for the rest of their lives. They were admitted to the Virginia bar together but parted ways soon afterwards. Swayne moved to Ohio, where he established a flourishing law practice and political career. As a Quaker, he strongly opposed slavery, and though originally a Jacksonian Democrat, he joined the fledgling Republican Party in 1854. Several years later he became Abraham Lincoln's first appointee to the United States Supreme Court, the first Republican to occupy a seat there. He served on the court for almost two decades, until he was well into his seventies, and over the years Foote occasionally called on his old friend for help with various problems, both political and personal.[5]

As Swayne left Virginia to seek his fortune in Ohio, Henry Foote contemplated his next career move, which eventually took him farther south. In 1798, the United States organized the Mississippi Territory, which included much of what would later become the states of Mississippi and Alabama. At the time, the area was the heart of the American Southwest, and with the end of the War of 1812, it began attracting settlers. In 1817, Congress split the territory into two parts. The western half entered the Union that same year as Mississippi, with Alabama achieving statehood two years later.

Alabama was only six years old when Henry Foote decided to relocate there, in the spring of 1825, and the southwestern frontier proved to be the perfect environment for the young, extroverted lawyer whose loud and abrasive personality was already beginning to develop. Alabama during the period was wide open in terms of business, politics, and general opportunity. It was a typically American frontier state filled with simple, hardworking recent immigrants as well as scores of opportunists looking to capitalize financially on the state's initial lack of a tight fiscal infrastructure. In his study of the Jacksonian period in the region, Joshua D. Rothman wrote that, in the new states of Alabama and Mississippi, "the institutions or customs that might have instilled civility and order were weak or nonexistent, and appearances were often deceptive, allowing the brash, the crafty, the venal, and the predatory to thrive." While there was money to be made in Alabama, doing business in the state could be chaotic. Many land titles were drawn up in haste, the fledgling frontier credit system was unstable, and legislators had not yet had the opportunity to create the statutes needed to define the financial parameters of almost any type of significant business pursuit. As a result, there was no shortage of tangled legal cases to be adjudicated, and lawyers were in great demand. Joseph G. Baldwin, a lawyer and author who witnessed Alabama's early development, later wrote, "There was no end to the amount and variety of lawsuits and interests involved in every complication. . . . Many members of the bar, of standing and character, from the other states flocked in to put their sickle to this abundant harvest."[6]

Leaving his home in Virginia behind, Henry Foote settled in Tuscumbia, Franklin County, in the northern part of the state. Nestled securely along the Tennessee River, the region around Tuscumbia was first settled around 1810, but the future of the town was secured after the War of 1812, when the United States government promoted a project to construct a military road connecting Nashville, Tennessee, with New Orleans, Louisiana. The road passed through Tuscumbia and instantly breathed life into the area. In April of 1816, Congress authorized $10,000 for the project and placed General Andrew Jackson in charge. Surveyors plotted the route and, after an additional $5,000 congressional appropriation, the massive construction project began in April of 1819. According to a Tuscumbia newspaper account, the undertaking included "an average of 300 men employed on the work, including sawyers, carpenters, blacksmiths, etc. who were amply furnished with oxen, traveling forges, and all tools and implements necessary." By May of the following year, much of the road was complete and was becoming more heavily traveled. At the time, Franklin County had a free population of 3,308 and a slave population of 1,667. Over the course of the next ten years, the county's total population doubled, and during the 1820s, signs of civilization began to show themselves in Tuscumbia with the construction of a school, a masonic lodge building, several churches, and a variety of mercantile establishments.[7]

Foote's arrival in Tuscumbia, which he later remembered as "a quiet and pleasant village," in 1825, marked the beginning of his professional career. Alabama was a new state, filled with opportunity for someone blessed with intelligence and a general determination to persevere. "This country was just settling up," one observer later remembered. "Emigrants came flocking in from all quarters of the Union, especially from the slaveholding States. The new country seemed to be a reservoir, and every road leading to it a vagrant stream of enterprise and adventure."[8]

Foote quickly set about the task of establishing himself as an up-and-coming man of the region. In the spring of 1826, paid announcements began appearing on the front page of the *Tuscumbian*, a local newspaper, stating that "Henry S. Foote, attorney at law, having fixed residence in the town of Tuscumbia, will in future attend the Courts of Lauderdale, Franklin and Lawrence counties and the Supreme Court of this state." As he established his law practice, he began cultivating personal and political alliances with other recent immigrants to the region, including brothers Platt and Stark Washington, local planters who could claim distant kinship to the nation's first president, and William W. Parham, who represented Franklin County in the Alabama legislature. Foote eventually established a partnership with another young attorney, John Caldwell. Caldwell was the son of Irish immigrants who had recently come to Alabama from Nashville. Like Foote, he would only stay in Tuscumbia for a few years before moving on. Foote's personal life also took a leap forward, in 1826, when he married another northern Alabama transplant, Elizabeth Winter, a woman six years his junior who had come to Tuscumbia with her family from Charles County, Maryland. In 1828, the couple welcomed their first child, a daughter they named Jane, after Henry's mother. The couple would raise six more children during a union that lasted until Elizabeth's death in 1855.[9]

Desperate for his voice to be heard above everyone else's, Foote began a newspaper, the *Tuscumbia Patriot,* and like many other prudent politicians of the time, supported the career of Andrew Jackson. A bona fide war hero and legend, following his crushing defeat of the British at New Orleans in 1815, Jackson was wildly popular in Alabama and the rest of the South. In addition to his military pedigree, Jackson had fashioned an irresistible political image of himself as "the hero of the common man," and many simple farmers of the region revered him as a role model. In the 1824, 1828, and 1832 presidential elections, Jackson garnered all of Alabama's electoral votes and won the popular vote by large margins.

In addition to praising the tenets of Jacksonian democracy in his newspaper, Foote also touted local politicians and issues that he supported, and he was involved in projects that helped shape the northern Alabama region. He was one of twenty-one founding trustees of LaGrange College, a Methodist school that later became Florence Wesleyan University and still later the University of North Alabama, and was also an early proponent of railroad building in the northern part of the state. Foote commented at length in his newspaper on Washington politics, reserving column after column for the comings and goings of Congress and for his own staid pronouncements on the nature of government in a republic. He was particularly keen on dissecting one of the most politically vexing questions in the new nation during antebellum period: At what point in a republic does the authority of the federal government begin and end and, conversely, at what point does state authority begin and end? In drawing up the United States Constitution, the founders had left plenty of room for debate on the subject, and the discussions in political circles on the nature and limits of state and federal power never waned. The issue of state authority versus federal authority became particularly explosive and even more complicated during the antebellum period, when southerners began using traditional states' rights rhetoric to defend the institution of slavery. As if he was already paving the way for his future discourse as a United States senator and as a governor, Foote disseminated his views on the subject from the moment he started his newspaper.[10]

The young editor was particularly agitated in 1827, when the state of Georgia came into conflict with the federal government and President John Quincy Adams over removal of the Cherokee Indians from the northern part of the state. The general arguments centered around whether the federal government or the state of Georgia had the ultimate authority to administer the Cherokee lands. At one point during the conflict, Georgia governor George Troup threatened to call out the state militia to combat any federal interference with the state's administration of the Cherokee holdings. Although negotiations quickly eased the crisis, Foote felt compelled to comment on the situation in his newspaper. In doing so, he for the first time publicly articulated his personal political philosophy with regard to the union of states and definitions of state and national authority, a philosophy that remained constant through more than three turbulent decades.

In general, he counseled "a spirit of moderation, on both sides," but he also felt strongly that the federal government should not be held hostage by the acts of one of its members and that every American's future was tied to a strong federal union of states. He called the refusal of the state of Georgia to adhere to federal authority, and the governor's threat to use military force to resist federal mandates, acts that seemed "to thrust this nation upon the brink of destruction, and to place in an awful endangerment the most exalted interest which appertain to human existence, the blessing of a free government." Using the type of rhetoric that he would use years later as a United States senator and as governor of one of the cotton states before the Civil War, he claimed that while states' rights should be upheld, the concept could only go so far in a republic and that, in the end, federal authority was the foundation of the national existence. While his comments in 1827 related to a potential military clash between the state of Georgia and the federal government that never happened, these events foreshadowed future sectional conflicts that would be all too real. "This recklessness about involving the country in civil war cannot be too strongly condemned," he editorialized, more than thirty years before the Confederacy was formed, "and we trust that this disgraceful example will never be repeated in our long history."[11]

While a fondness for national discourse gripped Henry Foote during the late 1820s, it did not soften political rivalries that he developed at the local level, where clashes of personality and ego could quickly generate lifetime feuds and grudges. Foote proved this was the case when he became involved in a potentially deadly dispute with Edmund Winston, a member of a large northern Alabama clan that would have a prominent place in Alabama politics for generations. The Winstons came to northern Alabama not long before Foote, with a formidable political pedigree. They were all descendants of Anthony Winston, a Revolutionary officer and Virginia politician who was a cousin of the famous patriot Patrick Henry. Immediately after their arrival in Tuscumbia, the Winstons immersed themselves in local and state politics and were already establishing themselves when Foote arrived on the scene.[12]

Apparently viewing the family as a threat or hindrance to his own political aspirations, Foote had a falling out with the Winston clan that came to a head in Tuscumbia during the summer of 1827. At one point, through his newspaper, Foote "assailed with great severity" the character of Edmund Winston, a local judge, leading one of Winston's sons to demand a retraction. Foote refused and, later, members of the Winston family attacked Foote and several of his friends on the street and a brawl ensued. One published account stated that the fight "grew out of a personal encounter between Mr. Foote and Stark and Pratt Washington on one side, and Edmund Winston and others of that celebrated family on the other, during which all of the participants were more or less injured." At least one shot was fired during the fracas, severely wounding one of the Washington brothers. "The game of knock down and drag out was played off in high style last week in Tuscumbia," one newspaper later reported. "Dirks and pistols were drawn and said to be freely used, many wounds inflicted but only one serious injury was sustained by a Mr. Washington from a pistol shot." After the fight, Foote challenged Edmund Winston to a duel.[13]

While Foote's attack on the Winston family in print sparked the feud, the conflict was also bred out of Foote's natural bluster, combined with the fact that both Foote and the Winstons came from Virginia families steeped in their own political traditions. The Footes were one of the first families of Fauquier County, Virginia, while the Winstons enjoyed great notoriety in their native county of Hanover. Coming from such backgrounds, Foote and Winston likely felt a sense of entitlement on some level in Alabama, a sense that their families' status in Virginia would translate into dominance of northern Alabama's rudimentary political infrastructure. "The disposition to be proud and vain of one's country, and to boast of it, is a natural feeling," frontier lawyer and author Joseph Glover Baldwin observed during the period, "but with a Virginian, it is a passion." Reuben Davis, another Foote contemporary, later remembered that "like all Virginians, Foote had inordinate state pride, and really believed that to be born there was a distinction in itself."

Foote and Edmund Winston were from families in Virginia that were comfortable with deference from others and uncomfortable with the concept of deferring to anyone. Thus, they were unlikely to give way to one another or to reconcile amicably once an insult was in the air. Both men had too much to prove, and too much to maintain, in a frontier setting where the social and political climate was in a constant state of flux. When Foote arrived in Alabama, he entered an area that was welcoming large numbers of new settlers but was far from civilized. Courts of law existed and were active, but the justice system was not yet finely honed. In the antebellum South, most states had antidueling statutes on the books, but on the frontier, the court of public opinion, or public perception, and notions of individual honor could trump the rule of law. Public reputation on the frontier was many times equated with general individualism and a quick response to challenges. Any man who practiced cautious deliberation when confronted by an enemy ran the risk of being branded a coward due to his lack of immediate reaction. It was a volatile and unforgiving social environment for anyone with political ambitions. "I found a vicious state of public sentiment existing in the Southwest when I went thither to reside," Foote later said, in an attempt to offer a brief explanation of his dueling, "and I weakly and criminally yielded to it."[14]

The Henry Foote–Edmund Winston duel took place in Hamilton, Mississippi, just across the state line, so both combatants could escape prosecution under Alabama's antidueling laws. According to the statutes of the period, anyone in Alabama who was involved in a duel and survived could face a thousand-dollar fine, a year in jail, and "be rendered incapable of holding any office of honor, profit, or trust, under the government" for five years. Both men fired a single shot and both were slightly wounded, Winston in the hip and Foote in the shoulder. Never one to let the lack of embellishment taint a good story, Foote claimed, many years later, that during this encounter he was wounded by a pistol that Winston had borrowed from Andrew Jackson. Whether this was the case or not, the duel dramatically altered the course of Henry Foote's life.[15]

While, from a technical standpoint, Foote may have exchanged pistol fire with Winston in Mississippi, Alabama authorities eventually held him accountable for violating the state's antidueling laws. Though he did not serve any jail time, Foote was temporarily disbarred in Alabama and forbidden to hold public office there. The legal minutiae of the case are unclear, but the Winston family may have used their formidable political influence to ensure that the authorities punished Foote while dealing lightly with their kinsman.

Already thinking about a public career and in need of making a living through a legal practice, Foote decided to leave northern Alabama for New Orleans, in the winter of 1830–1831. He arranged to form a law partnership in Louisiana with fellow Alabaman Seth Barton, a savvy attorney and legislator who was also looking to move out of state to what he believed were greener pastures elsewhere. While Barton eventually moved to New Orleans and flourished there, Foote never made it to Louisiana. On the way to the Crescent City, a stop in Natchez, Mississippi, changed his plans.[16]

Nestled comfortably along the Mississippi River, about a hundred miles north of the river's mouth, Natchez was founded in 1716—two years before the founding of New Orleans—on the site of the old French settlement Fort Rosalie. Permanent European settlement in Mississippi first took root in the Natchez District during the early eighteenth century, and the region passed through French, British, and Spanish dominion before finally becoming part of the United States. Cotton and other staple crops were cultivated in the district as early as 1721 in soil "exceedingly fertile, consisting of black mould, at least three feet deep on the hills, and much deeper in the bottoms."[17]

Though on the fringes of a wilderness, the district's location along the river gave Natchez planters easy access to markets, and with the invention of the cotton gin, cotton quickly became the region's primary export. Plantations developed and a considerable amount of wealth concentrated in Natchez, but only in the hands of a small minority of citizens. Activity along the river also allowed pockets of cosmopolitan culture to develop, and the city of Natchez eventually became a thriving sociocultural center on the American frontier. By the beginning of the nineteenth century, the city had a well-structured government and firmly entrenched political elite. Mississippi achieved statehood in 1817, with Natchez as the capital, and the district around Natchez claimed three-quarters of the state's assessed property valuation, along with the state's highest concentration of slaves. Although the state capital was moved to a more central location during the early 1820s, for years much of the state's political power rested in Natchez, in the hands of a small number of wealthy planters.

In short, when Henry Foote arrived in the city, in late 1831, he saw a thriving center of activity dominated by money and politics, a perfect spot for a smart, ambitious lawyer to cultivate a legal practice. "Natchez was at the time an eminently flourishing commercial city," he later said. "I found the judges of the courts and members of the bar all exceedingly polite and accommodating." In Natchez, Foote also found a reason to abandon his plans for settling in New Orleans, a major city where he could easily get lost in the crowd. From the time he first laid eyes on Mississippi, he sensed an easier path to notoriety and success, an opportunity to settle in a burgeoning frontier state where lawyers—and in many instances the rule of law itself—were in demand. Foote knew he could advance faster in wide-open Mississippi than in crowded New Orleans, where he would be a smaller fish in a bigger pond. As a result, he chose to stay in what he called "the young and rising" state of Mississippi, a decision he later remembered as "perhaps the very best thing I could possibly have done."[18]

While Natchez would remain the state's cultural center for years to come, it was not the only city of consequence in Henry Foote's Mississippi during the 1830s. Vicksburg, a developing port city on the Mississippi River, about seventy-five miles upstream from Natchez, had a steadily increasing population and a growing business community in need of legal services. Like Natchez, Vicksburg owed its existence to a high, imposing bluff along the meandering Mississippi River that was a natural location for a settlement. The French were the first Europeans to recognize the bluff's potential, constructing a fort in the area in 1719. The Spanish built an outpost called Fort Nogales—translated as "Walnut" or "Walnut Trees"—on the site in 1790. Eight years later, when the Americans finally gained possession of the region, the settlement that had grown up around the old fort was christened Walnut Hills, and in 1825 it was renamed and incorporated as Vicksburg, after local resident Newton Vick. The city grew along with the cotton kingdom of the antebellum period. Riverboats came and went from the Vicksburg docks, and an early railroad line linked the city with the state's interior. According to one observer, "After its incorporation a steady stream of robust citizenship of Virginia, the Carolinas, Kentucky, and some of the eastern states, poured into the town, until in 1835, it had expanded into quite a prosperous little city of twenty-five hundred or three thousand souls." Vicksburg would continue to grow, rivaling Natchez as a commercial center and eventually becoming a focal point of Union advances into the South during the Civil War.[19]

Not as cosmopolitan as Natchez or as quick to develop as Vicksburg, Jackson became an important city in Mississippi after the state capital was moved there in 1821. Named for Andrew Jackson, the city grew up on the site of a trading post established by French trader Louis LeFleur, on a bluff overlooking the Pearl River. The legislature authorized construction of a two-story brick statehouse in Jackson during the 1820s, which was replaced during the next decade with a larger, much more elegant structure. In 1832, a convention of Mississippi's leading politicians took place in Jackson for the purpose of drawing up a new state constitution.

If Natchez was a seat of culture in Mississippi during the 1830s, and Vicksburg a seat of commerce, Jackson was the state's political hub and a nesting place for lawyers and politicians looking to make their mark in government. Henry Foote's professional and personal life would revolve around Natchez, Vicksburg, and Jackson for many years as he became one of the region's best-known lawyers and politicians. Those cities would also host some of Foote's most prominent activities. Foote initially settled in Natchez for a short time before briefly moving his family to Vicksburg and finally to Clinton, a small town just west of Jackson. From there, he could easily access the state capital as well as the courtrooms and courthouses of the river cities.

As had been the case in Alabama, Foote made his presence known in Mississippi's expanding legal circles with lightning speed and, according to James D. Lynch's comprehensive 1883 history of the state's legal profession, "practiced law with much success for many years, both in the civil and criminal departments of the profession." Foote took part in a number of high-profile cases that received a great deal of local publicity, and it did not take long for his abrasive personality to generate controversy. "As a lawyer," Lynch remembered, "Foote was learned and astute. . . . His tenacious disposition rendered him exceedingly loath to accept defeat." While arguing a case at the Vicksburg courthouse, in 1833, he crossed paths with Seargent Smith Prentiss, another up-and-coming lawyer and politician of the era, in an encounter that led to not one but two duels.

A native of Maine, Prentiss arrived in Mississippi several years before Foote and established himself as a legal and political force in the state. He had few equals as a speechmaker and storyteller, and his wit in the courtroom was notorious. During the 1830s, he was one of the best-known political figures in Mississippi, and his formidable reputation preceded him wherever he went. "He was dramatic in style of delivery and in diction," one writer later remembered, "combining this with great logical power, subtle wit, and touching pathos." Joseph G. Baldwin, another Mississippi lawyer of the period, thought Prentiss had an innate talent for "knowing and being able to show people what was the law." In fact, as an orator, Prentiss had a great deal in common with Foote. Both were intelligent to the extent that many called them brilliant, both were exceptional public speakers, and both were relentless in an argument. Foote first met Prentiss in Natchez, several months before they crossed rhetorical swords in the courtroom, and he was impressed. "When I was first introduced to him," Foote later recalled, "Natchez was already full of his fame. He had delivered several speeches at the bar, which all agreed had never been equaled there."[20]

In early 1833, Foote and Prentiss found themselves in Vicksburg on opposite sides in a murder trial, with each man hoping to outshine the other in front of a packed courtroom. In an era when murder trials were sometimes considered a form of community entertainment, both men were determined to put on a great performance for the public. As the trial progressed, their courtroom showmanship became more dramatic and their exchanges more heated. According to some accounts, Foote at one point threw an inkstand at Prentiss, while others later stated that Prentiss grew so angry during the proceedings that he slapped Foote across the face. Regardless, by all accounts Foote, the more impulsive of the two men, felt that Prentiss insulted him during trial, and he challenged Prentiss to a duel. In his memoirs, Foote never stated what Prentiss said or did to him, but he did express regret at having issued the challenge. "I had a personal dispute at the bar with the famous S. S. Prentiss during a capital case," Foote later recalled. "His language, though sufficiently retaliated by me at the time, induced me to send him a challenge, which I ought never to have thought of doing. He promptly accepted, proved a far better shot than myself."

Prentiss, who was less rash than Foote, was cool to the notion of a duel but was honor-bound to fight, once Foote issued the challenge. "I regretted the occurrence as much as anyone," Prentiss wrote in a letter, not long after the event. "I neither sought the difficulty nor sent the challenge, but having received it under the circumstances that existed, I could not have acted differently than what I did."

The two men met at dawn on October 5, 1833, in Louisiana, just across the Mississippi River from Vicksburg. Just as Foote and Edmund Winston had fought their Alabama duel in Mississippi in hopes of sidestepping Alabama's antidueling statutes, Foote and Prentiss likely met in Louisiana as a means of getting around Mississippi's laws against the practice. As the duel commenced, Foote fired and missed, and then, according to Prentiss, "I threw up my pistol and fired, not intending to hit [Foote] at all, but . . . my ball, even as I threw up my pistol, hit him in the shoulder, slightly wounding him in the flesh."[21] Foote's wound was painful but not life threatening.

Both Foote and Prentiss escaped the duel with their lives, but the matter did not end there. Following the contest, some of Prentiss's friends began circulating malicious rumors about Foote's conduct during the duel, which led Foote to make countercharges against his rival. The end result was a second challenge, this one issued by Prentiss. The second Prentiss–Foote duel was marked with much more fanfare than the first, and much more intrigue. Before it took place, rumors began circulating that the authorities in Vicksburg were poised to stop the duel by arresting Foote and Prentiss, so the combatants left town and met in Natchez, where they boarded a boat that took them across the Mississippi River, again into Louisiana. Despite the change of venue, word of the duel continued to circulate and hundreds gathered at the dueling grounds to witness the event, drawn by what one observer described as "a prurient curiosity for the tragic."

Foote again fired first but missed, which bolstered his later admission, and the claims of others who knew him, that he was a terrible marksman. According to one source, after discharging his weapon, Foote "then stood, his left arm clasped across his side, his right arm hanging down. He neither blanched nor quivered, although the deadly aim of his opponent was upon him. Prentiss pulled the trigger, but the percussion cap exploded without firing the pistol."

The misfire of Prentiss's pistol led to a second exchange. Foote again missed, but this time Prentiss did not, wounding Foote severely in the right leg, just above the knee, a wound that would cause Foote to limp slightly for the rest of his life.

Oddly enough, Foote and Prentiss became friends after the duel. According to Foote, the men reconciled and within three months had established a friendship that would last until Prentiss's death, in 1850. Prentiss's brother later described the relationship between the former combatants as one of "warm personal friends," and not long after the duel, Foote publicly supported Prentiss in his successful campaign for a seat in the United States House of Representatives.[22]

Though Foote and Prentiss gave up dueling with one another after their second altercation, they met again in the courtroom during two notable Mississippi criminal trials of the 1830s. Only a month after the second duel, the two men took part in the murder trial of Alonzo Phelps, one of the most infamous outlaws of the region. Phelps was born in New England but, according to his own statements, fled south after he killed another man in a dispute over a woman. He roamed the southern reaches of the Mississippi Valley, shunning conventional society and supporting himself through a variety of criminal activities that eventually made him one of the area's most notorious highwaymen. Phelps was primarily a thief, but he did not hesitate to kill if the need arose. While no one ever knew exactly how many people he killed, popular conjecture at the time had the criminal committing at least eight cold-blooded murders during his career, and probably more. According to observers, Phelps certainly looked the part of a formidable outlaw. He was a tall, muscular man with a tanned complexion and wild red hair, who "evidently possessed of great vigor and activity." According to Foote, Phelps general countenance was "fierce and menacing," and "his keen gray eyes exhibited a curious blending of audacity and furtiveness."[23]

Phelps robbed and murdered a man outside of Vicksburg, and the state placed a $3,000 reward on the outlaw's head, leading to his capture. Authorities transported him in irons to the Vicksburg jail. The state chose Prentiss, assisted by several other lawyers, to prosecute the case. Foote, who was still on crutches as a result of his duel with the prosecutor, was chosen to lead the defense. The trial was a one-sided affair, with Foote unable to counter the charges made by the prosecution. In truth, there was little chance that any lawyer could have won an acquittal for such a well-known outlaw, and Foote likely signed on to the case because he knew it would generate publicity for his practice, regardless of the verdict.

According to Foote, his primary duty during the proceedings was to keep his client from going berserk and killing someone in the courtroom. The more Prentiss attacked Phelps's character and outlined the depravity of his crimes, the angrier the outlaw became. Finally, as Prentiss was giving his closing argument, Phelps leaned over to Foote and whispered a threat on Prentiss's life. "Tell me whether I stand any chance of acquittal," the outlaw reportedly told his attorney. "If my case is hopeless I will snatch a gun from the guard nearest me and send Mr. Prentiss to hell before I shall go there myself." According to Foote, he pacified Phelps with a lie, telling the agitated defendant that he should refrain from doing anything rash because an acquittal was still possible. The jury ultimately issued a guilty verdict and Phelps was remanded to jail to await execution. He was shot soon afterwards, while trying to escape.[24]

Foote was also involved in the Mercer Byrd trial, which drew a good bit of attention in Mississippi and the rest of the South and in many ways was a reflection of the times, peppered as it was with heavy doses of racial hysteria and political intrigue. Joel Cameron was a wealthy planter in the Vicksburg area who was notoriously cruel to his slaves and who had as a business partner future Mississippi governor Alexander McNutt. On May 5, 1832, three of Cameron's slaves clubbed their master to death, weighted down his body, and dumped it in a lake.[25] Locals later found Cameron's horse wandering free, and authorities, suspecting foul play, launched an unsuccessful search for the planter. Not long afterwards, a storm blew through the area, stirring up the water in the lake and causing Cameron's body to rise to the surface, where it was recovered. After an investigation, authorities arrested Cameron's slaves and the local courts of Warren County, where Vicksburg was located, hired Foote to prosecute the case.

"It appeared on investigation that this murder had been concerted for some time," Foote later wrote, "that the negroes implicated had assaulted Cameron with clubs as he passed early in the morning, on horseback, upon a narrow path." There was evidence against the men, and their status as slaves skewed the justice system against them from the beginning. Foote had little difficulty extracting a guilty verdict from the jurors who heard the case, many of whom owned slaves themselves. "The proof against [the defendants] was clear and conclusive," the prosecutor later recalled, "and all of them put under trial were convicted." The judge sentenced the defendants to death, but shortly before their execution they implicated as an accessory a local free black named Mercer Byrd. Once word got out, Byrd was arrested and tried for the crime, with great fanfare.[26]

Cameron's partner, Alexander McNutt, was the driving force behind the Mercer Byrd prosecution. Using his own money and influence, he hired Seargent S. Prentiss to prosecute the case. The key piece of evidence against Byrd was Cameron's watch, which was discovered buried in Byrd's henhouse. To many observers, it seemed like another open-and-shut case, but others were skeptical and believed that Byrd had been framed. "It is certain that the watch of the murdered Cameron was found in Byrd's hen-house," one witness to the trial wrote. "The fact of its being deposited there was disclosed by one of those who had been executed, but he did not assert that the secreting of the watch in that place was at all known to Mercer Byrd."

Byrd was actually tried three times, with the first trial ending in a hung jury and the conviction in the second being overturned on technicalities. The third and final trial drew the most attention, and drew Henry Foote into the courtroom—ironically, to defend Byrd rather than to prosecute him. Never one to shy away from a public spectacle, Foote volunteered his services for free. He knew that the trial would draw packed galleries and a great deal of press coverage, and he was also eager to face Prentiss again. Foote put on a good show for the packed courtroom, but he could not overcome the simple fact that Byrd was black and that, since the famous 1831 Nat Turner slave rebellion in Virginia, the racial climate in Mississippi and the rest of the South was increasingly tense.

Byrd was convicted and sentenced to the gallows, but, according to Foote, the condemned man made a startling claim just before he was hanged. Foote later stated that, on the day Byrd died, he revealed that it was actually McNutt, Cameron's partner, who was behind the murder. "He charged," Foote later claimed, "that Cameron had been murdered at the instigation of McNutt himself." The charges against McNutt were unprovable, but the gossip that he was somehow involved in Cameron's death "caused considerable popular commotion" at the time and circulated for years, fueled by the fact that McNutt married Cameron's widow seven months after the murder.[27]

In addition to taking part in a number of high-profile criminal trials during the 1830s, Henry Foote was a firsthand witness to the great Mississippi slave insurrection scare of 1835, one of the most terrifying events of the antebellum era for central Mississippi whites. A number of factors created the scare, including general friction between the North and the South over the slavery issue, the growth of the abolition movement in the North, and, at a more primal level, fallout from the Nat Turner rebellion in Virginia. The Turner rebellion, which resulted in the deaths of more than fifty men, women, and children, had terrified the white South. It added the ultimate element of racial terror to the mind-set of southern whites, who feared that one day the slaves would rebel in large numbers, indiscriminately killing any whites they saw, in an act of multigenerational revenge against those who for so long had held them down.

The fear was tangible, and it never completely abated, affecting southern life on a daily basis long after the initial shock of the rebellion dissipated. In most communities the fear simmered, but it could sometimes boil over, giving way to mob violence and lynch law. White Mississippians, like their contemporaries around the South, could be alarmed to the point of irrational action by even the most far-fetched rumor of slave rebellions supposedly taking place hundreds of miles away. In many locales, this gave way to the formation of local vigilante groups that dispensed extralegal justice on the whim of public opinion. Henry Foote later recalled that, during the great scare of 1835, Clinton, the town in which he lived, was not immune to the hysteria, and that on more than one occasion "the panic awakened was so great that night after night the women and children of the place were assembled at a central position, where they remained till daylight, while all the male citizens moved in armed squads over the settlement." As abolitionist activity in the North began to grow during the antebellum period, many southern whites perceived themselves as being under siege, and therefore a desperate siege mentality grew among them.[28]

There were few if any places in Mississippi where this type of mentality was more prevalent than in Madison County, a planter's haven and cotton-producing mecca, where, by 1840, the slave population outnumbered the free population three to one. Some planters lived on the property that their slaves cultivated, while absentee landlords controlled and cultivated other large holdings. "Immense bodies of rich land are being converted into cotton fields and negro quarters," one Madison County observer wrote in 1834, "leaving so sparse a white population as to preclude the possibility of building up anything like an interesting state of society." In short, Madison County was awash in cotton and slaves, and, as a result, awash in white anxieties over slave insurrections and other threats to the status quo. It was the perfect breeding ground for rumor and panic.[29]

Henry Foote was familiar with and well known in Madison County. He had traveled through the area on many occasions as it was geographically close to his own home. Madison County was immediately north of Hinds County, where Foote lived, and just east of Vicksburg, in Warren County, where the lawyer plied his trade on a regular basis. A scare over a potential slave rebellion in Madison County would certainly bleed over into Hinds and Warren counties and generate similar fears there among whites. Such was the case in 1835, four years removed from the Turner uprising in Virginia and two years after the founding of the American Anti-Slavery Society in New England. In the flowery prose of his personal memoir, Foote later described the insurrection scare in central Mississippi as "an extravagant and even maddening excitement" that had deadly consequences for both whites and blacks in the region.[30]

The genesis of the scare was apparently a pamphlet written by a criminal named Virgil Stewart. Stewart was a shadowy character who claimed to be part of a gang led by John A. Murrell, a regionally famous outlaw whose primary trades included slave and horse stealing. According to some accounts, Murrell and his men were experts at stealing and selling the same slaves to unsuspecting planters over and over again. In early 1835, Murrell was captured and convicted of thievery in Nashville, Tennessee, with Stewart turning informant and serving as one of the state's key witnesses. After the trial, Stewart left Nashville and came up with a scheme to profit from his time as part of the outlaw's gang. He wrote a heavily dramatized account of Murrell's activities as a highwayman, including claims that a sophisticated network of outlaws who were tied to Murrell still operated throughout the southern states, stealing slaves. According to one account, Stewart "traveled extensively through Mississippi and several adjoining States, and sold many thousands of his fearfully exciting and inflammatory book. . . . He was looked upon by many as a great public benefactor." Stewart's story was so sensational that editors throughout the South, always in search of a literary vehicle for selling more newspapers, began reprinting the most inflammatory portions of the pamphlet, complete with lurid embellishments.

What created the excitement in Madison County in the summer months of 1835 was Stewart's claim that members of Murrell's gang who lived in Mississippi were poised to start a slave rebellion in the central part of the state in hopes of somehow profiting from the chaos. The insurrection was supposed to take place on the Fourth of July, when holiday celebrations would presumably distract local whites and therefore make it easier for slaves in the area to congregate. Using Stewart's word alone as a source, one Mississippi newspaper spread the alarm by warning its readers that "individuals enjoying all the privileges of free citizens, have, with fiend-like madness, instigated the ignorant and generally contented Africans to rise against their fellow citizens and to engage in an indiscriminate butchery of every age and sex.[31]

As word of the supposed plot circulated in Madison County, local whites grew hysterical. "[We] have been under arms day and night," one man wrote, "expecting every moment to be burned up or have our throats cut by the Negroes. A dreadful alarm exists particularly among the females." On June 27, 1835, "a large and respectable meeting of citizens" was held at Livingston, at the time the Madison County seat of government, where resolutions were adopted appointing patrols and committees of investigation charged with gathering information on "the momentous crisis which has arisen." The investigation amounted to an exercise in mob rule and vigilante justice. A number of slaves and "a villainous band of white men" who were supposedly tied to Murrell fell under suspicion as the result of questionable confessions by a small group of slaves who had been viciously whipped. In addition to more than a dozen slaves, several whites, whose only crime may have been that they were new to the area, were eventually executed. During the period, one man reported, "About ten negroes and five or six white men have been hung without any form of law or trial, except an examination before the examining committee. They are still going on trying and hanging."[32]

Henry Foote became involved in the Livingston vigilante trials through one of the accused, a farmer and boatman named Angus Donovan. Donovan, who was white, was a native of Maysville, Kentucky, who had recently brought a boatload of farm produce down the Ohio and Mississippi Rivers to New Orleans. After completing his business, he sold his boat and slowly began his journey back home on horseback, stopping temporarily in Madison County. A transient quickly branded as an outsider, Donovan was an uncomfortable community presence who seemed to be a little too friendly with local slaves. Some claimed that Donovan was trading illegally with slaves, presumably for articles stolen from area plantations. At one point, the Kentuckian had also tried to intervene to stop the beating of a defenseless neighborhood slave, drawing even more suspicion from local whites. Even before the insurrection scare exploded, local residents had unsuccessfully tried to run the stubborn Donovan out of the region. As racial tensions peaked in Madison County in 1835, vigilantes found him to be an easy mark and quickly accused the Kentuckian of being a member of the Murrell gang, and therefore one of the white men behind "a diabolical scheme for the butchery of the whites."

Once in custody, Donovan realized that his life was in danger and that he needed help. Exactly who or what led him to contact Henry Foote is unclear, but Foote was considered one of the best young lawyers in the state, and his home in Clinton was less than twenty miles away from where the accused man languished in a small jail cell. Desperate, Donovan sent a note to the attorney, begging for representation. Foote was immediately skeptical, believing that Donovan's fate was already sealed and that no one in Donovan's position could ever escape mob rule in such a racially charged climate. "The poor fellow," Foote later recalled, "seems to have imagined that it was a real court that was about to examine into the case, and that a lawyer would be allowed to defend him before it."[33]

Still, Foote was never quick to shy away from a challenge. He felt a degree of sympathy for the young man being held and was also curious about exactly what was happening over in Madison County. As a result, he mounted his horse and headed for Livingston, where he found a dangerous, ill-disposed crowd more unruly than he had ever imagined. Foote was no shrinking violet, and certainly no stranger to confrontation, but he approached the situation around the Madison County courthouse with caution. "When I got to Livingston I saw a large multitude convened, composed almost altogether of excited white citizens," he later wrote. "I dared not name my business to anyone, for had I done so there was not much probability that I should have ever returned to my home again."

By the time Foote made it into the courthouse, an extralegal trial before the community vigilance committee had already begun and, as he suspected, there seemed to be little chance that Donovan would leave Madison County alive. Despite the lack of credible evidence against the accused, members of the committee were poised to execute him as a race traitor. Foote introduced himself to the committee, and when it finally came time for him to examine Donovan, the attorney cut to the chase. He knew that Donovan's incarceration was not the result of solid evidence but rather of the race-based fears of local whites. As a result, Foote chose to solicit from the accused man the only testimony that might soften the mood of the vigilance committee, the agitated onlookers in the courtroom, and the angry crowd outside. He hoped to take the racial anxieties that were at the heart of Donovan's problems and use those same feelings to Donovan's advantage. He would make an appeal to racial solidarity rather than racial division, in hopes of saving Donovan from the hangman's noose. In the process, Foote also hoped that he could avoid being lynched himself.

When his time to speak came, Foote rose slowly and began to pace in front of the accused in a dramatic display that was one of his trademarks. He then furrowed his brow, wheeled around, and confronted Donovan face-to-face. "You are a *white* man," Foote bellowed. "Now tell me, I beseech you, were you to witness a bloody conflict between the slaves of this country and the *white* people, on which side would you be?"[34] Emotional, and understanding the full ramifications of Foote's question, Donovan quickly answered that he would always side with his own color, with his own race, and that he would never turn on his own kind. After questioning Donovan, Foote sat back down, already convinced that the accused was doomed. "I felt for him most deeply," Foote recalled, "but what could I do?" In the end, Foote's examination of Angus Donovan was little more than a formality to the vigilance committee, who could now say that they had allowed the accused to mount a defense. In less than half an hour, the committee found Donovan guilty of being "undoubtedly the emissary of those deluded fanatics at the North, the abolitionists," and had him executed.[35]

Disturbed by what he had seen in Livingston, Foote found similar events unfolding when he returned to Clinton. In Foote's hometown, a vigilance committee had tried a local free black named Vincent for inciting insurrection, on the flimsy grounds that "a considerable quantity of powder and shot had been found in his possession." The committee originally sentenced the man to a severe whipping, but after word of their ruling leaked out, an angry crowd assembled in town demanding that the man be executed. "Vincent was carried out to receive his stripes," a local newspaper reported, "but the assembled multitude were in favor of hanging him. . . . A vote was accordingly fairly taken, and the hanging party had it by an overwhelming majority." Bowing to public pressure and fearing for their own safety, the committee quickly changed the sentence to death. "I never saw people so blind with excitement in all my life," one observer wrote in a letter to a friend. "The populace, breathing fury and vengeance, are up for blood."

The former slave had been owned by Robert Bell, a deceased friend of Foote's, who had freed the man in his will. When Foote reached Clinton, he found Bell's widow weeping hysterically, trying to speak up for her former slave and save him from the gallows. More comfortable speaking before the crowd in his hometown, Foote interceded on the widow's behalf, attempting to quiet the mob minutes before the execution. Again, Foote was unsuccessful. Vincent was hanged and Foote, dejected, returned to his home. "I remember to have at this moment consulted with my family," he later stated, "whether we should not at once leave a region so replete with scenes of sorrow, and so full of danger to those who relied on the laws of the land for protection and security."[36]

Foote and his family remained in Clinton, but the violent mob action that he witnessed affected the lawyer. During the insurrection scare, many normally placid citizens had literally been driven to murder by simple rumor and innuendo. Fear had spread among them like a highly contagious and incurable disease that, instead of wreaking havoc on their bodies, wreaked havoc on the world around them. Though certainly capable himself of manipulating a crowd, Foote forever after remembered the horrors of an excited crowd whose rage had grown beyond their own control. Later, as governor of Mississippi and in the United States Senate during the 1850s, he would warn others about the dangers of mob action as he defended the union of states against those who he believed were trying to tear it asunder to promote their own agendas in a similar time of racially charged unrest. Just as he placed himself in physical danger by speaking on behalf of Angus Donovan and of his friend's former slave Vincent in the 1830s, he would place himself in grave political danger by speaking out against secession a generation later. Rather than vigilantes who feared insurrection, he would later face fellow southerners terrified that the entire institution of slavery was in danger. Just as he had gone against the grain defending the accused during the insurrection scare of the 1830s, he would defy the mounting secessionist sentiment in the South that ultimately led to civil war. Like the central Mississippi mobs of the 1830s, the secessionists and their followers during the 1850s would parlay the collective fear of the masses into harsh action. "In no community in Christendom," Foote later surmised, in a moment of reflection, "can the public mind be reasonably supposed."[37]

A third case that Foote took part in during the insurrection scare had political overtones, and his involvement seemed to confirm that, by 1835, he was recognized in Mississippi's highest legal circles as an expert speaker and counselor. The case involved plantation owner Patrick Sharkey, who lived in Fleetwood, Mississippi, a small community near Clinton and not far from the Hinds–Madison county line. Sharkey served as justice of the peace in Hinds County and chaired a local vigilance committee that was also investigating the potential for slave insurrections. Unlike some of his contemporaries who obsessed on the notion that local slaves were about to rise up, Sharkey was a man of more even temperament. A veteran of the War of 1812, he was a cautious man in his midforties when the insurrection scare took place, and he rarely leaned toward reactionary action, no matter what the situation. In fact, he seemed to have suspicions that the entire idea of a slave rebellion led by white outlaws was exaggerated. The vigilance committee that he chaired released most of those who came before it, choosing to recognize rather than ignore that there was little or no evidence against them.

During the scare, members of the same Madison County vigilance committee that tried and executed Angus Donovan came into Hinds County to capture two men who they suspected of conspiring with slaves near Livingston. As justice of the peace, Sharkey refused to surrender the men as there was no real evidence against them and it was apparent that the posse was more interested in lynching than in impartial hearings. The interlopers from Madison County were furious, accusing Sharkey of being "soft on slavery" and "an enemy of Mississippi," and they pledged to take him back to Livingston and place him on trial as a coconspirator. In an attempt to capture Sharkey, they staged a nighttime raid on his home, during which Sharkey was wounded in the hand, shortly after fatally wounding one of the men from Madison County.

Though he drove the intruders away, Sharkey, seeking protection, eventually surrendered himself to the local vigilance committee in Clinton. The committee included men he had long known, and who had long known him, and it was to these men that he wanted to tell his side of the story. While being held in custody, he also played his trump card, contacting his cousin William Sharkey in Jackson, who happened to be chief justice of the Mississippi supreme court. William, in turn, contacted Henry Foote. At the time, Foote was in Jackson on business, staying at a downtown hotel. "He came suddenly to my room at the hotel one day, around noon," Foote later wrote of William Sharkey's request, "and showed me a letter he had just received from Mr. Patrick L.

Sharkey, his first cousin." The letter outlined the circumstances and appealed to William Sharkey for help. After showing the letter to Foote, the chief justice asked Foote to travel to Clinton with him and advocate on behalf of his cousin.

Together, the two men traveled the dozen miles between Jackson and Clinton and spoke to the vigilance committee, asking them to release Patrick Sharkey. The committee listened to the two lawyers and agreed to do so, knowing full well that Sharkey, a successful planter and slaveholder as well as a law enforcement official, would never be involved in a scheme to arm and agitate slaves. In addition to acquitting the man of wrongdoing, the committee vowed to protect Sharkey from anyone coming into the county to do him harm. William Sharkey was grateful for Foote's help, and the chief justice became one of Foote's political allies as a result of the affair. Later, after the general hysteria of the period died down, Foote also helped Patrick Sharkey win a $10,000 judgment in a lawsuit filed against those involved with the Madison County vigilance committee.[38]

Henry Foote was involved in a high-profile murder case several years later that was rooted in politics and perceptions of public honor. In 1830, a physician named James Hagan emigrated from Ireland to the United States, settling first in Virginia and then, by 1836, in Vicksburg, Mississippi, where he established a newspaper, the *Vicksburg Sentinel*. Although he practiced medicine, he gained greater notoriety as a rough-and-tumble journalist, described by one source as "a most powerful writer, particularly of satire and ridicule . . . one of the most famous characters in Mississippi journalism."

In 1844, Hagan published a series of particularly vicious articles accusing Mississippi attorney general George Adams of corruption. In response, Adams's twenty-two-year-old son, Daniel, attacked Hagan one night on the streets of Vicksburg. During the tussle, Hagan apparently began choking Adams, at which point Adams drew a pistol and killed the unarmed man. Adams surrendered himself to authorities and confessed to the killing, claiming self-defense.

Daniel Adams's father, the attorney general, hired three men who he believed were among the best attorneys in the state of Mississippi at the time, future judges George S. Yerger and John I. Guion, and future Mississippi governor Henry Foote, to defend his son. During the trial, Foote railed against Hagan, ironically using the same sort of rhetoric that his political opponents would one day use against him. Foote vilified the editor as a demagogue with a poisonous agenda designed to breed conflict. "I do not think that any other editor that this country has produced," Foote said, "has been known with impunity to indulge, for so long a space of time, as freely as Dr. Hagan, in language of the harshest personal invective." The attorney also called the *Sentinel* "an object of mingled dread and hatred to large numbers of peace-loving and law-respecting people."[39] While the Vicksburg newspaper was indeed well known for personal attacks, many other newspapers in the region participated in the same type of activity, and Foote himself was also known for similar public attacks on his enemies.

As for the accused assailant, Foote portrayed him as a frightened victim. With dramatic flair, the attorney claimed that, after the argument on the street in Vicksburg, it was actually Hagan who attacked Adams, and that Adams, fearing that his own demise was at hand, had no choice but to pull his pistol. The jury agreed with Foote's interpretation of events and "retired but seven minutes" before acquitting Adams of murder. It was a legal and political victory for the lawyer. Not only had he helped gain the release of the son of Mississippi's attorney general but also Daniel Adams himself went on to have a great deal of political influence in the state in his own right.[40]

It was no coincidence that Foote enjoyed being involved in trials with political implications. As he made a name for himself in legal circles in Mississippi, he was building political networks for future use. Along those lines, he also knew that one of the best ways for a politician to have his voice heard, and one of the best avenues for influencing public opinion, was through journalism. As he had done in Alabama, he established a newspaper in Vicksburg, the *Mississippi Advocate*, shortly after arriving in Mississippi, and he later started the influential *Mississippian*, in Jackson, with his brother-in-law Reuben Catlett. He and Catlett eventually gave up their interests in the *Mississippian*, and the new editors, ironically, would become some of Foote's harshest public critics.

Regardless, Foote was well established in Mississippi by the time he was in his late thirties. He seemed to know everyone in the state who mattered, and everyone seemed to know him. While his demeanor bred friction with those who opposed him in the courtroom, even his detractors could not argue the point that he had become a significant voice within the state. "His talents were of a high order," one observer noted, "and whether a lawyer, politician or orator, he was equally conspicuous and popular in the sphere of his labor."[41]

2

The Emerging Politician

Foote had an unusual command of language, and was especially
gifted with a power of arranging historical facts, and
deducing from them political principles.
—Reuben Davis

HENRY FOOTE HARBORED POLITICAL AMBITIONS that matched, or perhaps
even exceeded, his strong drive to succeed in the courtroom, and he seemed to
be in the right place at the right time to realize his political goals. The political
climate of Mississippi in the decades immediately after statehood in 1817 was
tailor-made for a man like Foote. Rough, unrestrained frontier politics was
the order of the day in an atmosphere of rapid social evolution. When Foote
arrived in Mississippi there were many shifting dynamics in place that guaranteed public men of the period a wild political ride.

Although Natchez had been the center of Mississippi politics and culture
for years and would be the home of many wealthy and influential individuals
for years to come, the elite who had ruled the state were losing their grip by
the time Foote entered the fray. During the 1820s and early 1830s, the removal
of the Choctaw and Chickasaw Indians opened millions of acres of central
and northern Mississippi for white settlement, and the state's interior began to
fill up with people. Soon, the new arrivals outnumbered the Natchez elite by a
considerable margin and began to clamor for control of the state government.[1]
Most of the new settlers revered Andrew Jackson as both a national military
hero and a frontier politician. They also personified the central tenets of "Jacksonian democracy," a somewhat loaded term that came to describe a general
expansion of the electorate during the period and the idea that every adult
white male, regardless of status, should have access to the political process. The

expansion of popular democracy during Jackson's two terms led many to call his tenure as president "the era of the common man," when theoretically even the poorest males among the lower classes of whites had a political voice.

The most visible signs of a significant shift in the political winds in Mississippi came during the 1820s, when legislative representatives from recently settled areas forced the removal of the state capital from the Natchez region to Jackson, in the central part of the state, and in 1832, when Mississippi adopted a more democratic constitution that would carry it through the Civil War. The new constitution did away with property qualifications for voting and holding office, and the settlers who were pouring into the state were prepared to take full advantage of this change in franchise requirements. By the time Henry Foote arrived in Mississippi, the political structure that had allowed a relatively small clique of wealthy individuals from the Natchez region to rule was beginning to collapse. In its place was a new system whose leaders would have to rely on popular support. They would have to be able to sway the masses to vote for them. In this more democratic environment, those who sought to control politics in the state would have to have new talents and the ability to use those talents effectively in competition with one another. On the stump, they would have to interest, amuse, and excite crowds as performers. They could still act on principle, but they would also have to be actors playing a role that they hoped would appeal to the people. If governing was a science, the process of getting elected was about to become an art whose practitioners routinely blurred the lines between substance and facade.[2]

In Mississippi, the Jacksonian era was very combative as politicians of every sort vied for state and local offices. Despite Jackson's personal popularity in the state, support for him was not universal and his followers still faced significant class-based opposition from the wealthy Natchez elites. While they may have admired his war record, it was difficult for many in the state's wealthier economic and social strata to support such a rough candidate against more well-educated, dignified statesmen like John Quincy Adams or Henry Clay. The Natchez elites also bristled at the prospect of ordinary citizens taking an active role in state government. To many conservative Natchez politicians, Jackson was a symbol of everything they feared in terms of political reform and popular participation in the political process. They disparaged Jacksonian democracy as "mob rule" and, as a result, most supported Jackson's opponents at the national level, eventually forming the nucleus of the Whig Party in Mississippi during Jackson's second term.[3]

Adding to the chaos of frontier politics in Mississippi during its formative years was the fluid nature of competing political factions in the state and the absence of a competitive two-party political system. As was the case nationally, the old Federalist Party had died out in Mississippi, leaving the Jeffersonian Republicans (also called the Democratic-Republicans) as the only existing party with national credentials. Politicians with different political philosophies operated, at least for a time, under that moniker, with intraparty factions competing for supremacy. Legislative elections in Mississippi underscored the absence of competing political parties and tightly focused political organizations in general. Legislators won elections for a variety of reasons, but at the heart of any victory was a candidate's stand on local issues, coupled with the force of his personality while on the stump.

As settlers of a frontier state, Mississippians tended to view most national issues as secondary in nature. They lived in an isolated environment where the immediacy of local concerns took precedence over political squabbles occurring hundreds of miles away. As a result, political movements tended to form at the local level around individual leaders, county interests, or a single issue. For most Mississippians, terms such as *party* or *faction* were synonymous with self-interest and treachery. During the 1820s and beyond, candidates often tried to emphasize their own political autonomy and individuality while branding their opponents as scurrilous puppets obligated to carry out a factional agenda once elected. During one election season of the period, a Vicksburg newspaper typically praised a candidate that it endorsed by pointing out his "determination to take an independent stand, and not suffer Mississippi to be the quiescent dupe of a faction or a party."[4]

In this frontier environment, emotionally charged personality politics was the order of the day. During the 1820s and 1830s, most of Mississippi's population was not native to the region. New settlers occupied the old Indian lands in the central and northern parts of the state, and while many had immigrated in family groups, extended kinship and friendship ties would take at least another generation to develop. This social vacuum affected politics in that, to get elected, candidates had to depend on the force of their personalities rather than on established social or political relationships. Only the Natchez area in the southwestern part of the state held a concentrated population with a cohesive political infrastructure, but its dominance was waning. More and more settlers occupied the old Indian lands, but most still lived on small farms in isolated, rural areas. This left Mississippi with no entrenched, statewide political networks to influence the choice of candidates or the nature of the issues placed before the public.

This environment bred certain traits among Mississippi politicians of the period, traits that Henry Foote seemed to be born with. Because they lacked organized party support, candidates had to build campaign organizations around their own individuality. In essence, they had to become their own party, whether running for state or local posts. They had to have strong oratory skills and a combination of wit and bluster to attract voters and distinguish themselves from their rivals. Because their fortunes were linked to their individuality, candidates posed themselves as uncompromising, and campaigns frequently became highly charged personal duels. Such an environment bred confrontation in that even the simplest dispute between two individuals running for office could bring personal honor into question. This attitude colored political discourse on all levels, particularly as slavery-related sectional tensions increased.[5]

Grounded in personality politics and intrastate sectionalism that pitted the haves of the old Natchez District against the have-nots elsewhere, Mississippi offered fertile political soil for the growth of Jacksonian democracy. In Mississippi, the movement manifested itself through the direct personal appeal of Andrew Jackson, and Jackson's personal popularity in most circles overwhelmed his stand on individual political issues. Jackson was revered in Mississippi as a war hero, and Mississippians also related to Jackson as the product of a frontier society. They took seriously the so-called rise of the common man that he embodied.

Mississippians also admired Jackson as a fellow westerner who shared their views concerning Indians, especially Indian removal. The more recently settled areas of the state were filled with citizens who credited Jackson personally with removing the Choctaws and Chickasaws and thus allowing white settlers to build homes and start new lives. When compared to their love for the man, most Mississippians had little interest in his position on national issues such as those dealing with the Bank of the United States, the tariff, or nullification. To the simple farmers in the state, many of whom were recent immigrants to the frontier, he was the quintessential American hero.[6]

Throughout his presidency, Jackson retained significant support among Mississippians, and to the practical politicians in the state, the Jacksonian movement proved irresistible. "I found myself a Democrat without being able to explain why I was of that party," wrote one political operative of the period. "I began . . . as a follower of Jackson." State and local elections in Mississippi could be won or lost on the single question of a candidate's wholesale support for the president. Many candidates came into office on Jackson's coattails, while others lost elections because their support for Jackson came into question. During some campaigns, candidates discounted the issues and instead merely concentrated on "out-Jacksoning" one another.[7]

Henry Foote began building his political résumé in Mississippi during the early 1830s, a time when Jackson was at the height of his fame. It took Foote some time to break through and separate himself from the pack of state politicians who were jockeying for positions on the frontier, but when he did break through, he did so with a flourish. Foote owed his success to his innate intelligence and a personal drive that never allowed him to accept failure. He was also fearless and willing to say anything to anyone at any time if he thought it might help his cause. Like other good politicians, Foote had the ability to judge what people wanted to hear during a given political season and to alter his rhetoric accordingly. He could be charming, but more often than not he was very aggressive, sharply focused in his attacks, and more than willing to speak louder and longer than his opponents if necessary. He was a colorful character who could draw a crowd, and his stump speeches came to be viewed by many as more of an event than a mere public appearance by a politician. "Young Foote entered the front list of contestants for position and for fame," one contemporary later wrote of Foote's early years. "He was ready for every form of combat, whether mental or physical."[8]

In almost any communicative situation, whether it required a quiet chat or an animated tirade, Foote proved to be a master. In private conversations, he seemed comfortable with all classes, from the rich and powerful to the ordinary. He had the ability to charm women and men alike and, according to one source, "his conversation was said to be delightful. Wherever he went he was in the center of social activity." With regard to his public speaking, many of his contemporaries were quick to notice his tight grasp of the English language and his effortless command of the spoken word. James O'Meara, a journalist who knew Foote, described him as a "fascinating speaker" who was "gifted in speech, persuasive in address, invariably polite [and] prone to imagery in his conversation and popular harangues." Another acquaintance lauded the Mississippian's oratory as the perfect "fusion of reason and passion that go to make up true eloquence." When challenged, Foote's weapon of choice was satire, which he used deftly on many occasions to reduce opponents to objects of ridicule. Reuben Davis, a Mississippi congressman who was friendly with Foote, later remembered a debate during which an opponent verbally attacked Foote and, in response, Foote rose to the podium and "assumed his most courtly, kind, and eloquent manner, but all the while the lash of his satire descended, and every stroke was received [by the crowd in attendance] with perfect yells and shouts of laughter."

Foote also used his personal appearance to his advantage. He had red hair, but from an early age was balding, and his five-foot-eight-inch frame was rather slight, giving no outward sign of the fierce intellect and tenaciousness that inevitably caught those opponents who did not know him off guard. Once on the stump or "on the battlefield of joint debate," he could be as animated as the situation required. "His quick, light, springy step proclaimed his physical and mental activity," one observer wrote, "while his finely shaped forehead and well-developed head told of the great potential energy of his intellect." J. J. Peatfield, another journalist of the period, was more succinct, describing Foote simply as "vigorous, energetic, and capable of great endurance."

Foote did not become a respected and sought-after public speaker by accident. He spent years honing his rhetorical skills, and he viewed speechmaking itself as an art form. He read voraciously the work of the great classical philosophers and politicians and was particularly enamored with the great political communicator Cicero. "Cicero has told us," Foote once wrote, "that the 'eloquent speaker is a man who speaks in the forum and in civil causes in such a manner as to *prove*, to *delight*, and to *persuade*.'"[9]

But of course Foote had his detractors. Throughout his almost fifty-year career in politics, his enemies accused him of being little more than an obnoxious self-promoter and a man with few guiding moral principles, a self-centered opportunist whose primary joy in life was hearing his own voice, usually at a high volume. Some of these charges were true, though with some qualifications. Foote was indeed a great self-promoter, but probably no more so than any successful politician of his era or any other. Politics in a democracy is a business of self-promotion. Before great thoughts can be considered or great pieces of legislation can be enacted, members of any legislative body, state or federal, must get themselves elected. Before they can become pillars of the legislative system, they must first convince a majority of their constituents that they deserve the honor, and most will do this by any means necessary. During his lifetime, Foote shifted his party affiliations to meet his needs at the time. At various points he called himself a Jacksonian Democrat, a Whig, a Union Democrat, a Confederate Democrat, and even after the Civil War, a Republican, seeming to confirm his critics' complaints that he was a man of gross political vacillations.

However, Foote did have an ideological compass before the Civil War. He was interested in promoting the career of Henry Foote, but regardless of all of the twists and turns of his public life, he never abandoned his belief in the Union. From his earliest political pronouncements in the 1830s, he trumpeted the value of the union of states, and he did so for the next twenty years, as the nation was coming apart at the seams. He stuck to this course during the 1850s, under mounting criticism in Mississippi, and was able to get himself elected governor in 1851 by lambasting states' rights advocates who promoted secession over compromise on the slavery question. As a Confederate congressman during the war, he was never comfortable with the Confederate government, and many in the Confederate hierarchy hated him. Writing later of the Civil War era, Foote summed up his position by stating that "I had long before this period become satisfied of the absurdity as well as the criminality of all attempts to break up the Federal Union, and I had always been of the opinion that nothing could justify armed opposition to the [United States] Government."[10]

Foote made two failed attempts at elected office during his early years in Mississippi. In 1832, the state legislature, by this time dominated by members from outside the Natchez area, called for a convention to adopt a new, more democratic constitution that better reflected the ideals of the Jacksonian era. Foote saw this as an opportunity and began using his newspaper, the *Mississippian*, to promote himself as a delegate to the constitutional convention and to promote his own ideas. Up to this point, property qualification for voting and holding office had been the rule in Mississippi, and there were many appointed offices that were traditionally "passed around" by members of the Natchez elite. The new constitution expanded the franchise and allowed for more elected offices. In a newspaper column designed both to express his Jacksonian beliefs and to curry favor with the masses, Foote wrote of his "belief in the faith of the people to govern themselves" and stated that the electorate should choose "all important public officers." He promoted "his attachment to the Jackson Party in national politics" and his earnest belief in "unlimited exercise of the right of suffrage."

Foote was particularly interested in promoting the idea of an elected judiciary, and he made this the cornerstone of his first campaign for a public office in Mississippi, a race to become a delegate to the upcoming constitutional convention. The seat Foote pursued was an important one, representing a large Mississippi River district that included Vicksburg. His opponent was Eugene Magee, a Vicksburg lawyer with a well-established practice in partnership with a local judge. As the western boundary of the district was a long stretch of the Mississippi River, Foote frequently traveled from stop to stop by boat as he took his message to the public. The campaign was grueling, with Foote later remembering that he traveled the river "in a common dug-out," soliciting votes at riverbank gatherings and subsisting on river water, cheese, smoked venison, and "an occasional small supply of very indifferent bread." Foote campaigned hard until the very end but lost the race by a small, forty-vote margin. Despite the defeat, the results represented a good showing for the upstart politician who, after the fact, blamed the outcome on his status as "a young gentleman who had not lived long enough in Mississippi." Although he lost the contest, he had taken on a formidable opponent and held his own in his first campaign, and the experience raised Foote's profile in the area. The local political community took notice, and the race established his reputation as a tireless campaigner. More significantly, it further galvanized what he described as his "ambitious hopes," whetting his appetite for more political competition.[11]

The years 1832 and 1833 were pivotal in the history of American politics. Still barely fifty years old, the United States government experienced during these years a tremendous constitutional growing pain called the Nullification Crisis. It was a crisis produced by several highly charged factors, including the perpetual republican debate over the limits of state and federal authority, friction between the North and the South related to the national tariff and slavery, and a personal rivalry between President Andrew Jackson and the South Carolina politician John C. Calhoun. At the heart of the crisis were arguments related to whether a state had the right to void, or "nullify," a federal law if residents of that state believed that the law was offensive and unconstitutional.

The idea of nullification rested on foundational states' rights concepts that had dominated antebellum political thought in the South for generations. For more than a century before the Revolution, many Americans held fast in their opposition to the centralizing tendencies of the British monarchy. The colonies themselves were settled as separate political bodies, and through the years they developed individual commercial, economic, and political identities. Sectional divisions, while not yet sharply delineated, were already visible. A growing dependence on slavery marked the southern economy and skewed, to one degree or another, the region's infrastructure at every level. The rural nature of the southern colonies also bred a more distinct sense of community. Isolated neighborhoods, removed from the rule of law, found self-definition in their local autonomy. In a political context, these characteristics became deeply engrained in southern culture over time.[12]

The American victory at Yorktown and the subsequent Treaty of Paris in 1783 marked the end of one great struggle and the beginning of another. With independence won, Americans faced the monumental task of crafting abstract notions of civic virtue, liberty, and self-determination into a viable, working government. They labored in a postwar environment fraught with conflict. The Revolution dispatched British rule and, in so doing, eliminated the common enemy that had helped bond the colonies. Economic diversity and discordant political visions threatened the already fragile union of states. Traditional prejudices against centralized government still existed, as did the concept that a republic could not function properly in a large geographic area.

In effect, the American Revolution gave way to an American evolution— the ongoing process of defining the nature of the American republic. Paramount among the problems faced by the framers of the new government was the role of state sovereignty in the American constitutional structure. State sovereignty at the expense of a national political entity had undermined republicanism under the Articles of Confederation, rendering the articles ineffective as anything but a general vehicle for cooperation among the states. The issue would produce heated debate during the ratification of the Constitution, debate that would continue through the early national period and be carried on, in one form or another, by the framers' political descendants, through the nineteenth century and beyond.[13]

In 1828 and 1832, Congress passed protective tariffs that were supported in the North and despised in the South. Northerners supported high tariffs on the grounds that they helped promote and protect domestic manufacturing, while southerners, fully attached to their agricultural economy based in cotton production and slavery, viewed them as devices that gave the North an unfair economic advantage. At the national level, John C. Calhoun hoped to use the South's hatred of the tariff as a political base for himself. He had run successfully as Jackson's vice president in 1828, but the South Carolinian and the old war hero from Tennessee hated one another. Calhoun hoped to use the tariff issue to rally the South against Jackson. While it would be a tall task, Calhoun hoped to convince southerners to forget about Jackson's war record and to see the president as the head of a federal government that was imposing an unfair and unconstitutional tariff on the southern states. He hoped to convince Americans that Jackson had abandoned his roots as a hero of the common man in favor of an oppressive agenda that included a dominant federal government that cared little for the rights of the individual states and their citizens. In doing so, Calhoun, one of the great political thinkers of his era, crafted a controversial theory that revolved around the claim that an individual state did not necessarily have to abide by all federal laws, that a state could *nullify* a law passed by the national congress if that state believed that the law was unconstitutional. Accordingly, if the federal government insisted on forcing the offensive law onto the states collectively, by somehow having it added to the Constitution as an amendment, individual states had the right to end their association with the Union through the secession process.

With Calhoun's blessing, his home state tested this theory by calling a convention in 1832 and voting to nullify the recently passed federal tariff. This generated a showdown between South Carolina and the federal government, and between Jackson, who called nullification treason, and Calhoun. Calhoun tried unsuccessfully to rally the rest of the South behind South Carolina and the nullification concept, but Jackson's hold on the region proved too strong. Once nullification became an issue, Jacksonians set upon a simple but effective course to neutralize Calhoun's argument linking the president with detrimental federal intervention in state affairs. They cast the nullifiers as villains bent on destroying the Union for their own purposes, and they further argued that a severed Union would create economic ruin and leave the South vulnerable to outside attacks. By contrast, they linked the president to the security that the Union provided. "The scales are now balancing in fearful equipoise," one Jackson ally in the South said, "liberty and union in the one hand, anarchy and despotism in the other. . . . The very fabric of our government is rocking on its foundation."

Most southern politicians were not willing to cross Andrew Jackson in favor of Calhoun because their constituents supported the old war hero in large numbers. A compromise eventually diffused the situation, but not before a small but strong states' rights movement began developing in the South. It was a movement that would come into full flower during the 1850s and eventually lead the southern states out of the Union and into civil war. In Mississippi, Henry Foote maneuvered through the period like a master, establishing himself at the state level while also advancing his national aspirations. Promoting his long-term commitment to the Union, he called nullification an "absurd theory" and allied himself with Robert J. Walker, Jackson's leading political operative in the state.[14]

Born into an affluent Pennsylvania family in 1801, Robert Walker entered politics soon after graduating from the University of Pennsylvania, at the head of his class, in 1819. Within a few years he was deeply involved in the Jacksonian movement in Pennsylvania, giving speeches and writing letters and newspaper editorials. Highly ambitious, Walker was determined to make his mark in politics. As Jacksonianism swept the nation, he saw his chance and never failed to capitalize on his early association with the phenomenon. Following his older brother and a number of other prominent Pennsylvanians who moved to Mississippi to make their fortunes, Walker relocated to Natchez in 1826. He practiced law with his brother and became involved in land speculation and other business dealings.

Realizing that the political influence of the Natchez region was waning in the face of thousands of new settlers entering Mississippi—the so-called common men who helped fuel Andrew Jackson's political career—Walker established himself as the state's leading Jacksonian. He helped organize a Jackson Association with like-minded politicians and was among a group that established a Jacksonian newspaper. Acquiring a reputation as something of a political miracle worker, Walker was able to shrewdly position himself, through his support for Jackson, as a friend of the common man, while still maintaining his ties to the elite of the Natchez area. During the presidential elections of 1828 and 1832, Andrew Jackson's political victories were also victories for Walker, establishing him as one of Mississippi's most influential politicians.[15]

Walker and Foote had been acquainted for some time, as a result of their legal work, and Foote knew that by cleaving to Walker politically, he was firmly attaching himself to Andrew Jackson's coattails. "When the dogma of nullification was suddenly broached by the politicians of South Carolina," Foote later recalled, "Mr. Walker came forth at once, in the newspapers and elsewhere, as the stern and uncompromising supporter of General Jackson." Foote also condemned nullification and defended the federal union in speeches and in letters to newspapers in the state. He made a name for himself during the nullification debates in Mississippi as a fearless Jacksonian crusader who was willing to take on all comers, regardless of their status or stature. At a large gathering held in Raymond, Mississippi, in 1833, Foote verbally harangued former state senator Samuel B. Marsh, an outspoken advocate of nullification, as an "intermeddling, mischief-making coward," and he later got into an altercation with United States representative Franklin Plummer, a Walker rival who was critical of Jackson. Foote and Plummer got into a public shouting match, during which Plummer questioned Foote's integrity and called him a liar. Foote responded by threatening to challenge Plummer to a duel, at which time the representative backed down.[16]

Behind the scenes, Foote also joined Walker and others in a business venture involving land speculation. On September 27, 1830, the Choctaw Indians ceded to the federal government their remaining lands in Mississippi—around eleven million acres—through the Treaty of Dancing Rabbit Creek. The treaty opened all of the old Indian lands for settlement and created opportunities for land speculators, who gambled that the price of land in Mississippi was about to go up. Sensing the opportunity for a financial windfall, Robert Walker partnered in a speculative enterprise with William M. Gwin, a physician and up-and-coming politician who later represented Mississippi in the U.S. House of Representatives. Walker and Gwin quickly put together a syndicate to gain control of more than seven hundred thousand acres of the recently ceded Choctaw land.

Among the first men that they approached to be part of the organization were future Mississippi governor John Anthony Quitman; Joseph Davis, brother of future U.S. senator and president of the Confederacy, Jefferson Davis; and Walker's political ally Henry Foote. Each member of the group was allowed to purchase $1,000 worth of shares in the project, and eventually about one hundred fifty other speculators from Mississippi, Alabama, and Tennessee were involved in the deal. When the dust settled and the land was sold, each member of the syndicate, on average, realized a modest profit on their initial investment. The project drew Foote and Walker closer together and also allowed Foote to circulate among what some referred to as the "Mississippi Regency," the state Democratic leaders who influenced much of Mississippi's money and politics.[17]

In 1834, Walker decided to challenge incumbent George Poindexter for his seat representing Mississippi in the United States Senate. Poindexter, up to that point, was the young state's most powerful politician. He was elected to the Senate as a Jackson supporter in 1830, but he subsequently had a falling out with the president and the two men became sworn political enemies. Walker knew that Poindexter's break with Jackson left the senator vulnerable in the state, and he planned to exploit the situation. Henry Foote signed on to be one of Walker's chief spokesmen and also filed to run his own campaign that year for chancellor of the state.

Walker and Foote toured Mississippi together, and although Foote's campaign for chancellor failed, he was an integral part of Walker's successful effort to unseat Poindexter. Foote railed against Poindexter wherever he spoke, emphasizing the senator's disloyalty to the president. While Walker won the race, many who heard both men speak during their many public appearances together judged Foote the superior orator. One observer called Foote "a bold and fearless man, who inspired [Walker] with his own courage." In the end, Walker defeated Poindexter, forcing him into retirement, and Foote made a name for himself as one of the best public speakers in the state, if not in the entire South. "He is the greatest man in our state. I mean, the most talented," prominent Mississippi newspaper editor George R. Fall wrote of Foote in a letter to future president James K. Polk. "He is a favorite of the friends of Andrew Jackson in Mississippi; has been their main pillar on the stump and with the pen [and] has toiled night and day for the last eight years to keep the administration star in ascent."[18]

The fallout from Walker–Poindexter race had a very ugly and violent by-product, in which Henry Foote was indirectly involved. In November of 1835, Charles Lynch was elected governor of Mississippi, and the following January he was installed as the state's chief executive. The night of the inauguration, most of Mississippi's leading politicians attended a party in Jackson honoring Lynch. Because of all the recent political squabbling, tensions were running high, and at one point during the affair, George Poindexter climbed on top of a table and began making a spontaneous, alcohol-induced political speech criticizing Andrew Jackson. William Gwin's brother, Samuel, a staunch Jackson supporter and close friend of Walker and Foote, took offense and began launching hisses and catcalls at the former senator. In turn, Poindexter's friend and former law partner, Isaac Caldwell, shouted insults at Gwin. The men exchanged more heated words and Caldwell eventually challenged Gwin to a duel.

The two men met several miles outside of Jackson a few days later, each armed with multiple pistols. Gwin chose Foote, a friend and fellow partisan in the Walker political machine, to serve as his second during the confrontation, which was witnessed by around four hundred local residents. "We proceeded to the grounds at the time agreed upon," Foote later wrote, "and found the adverse party already there and a vast concourse of citizens in attendance. All the neighboring villages had poured out the tide of population to take a view of the expected combat." Once the duel began, the onlookers witnessed a grisly scene. The terms agreed upon for the duel were "thirty paces distant . . . each contestant given the privilege of advancing," meaning that the combatants did not have to remain stationary and could fire multiple shots from multiple weapons. They could move around and even rush one another while firing, greatly increasing the odds that one or both of the men would be hit. After firing several shots, Gwin killed Caldwell, but not before Caldwell shot Gwin in the chest. The wound was serious but not immediately fatal. After the duel, Gwin never fully regained his health, and he died less than two years later from the effects of the contest.[19]

After the 1834–1835 election cycle, Foote resumed his law practice full time and eventually opened an office in Clinton, a few miles outside the state capital, in partnership with Anderson Hutchinson and Daniel R. Russell. Foote was by then well known in the state. His firm never lacked for business, and according to one source his "professional receipts were as much as $10,000 per year," a considerable sum for the period. While Foote made good money through his talents as a barrister, he also spent a great deal and "laid up but little, having a numerous family." Generous to those he liked, he was quick to lend out funds or guarantee the notes of acquaintances, with one source later recalling that Foote routinely lost money after "having had to advance considerable sums in payment of the debts of friends for whom he had become security." Regardless, Foote had a reputation as a master of the courtroom with an ability to convince any jury of almost anything at any time. Obviously impressed with the Foote's abilities, fellow attorney James Daniel Lynch later wrote that Foote "was engaged in many of the most important criminal cases that occurred in the state during the time of his practice at the bar of Mississippi, and acquitted himself with ability and remarkable success. His main professional strength lay in his capacity for captivating the minds of the jury."[20]

While Henry Foote maintained his reputation as an aggressive attorney, his political maneuvering never ceased. He had yet to win an election in Mississippi, having been defeated in races for constitutional convention delegate in 1832 and state chancellor two years later, but most observers believed that these defeats were primarily the result of his having only recently settled in the state. Foote angled for an appointment as a federal judge through his relationship with Senator Walker but met with little success in a crowded field of fellow Jacksonian office seekers. Finally, as Andrew Jackson's second administration drew to a close, the president appointed Foote to a federal position as surveyor general of the lands south of Tennessee. In Mississippi, the Democratic press applauded the selection, stating that Foote was "known as a prompt, energetic and business-like man, and is well qualified to discharge the duties of the office."

Foote took the appointment and opened a federal land office in Jackson but, despite praise from the newspapers, he was not cut out for life as a low-level federal bureaucrat. Compared to his life as a political operative in the rough-and-tumble world of frontier politics, the job was boring. His confrontational personality also brought him into conflict with other bureaucrats and he soon fell out of favor with officials in the Government Land Office in Washington. The federal appointment represented a slight but significant diversion from the career path he had set for himself, which was to be a dominant figure on the Mississippi political scene and to perhaps become a national voice one day. He stayed in the position for less than two years, resigning to run for the state legislature in the spring of 1838.[21]

After taking the federal appointment, Foote tried to remain actively involved in political affairs in Mississippi, which were becoming decidedly more complicated. As was the case nationally, a bona fide two-party political system was emerging in the state as the Jacksonian era came to an end. The development of the Whig Party in Mississippi paralleled the party's development as an anti-Jackson coalition at the national level. Mississippi Whigs included a loose coalition of the old Natchez elite who had never been enamored with the "democratization" of politics during Jackson's tenure and disaffected Jacksonian politicians who abandoned the Jackson camp over issues such the distribution of federal patronage in the state and nullification. The party gained strength during the last half of Jackson's second administration, and after the president left office, the Mississippi Whigs and Democrats were evenly matched for several years. Reflecting the nature of the era's competition for supremacy, the state's House of Representatives was majority Democrat in 1837, evenly matched in 1838, Whig in 1839, Democrat in 1840, Whig in 1841, and Democrat again in 1842.[22]

The new Whig Party rivaled the Democrats so quickly in Mississippi for several reasons. First, it included among its leadership many notable politicians who had been networking in the state for years. More importantly, Jackson's departure from the White House leveled the political playing field. The president's policies had alienated some of the state's Democrats, who, with Jackson's personality removed from political consideration, could now voice their opposition to the party rather than to the man himself. Finally, Mississippi's basic political climate made it virtually impossible for one party to dominate the other. The state, and the South as a whole, had a strong antiparty tradition. Parties were viewed with suspicion by many as vehicles for the type of concentrated political power that was always a threat to republican ideals and the autonomy of rank-and-file white male citizens. These concerns were particularly acute in the South's slave-based culture, where the terms *master* and *slave* transcended the physical boundaries of plantations.

As a result, the coalitions that would operate under the party labels of Whig and Democrat were never stable in composition during their early years. Single-issue debates and personalities often trumped party loyalty, and while most of the core leadership of both groups consistently defined themselves with these labels, such self-definition was often superficial. Both parties contained various cliques that backed individual party leaders or promoted a particular agenda that was not universally partisan. In addition, the men who led both parties were usually of the same economic class and cooperated with one another in areas that promoted their common interests.

Among Mississippi's voting population in general, party loyalty was even more tenuous. After the adoption of the 1832 constitution that expanded franchise, voter participation increased dramatically. During the presidential election year 1840, 88 percent of eligible voters in the state went to the polls—up from 28 percent in 1832 and 64 percent in 1836. This large mass of voters represented diverse interests that could not be rigidly placed within the confines of a two-party political system. According to one cynical nineteenth-century observer, in Mississippi, "about one half of those who vote look upon the privilege as worthless unless they can use it to gratify a personal hostility or religious antipathies, or to inflict injury on what they hate." In such an environment, the parties functioned as a tool for general organization at the state level and as a means for organizing support for candidates in national races, but for little else.[23]

The 1836 presidential election season was notable in that several candidates vied for the spot as Jackson's successors. Prominent among them was Jackson's vice president, Martin Van Buren, the eventual Democratic nominee, and Whig candidates led by war hero William Henry Harrison and Tennessee senator Hugh Lawson White, a former Jackson ally who had broken with the president during his second administration. In Mississippi, Foote flirted with White and the Whigs before throwing his support behind Van Buren.

Foote's early leanings toward White represented a political testing of the waters by a cautious politician seeking to keep all of his options open. The slavery issue was beginning to create regional fissures in the national Democratic coalition, and in the Deep South, many Democratic politicians were not completely comfortable with Van Buren. As a New Yorker, the vice president had roots in the North, where the abolition movement was steadily growing. In addition, Van Buren's great political enemy at the national level was John C. Calhoun, the formidable South Carolina senator viewed by many as the South's standard-bearer on issues related to slavery and states' rights. In contrast, White's candidacy was designed to appeal to southerners, and the Tennessean went to great lengths to promote southern unity during the campaign.

Always striving to come down on the winning side, Foote tried to gauge early on whether White could put together an effective national coalition and how White's message would play in Mississippi. Foote was also frustrated as a result of his failure to advance as part of his state's crowded Democratic organization, where dozens of ambitious men perpetually jockeyed for position. Foote was a well-respected stump speaker and he maintained a lucrative law practice, but for all of his work for the Democratic Party in Mississippi, his only reward, so far, had been a federal appointment to a job for which he was not well suited. Still, more comfortable in general among the Democrats and sensing that Van Buren would win the election, Foote eventually abandoned White in support of the Democratic ticket.

While Van Buren's association with Andrew Jackson garnered him a great deal of support in Mississippi during the 1836 election season, some state leaders were suspicious of the New Yorker's motives and agenda. The Nat Turner rebellion, still fresh in the minds of many, along with the founding of the American Anti-Slavery Society and the general increase in abolitionist rhetoric in the nonslaveholding states, alarmed Mississippians and made them fundamentally suspicious of politicians from the North. Many Democratic leaders in the southern states either sent representatives to meet with Van Buren or corresponded with him in hopes that he could clarify his position on slavery, and Mississippi was no exception. Van Buren's enemies in the state, both within his party and among his Whig rivals, had been disparaging him in the press, bringing into question his character and his motives for wanting to become president as they related to the slavery issue.

To counter these attacks, Van Buren's supporters wanted to send a Mississippian to meet with the candidate and to get from him definitive assurances that he was sympathetic to the state and to southern concerns, should he become president. State leaders chose Foote to make the trip and, upon his return, to canvas Mississippi, promoting Van Buren for president. "It was judged in Mississippi to be expedient," Foote later wrote, "that someone should be deputed to Albany—where Mr. Van Buren was then temporarily sojourning—for the purpose of obtaining some explanation from his own lips elucidatory of certain disputed points in his history." These "disputed points" all related, to one degree or another, to slavery, and while Van Buren would one day run for president representing the Free Soil Party, during the 1836 election cycle he placated the South by expressing his support for slavery in the District of Columbia and through his general position that the national congress had no right to interfere with the institution in the southern states. "I must go into the Presidential chair," Van Buren wrote at the time, "the inflexible and uncompromising opponent of any attempt on the part of Congress to abolish slavery in the District of Columbia, against the wishes of the slave-holding states; and also with the determination, equally decided, to resist the slightest interference with the subject in the states where it exists."[24]

By his own account, the trip to visit Van Buren was memorable for Foote, particularly after he reached Norfolk, Virginia, by rail and boarded a steamship headed up the James River toward Richmond. Ever the extrovert, Foote fell into conversation with several Virginians who were active supporters of the

Whig Party and who, like Foote, were not shy about sharing their thoughts on the political climate of the day. Once they found out that Foote was on his way to see Van Buren, the discussion grew more heated, and what Foote later described as "a calm and courteous colloquy between us" turned into "a boisterous and excited controversial dispute."

After a while, one of the Virginians insisted that Foote accompany him to another part of the steamer to meet John Tyler, who was also a passenger. At the time, Tyler, the former Virginia governor and future president, had recently resigned from the United States Senate and was a candidate for vice president as Hugh Lawson White's running mate. Tyler seemed pleased to meet Foote and quickly settled into conversation with him. Unlike his discourse with the other Virginians, Foote's political discussions with Tyler were calm and to the point, and the Mississippian uncharacteristically deferred to Tyler, who was fourteen years his senior, preferring to listen to the veteran lawmaker rather than drive the conversation. "Being really very anxious to hear him talk," Foote later recalled, "and being altogether unwilling to change the tone of our conversation . . . I cautiously avoided making any issue with him whatsoever." Upon reaching Richmond, Tyler gave Foote a brief tour of the city before the two men parted company.[25]

Foote stayed the night in Richmond and continued his trip by rail the next day, eventually arriving in Albany, New York, for his meeting. Whereas Foote's conversation with Tyler had been political but somewhat informal, due in large part to being unexpected, Van Buren was prepared for Foote's arrival and to sell himself and his programs to Foote so that Foote could go back home and sing the candidate's praises to Mississippi Democrats. "I found Mr. Van Buren in excellent health and spirits," Foote later reported. "He met me very cordially, took me to several interesting places in the city, and invited me to dine with him at 5 o'clock." The dinner included several other prominent New Yorkers, including Governor William L. Marcy, a staunch Jackson ally; U.S. senator Nathaniel P. Tallmadge, who had been elected in 1833 as a Jacksonian Democrat; veteran New York judge Reuben H. Walworth; and Van Buren's son John, an Albany attorney and Yale graduate. The group wined and dined Foote, flattering him in general and assuring him that Van Buren stood for the Jacksonian principles that had appealed to so many southerners and had helped the general win two elections.

Convinced of Van Buren's sincerity, Foote returned to Mississippi as an "expert" on Van Buren's candidacy and met with other state leaders to plot a course of action. He then organized a speaking tour, during which he made impassioned speeches on the vice president's behalf. While the Whigs showed significant strength in the state, Van Buren ultimately carried Mississippi and won the presidency. The state's Democratic press again praised Foote's efforts as a campaigner and "a prominent member of the Democratic Party."[26]

Not long after Foote canvassed the state lauding Van Buren, he participated in another duel. The contest took place near Columbus, Mississippi, and his opponent was Osmun Claiborne, a retired naval officer and a member of one of the most prominent families in Natchez. The Claibornes had moved to the Natchez region from Virginia around the turn of the nineteenth century and had firmly established themselves among the local gentry. Claiborne's father served as a brigadier general in the United States Army during the War of 1812, and his uncle, William C. C. Claiborne, was the first governor of Louisiana and a United States senator.

According to Foote, Claiborne issued the challenge, but the cause of the duel is unclear. Neither man was fatally injured after, according to one account, "the parties fired at each other five times with pistols, [with Foote] wounding his antagonist slightly three times." Foote himself later recalled that "after five shots having been exchanged, the affair terminated without the least personal injury to myself, my adversary having been disabled by my fifth shot, which entered his hip." Claiborne's wounds were not serious and he went on to live for another eight years.

At this point in his life, Foote—along with many other politicians—seemed to no longer worry about breaking antidueling statutes. By the time he became prominent, the ritual was so fully ingrained in the South as a means for men of substance to defend their personal honor that law enforcement often ignored the illegality of the practice. Many local sheriffs or constables felt that they had little to gain by arresting prominent men, and local prosecutors knew that convicting duelists was a difficult chore. Many witnesses refused to give damning testimony related to the combatants, while others refused to offer any testimony at all, believing that a duel was strictly a personal matter that government officials should stay out of.[27]

Despite his work for the Democratic Party in Mississippi, political expedience trumped party loyalty in 1838, when Foote resigned his post as surveyor general to run for the state legislature, representing Hinds County. Hinds was one of the state's predominantly Whig counties, and though still a Democrat in practice, Foote chose to run as a Whig for the position. It was an uncomplicated decision based in practical opportunism, and it would not be the last time that Foote manipulated Whig support during an election season. In an era where personality regularly trumped party affiliation at the local level, Foote was able to mount a smoke-and-mirrors campaign as a Whig, through the force of his campaign rhetoric.

Before he could do so, however, he had to clear up a nagging legal detail related to a duel from his younger days. Mississippi's dueling laws excluded anyone convicted of dueling—as Foote had been in Alabama—from holding public office. For someone like Foote, whose standing in his party was secure, wiping away a past indiscretion like his contest with Edmund Winston was merely a technical matter, remedied by a general amnesty granted by the state legislature. Such pieces of legislation were not uncommon in a state where dueling was governed by laws that were many times ignored. Using his contacts in the statehouse, Foote lobbied for a "full and complete amnesty" for his past indiscretions related to dueling, which he received on February 16, 1838.[28]

Amnesty in hand, Foote won the election and took a seat in the Mississippi legislature. He served a single term in that body and, with regard to legislative matters, he won both popular acclaim from many and an acute disdain from some by successfully sponsoring a temperance bill. The bill was officially titled "An Act for the Suppression of Tippling Houses, and to discourage and prevent the odious vice of drunkenness," but critics called it simply the Gallon Law, because one part of the legislation prohibited the sale of alcohol in quantities less than one gallon. The law in essence forbid the sale of spirits by the drink and outlawed the distribution of liquor by political candidates seeking public office. News of the new law created a stir in Jackson, with Foote facing the wrath of local saloon keepers and their patrons as well as of local newspaper editors, who denounced the legislation as an "outrageous infraction of personal liberty." At a rally near the state capitol building, rowdy critics of the law cursed Foote's name and hung him in effigy.

Foote was unmoved by the protest and called the gathering and his symbolic execution "amusing and gratifying." Foote apparently backed the law because he sincerely believed in the idea of temperance. Throughout his career, he consistently spoke about the evils of alcohol and condemned its sale and distribution. "How many men," Foote wrote, "who once enjoyed social respectability have been sunk in cureless infamy by habitual indulgence of stimulating liquids?" Always conscious of public perception, he also knew that his sponsorship of the law made for good politics because it allowed him to take the moral high ground on an emotional issue that many nondrinking voters paid attention to. The legislation also garnered Foote a small amount of national attention as his sponsorship of the bill earned him accolades from the American Temperance Union.[29]

Though technically elected as a Whig, Foote remained loyal to the Democratic Party and made no secret of his affiliation. He seemed to suffer no immediate ill effects from taking on a Whig facade, but it left him open to critics who later questioned his loyalties and disparaged him as a "party-switcher." All was apparently forgiven by the 1840 presidential campaign season, when he dropped the Whig label and the Democrats chose him to replace a recently deceased Van Buren elector. Several years later, a Democratic newspaper would explain away Foote's dalliance with the rival party, telling its readers that "once in his life, for a few months, he withdrew his support from certain Democratic measures . . . but not long enough to have voted the Whig ticket in any general election. This solitary deviation he has always regretted."

Other than his promotion of temperance, Foote's one term in the state legislature was uneventful with regard to actual legislation, but during this period he was very active around the state, giving speeches and attending rallies. The press began taking note of Foote's comings and goings, drawn to him primarily because he attracted growing crowds and because his addresses were "entertaining . . . alternately sarcastic, eloquent and amusing" and filled with "a great deal of ornament and play." Foote obviously enjoyed being noticed, and it soon became apparent that his energies and bold personality could never be confined solely to the Mississippi capitol building in Jackson. While filling a seat in the state legislature was a terminal goal of many local politicians of his era, for Henry Foote, the floor of the Mississippi House of Representatives was far too small a stage.[30]

3

Temporary Texan

I had gone [to Texas] on a mingled trip of pleasure and business.
—Henry Stuart Foote

ON DECEMBER 29, 1845, U.S. President James K. Polk signed legislation bringing Texas into the Union as the twenty-eighth state. It was an event that marked the culmination of more than two decades of American fascination with the region. For most adult Americans living in the first half of the nineteenth century, it was impossible to ignore Texas. It was a vast area of great topographical and cultural diversity, a land of endless horizons where a man might make his fortune or, if needed, disappear. To some Americans, Texas was a lawless but tamable frontier, ripe for settlement and exploitation, while others viewed it with excitement as a land of mystery and intrigue.

American expansion into Texas and the rest of the West was driven by a general political, economic, social, and religious philosophy—Manifest Destiny, as it came to be called—that emerged during the period to justify the goal of United States dominance from the Atlantic to the Pacific. Before becoming president, John Quincy Adams summed up the general tenets of Manifest Destiny, in 1811, when he wrote in a letter to his father, former president John Adams, "The whole continent of North America appears to be destined by Divine Providence to be peopled by one nation, speaking one language, professing one general system of religious and political principles, and accustomed to one general tenor of social usages and customs."

While lofty pronouncements about God's role in spreading American influence across the continent helped fuel Manifest Destiny, so did a host of economic, political, and social realities, including greed for new land and traditional American beliefs related to the superiority of Anglo-American culture.

The status of Texas also generated great political controversy in the United States in an era when slavery was driving northerners and southerners farther apart. Leaders in the slaveholding states who sought to expand the cotton kingdom into the West were particularly enamored by Texas at a time when many of their counterparts in the North hoped to keep slavery in check. In the end, Texas entered the Union as a slave state, aggravating sectional tensions as it stretched the southwestern borders of the United States.[1]

Like others interested in national affairs, Henry Foote had been keeping up with events in Texas for some time. Americans in Texas began agitating for self-government during the 1820s, and by the next decade the status of Texas was a major component of American political discourse. Like Foote, southerners in general were sympathetic to the Texas revolutionaries during their struggle to break free from Mexico, and many of the Texans in the revolutionary army were southern transplants. Most southern politicians, especially those from the Deep South cotton states, supported the revolution and hoped that an independent Texas would one day become part of the United States. With the outbreak of hostilities in the region, volunteers from around the South went west to fight with the revolutionaries as southern communities large and small held political meetings and fund-raising rallies to support the effort. "We feel quite gratified in being able to say to our readers that the spirit of enthusiasm is now burning with increased vigor," one Mississippi editor crowed at the time, "and many brave and gallant young men have equipped themselves and started to the aid of the suffering Texans."[2]

In retrospect, the Mexican government almost invited revolution through policies that it instituted soon after Mexico achieved independence from Spain, in 1821. In what was one of the greatest political miscalculations in the history of North America, the new Mexican government invited Americans to come and live in Texas, then one of the Mexico's northern provinces, in an attempt to populate and stabilize the region. The Mexican government set up the *empresario* system, hiring American agents and giving them the rights to vast acreage in exchange for their help recruiting into the region settlers from the United States. These new setters would have exemptions from taxation and could start new lives if they agreed to swear loyalty to Mexico, abide by Mexican law, and convert to Catholicism.

The plan was doomed from the start, and the *empresario* system soon crumbled. Instead of an orderly migration, what amounted to a land rush took place.

Still in economic distress following the financial Panic of 1819, thousands of settlers from the United States poured into Texas in search of opportunity. Land speculators also fueled the fires of immigration as well as the eventual push for Texas independence and annexation to the United States. Even after Mexico banned further immigration from the United States, in 1830, the settlers kept coming, mostly from the South and many with slaves, in direct violation of Mexican law. By the eve of the revolution, the southern Texas settlers were growing cotton and the institution of slavery was firmly established there.[3]

Fighting between Texans seeking self-determination and Mexican forces began in earnest in 1835, and the following year Texas declared independence. During the revolution's climactic Battle of San Jacinto, on April 21, 1836, the Texans captured Mexican dictator Antonio López de Santa Anna and forced him to sign a peace treaty, paving the way for Texas independence. While the treaty officially ended the revolution, it heightened the political maneuverings and intrigues related to the relationship between Texas and the United States. The major questions at hand involved America's official recognition of Texas as a sovereign nation and whether Texas would become part of the United States as a new slave state. Many thought that annexation might bring on a war between the United States and Mexico. Others, especially many northerners, saw the addition of Texas to the Union, in political terms, as a significant expansion of slavery. Conversely, many in the South favored annexation for that same reason, leading to heated debates on the subject in Congress.

In the United States Senate, there was no greater champion of the Texas cause than Mississippian Robert J. Walker, Henry Foote's political ally. Walker was certainly a proponent of expanding the cotton kingdom into the West, but he also had personal, self-serving reasons for promoting Texas annexation. Walker and his brother Duncan were involved in land speculation in Texas, a venture which would likely become more lucrative if Texas broke away from Mexico and became part of the United States. Duncan Walker, in 1834, purchased a substantial amount of land in Texas and subsequently transferred ownership of some of the property to his brother. Not long afterwards, Mexican authorities captured Duncan and put him in prison for allegedly agitating for Texas independence, and while he was incarcerated his health declined. Eventually released, he never fully recovered from the ordeal and he died not long afterward.

The episode left Robert Walker with a deep hatred for Mexican officials and a deep desire to increase the profitability of his Texas holdings by promoting Texas independence and annexation, which he did with fervor. Walker advised his political friends in Mississippi, including Henry Foote, about the advantages of purchasing land in Texas and about where the land with the most potential might be located. As a result, a handful of well-connected Mississippians began buying up hundreds of thousands of Texas acres. While he hoped to make significant profits through land speculation, Walker's concerns related to Texas were also political. His constituents in Mississippi heavily favored annexation, and because the Texas question was tied to slavery, it was an emotional issue ripe for exploitation. Walker knew that his political future was tied to his maintaining popularity in his home state, where constituents viewed his high-profile support of Texas as support for cotton, slavery, and a general way of life that they held dear. As a veteran politician, Walker knew how to use this situation to his advantage. In addition, his support for Texas enhanced his national reputation and garnered him support across the South as other southern states clamored for the admission of Texas into the Union.[4]

After the revolution, Walker went to work in the Senate, promoting American recognition of Texas independence. He worked on the issue with such focus that some jokingly labeled him the new country's unofficial representative in Congress. He sponsored the legislation seeking congressional approval for the recognition of independent Texas, which passed in March of 1837 after a great deal of debate. Grateful leaders of the new republic invited Walker to Texas to tour the San Jacinto battlefield and address a large crowd of well-wishers. He later addressed a joint assembly of the Texas congress, where he was applauded by its membership. "You were our champion in our direst conflict with the enemy," one Texan told Walker, "and to you, sir, are we now mainly indebted for the rank we hold amongst the nations of the world." The next year, Texas representatives sought and received permission from Walker for the preparation of a stone bust of the Mississippian to be placed in the Texas capitol.[5]

Henry Foote kept a keen eye on events in Texas during this period. Like Walker, he believed that the United States should annex Texas, but he was also interested in any financial and political opportunities that Texas might offer him personally. Foote's interest in Texas dated back to 1835, the year the revolution began, and was directly tied to his relationship with Walker. Foote followed Walker's lead with regard to his expansionist views and involvement in the Southwest, claiming later that he was "burning with zeal" for Texas. In Mississippi, Natchez was a focal point for Texas support as a number of the city's elite saw the opportunities that an independent or annexed Texas might afford men with capital, and Foote used his many Natchez connections to promote the Texas cause. Not long before the revolution began, Foote accompanied Felix Huston, a Natchez lawyer who eventually commanded troops in the revolutionary army, to New Orleans for an early meeting to "foster public sentiment favorable to Texas."[6] Foote then left on a speaking tour through Mississippi, promoting the Texas cause.

Once the revolution ended, in April of 1836, Foote left the state on a fund-raising trip that took him to New York, where he met with Memucan Hunt, a political operative representing the Texas government. An officer in the Texas army who also owned a plantation in Madison County, Mississippi, Hunt was soliciting resources from some of New York's wealthiest men, including John Jacob Astor. "The affairs in Texas were still in a feeble and tottering condition," Foote later wrote. The fledgling republic was "still menaced by invasion from Mexico" and was "exceedingly deficient in moneyed resources."[7] Armed with promissory notes guaranteed by a wealthy Natchez planter, Foote helped arrange a line of credit through the Bank of America in New York for the purchase of arms and ammunition for Texas.[8] He was also among a delegation that went to visit Astor.

The visit to John Jacob Astor's New York home was memorable for Foote but ultimately unsuccessful. Foote was accompanied by Hunt and Samuel Swartwout, a man of questionable reputation who, years before, had been a confidant of Aaron Burr and who, within a few years, would be charged with embezzling more than a million dollars from the Port of New York. A well-connected Jackson supporter, Swartwout was an active campaigner on behalf of Texas and was involved in a variety of business enterprises, including Texas land speculation. Through his business connections he was able to arrange a meeting with Astor, who was by then an old man in his seventies. "Now, Mr. Astor lived at a beautiful place," Foote later recalled. "The company mentioned were received by Mr. Astor in his front piazza. The day was intensely hot and the old gentleman was cooling himself in the fresh breeze from the bay. . . . Suffice it to say that those who represented Texas on this occasion did all in their power to persuade the illustrious banker that he had a fair chance to immortalize himself by advancing to the rescue of a people struggling for liberty." The pleas from the delegation fell on deaf ears as Astor refused their requests. He used as an excuse the claim that, because of his age, he had already transferred the bulk of his fortune to his children and therefore had no spare funds on hand. After further conversation, he rather brusquely dismissed the group, complaining to them that "not a day passes over my head that some application is not made to me for money."[9]

Because of his association with Robert Walker, Foote was seen as a political champion of the Texas cause, which led to his meeting and mingling with many politically and financially prominent Texans. He had already dabbled in Texas land speculation through his Walker connection, and in 1838 he entered into a business arrangement that included members of the Texas political elite. In one Galveston shipping enterprise, Foote was involved with Texas president Mirabeau Lamar, revolutionary hero Moseley Baker, newspaper publisher Gail Borden, and Texas treasury secretary Richard Dunlap. Foote acquired land in Refugio County along the Texas coastline and on a long, thin island situated strategically in Matagorda Bay.

The following year, he visited Texas, hoping to bolster his political and professional contacts, although he later downplayed the journey as "a mingled trip of pleasure and business." Foote arrived in Texas with his wife on March 9, 1839, and immediately began making the rounds. One of the first events that he attended was a dinner honoring former South Carolina governor James Hamilton, whom President Lamar had recently appointed loan commissioner of the republic, a job that revolved around the sometimes herculean task of securing financing for the Texas government. The banquet took place in Houston, which was serving at the time as the temporary capital. According to Foote, the dinner "was served up to a numerous concourse of congenial and accomplished guests in the lower rooms of a large building in Houston then used as the statehouse. A merrier or more agreeable party I have never witnessed." More parties followed, at which Foote "met many gentlemen not unknown to fame." Using his trademark mixture of bluff, bluster, and eloquence, he joined the social circle of many important Texas officials, including President Lamar.[10]

Mirabeau Buonaparte Lamar was a native Georgian born into a prominent political family. After an early career as a state senator and newspaper editor, he moved to Texas in 1835. He joined the revolutionary army and distinguished himself while leading cavalry at the climactic Battle of San Jacinto. His success led to his appointment as secretary of war in the provisional government of Texas, and after the revolution he ran successfully for vice president of the new republic. Sam Houston was elected president, and he and Lamar did not get along well. Under Texas law, Houston could not succeed himself, and Lamar won the presidency in 1838. Foote and Lamar had first crossed paths briefly some years earlier, and by the time they met again, Foote was already known to most Texas officials through his association with Robert Walker and through his fund-raising efforts for the republic. Upon becoming president, Lamar appointed to his cabinet several men with whom Foote was well acquainted, including Secretary of the Navy Memucan Hunt, Secretary of the Treasury Richard C. Dunlap, and secretary of war and future Confederate general Albert Sidney Johnston.

Lamar also knew the value of history. A writer and poet himself, he had toyed with the idea of composing a history of Texas that would tell the story of the new republic and, at the same time, promote his political agenda. To this end, he collected a good bit of research material, but he never had the time to produce a manuscript. Always the politician, he also knew that a history promoting the political agenda of Mirabeau Lamar could not be written by Mirabeau Lamar. He would have to find someone else, someone who was supposedly impartial, to produce the book, if the book was going to be credible.

Henry Foote's reputation as an orator and writer had preceded him to Texas, and he seemed to be the perfect choice to produce the work. Not only was Foote highly literate and an expert at expressing himself with pen and paper but also he was ambitious enough to undertake the project, if for no other reason than that it would ingratiate him with Lamar and the Texas high command. Lamar's associates flattered Foote as they solicited his help. "It is due to the cause of liberty that a true narrative of Texas independence should be submitted to the world," a committee of Lamar partisans wrote publicly to Foote. "Appreciating your great literary attainments, your high standing, the independence of your character and your devotion to the cause of liberty, we respectfully ask if . . . [you will] prepare for the world a history of Texas." Lamar political ally Thomas Jefferson Green cut to the chase in his private observations, writing to the Texas president, "I know the history of our young country full well and know too that these facts only want telling by the *proper* persons and in the *proper* way—upon this matter let me refer you more particularly to our friend Foote, with whom we have talked freely."

Foote accepted the commission—his ego would not allow him to turn it down—and Lamar provided him with the research material collected over the years, as well as some finished manuscript pages, some of which Foote likely used word for word. Many years later, Foote wrote that Lamar indeed contributed "most of the material for such a work, and . . . fifty or sixty experimental pages," along with "copious memoranda provided by others with authority to use the whole in such form as I might deem judicious." Despite the fact that Lamar and his operatives had issued the invitation to write the book and had supplied the bulk of the research material, Foote always claimed publicly that the book he produced was "thoroughly impartial." With the goal of producing a history that would quickly help Lamar and his administration, the prolific Foote took the material provided by Lamar and others back to Mississippi and finished the primary draft in six months.[11]

Henry Foote's book was one of the first Texas histories ever produced, and it would be quoted in other works related to Texas history up to the present day. The massive manuscript chronicled important events in the history of the republic and details about the exploits of many early Texas personalities, but, despite the author's claims to the contrary, it was far from impartial. From the front cover to the back page, the manuscript was agenda driven. Even before opening the book, the full title, *Texas and the Texans: or, Advance of the Anglo-Americans to the South-West; Including a History of Leading Events in Mexico, from the Conquest by Hernando Cortes to the Termination of the Texan Revolution,* coveys the harsh anti-Mexican prejudices of the author.

Foote was one of the first writers to propagate many of Texas history's great myths, couching the independence movement in strict terms of a moral struggle between good and evil, romanticizing the exploits of Texas heroes, and condemning Mexican authorities as villains. "That struggle from the outset was essentially a moral struggle," he wrote. "It was, in addition, a struggle for constitutional rights—a war for principles." Accordingly, in Foote's assessment, the chivalrous American population in Texas had "simultaneously sprung up as if roused by the voice of a trumpet from on high, and vowed to put down the vulgar tyrant." The unabashed Anglocentric work slurred the Mexican people as members of a "degenerate and enervated race" and expressed "a profound contempt for the whole Mexican race as antagonists for the war." The author also discounted, through omission, the impact of slavery and the potential spread of the cotton kingdom on the Texas independence movement, giving it only a brief, passing acknowledgment throughout the work. Foote's racial and ethnic prejudices were not unusual for his time; indeed, the target audience for his book would likely agree with many of his sentiments.[12]

Foote's book, by far, generated the most controversy in the realm of Texas politics. While there were a handful of other writers working on Texas histories at the time, the Mississippian was specifically commissioned to produce a book with a political agenda. It was biased by design, at least as far as the portrayals of individual Texas personalities were concerned. It was supposed to promote one faction over another, to tear down some while lifting up others. Still, the book was of significant value. The partisanship within its pages was apparent, but it also provided a solid record of many pivotal events and included a good deal of original correspondence from men who were creating Texas history through their actions. Political predispositions hurt the work's credibility in some circles, but the book was still a fascinating read for those who knew and were interested in the comings and goings of the region's governing elite.

While other characters played a role in the narrative, the relationship and rivalry between Sam Houston and Mirabeau Lamar dominated the political message in Foote's Texas history. As is the case with most successful political upheavals, the two revolutionaries became politicians once their revolution ended, with both vying for political dominance in the new Texas republic. Houston's fame as the victorious leader of the Texas Army was unmatched in the fledgling nation, and Lamar struggled mightily to compete with the hero in the political arena. When Lamar took office after Houston, in late 1838, he reversed many of Houston's policies and sought to tarnish Houston's image, using surrogates like Foote.

It was obvious to anyone who read Foote's history that it was designed to support Lamar and discount Sam Houston as a political leader, and even as a soldier. The heroes of the Mississippian's tome were men such as the martyred Alamo defender William Travis, whose deeds and death "have made his name a talismanic word for freemen battling for their rights in all countries under the sun," and the "bold, resolute, energetic" Branch T. Archer, Speaker of the Texas House of Representatives and secretary of war under Lamar. Foote also devoted space to Ben Milam, another Texas martyr, who died during the Siege of Béxar. "His memory will be dear to Texas," Foote wrote, "as long as there exists a grateful heart to feel, or a friend of liberty to lament his worth." The book also cited the "gallant and daring conduct" of Lamar during the conflict and spent a significant amount of space defending the Lamar presidential administration.

While *Texas and the Texans* paid full homage to a constellation of Texas heroes, it was much less generous to Sam Houston. Foote complimented Houston throughout the work, but usually through veiled references that, in the end, seemed to question the commander's resolve and his ability to plot and carry out military strategy. The narrative subtly seemed to suggest that, during the revolution, Houston was an indecisive commander who had been pressured by others to fight the pivotal Battle of San Jacinto, the clash that had made him a Texas legend.

The hatred that Foote harbored for Houston was political, but over time it seemed to turn personal. Toward the end of Lamar's term as leader of Texas, a movement began to once again place Houston at the head of the government.[13] In a letter to Lamar written from Jackson, Mississippi, in November of 1839, Foote viciously attacked Houston, who had recently passed through the area. "Sam Houston passed through this county in my absence," Foote wrote. "Public expectation was greatly disappointed by his rhetorical efforts in Mississippi & his vulgar egotism and barbarous vanity are now spoken of freely in the language of unsparing ridicule."[14]

Foote's experiences in Texas led him to consider permanently relocating to the new republic, although he recognized that such a move would be a gamble. On the one hand, he had established political contacts with many important people in Texas. He was well acquainted with President Lamar and his cabinet and was especially friendly with Memucan Hunt, the Texas secretary of the navy. At one point, Hunt suggested to Lamar that, should Foote relocate, he might be a good addition to the cabinet, perhaps even as secretary of state. Foote also owned land in Texas that was potentially valuable, and he could establish a law practice there with relative ease.

On the other hand, there were signs that Lamar's administration was in trouble. As president, he had set an ambitious agenda that included the creation of a public education system, removal of Native American populations from the region, and expanding the republic's borders, but under his leadership the Texas economy declined significantly. Inflation was rampant and the public debt more than tripled during Lamar's administration. The crisis deepened as the government attempted to provide economic relief to the country by simply printing more paper currency. As Lamar's term as president was drawing to a close, a move was already afoot to bring Houston back to the presidency. Foote had in effect hitched his wagon to Lamar's star and, more importantly, to Lamar's political network. Should Lamar fall out of favor with the public, and should Houston once again become the president of Texas, Foote would lose much of his political leverage and could potentially find himself on the outside looking in. Problems with land claims, some dating back to the period when Mexico controlled region, also threatened Foote's interests in land speculation, should he lose his important political contacts in the government.

In Mississippi, moreover, Foote was well known, both as an attorney and a politician. He had already put down political roots there and owned significant property in that state. If anything, his dalliances in Texas had enhanced his reputation in his home state as a man with national interests and a broad worldview. Mississippi was the safer choice for Henry Foote, but in Texas lay adventure and a sense that, with just a little luck, anything was possible for a person with the proper drive to succeed.

Apparently wrought with indecision, Foote posted a letter from his Hinds County, Mississippi, home to Lamar in late 1839, expressing his views on relocation. "My friends say stay here . . . that I must not leave them," he told the Texas president. "The state of the country is such, and the professional harvest so inviting that I am a little hesitating about it; not withstanding everything I saw when among you." As time wore on, however, it seemed that Foote had decided that moving west was worth the risk. He sold his plantation home in Clinton, made arrangements to purchase a house in Velasco, a bustling hub of activity near Houston, and began telling his Texas friends to expect him soon. He also made plans to establish a law practice in Austin, the new national capital, with his Mississippi law partner, Anderson Hutchinson, another recent Texas immigrant. By April of 1840, notices began appearing in Texas newspapers announcing the eminent relocation of the law firm Anderson and Foote to Austin, with the caveat that "Henry S. Foote after closing the unfinished business of the firm, and of the partners in Mississippi, will remove permanently to the Republic."[15]

Despite the notices in the newspaper, Henry Foote and his family never permanently relocated to Texas. Foote apparently changed his mind during the early summer of 1840. By that time it was apparent that the Lamar administration was teetering. The Texas economy was in a shambles and it was becoming even more likely that Foote's enemy Sam Houston would soon reclaim the presidency. Should that happen, Foote would lose most of his political contacts in the government and would risk being subjected to Houston's personal wrath. Foote's friendships with the Lamar regime were common knowledge, as was his personal distaste for Houston. Many people also knew that Foote was preparing a Texas history designed to be critical of Houston while promoting Lamar. A man known for holding grudges, Houston would likely never forget the Mississippian's role in efforts to tear him politically asunder. As a result of these shifting political tides in Texas, Foote suddenly decided to sell the house that he had just acquired in Velasco and to purchase a new home for his family in Raymond, Mississippi, just a few miles from Clinton and still within a day's travel of Jackson, Vicksburg, and Natchez.

Constantly active, Foote was in Philadelphia during the latter months of 1840, overseeing publication of his Texas history by Thomas, Cowperthwait and Company. Production of the book was somewhat rushed, in hopes of getting it out before the Texas elections of 1841. While Lamar was barred from running for a second consecutive term, his administration supported vice president David G. Burnett against Houston. Foote later admitted that his book was "written in great haste, and amid numerous other absorbing and perplexing avocations," and that he considered it "in point of literary execution as exceedingly imperfect."[16]

In the end, *Texas and the Texans* had little if any effect on the race for Texas president, which Houston won in a landslide, vindicating Foote's decision not to settle in the republic. The publication of the book did create lifelong bitter feelings between Foote and Houston, who later served together in the United States Senate. "[Foote] is a bad and base man," Houston later wrote to his wife, "and has no regard for truth or honor." In his inaugural address, the new Texas president ridiculed the Mississippian's Texas history, telling the assembled throng, "I would simply remark that I have reviewed the book referred to, at my leisure, and that I found very little orthodox there. I will name the book the *foot history*. I call it the *foot* history because it will be more *footed than eyed*."

In the press, contemporary reviews of the book were mixed, recognizing it as a decent chronicle of events but also deeming it suspect because of its biased perspective. In Mississippi, one editor called it "a racy, humorous and graphic work, executed with much ability and literary skill," while the *Daily Picayune* in New Orleans claimed the book was "highly interesting and useful."

Despite praise for Foote's literary prowess in some circles, it was impossible to ignore the book's political implications. Nineteenth-century journalist and early Houston biographer Alfred M. Williams later reflected that *Texas and the Texans*, which was originally published in two volumes, was written "in the style of a controversial and oratorical pamphlet," with its primary value lying "in the journals and accounts of participants in the events." One modern historian summed up the work by stressing that Foote "went beyond history and literature to produce a parody of both form and substance," becoming "the first, intentionally, to treat the subject of Texas history, and particularly modern history, as heroic myth." While not considered a classic, or even a completely accurate, record of Texas history, parts of Foote's tome would be quoted and noted in future Texas histories for the next hundred and fifty years.[17]

Despite the enmity of Sam Houston and the misgivings of others, the book helped give Foote a national reputation. During the early 1840s, the status of Texas consumed many national politicians and a good many average Americans. There were a number of questions involved, some dealing with domestic concerns and others related to the place of the United States in the world's geopolitical pecking order. Even as the Texans were fighting their revolution, prudent American politicians were already debating the notion that Texas would one day become part of the United States. Expansionists used Manifest Destiny as their battle cry, claiming that it was only a matter of time until the nation reached its full, divinely sanctioned potential by stretching from the Atlantic Ocean to the Pacific.

Others were far less excited about the prospects of Texas joining the Union. Northerners winced at the thought of expanding the southern cotton kingdom into Texas and beyond. They linked expansion into the region once controlled by Mexico with the expansion of slavery and did not want to create a situation in which the slave states could one day have an advantage in Congress. For the same reasons, many southerners were eager to see slavery expand and thus supported the addition of Texas.

There were also those who were worried about national security. Some believed that annexation might lead to war with Mexico, as the Mexicans were firm in their claims that they one day would retake what they called their "northern province." In addition, after the revolution, the Texas government was in dire financial straits and therefore vulnerable to outside influences from abroad. The British, in particular, were interested in forming an alliance with

Texas, in which Britain would be the senior and more dominant partner. In so doing, the British could offer the Texans financial relief in exchange for a foothold on the North American continent that would halt further American western expansion. An Anglo–Texan alliance would also make it impossible for the United States to carry out its plans to dominate the Gulf of Mexico and could potentially place the important port of New Orleans at risk. While northern politicians were concerned about an alliance between Britain and Texas, southern solons were frantic because they believed that the alliance might lead to the end of slavery in Texas, which would also end the southern dream of an expanding cotton kingdom and provide another avenue of escape to runaway slaves.[18]

All of these issues were in play when Henry Foote published his massive two-volume history of Texas in 1841. The sheer bulk of the manuscript, coupled with the gravity of the debate over Texas, gave Foote an air of authority in many circles. During the period when the book was being produced in Philadelphia, a number of influential men and politicians sought Foote out to get his views on the Texas situation. They knew that Foote had been to Texas and had mixed with many of the political leaders there. The list of those who sought an audience with the Mississippian was impressive: Pennsylvania congressmen Joseph and Charles Ingersoll; noted physician Robley Dunglison, who had once been Thomas Jefferson's personal doctor; U.S. senator and future vice president George M. Dallas; Richard Rush, who had served as John Quincy Adams's secretary of the treasury; and Nicholas Biddle, the former president of the Bank of the United States, who had fought the famous Bank War with Andrew Jackson. "I met with many excellent and accomplished gentlemen," Foote wrote of his stay in the city, "all of whom were eager to gauge the political climate in Texas and the prospects of annexing the new republic." Foote became particularly friendly with Biddle, an ardent expansionist who "advocated most earnestly the immediate admission of Texas [to the Union]." Several years later, as a member of the United States Senate, Foote would be a staunch supporter of western expansion, to the extent that he suggested annexing all of Mexico after the Mexican War. Upon reflection, he later admitted that many of his senatorial views on expansion and the West in general had been shaped by his conversations with national political figures while in Philadelphia.[19]

After the publication of his Texas history and Sam Houston's victory in the presidential race, Henry Foote dramatically reversed course. He left Texas and the Texas political arena as quickly as he had arrived on the scene. He sold or abandoned most of his Texas property and returned to Mississippi, his home base. Like many other southern Democrats, he also became a firm advocate of Texas annexation as a way to promote the expansion of slavery and the southern agenda in general. He gave speeches on the subject all over the state, telling his fellow Mississippians that "it is wise and expedient to annex Texas at the earliest opportunity."

The move back home was typical of Foote, who, throughout his career, exhibited a personality and work ethic fraught with contradictions and odd simultaneities. He tended to focus with incredible precision on whatever issue was at hand while also maintaining a sense of recklessness. He was undoubtedly fearless, but he was also insecure and quick to abandon a project that did not provide immediate gratification. Acting on impulse, he had the keen ability to both build and burn bridges with other men, all at the same time. "He was erratic and in many ways eccentric," one contemporary later wrote. "Like a brilliant comet making its first pathway in the political heavens, the periodicity of his orbital motions could not be calculated."[20] If asked, most who dealt with Foote in Texas probably would have agreed with that assessment.

4

Senator Foote

I am for the Constitution. I am for the Union
as provided for and delineated in that sacred instrument.
—Henry Stuart Foote, March 5, 1850

HENRY FOOTE RETURNED TO MISSISSIPPI after his Texas adventure with his ambition, enthusiasm, and spirit for rhetorical combat intact. In his late thirties and approaching the height of his powers, he remained committed to his law practice, to the Democratic Party, and to the focused political interaction with others that seemed to be his lifeblood. During the early 1840s, he hit his stride as a force in the courtroom and as a manipulator of votes, bending popular opinion in the jury box and the electorate to his will on a regular basis. In politics, he developed into "a popular leader of his party" and, according to one observer, "acquired widespread fame as a debater" during the presidential campaigns of the era. In a more succinct assessment, early Mississippi historian Dunbar Rowland called him simply "the most formidable orator in the Democratic Party in Mississippi."

Even before he concluded all of his Texas business, Foote carved out time to make several speeches in Mississippi on behalf of Democratic candidate Martin Van Buren, who was running against Whig William Henry Harrison during the 1840 election season. In late July 1840, Foote gave what one Democratic newspaper called "an able, eloquent, and patriotic address" at a raucous meeting held in Madison County, which almost turned into a riot when local Whigs attempted to disrupt the proceedings. Two weeks later, he debated George S. Yerger, one of the state's leading Whigs, at Vicksburg, and by all accounts carried the day. Foote hammered away at the Whig position as Yerger attempted to laud the abilities of Harrison. Coupling his relentless wit with a focused display of political intellect, Foote eventually drove his adversary into submission. According to one observer, "No one who knows anything about the two men will compare Yerger and Foote. It is like comparing the taper's glimmer with the sun's broad glare." Foote's effectiveness was praised by Democrats across the state, but it predictably drew fire from Whig newspapers. In Jackson, the *Southern Sun* claimed that Foote was "now at heart a malignant partisan, as his language and antics clearly show" and likened his speechmaking skills to "monkey motions."[1]

While canvassing for the Democratic Party in Mississippi, Foote also had a notable encounter with an old courtroom adversary who had become a friend, Seargent Smith Prentiss. At the time, Prentiss was a mainstay of the Whig Party in the state, having served in the state legislature and recently run an unsuccessful campaign for a seat in the United States Senate. His name was still synonymous in legal circles with the perfect blend of tenacity and eloquence. Prentiss was traveling on behalf of William Henry Harrison and preaching the Whig message to crowds around the state. He and Foote were scheduled to debate one another at Gallatin, a south Mississippi hamlet thirty-five miles from the state capital.

By all accounts, the debate was a spirited struggle that for hours held the interest of an active crowd that cheered, booed, hissed, laughed, and yelled through the entire proceedings. It was a rhetorical marathon that lasted for an entire day. "Before a vast crowd of ladies and gentlemen," Foote later remembered, "the conflict continued for eleven hours; the speeches being delivered alternatively." At the end, the crowd cheered the exhausted men. Despite their differences on the stump, Foote and Prentiss were personally cordial to one another during the encounter. They eventually retired for the evening to meager accommodations, actually sleeping in the same room at a small local inn, and left Gallatin together the following morning. Of the scene, Foote later recollected, "We slept amicably in the same room that night, in a little log tavern at Gallatin, and traveled in company next day, lunching on the road-side before we parted company for our respective homes." While their paths would cross briefly from time to time over the next few years and they would occasionally exchange correspondence, Foote and Prentiss never shared a stage, stump, courtroom, or dueling ground again. Prentiss later moved to New Orleans and practiced law there until his untimely death, in 1850, at the age of forty-two.[2]

During the early 1840s, Foote refocused his attentions on his Mississippi law practice and on land speculation. He was also a popular public speaker and maintained the ability to draw a crowd wherever he gave an address. In Mississippi, at least, Henry Foote was famous, a personality who sparked interest all over the state. His ability to communicate with the masses was, by many accounts, astonishing, and he was also a great self-promoter. Important men sought him out as an advocate and to untangle sensitive legal issues. Politicians too sought him out, for advice and support. He was prolific in his comments on issues of the day, making speeches, writing newspaper editorials, and in general keeping his name before the public and his opinions in the realm of public discussion.

Like other ambitious politicians of his era, he attempted to create a humble facade when directly discussing his political wants, claiming on many occasions that he was not a man who sought high office. However, anyone who knew Foote usually drew the opposite conclusion. To most of his contemporaries in the public arena, it was obvious that Foote was constantly angling for some type of future political success. His legal work financed his political maneuverings, as did his real estate ventures, which including buying and selling thousands of acres, spread over several Mississippi counties, during the 1840s.[3]

Henry Foote would need every penny that his law practice and his ventures in land speculation could produce. Outwardly, at least, he seemed to have a dangerously cavalier attitude with regard to money, running up bills almost as fast as he generated income. As a lawyer and politician, he often traveled on his own dime, and his travels were extensive. In addition to the funds needed for his political comings and goings—fees for hotel rooms, transportation, meals, and the like—he also had to support a domestic household that continued to expand. During the 1840s, Henry Foote and his wife, Elizabeth, completed their family, which eventually numbered seven children. Their second daughter, Annie Elizabeth, was born in 1834, soon after the couple moved to Mississippi. Two more daughters followed, Virginia Cecilia, born in 1835, and Arabella, born in 1837. In 1840, Henry Foote and his wife welcomed their first son, Henry Stuart Jr., into the world. Three years later, another son, Romilly Erskine, was born, and in 1848 the Foote family was completed with the birth of their youngest child, William Winter. In addition to clothing and feeding his children, Foote was determined that they should receive a good education, including training in the social graces, which required more funds for schooling. Much of Foote's frantic personality and drive was a product of his own ego and a hunger to be perceived as a success by others, but he also needed considerable sums of money to meet his household overhead.[4]

As the presidential election season of 1844 drew near, Foote maintained a grueling professional pace. On January 8, 1844, he met with fellow Mississippi Democrats at the state convention in Jackson, where, after sometimes strained discussion, they eventually threw their support behind Martin Van Buren as the potential nominee for the national party. While many Mississippians still distrusted Van Buren because of his northern roots, practical wisdom held that Van Buren should be accepted for the sake of national party unity.

However, indicative of a growing states' rights faction within Mississippi Democratic circles, there was significant support at the convention for states' rights ideologue John C. Calhoun of South Carolina, though not enough to win official state party support. Among those backing Calhoun was a rising planter and politician named Jefferson Davis. The convention eventually elected Davis, along with Foote and four others, as delegates to the Democratic National Convention in Baltimore, and afterwards Foote, Davis, and John A. Quitman, another formidable Mississippi politician, all gave speeches in the state capital on the importance of Texas annexation to the United States. It was one of the key issues of the upcoming campaign and probably the most important issue in the minds of many southerners.[5]

After the convention, Foote embarked on a whirlwind speaking tour of Mississippi, promoting the Democratic Party. At rallies, he usually spoke louder, longer, and with more flair than anyone else, inspiring waves of applause. "No man occupies a stronger position in the affections of the Democracy," one correspondent from the *Free Trader* in Natchez wrote of Foote. "He has a long head, a big heart, and an unqualified spirit." Deemed by many a Texas "expert" because of his recent dealings there, Foote usually spoke with great emotion on the need for annexation, framing his arguments in purely sectional terms.

As with many other southern solons, Foote's oratory became more focused and pointed whenever the subject of slavery reared its head during discussions. He claimed that the Texas question was actually "the abolition question in another form" and that Texas must be annexed to spread slavery, the cotton kingdom, and the southern way of life. Those who were against annexation, he said, such as "the friends of abolition in both the United States and England," had a nefarious agenda that involved eventually ending slavery by not allowing the institution to grow. With great passion he argued that the admission of Texas to the Union was essential to the protection of slavery over the long term, and that "it would be suicidal in the South" to pursue any other course. "Foote's speech was a most triumphant vindication of the rights of the South," one Democratic correspondent wrote after attending a rally, "and of the right policy and necessity of immediate annexation."

It was easy for Foote to place annexation in the context of the slavery debate, and it was an effective rhetorical tactic used by many southern Democrats of the period. By doing so, he boxed in his Whig rivals, whose national party opposed accepting Texas into the Union and whose national leaders included men sympathetic to the abolition movement. Foote browbeat Mississippi Whigs again and again for the sins of their national organization, casting state Whig leaders—many of whom were actually major slaveholders—as being soft on abolition. Whig speakers found it difficult to counter Foote's accusations, and the Whig press in Mississippi could only resort to name-calling, variously referring to their Democratic rival as a "shuffling jackal," a "bar room dema-gogue" and "half a maniac, not worthy of notice." As for Foote, he seemed to draw strength from the insults, and even more confidence from the knowledge that he had the upper hand.[6]

The presidential election of 1844 set in motion a chain of events that even-tually led Foote to a seat in the United States Senate. The election season was fraught with intrigue at the national level, especially among the Democrats. The experienced statesman Henry Clay emerged as the Whig candidate, but when the Democrats met at their convention in Baltimore, chaos ensued. Mar-tin Van Buren, though the favorite for the Democratic nomination, alienated many Democrats, particularly southerners, by refusing to endorse the annex-ation of Texas. At the time, southern politicians like Foote were fixated on the issue. In Mississippi, less than two years earlier, the state legislature had adopted a resolution demanding that "our Senators in Congress be instructed and our Representatives requested to use their best exertions to procure the annexation of the Republic of Texas to the United States." The annexation issue proved to be an Achilles' heel that Van Buren's opponents exploited, par-ticularly after a letter surfaced in which the former president stated that he was opposed to the annexation of Texas unless Mexico agreed. Van Buren's southern support began to melt away as important politicians from the region turned their backs on him.

Sensing Van Buren's vulnerability, proslavery ideologue Senator Robert J. Walker of Mississippi began laying the groundwork to block the candidate's path to the Democratic nomination. Using a practiced, carefully honed ability to wheel and deal, Walker and his friends, in May of 1844, persuaded the Democratic convention to adopt a rule stating that any presidential nominee must garner two-thirds of the convention's votes rather than a simple majority. Though not disqualifying Van Buren outright, the rule created a situation in which the former president would find it virtually impossible to collect enough votes to win. It also made it difficult for Van Buren's chief rival, Lewis Cass of Michigan, to muster the needed support for a victory.

After eight ballots with no nominee, the need for a compromise candidate was apparent. Walker and other southerners promoted expansionist James K. Polk of Tennessee, who subsequently became the Democratic standard-bearer. Eventually elected president, Polk rewarded Walker for his efforts by appointing the Mississippian to his cabinet as secretary of the treasury. By association, the appointment helped Henry Foote's political future, as he and Walker had a long-standing relationship. In addition, once Walker was named to the Polk cabinet, his United States Senate seat became available.[7]

After the national convention, Mississippi Democrats mobilized in support of Polk and of one of the key planks in the Democratic platform, Texas annexation. Henry Foote was selected as one of the state's six Democratic presidential electors, and he immediately began giving speeches in support of his party's nominee and of vice presidential nominee George M. Dallas. In late July of 1844, Foote was on hand at a large, two-day meeting held at Davis' Mill, a small community situated at a strategic crossroads just south of the state line dividing Mississippi and Tennessee, which drew crowds from both states. According to one account, it was "an immense gathering of people," around eight thousand strong, that was part political mobilization and part county fair. During the two-day affair, around a dozen politicians from Tennessee and Mississippi addressed the crowd, which between speeches was well fed with barbecue lunches and dinners. The schedule had Foote speaking at the end of the second day, followed only by Jefferson Davis, meaning that Foote and Davis would give the last two speeches at the gathering.

The fact that he had to speak before Davis likely rankled Foote, who would have preferred the more conspicuous closing spot on the program. It also seemed to motivate him as an orator. Many at the gathering later maintained that, at the Davis' Mill rally, Foote gave one of his finest performances as a political speaker. According to Foote's friend Reuben Davis, an eyewitness who had given a speech the previous day, "Foote opened with the most effective speech I ever heard him make. . . . Denunciation and ridicule were the weapons [he] used." The crowd of primarily Democrats went wild as Foote attacked the Whig positions and "applause rolled up in great waves like the swelling sea."[8]

During the 1844 campaign season, Foote drew large crowds wherever he spoke. Texas annexation was the key issue of the period, and most Mississippians viewed Foote as an expert on the subject because of his travels around the Lone Star Republic. Though always feigning humility with regard to his authorship of *Texas and the Texans*—often claiming that it was only a minor work—Foote never failed to mention the Texas history during his speeches, in an effort to gently remind those listening of his expertise. As he traveled the state, Foote exploited to his advantage the anxieties of his audiences with regard to the annexation of Texas and their concerns over the growing abolition movement in the North. At a meeting in the town of Pontotoc, he "took up the Texas question," and "presented the most convincing facts and arguments to prove that the annexation of Texas is indispensable to the peace, happiness, and security of the South . . . and to the southern institution of slavery." Several days later, at a gathering in Aberdeen, he assured a boisterous crowd that Texas "will become a great cotton growing region" and that all opposition to annexation "originated with abolitionists of the North," who hoped to curtail the expansion of the cotton kingdom and end slavery. During the month of August in 1844, Foote gave speeches at various locations almost every day, sometimes with other Democrats and sometimes as part of debates with local Whig leaders who supported Henry Clay.[9]

Of course, Foote was not without enemies or rebukes from Clay supporters along the campaign trail. The more speeches he gave, the more the Whig press in Mississippi took notice of him, launching desperate counterattacks in hopes of stopping the Democrats' momentum in the state. After one speech in Port Gibson, a Whig stronghold where Clay was held in high regard, the local Whig organ lambasted Foote's "quirks and quibbles, misstatements and concealments" and lampooned his theatrics and his past history as a "renowned political changeling" who had once run for the state legislature under the Whig banner. "We had expected something extraordinary and were not disappointed," the *Port Gibson Herald* told its readers. "With the eloquent gestures of a galvanized frog, and the argumentative ability and tact of a pettifogging attorney, [Foote] poured forth a torrent of abuse upon Mr. Clay and his friends, branding them as abolitionists and allies of abolitionists.[10]

Although the newspaper's language was partisan and designed to hurt Foote, the basic charge of demagoguery was true. As was the case throughout the South, more and more conservative Democrats were using the politics of fear to attract voters and increase their personal political power. By the 1840s, the slavery debate was coming to the forefront of national politics, and it was also having a great psychological impact on white southerners. As a result, the perceived threat to the institution of slavery was an effective tool for ambitious Democrats because it instantly drew a great deal of attention and united most white Mississippians, rich or poor, regardless of whether they held slaves.

Throughout the South, racism left most whites in a dilemma that would not reconcile itself. Although literally surrounded by blacks, they could not conceive of a society in which the races were equal. Slavery defined the self-perception of every white southerner. For the planter elite, it signified power, status, and paternalistic control not only of their slaves but also, as fellow dependents in the household, of their wives and children as well. The ability of white males to hold property established the social order in the South, and this included claims over their dependents, based in both custom and law. For the large planter, a disruption of the slave system meant a disruption of his societal authority and the "natural" relationship between the male head of the family and his charges.[11]

The impact on poorer, nonslaveholding white males was similar. Though not directly involved as slaveholders, they recognized the social impact that the demise of slavery would have on their world. Regardless of their economic condition, they drew strength and self-esteem simply from the fact that they were white males and heads of their own households. Their white skin bonded them to their more affluent planter neighbors, with whom they periodically interacted. "So far as my own state is concerned," Foote opined during the period, "the non-slaveholders among us are as true to the South, her honor, and her interests, as the slaveholders themselves. I cannot doubt it." They recognized the importance of property as the traditional barometer of independence and feared a future in which they might compete with free blacks for land or in the labor market. From a psychological standpoint, the South's slave-based society allowed poorer white males the comfort of viewing themselves as free men in a society where most of the population—white women and children, along with slaves—were denied the full rights of citizens. They defined their own independence through the bondage of others and believed that the demise of slavery would irreversibly harm their position in southern society. "With us the two great divisions of society are not rich and poor," John C. Calhoun claimed, as he tried to justify the system in 1848, "but white and black; and all the former, the poor as well as the rich, belong to the upper class, and are respected and treated as equals." Of course, the small farmers' race-based equality with wealthy planters was illusory, but their fears were ripe for exploitation by secessionist politicians as sectional tensions increased.[12]

Henry Foote was a part of this world, and he knew how to maneuver through it. Like other southern politicians of the era, he saw the fears generated by abolitionist agitation in the North as a vehicle through which he could excite crowds and draw their support. He had witnessed the power of that fear firsthand in Mississippi during the slave insurrection scare of 1835, and he knew that harnessing that fear could create for him an effective campaign tool. Like most southerners in general, Foote believed that slavery, or "our favorite domestic institution," as he sometimes referred to it in speeches, was the key to the South's social, political, and economic vibrancy. He also saw nothing "in the system of domestic slavery intrinsically degrading." Foote himself was a slaveholder—reportedly owning as many as twenty slaves during the 1840s, though records indicate that he owned only four by 1860—and he argued many times during the era that the United States Constitution sanctioned slavery by guaranteeing citizens the rights to their "property." Like other southerners, one of the primary components of his interest in Texas had always been the potential for expanding the South's slave-based cotton culture to the West. As the Democratic Party in Mississippi became more radicalized via the slavery debate, Foote went along with it. States' rights and criticism of the abolition movement became standard parts of his rhetoric, just as it was for other prominent Mississippi politicians of the era. What made Foote unusual, however, was the fact that, while he maintained his proslavery sentiments, in the end he would not let them diminish his dedication to preserving the Union.[13]

The 1844 presidential campaign in Mississippi was a pivotal event for Foote. He turned forty during the campaign year, a milestone that seemed to add gravitas to his already solid stature as a prominent member of the state's political community. During the campaign he also became better known at the grassroots level. While many Mississippians knew Foote's name and reputation prior to the campaign and had seen his name over and over again in newspapers, they actually got to meet Foote and experience for themselves the force of his personality as he moved around the state in support of the Democratic ticket. During the canvas, Foote gave speech after speech, day after day, in dozens of Mississippi communities. He shook countless hands and experienced ovation after ovation when he spoke. In doing so, he created an ever-expanding base of political support for himself that would benefit him in the future. According to one observer of the period, on the stump, Foote's "fluency and fancy were inexhaustible" and afforded him a great deal of attention. Rather than a mere politician who gave interesting presentations to the public, Foote would emerge from the 1844 campaign season as a bona fide political celebrity in Mississippi, a man whom more and more people would sacrifice their free time to see.[14]

The year 1844 was also significant in that it witnessed the origins of a rivalry between Foote and Jefferson Davis that would eventually turn very bitter and, on at least one occasion, violent. The origin of the Foote–Davis feud was rooted in an 1844 court case in Madison Parish, Louisiana, just across the Mississippi River, not far from Vicksburg. The case involved charges of malfeasance against local district court clerk John T. Mason, and the plaintiffs hired Davis's brother-in-law David Bradford to plead their case. Bradford was a well-known attorney in the region and former superintendent of the United States mint in New Orleans. He came from a prominent Pennsylvania family, and his father had been one of the leaders of the famous Whiskey Rebellion.

In the courtroom, Bradford attacked the character of Mason, and Mason took great offense, leading to a confrontation between the two men. On March 12, 1844, Mason and Bradford met on the streets of Richmond, Louisiana, and, in what contemporary accounts say amounted to a duel, Mason gunned down Bradford, fatally wounding him with a single shotgun blast. "On Wednesday last the parties met on the street," the Richmond *Compiler* reported at the time, "[and] the result of that meeting was the instant death of Mr. Bradford, occasioned by the discharge of a double-barreled shotgun in the hands of Mr. Mason." Once news of his brother-in-law's death reached Davis, he quickly made his way to the Bradford home, where he collected his widowed sister Amanda and her children and took them back to the Davis plantation.[15]

Mason was indicted for murder and went to trial the following May. He hired a team of attorneys to defend him, led by Foote, who crossed the Mississippi River into Louisiana to take part in yet another high-profile trial. Because both Mason and Bradford were well known in the region and their violent encounter was played out in public, an unusually large number of spectators assembled to watch the trial. The proceedings lasted three and a half days, and newspapers praised Foote's efforts, stating that "perhaps so great a display of learning and ability has never before been witnessed in this parish." Foote made the closing argument in Mason's defense and apparently dazzled the jury, whose members acquitted the accused after two days of deliberation, ruling that the killing was an "excusable homicide." As was his way, Foote was quick to trumpet his success to anyone who would listen, which likely angered Davis and his entire family, who naturally felt that Bradford's killer should be punished.[16]

The friction between Foote and Davis became noticeable once the 1844 presidential campaign season began a few weeks later, mainly because they were often in such close proximity to one another. As prominent Democratic voices in the state, the two men shared stages around Mississippi, giving speeches in support of Polk, and on a few occasions even traveled to rallies together, but there was no love lost between the two. In addition to the animosity generated by the court case, Foote and Davis also did not get along because they were two different types of people. Foote was loud, sometimes rude, and enamored by the sound of his own voice. He enjoyed playing to a crowd and relished the hoots, hollers, and applause of his audiences during his speeches. He enjoyed verbal combat—perhaps too much—and took pride in his ability to berate opponents into submission. Davis, on the other hand, had a calmer temperament and in public debate expected a certain level of decorum. He held himself aloof to the point that many considered him arrogant, and he expected deference from most of those around him. While Foote specialized in the raucous personal attack on opponents, Davis viewed such spectacles as distasteful. One politician who saw both men speak highlighted the contrast, describing Foote's presentation as "a fiery torrent of fierce invective and brilliant declamation," while describing Davis's more controlled, focused discourse as "lucid argument and poetic fancy . . . dignified and commanding, soft and persuasive." Davis looked down on the type of unsophisticated bombast that sometimes carried the day for Foote and men like him, while Foote resented what he perceived as Davis's sense of self-importance and entitlement. In addition, while both men spoke up for the dominant Democratic Party in their state, they were also rivals within the party, ambitious men with national aspirations who were

destined to cross paths again and again in the future. A year after Foote and
Davis helped James K. Polk carry Mississippi on the way to the White House,
Jefferson Davis won election to the U.S. House of Representatives. Not to be
outdone, Foote soon afterwards unexpectedly leveraged himself into a seat in
the United States Senate.[17]

Polk carried Mississippi, which should have put both Foote and Davis in
a celebratory mood. Instead, the victory for the state's Democrats caused yet
another fissure in the relationship between the two men. Once the votes were
tallied, the state's electors, including Foote and Davis, had the responsibility
to choose an official messenger to take the election results and deliver them by
hand to Washington. It was a patronage position that carried with it a certain
amount of prestige. Foote pressed for the electors to choose a young attorney,
David C. Glenn, for the position. Glenn was the nephew of Joseph Chalmers,
the Democratic United States senator from Mississippi who had been appointed to finish Robert Walker's term after Walker's appointment as Treasury
secretary. Chalmers would soon retire, leading to Foote's election to the open
seat. Glenn had just begun practicing law in Hinds County and within a few
years would be elected Mississippi's attorney general. While Foote lobbied for
Glenn, Davis promoted his own man, Warren County physician Lloyd Selby.
Selby was a Davis ally who, in addition to his duties as a doctor, edited the
Vicksburg Sentinel.

To Foote's great irritation, Selby won the honor. "I labored hard to have
[Glenn] sent to Washington," Foote later wrote. "Unfortunately for him, Mr.
Jefferson Davis was a co-elector, and he succeeded in defeating my wish upon
this subject, and procuring a favorite of his own to be appointed in his stead."
Though the incident was minor when compared with what would come later,
the conflict over the choice of their state's electoral messenger in 1844 was indicative of the general relationship between Foote and Davis. If Foote was for
something, Davis was against it, almost as a matter of routine, and vice versa.
Any dispute, large or small, between the two men usually made the transition
very quickly from the political to the personal. "Foote and Davis were soon at
daggers' points," Robert W. Winston, a contemporary and early Davis biographer wrote of the fallout from the 1844 election. "From this time forth no love
was lost between H. S. Foote and Jefferson Davis."[18]

Henry Foote's aggressive personality, combined with a favorable mix of
luck and circumstance, led to his ascent to the United States Senate. Before his

canvas for Polk, Foote was a well-known political commodity in Mississippi but was not seen as a favorite to achieve national office. He was more maverick than mainstream, and while he was among the most effective political speakers in the state, other ambitious men were in line in front of him, and their constant jockeying for position usually left Foote out in the cold. Foote was popular among the people but his abrasive tendencies made it difficult for him to establish his own political network in an era when state legislators chose United States senators. He was anything but subtle, which generated admiration in some circles but hatred in others. He was too direct in a profession where nuanced conversation or rhetoric sometimes carried the day. Even many among his admirers viewed him as a loose cannon, entertaining and dependable on the stump but not yet tested in a national political body where important, rational decisions had to be made on a regular basis.

While the Polk canvas did not remake Foote completely, it helped combat some of these negative perceptions. No one could say that Foote was not a tireless worker, nor could they say that he was not well versed in the national issues around which the presidential campaign centered, particularly those dealing with Texas. After a speech in Macon, Mississippi, the Macon *Jeffersonian* reported that Foote "made the most powerful and unanswerable arguments we ever heard, sustaining the great principles of the Democratic Party, and exposing the duplicity with which the Whigs acted, and the unsoundness of their principles" before retiring "amongst the most tremendous cheering."[19]

The Mississippi senatorial campaign of 1845–1846 initially involved several of the state's political luminaries, with former governor Alexander McNutt leading the way. Like Henry Foote, McNutt was a Virginian by birth who had come to Mississippi to make his fortune in the 1820s. He practiced law in Vicksburg and, in 1835, won election to the state Senate. In 1837, he became president of the Senate and eventually ran successfully for governor that same year. He served a second two-year term and left office in 1842. According to contemporary accounts, McNutt was a convincing speaker who used a mix of wit, humor, and traditional political bluster to sway crowds. A large man with a booming voice, he had a particular skill for deflecting unpleasant truths about himself and took an almost perverse pleasure in altering or misrepresenting facts to meet his needs. McNutt was also a heavy drinker who, according to one observer, had a penchant for "looking into the wine cup when it was red." Foote, who hated McNutt, later described him as "much renowned as a liberal consumer of both meats and strong drink." Regardless of his faults, McNutt was very popular with the people, though not nearly as popular with other prominent Democrats in the state. He seemed to have a nasty habit of criticizing other state leaders, to the point that he alienated many of them. According to nineteenth-century historian J. F. H. Claiborne, McNutt had an "exuberant vanity" that manifested itself in "unkind denunciations of a number of leading men of his own party." In some ways he was like Foote in that his rough-and-tumble ways appealed to crowds but were also quick to generate enemies.[20]

McNutt's enemies conspired against him in the race for the Democratic nomination for the U.S. Senate, in what amounted to a contest between the McNutt faction of the Mississippi Democratic Party and several other Democratic candidates, who led the anti-McNutt faction. As Foote later stated, when McNutt announced his candidacy for the Senate, it "gave a good deal of uneasiness to several gentlemen who were already known to desire the senatorial position." These included John A. Quitman, former president of the Mississippi Senate, who served for a few weeks in the 1830s as acting governor of the state; sitting governor Albert Gallatin Brown; congressman Jacob Thompson; and former congressman William M. Gwin, all of whom began their political careers in Jacksonian-era Mississippi. Foote, who was not originally considered a candidate, was closest to Gwin. Both men were part of Robert Walker's organization and had campaigned together for Andrew Jackson during the 1830s. They would have a long association and, until his death, Foote considered Gwin "an old and valued friend." In the end, most believed that the contest would boil down to a match between McNutt and Quitman, who seemed to have a great deal of support in the legislature.[21]

With the exception of McNutt, all the candidates began the campaign in a way that would likely seem odd to many today. They campaigned by not campaigning themselves. Instead, they chose to follow the old adage that "the office should seek the man" and not vice versa. This tradition, which in the United States dated back to the founding fathers, dictated that an open, aggressive pursuit of political power by an individual was unseemly and that a candidate should only begin a tireless campaign after being asked or persuaded to run by a significant number of concerned citizens. Such a course would allow the candidate to maintain the facade that, no matter how rigorously he campaigned before the public, his running for office was a selfless act of acquiescence to the will of his constituents rather than a self-centered grab at political power. In the end, of course, promoting the pursuit of political power as a selfless act was usually little more than political theater that ignored the behind-the-scenes posturing and deal making that was a mainstay of the democratic process.

Possessing a huge ego and believing that his best chance to win the seat was to campaign early and aggressively, McNutt ignored the tradition of remaining removed from the electoral process. He began traveling the state, giving speeches and denouncing his opponents with great fervor. Quitman, who most Democrats believed had enough support in the legislature to be McNutt's chief rival, became the former governor's prime target for abuse. Rather than answer McNutt directly, Quitman and the other candidates decided to remain aloof and send out a surrogate, someone who had enough force as a public speaker that he could match McNutt rhetorically, blow for blow. Pursuit of this strategy was also the product of more practical concerns. "Mr. Gwin had no time for a canvas," one observer later wrote, "and Quitman would have been no match for McNutt [in a debate]."

Quitman and Gwin, in particular, believed that Henry Foote was the man that they needed to go out and do the dirty work of tearing McNutt down. According to J. F. H. Claiborne, "Of all the public men in the state, Foote was the best fitted for the encounter. He knew the inconsistencies of McNutt, and was utterly indifferent to his own. . . . McNutt told jokes; Foote recited epigrams." Because Foote also had a history with McNutt and disliked the former governor immensely, Quitman and the others knew that Foote would not hold back in his attacks.

Foote later claimed that he had at first turned down the offer to go up against McNutt, and that he had to be convinced. Considering Foote's personality, this was at best a suspicious claim. While he could be very overbearing at times, Foote was a smart politician who could not help but recognize the invitation to canvas the state as an opportunity. It gave him an excuse to keep his name before the electorate and, because he himself was not a candidate, he was free to say almost anything he wanted without repercussions. It also allowed him to posture himself as a man who, rather than campaigning for himself, was involved in the public service of generating discourse before the public about important issues of the day. "McNutt presented himself to the people as a patriot assailed by a triumvirate of ambitious aspirants for favor without regard for principle," one observer later recalled, "[while] Foote appealed to them as a disinterested guardian of the public purity, and the generous champion of his absent friends."[22]

The canvas crossed the state, with McNutt always speaking first and Foote following him in rebuttal, though the men never shared the stage at the same time. McNutt's strategy involved speaking his piece and leaving the scene, not even acknowledging Foote's presence. "McNutt would never notice Foote," attorney Jehu A. Orr observed, "and silently treated him with profound contempt. He would open his speech at 11 o'clock and speak until 3, gather up his papers and leave without alluding to Foote in any way or paying the slightest attention to him." Foote's speeches usually lasted an hour or less, during which time he would defend Quitman by emphasizing the candidate's commitment to southern traditions and institutions, particularly the institution of slavery. "I have defended you on each occasion," Foote wrote to Quitman at the time, "and presented you as a gentleman, a scholar, an old and approved public servant, and a staunch, fearless and unexceptional State Rights Democrat of the true Jeffersonian and Calhoun school. I carried the war into Africa in all cases." Foote tried to get Quitman himself to appear at a rally in Columbus, Mississippi, but Quitman refused, preferring instead to let Foote do the heavy lifting of the campaign.[23]

As Foote and McNutt crisscrossed the state, Foote's personal ambitions began to take on a momentum of their own. While promoting Quitman's candidacy, Foote was also, in effect, promoted himself before "dense crowds" of people who were "greatly interested in this memorable contest." The audiences loved Foote's haughty ways and his use of sly humor, and it would have been impossible for a shrewd politician like Foote not to notice that his own popularity among Mississippi's citizens seemed to be growing with each stop on the tour. The canvas ended in December of 1845, and by the time the Democratic caucus met in Jackson the following January, it was apparent that Foote was no longer just a spokesman for other candidates. He was a candidate himself, despite outward claims that he did not want the office.

By the time the caucus began deliberations, Gwin had withdrawn from the race, and none of the other announced candidates besides Quitman had significant support. Many legislators who were more interested in stopping McNutt than in personally supporting one of the other candidates began to view Foote as a viable alternative. On the first ballot, no one received the two-thirds majority needed for victory, but McNutt led the field with twenty votes and Foote ran a surprisingly close second, with eighteen. Quitman trailed in third place, with sixteen votes, followed by Jacob Thompson, with fifteen, and

Governor Brown, with nine. McNutt led on the next five ballots, as supporters of Quitman and the others began to rally around Foote as the primary "stop McNutt" candidate. Foote won the Democratic nomination and then handily defeated the Whig nominee, George Winchester, by a vote of 93 to 35 to become senator-elect.

On January 23, 1846, the *Grenada Dollar Democrat* summed up the events of the day in the state capital by reporting, "Before the people McNutt and Quitman were considered the only prominent aspirants for the senatorial seat; Foote was hardly ever thought of. . . . But the [members of the] convention have fulfilled the scriptural prophesy 'the last shall be first.' Foote is at the *head* of the ladder of political preferment and McNutt is at the *foot*." Although he would not take office for another year, when the seat officially became vacant, Henry Foote was about to become a player in national politics.[24]

Toward the end of his life, Henry Foote did his best to claim that there was no premeditation involved in his rise to the United States Senate. He maintained that his elevation to national office was the result of a combination of fate, timing, and a lifetime of work for the Democratic Party in Mississippi. In his memoirs, he was obviously sensitive to the perception that he had somehow stolen the Senate seat from Quitman in an act of betrayal. Foote emphasized that it had been Quitman himself who suggested that Foote tour the state on his behalf and not the other way around. Foote claimed that he had been a Quitman supporter all along and that the Democrats in the Mississippi legislature effectively thrust the office of United States senator upon him by insisting that he take the Democratic nomination. Furthermore, he claimed that he had warned Quitman in advance of this possibility. Foote later wrote that, before the canvas, he speculated to Quitman that the strategy of sending out a surrogate to take on McNutt might backfire, and that "if you force me into this painful and arduous struggle the probability is that I may be chosen senator." In other words, Foote later tried to portray himself as a loyal Quitman supporter who had done everything in his power to promote Quitman until the legislature gave him no choice but to take the nomination.[25]

Foote's later claims were, at best, revisionist history and more likely outright falsehoods. At any time during the campaign, even after the legislature began its selection process, Foote could have made it known to his supporters that he did not want the office and would not serve if elected. He could have disqualified himself and urged his supporters in the legislature to vote for Quitman. By the time he became a United States senator, Foote had been a hyperambitious politician for more than twenty years, an aggressive self-promoter who did his best to keep his name before the public, never missing an opportunity to make a speech or engage in a debate. He attacked his opponents with the fervor of a man who refused to let other men stand in his way, and observers of the period universally recognized his talents as a master of public discourse. At some point during the 1845 canvas, Foote must have realized that his own standing in the state was rivaling that of Quitman and the other candidates, and that when the time came for the state legislature to vote, there was a good chance that he could be chosen over Quitman for the Senate seat.

This may have been his plan all along. By all accounts, Foote campaigned like a man running for office, even though he was not a candidate himself, and other political observers of the period were not fooled by Foote's claims to the contrary. Paying a backhanded compliment to Foote's work ethic, politician John Guion wrote sarcastically to his friend Jefferson Davis, "Truly perseverance will accomplish much! A seat in the Senate of the U.S. has been the goal of Foote's ambition for many years." Surprised by his loss, Quitman was angry and resentful. One of Quitman's early biographers wrote afterwards that the failed candidate was "deeply stung with what he considered ingratitude, and had good reason to consider treachery, and for a period he expressed himself with bitterness." He blamed the men who he thought were his allies in the legislature, as well as Foote, who he would eventually face again.[26]

The period between Foote's election as U.S. senator in January of 1846 and his official installation in early 1847 was a busy time. A number of national events took place that dramatically altered Mississippi's political landscape and had a great impact on the South and the nation as a whole. Paramount among these was the outbreak of the Mexican War. The war with Mexico was a catalyst for the problems that were beginning to separate the free states from the slaveholding states. It involved the potential for American acquisition of vast western territories, and the eventual need to determine the status of slavery in these territories would help tear the country apart.

The war began as a border dispute after the United States acquired Texas. Mexico claimed that the Nueces River represented the southern border of Texas, and therefore of the United States, while the Americans claimed that the border was farther south, along the Rio Grande. President Polk sent troops to defend the Rio Grande in what the Mexicans viewed as an invasion of their territory, making some type of clash inevitable. Who actually fired the first shots was disputed, but the United States declared war on May 13, 1846.

The war generated great excitement in the South as the region's political leaders, inspired in part by the recent annexation of Texas, set their sights on acquiring more Mexican territory to further expand the cotton kingdom. The war and its outcome would accelerate the process of bringing the slavery debate in the United States to a head and, in so doing, light the fuse that would lead to the Civil War. Men from all over the South volunteered to take part in the war effort against Mexico, including two important men from Mississippi, neither of whom cared for Henry Foote. Both Jefferson Davis and John Quitman took part in the war effort, and both returned home to Mississippi as war heroes with enhanced reputations. This likely concerned Foote, who recognized that their increased popularity and stature in Mississippi might come at the expense of his own.

Foote was especially displeased that Davis received so much attention as a result of the war. The two men disliked one another already, and Foote certainly perceived Davis as a formidable rival. Although Davis usually tried his best to ignore Foote, there was little doubt that the outspoken politician was a constant irritant to the future Confederate president. Like Foote, Davis made the most out of his 1844 Mississippi canvas for James K. Polk. Popular on the speaking circuit, he won election to the U.S. House of Representatives in November of 1845, but he served only six months before resigning to join the war effort. He recruited a regiment of Mississippians, dubbed the Mississippi Rifles, and commanded the men as colonel at the Battle of Monterrey, in September of 1846, and at the Battle of Buena Vista, the following February. Wounded at Buena Vista, Davis returned home to convalesce and, on August 10, 1847, Governor Albert Gallatin Brown appointed the now full-fledged war hero to complete the term of recently deceased United States senator Jesse Speight. The following January, the state legislature elected Davis in his own right to a six-year term in the Senate, where he would serve uneasily alongside Foote representing Mississippi.[27]

Quitman also gained national acclaim as a result of the Mexican War. Ten years older than Davis, Quitman volunteered for service, commanding Mississippi militia with the rank of brigadier general. He served under Zachary Taylor during the northern Mexico campaign of 1846 and with Winfield Scott in the campaign against Mexico City the following year. Quitman's command was the first to enter the Mexican capital after its surrender, and Quitman was appointed civil and military governor of the city. Quitman's wartime service actually put him at odds with Davis, as both men had significant egos and both knew that a war record was always a significant political asset. At Monterrey, Davis served under Quitman and, later, as far as Quitman was concerned, tried to hoard the glory associated with the American victory, building himself up at the expense of his commanding officer. Though he did not make the charge publicly, Quitman wrote privately that Davis "claims the merit of having done everything" during the battle, and that in Davis he observed "an envious disposition and a selfishness which I have rarely witnessed." Ironically, Quitman's service during the war ultimately drew him closer to Foote, at least in a political sense, in that neither man cared for Davis. Shifting hatreds and mutual distrust would characterize the rocky Foote–Davis–Quitman relationship for years as they met one another in the political arena, with Foote always trying his best to play Quitman and Davis against one another.[28]

On November 11, 1847, Foote and Davis boarded the steamer *Ben Franklin* at Vicksburg to travel to Washington, DC, where they would take their seats representing Mississippi in the United States Senate. They traveled together only out of necessity and convenience and because they were on their way to serve in the same body. The two men did not enjoy each other's company and, aside from formal settings aboard the ship or in port along the way, would not socialize with one another during the trip. They traveled up the Mississippi and then the Ohio, passing Louisville, Cincinnati, and Pittsburgh before finally arriving in Washington on November 25.

As was the custom in an era when most members of Congress did not keep permanent offices or residences in the nation's capital, both men immediately sought out lodging. Having already served in the House of Representatives, Davis was familiar with the Washington social scene and knew the prominent places where an up-and-coming politician should stay and be seen. He briefly took a room at the fashionable Gadsby's Hotel and then settled into Owner's boardinghouse on Pennsylvania Avenue, near Third Street, "opposite the north gate of the Capitol." The property included a dozen "well-furnished and comfortable apartments" and had been boarding members of Congress since the days of Andrew Jackson. Owner's also maintained public rooms where boarders could meet with one another for idle chatter or more serious political discussions. Foote took up residence a few blocks away, at Smallwood's boardinghouse on Virginia Avenue, also near Third Street. Smallwood's was comfortable but it was not as large or as close to the capitol as Owner's.[29]

On Christmas Day 1847, the simmering rivalry between Foote and Davis finally boiled over, manifesting itself in a physical confrontation. That morning, Foote left Smallwood's and stopped in at Owner's for some holiday socializing. In addition to Davis, a number of other politicians lived at the boardinghouse, including Howell Cobb of Georgia, Abraham Venable of North Carolina, Sampson W. Harris of Alabama, Ohio representative John K. Miller, and John L. Robinson and William W. Wick of Indiana. Shortly before lunch, Foote and some of the other men, including Davis, settled into the boardinghouse's large sitting room and a conversation developed regarding the western expansion of slavery in the United States, an explosive issue that was beginning to dominate public discourse in Washington as the Mexican War played out.

According to Davis, the men discussed the merits of "squatter sovereignty," the idea that the people of a particular state or territory had the right to determine whether their state or territory should have slavery. Many saw it as a way that northerners and southerners might be able to compromise on the slavery issue. Foote was open to this line of thinking, while Davis favored extending the Missouri Compromise Line to the Pacific Ocean, prohibiting slavery above the line and allowing it below. Foote likely took great pleasure in taking a position opposite the notoriously smug Davis, who, according to one observer, "assumed in a decidedly dictatorial manner to speak for Mississippi." Though at the time no one recorded what was actually said, Foote apparently challenged Davis's opinions in what Davis later termed "offensive language."

Exactly what happened after that depends on whose account one believes. Davis later claimed that he landed the first blows, writing that he attacked Foote and "whipped him until I was pulled off." After Foote continued using abusive language toward him, Davis stated that he broke away and attacked his fellow Mississippian a second time. "I knocked him down, jumped on him and commenced beating him, when the gentlemen in the room again pulled me off." Foote later maintained that it was he who struck first, and that it was Davis's "presumptive arrogance" that "compelled me to slap him in the jaw," leading to the fight.

In a dispute such as the one between Davis and Foote, the question of who struck first was always important, as the initial blow created a chain of events that spoke to the combatant's personal honor. If a "gentleman" struck another "gentleman" and the injured party accepted the assault and did nothing about it, he risked being deemed a coward in the eyes of his peers. In Washington, DC, an ego-driven environment where honor and violence were sometimes linked together, a personal assault amounted to a personal challenge, and to dismiss the challenge without meeting it was considered unmanly. As a result, had Davis struck the first blow, it would have been up to Foote to respond to the challenge, and apparently Foote did bring up the subject of a duel during the altercation. "I proposed to him to go into my room and lock the door," Davis later recalled. "He asked me if I had coffee and pistols for two. I told him I had no coffee, but pistols."

The duel never materialized, and, according to Davis's account, "after much blarney that [Foote] always had on hand, it was urged by the friends present that the matter should be dropped as a Christmas frolic." Of course, Foote's later accounts of the events were different and always portrayed Davis in as negative a light as possible. Foote claimed that he struck Davis first and that Davis did little or nothing about it, thereby inferring that Davis was a coward. As late as the 1870s, Foote still relished any opportunity to bring up the story and disparage his old rival, claiming that he had hit Davis first and that he was still waiting for Davis to respond. "My whereabouts may be easily found by [Davis]," Foote, with characteristic dramatic flair and sarcasm, wrote to a newspaper in 1874. "He knows, as thousands of others know, that for a full twenty years I have stood ready to accord to him such satisfaction as he might deem necessary to his deeply wounded honor."

No objective firsthand accounts of the Foote–Davis altercation exist, as everyone in the room at the time agreed to keep the matter to themselves. The two combatants found it prudent to drop the matter, and Foote, in what everyone at the time knew was an outright lie, claimed that he harbored no hard feelings. After the Civil War, former congressman Abraham Venable of North Carolina, who was at Owner's when the dispute took place, wrote a brief recollection of what happened. Venable was not present as the fight occurred but entered the room shortly afterwards. "I at once perceived that there was some restraint upon the company, and was informed that a personal difficulty had occurred between Mr. Davis and Mr. Foote—that blows had passed and that the parties had been separated by the interference of the gentlemen then present—It was agreed that further proceedings should be stopped and that the relations of the parties be restored as theretofore if the whole matter would be regarded as secret and never divulged by anyone—Mr. Foote declared that he bore no malice." The matter was kept confidential for a while, but not forever, with the claims and counterclaims between Foote and Davis about the incident going on for years.[30]

On December 6, 1847, Henry Stuart Foote was sworn in as a member of the United States Senate and, as a man who relished the limelight, his timing was perfect. The nation was creeping toward a crisis, the consequences of which were unthinkable at the time. Slavery and the host of other issues that the institution spawned were beginning to split the country and, for the next decade, statesmen of the period would struggle unsuccessfully to allay the crisis. This created a climate of unease and tension in the national capital, above and beyond the norm. Foote also arrived in Washington at a time when Congress was on the cusp of great generational change. Older members who represented the second generation of American political leadership after the founding fathers—iconic figures like Henry Clay, John C. Calhoun, and Daniel Webster—were disappearing from the scene or were on their last legs. At the same time, a younger group of politicians, including men like Stephen Douglas, William Seward, and Foote's rival Jefferson Davis, were poised to take the reins of leadership in Washington. Born in the nineteenth rather than the eighteenth century, they represented the modern generation of American political leaders—Henry Foote's generation—who would dominate the scene for years to come.

On the floor of the Senate, looking out from the Senate president's chair, Foote occupied the first seat to the right of the center aisle, in the second row, placing him near the middle of the room. The seat directly in front of him was vacant, but directly behind were the desks of Chester Ashley of Arkansas and Lewis Cass of Michigan. Hopkins L. Turney of Tennessee sat on one side of Foote, and on the other side, just across the aisle, sat Louisiana's Henry Johnson. The new Mississippi senator's initial committee assignments in the 30th Congress included the Committee on Private Land Claims, the Committee on Roads and Canals, and the Committee on the District of Columbia.[31]

As Foote arrived in Washington, it was obvious that the gulf between the North and the South was widening. The Mexican War was winding down, and Pennsylvania Democrat David Wilmot had inflamed national passions and gained lasting historical notoriety by introducing in Congress an amendment to an appropriations bill that would have prohibited slavery in any territories acquired from Mexico as a result of the conflict. While the Wilmot Proviso never came to a vote in the Senate, southern statesmen took it as a direct assault on their constituents' rights within the Union. The push for southern unity by ideologues led by John C. Calhoun of South Carolina grew in intensity, and after the Senate ratified the Treaty of Guadalupe Hidalgo, ending the war, Calhoun issued a stern warning that "the slave question will now come up and be the subject of deep agitation." Furthermore, he added, the South risked all if it did not respond immediately, so the time to fight was at hand. The South Carolinian hoped to unite the South through a tightly knit consensus among southern congressmen, based on the fundamental principle of no federal interference with slavery in the territories. He authored "The Address of the Southern Delegates in Congress, to Their Constituents," a document that emphasized states' rights, racial solidarity, and, in general, the need for southern whites to circle the wagons to protect slavery against northern abuses. He counseled that only a united front would allow the slaveholding states to advance their cause in Congress, and the first step in such a process should be the call for a great convention of the slaveholding states.

Foote dutifully aligned himself with Calhoun and the other southerners. "Be not at all uneasy as to our harmonizing hereafter upon every branch of the slavery question," the Mississippian wrote to Calhoun. "I shall not fail to show, on all occasions, a suitable and just deference for your judgment on the whole subject." While Foote would certainly maintain "harmony" with other southern politicians over the protection of slavery, he would eventually break with Calhoun and steer his own course away from rash action.[32]

Foote wasted no time making his presence known on the Senate floor, giving his first major address to his colleagues on January 19, 1848, just six weeks after being sworn in. He lived up to his reputation with a long-winded speech about the Mexican War and the future of the West. Foote's choice of topics was no surprise, as the war effort, American western expansion, and the status of slavery in the West were the burning issues of the day. Foote wanted to participate in the high-profile debates on all of these subjects and, perhaps more importantly, be perceived by the Washington, DC, press corps as being a knowledgeable and important contributor.

Having written his massive history of Texas, Foote had voluminous notes on the region as well as on the history of Mexico, and he had previously delivered many speeches on western expansion. He could craft a lengthy address on the subject quickly and with relative ease. As a bill related to additional military expenditures for the Mexican War made its way through Congress, Foote took the opportunity to speak in favor of it and, in so doing, pontificate on a wide range of subjects related to the war effort. A southern expansionist of the first order, Foote defended the war, discounting as nothing more than "a furious band of unblushing demagogues" those who dared to criticize Polk. He stated that war was inevitable and was provoked by Mexican actions along the Rio Grande, and that "the patriotic citizens of this Republic, almost everywhere, heartily approve the whole course of the administration thus far in the management of this war." He spoke of the "glorious battles of Palo Alto, Resaca de la Palma, Monterrey, and Buena Vista," peppered his rhetoric with references to Demosthenes and Hannibal, and quoted Shakespeare and the founding fathers. He heaped felicitous praise on General Zachary Taylor for his military prowess and brought into question the patriotism of those who believed that the war was nothing more than an exercise in American imperialism.[33]

Foote also promoted the annexation of most of Mexico to the United States as the war wound down, and he was part of a brief "All Mexico" movement that temporarily took root during the period. The idea of annexing all of Mexico was controversial, to say the least. From an economic perspective, some southern Democrats favored the idea as a way to expand the cotton kingdom, while others, like John C. Calhoun, opposed full annexation because it would make citizens of throngs of Mexicans, whom he considered to be members of an inferior race. "We have never dreamt of incorporating into our Union any but the Caucasian race," Calhoun stated, "the free white race."

Meanwhile, many Whigs were cool to the idea of western expansion, predicting correctly that it would reopen the slavery debate in a very volatile way that might threaten the Union. Most northern abolitionists naturally opposed the annexation of Mexico because they wanted to halt the spread of slavery. There was also considerable concern in Washington and elsewhere that, if Mexico were not annexed, the country's weakened state after the war's end would leave Mexico vulnerable to European interests, perhaps giving Britain an opportunity to gain a foothold in the region. Mexico held natural resources and mineral wealth coveted by both the Americans and the Europeans, and many felt that the potential for increased British intrusion represented a threat to U.S. national security and its dominance in the Western Hemisphere.[34]

Though Foote often disparaged the Mexican people, referring to them in his Texas history as "that enervated and degraded mongrel race," his prejudices did not outweigh his belief in Manifest Destiny, the spread of the South's cotton empire, and the need to exploit Mexico's resources and people. He had already corresponded with his old rival John A. Quitman on the subject. Despite their differences, Foote and Quitman maintained a reasonably cordial relationship for a short time after Foote entered the Senate, with their mutual dislike for Jefferson Davis serving as the glue that held the otherwise tenuous relationship together. By this time, Quitman, a southern states' rights ideologue, was a bona fide war hero with a great interest in annexing all of Mexico to the United States. "I speak to you boldly," Quitman wrote to Foote, regarding Mexico, "hold on to this country. It is destiny. It is ours."

Foote agreed, arguing before the Senate that Mexico should be annexed and divided into territories in the traditional American manner and that, after a period of "gradual civilization and Americanization," the Mexican territories might become states. He was clear to maintain, however, that before this process took place, the United States should establish a list of priorities, at the top of which included "securing the mining districts from encroachment from any quarter, the introduction of our system of import duties," and the declaring of millions of acres in Mexico "public lands," which would be open to American settlement and commercial exploitation. Foote's arguments before the Senate also made it clear that, while former Mexican provinces might become states under his plan, true control of Mexico would remain Anglocentric to create a "perfect social order throughout the whole extent of the region." Eventually, the Treaty of Guadalupe Hidalgo ended the All Mexico movement, annexing only the country's northern provinces to the United States, but not before Foote had his say on the issue.[35]

As was his nature, Foote was quick to challenge those in the Senate whose views differed from his own, and many times his verbal attacks crossed the line from political to personal, just as they had always done in squabbles large and small. At one point during debates on the Mexican War and annexation, Foote seemed to question the patriotism of George E. Badger, a Whig from North Carolina who opposed going to war with Mexico, and he participated in a tense exchange with Delaware senator John M. Clayton, another antiwar Whig, over military appropriations. Foote could be aggressive to a fault, making enemies when he did not have to. In his speeches, he lavishly praised those with whom he agreed, and those who agreed with him, and with equal fervor denigrated those taking opposite views, to such a degree that it was afterwards difficult to mend fences. "For power of biting sarcasm," one newspaper of the period wrote, "Senator Foote stands almost unequalled."

Foote tended to focus on the immediate political battles at hand without thinking through the long-term effects of his actions. He seemed unable to overcome the heat of an argument and envision a point in the future when a foe on one issue, on one particular day, might later be willing to bargain with him on another subject. This was part political strategy, in that Foote believed that if he could drive an opponent to lose control of his emotions he could win an argument, or at least discredit that opponent to some degree. The only problem was that it tended to alienate that opponent forever, making him unwilling to work with Foote on anything else. "Foote could smile while his opponent was boiling with rage," one observer noted. His traits as a speaker included "indomitable audacity, a proud haughtiness . . . an arrogance which reduced his companions to subalterns." "Doubtlessly he enjoys it," wrote another. "He utters the drollest and bitterest things, with a look of innocent simplicity that adds infinitely to the effect."[36]

During his first months in Washington, Foote's and John Quitman's mutual animosity toward Jefferson Davis led Foote to advocate on Quitman's behalf in the Senate. In Mexico, Quitman had commanded volunteers as a brigadier general and had received a brevet appointment to major general of volunteers as a result of his service at Monterrey. However, the brevet was held up and never received official sanction, even though he later received a promotion to major general in the regular army. President James K. Polk dismissed the issue, but to Quitman it was a matter of honor, and he believed that if his brevet did not receive official sanction it would somehow tarnish his accomplishments at Monterrey. Quitman lobbied Polk to correct the oversight, and the request ended up in the Senate Committee on Military Affairs, where, to Quitman's great chagrin, Jefferson Davis served as acting chair. Davis blocked the progress of the nomination through inaction, frustrating Quitman and causing him to solicit Foote's help.

Happy for any chance to prod Davis, Foote took up the cause, soliciting the aid of Illinois senator Stephen Douglas to help get Quitman the brevet. Foote and Douglas took Quitman to the capitol building and demanded that the Committee on Military Affairs take action. At one point, Foote and Davis had yet another heated verbal confrontation, with Foote threatening to go back to Mississippi and make an issue of the situation. "Very bitter words were spoken on this occasion between Mr. Davis and myself in the hearing of our brother Senators," Foote later recalled, "and I did not hesitate to charge him with illiberality and injustice toward a meritorious comrade in arms, and I even menaced him with the exposition of his unworthy conduct to our constituents in Mississippi."

In the end, Quitman received his brevet for meritorious service and Foote got the satisfaction of forcing Davis to do something that he did not want to do. The whole episode was also a case study in Foote's abilities as an opportunist. Foote easily could have ignored Quitman's request, but instead he used it to his advantage. He enhanced his own status by coming to the aid of one of his state's most revered military figures, and at the same time he placed one of his political rivals in his debt. Quitman now owed Foote a favor that Foote presumably could cash in at some point in the future.[37]

In the Senate, Foote often tried to involve himself with issues related to world affairs, so much so that he was twice elected chairman on the U.S. Senate Committee on Foreign Relations. While the United States was no longer entangled in a war, a good many delicate diplomatic matters were in play during the late 1840s due to the revolutionary climate in Europe at the time. One of the first foreign issues that Foote heavily debated was whether the United States should establish a strong diplomatic relationship with the Papal States in Italy. The issue was contentious, as many viewed the establishment of diplomatic relations with the Papal States in strictly religious rather than political terms, as if doing so would establish diplomatic ties to a specific religion rather than a political entity. The 1846 election of Pope Pius IX, who was at the time considered a reformer who favored increased political tolerance in the region, sparked increased congressional interest in establishing both diplomatic and economic ties. At stake was a small but potentially lucrative trade with the Papal States in cotton, sugar, and tobacco.

In late 1848, President Polk pressed for official U.S. recognition, stating during an address that "the interesting political events now in progress in these states, as well as a just regard for our commercial interests, have, in my opinion, rendered such a measure highly expedient." Most Democrats, particularly Polk's close friends in Congress, approved of official recognition and backed the idea of sending a chargé d'affaires to represent American interests, but there was also significant opposition to the idea. The anti-immigrant, anti-

Catholic "Know-Nothing" movement was gaining steam during the period as large numbers of Irish Catholic immigrants found their way into America's major cities. In a long address before Congress, Lewis E. Levin, a Know-Nothing representative from Pennsylvania, claimed that recognition of the Papal States was part of a larger plot to give American Catholics leverage to eventually "change the fundamental law, and make the Roman Catholic religion the established religion of the [United States]."[38]

Foote's political rhetoric occasionally included religious references that were general in nature and meant to help him maintain a "God and country" image before the electorate. He tended to sidestep serious debates on religion to avoid being pinned down. Like any prudent politician, Foote knew that while taking sides in a religious debate might forever endear a speaker to one group of believers, it could just as easily alienate him from another. Foote was a staunch defender of Polk's administration and promoted recognition of the Papal States on the Senate floor. Well aware that the most volatile component of the recognition debate revolved around religion, he addressed the issue directly and with skill. Navigating a safe course, he was careful not to criticize, offend, or insult either Protestants or Catholics during debates, sticking instead to broad themes that dealt with freedom of religion and separation of church and state, traditional American principles that anyone reading accounts of his speeches in a newspaper could easily understand. Although Foote, who did not regularly attend church, self-servingly cast himself as an unbiased Christian in the mold of the founding fathers, the recognition debate saw him make some rare public pronouncements of his religious views. "I am not a member of any church [denomination]," he stated at one point. "I have only had the honor of being born in a Christian country and have always paid—as I trust I have felt—a decent respect to the religion of my forefathers. . . . In the success of Episcopalians, Catholics, Methodists, and all other denominations, I have sympathized with equal warmth." Foote went on to defend the pope himself as a "champion of freedom" and as a visionary who promoted civil and religious liberty.[39]

As debates on recognition of the Papal States progressed, Foote became involved in an exchange with New Hampshire senator John P. Hale, establishing a permanent, adversarial relationship between the two men. Like Foote, Hale was aggressive, abrasive, sarcastic, and unwavering in public debate, but the two senators could not have been more different in terms of political philosophy. Foote was a proslavery southerner, firm in his support of the "peculiar institution" and quick to attack those who would threaten it, while Hale was a staunch abolitionist who helped create the Free Soil Party and would later serve as the party's presidential nominee. Foote had championed Texas annexation, the Mexican War, and the western expansion of the cotton kingdom for the Democrats, while Hale had severed his ties with the Democratic Party over those same issues.

Hale charged that the Polk administration's support for recognition of the Papal States represented nothing more than political pandering and that the Democratic Party was simply "fishing for Roman Catholic votes" for the next election cycle. In an indignant flourish, Foote responded that Hale's charges were "absurd and malignant, and incapable of any support whatever from anything that can be called evidence." He also advanced a geopolitical argument by linking the liberal Pope Pius IX to the democratic reform movements that were sweeping through Europe at the time. In the end, Henry Foote came down on the winning side, with Congress approving official recognition of the Papal States.[40]

Despite Foote's rhetoric to the contrary, his successful support for recognition of the Papal States was not a function of his admiration for the pope or his commitment to religious freedom and the universal rights of all denominations. His interest in the issue proved purely political and devoid of any moral underpinnings. Several years later, the Mississippian would become involved with the anti-Catholic Know-Nothings in an effort to promote his own political future, and he was known to make anti-Semitic remarks, casting serious doubt on the self-serving claims that he was free from prejudice and a champion of religious freedom.

Foote had been laboring for the Democratic Party for decades, canvassing Mississippi and elsewhere for state and national Democratic candidates. He made impassioned speeches for James K. Polk during the 1844 election season and proudly cast his vote for Polk as a Democratic elector. The Polk administration, led by Secretary of State James Buchanan, favored opening diplomatic relations with the Papal States, and Foote took up the cause to support the president's wishes and to defend the Democratic administration's policies. In addition, it seemed at the time as if the Papal States might provide another market for U.S. exports, most notably southern cotton, once diplomatic relations were established. As a southerner and a man who longed to be perceived nationally as one of the chief political spokesmen for the South, any proposal that seemed to benefit cotton producers usually caught Foote's attention and led him to fully support the cause.

Foote was also involved in debates related to official United States reaction to the 1848 revolution in France. The revolution overthrew French monarch Louis Philippe and established the French Second Republic, ushering in a period of broad political upheaval throughout Europe that many American officials cheered and others were wary of. Once the revolution in France took place, the issue of whether to officially recognize and congratulate the new French government became an important question in the halls of Congress. The Polk administration favored recognizing the new government, as did many other national politicians, but some saw such action as premature. After a resolution congratulating the people of France "upon their success in their recent efforts to consolidate liberty" was introduced in the Senate, debates on the subject began. Some senators, like John Milton Niles, a northern Democrat from Connecticut, were skeptical about whether the new government in France would actually "consolidate liberty" in the form of creating a more democratic environment in the country. The idea that the French were presumably in the process of establishing a more democratic republic was universally applauded by American lawmakers, but some wanted to wait and see the new government and its policies take shape before issuing official statements.[41]

Others, particularly northerners with abolitionist sympathies, believed the revolution should be lauded and taken at face value, particularly since the new French government was committed to abolishing slavery in France's colonial possessions. Henry Foote's emerging nemesis in the Senate, the abolitionist John P. Hale, complicated the debate by introducing an amendment to the original resolution that would have congratulated France on establishing a new government and on "instituting measures for the immediate emancipation of the slaves of all the colonies of the republic." As always, bringing slavery into any discussion of issues large or small immediately put southerners on guard. The provocative amendment was voted down, but not before it created a stir that led to sharp words between northern and southern senators.[42]

Along with his southern brethren, Henry Foote defended the cause of slavery and the South during discussions. While Foote supported recognition of the new French regime because of his sympathies for the movement and because it was the position of the Polk administration, the feisty Mississippian was also sensitive to his place in the pantheon of southern leadership. In his comments before the Senate, he defended his region's "domestic institutions" to their core and chastised northerners for introducing the issue of slavery in America into discussions related to the freedom and liberty of the French people. In so doing, he also made one of his first public senatorial pronouncements on the subject of slavery's threat to the Union. The question of domestic slavery in the South, Foote argued, "is one that involves some of our dearest interests, our strongest sensibilities, and puts in peril the Union itself." He went on to condemn the "long, factious, disorganized harangues" of northern abolitionists, who he believed were determined to "conjure up a hurricane" that would destroy the country and "bring down upon the South all the horrors which our enemies have long desired us to experience."[43]

Foote was not satisfied to confine his remarks on the subject to the Senate floor. Seeking a broader forum that would give him more personal notoriety in Washington, he made certain that he was on the schedule to speak at a major public rally celebrating the new French government, on the evening of April 15, 1848. In doing so, the Mississippian knew that he was playing to his strengths. Although Foote liked to see his name in the newspapers, he knew that he was at his best on the stump, appealing directly to large crowds of people. The sarcasm, invective, and emotion that so often punctuated his remarks and drew cheers from audiences did not translate as well to the cold written word. Foote enjoyed the give-and-take between himself and the public and treated his political appearances more as political *performances.*

The rally celebrating the ascendance of a new democratic government in France began with a large parade that ended at Washington's Lafayette Square. According to one report, the event "drew an immense crowd. *Marseilles Hymn* was sung, many of the houses were illuminated and torch-light processions moved through the streets amid the shouts and rejoicings of the multitude." Another stated that the lively Washington crowd numbered in the thousands and that "the whole city presents one scene of glorious enthusiasm on the occasion of celebrating the late revolution in France." At the park, bonfires, multicolored lanterns, and torches lit both the stage and the surrounding area, creating the perfect environment for a Foote address. He gave a speech that was typically southern in that it defined the irony, hypocrisy, and irreconcilability of a slaveholder promoting the concept of democracy and self-determination. "The age of tyrants and slavery is rapidly drawing to a close," Foote said, in reference to France, and "the happy period to be signalized by the universal emancipation of man from the fetters of civil oppression, and the recognition in all countries of the great principles of popular sovereignty, equality and brotherhood is, at this moment, visibly commencing."[44]

As was the case with other southern lawmakers who spoke thematically on freedom, liberty, and democracy in antebellum America, the irony that he was using the language of abolition seemed to be lost on Foote. It was not, however, lost on members of the abolitionist community in the North. Horace Mann, in particular, was quick to quote Foote, frequently in tongue-in-cheek fashion, when pointing out southern hypocrisy related to the slavery issue. A newly elected Whig congressman representing Massachusetts, Mann was known, among other things, for his strong opinions on slavery and as an education reformer. Two months after the Washington rally, Mann was busy defending Daniel Drayton and Edward Sayres, who were indicted on numerous counts of aiding escaped slaves. Their high-profile case involved seventy-seven slaves who had attempted to escape Washington, DC, aboard the schooner *Pearl*. It was the largest escape attempt by slaves in American history, and the press followed the trial with great interest. During the proceedings Mann quoted from Foote's speech, peppered as it was with references to freedom and liberty, and then sarcastically suggested that the Washington slaves may have gotten the idea of running away from people like "the great Mississippi senator."

When word of Mann's courtroom comments got out, other abolitionists hailed Mann's use of a prominent southerner's remarks as an indictment of southern hypocrisy. "Will anyone be surprised after this," Harriet Beecher Stowe wrote after the furor subsided, "that seventy-seven of the most intelligent slaves, male and female, in Washington City, honestly taking Mr. Foote and his brother senators at their word, and believing that the age of tyrants and slavery was drawing to a close, banded together and made an effort to obtain their part in this reign of universal brotherhood?" Foote himself did not respond publicly to the incident or the use of his speech by abolitionists, but one reporter commented at the time that the senator would be "considerably startled" at the claim that the escape attempt was "the consequence of his speech."[45]

Despite the contradictions between the liberty that he praised and the institution of slavery that he promoted, Foote continued to support European revolutionaries and the revolutionary movement in general. In 1850, Congress took up the question of how the United States should respond to the struggles of Hungarian revolutionaries who sought to free themselves from Austrian rule. Foote, who by this time chaired the Senate Committee on Foreign Relations, suggested on the Senate floor that the United States should cut off diplomatic relations with Austria in support of the Hungarians. As had been the case with debates over French recognition, northern abolitionists again tried to use the issue of freedom in Europe to make points about slavery in the United States. This made some southern congressman wary of embracing the Hungarian cause too tightly, but not Foote, who consistently praised the Hungarian revolutionaries and their leader, Louis Kossuth.

In February of 1851, Foote successfully introduced a joint resolution empowering the president to send an American naval vessel to Turkey, where Kossuth and other revolutionaries were living in exile, and bring the group back to America.[46] The ship collected Kossuth and his colleagues and, after several stops, including a successful visit to England, made its way into port at Staten Island, where the revolutionaries received a hero's welcome. "Salutes were fired, flags were given to the breeze, and the people rushed to the wharves by the thousands," the *Baltimore Sun* reported. "The city will be in a tremendous state of uproar all day."[47]

For Foote, Kossuth's visit posed a problem in that it forced the Mississippian to straddle a very rickety fence. Though he was politely received in Washington, DC, Kossuth's visit was polarizing. Abolitionists couched the visit in terms that promoted their interests, praising the Hungarian's commitment to universal liberty. They saw him as representing a beacon of freedom in the universal sense, a symbol of all peoples who hoped to rid themselves of the shackles of oppression. At the same time, to southern slaveholders, and particularly to the more conservative members of the region's political community, Kossuth's arrival sent up yet another red flag. Though they routinely ignored the conflict inherent in the existence of a slaveholding society within a nation founded on democratic principles, they now were faced with the contradiction on a daily basis and therefore were uncomfortable with too much talk of freedom, justice, and human dignity.

Foote was caught in the middle. He hoped to further his national reputation as a statesman and authority on foreign policy by promoting Kossuth, but he did not want to do so at the risk of alienating his homeland. As the Hungarian leader was arriving in New York, Foote introduced in the Senate what turned out to be a controversial resolution to organize a grand reception for Kossuth to officially congratulate him on his arrival in the United States and to "tender to him, on the part of Congress, and in the name of the people of the United States, the hospitalities of the Metropolis of the Union."[48]

The resolution set off a firestorm in the Senate. Abolitionists pushed to amend it to reflect their interests, while some southerners, who had by this time had their fill of discussion on the universal rights of man, sought to defeat it outright. Foote called for unanimous consent on the issue, but it was immediately apparent that the resolution was in trouble. Among the most prominent southerners speaking out against it was William C. Dawson of Georgia, who argued that an official reception like the one that Foote proposed should be reserved for someone who has rendered great and measurable service to the United States. While claiming that he held a great respect for Kossuth as a person, Dawson told his colleagues, "I see nothing in the character of this distinguished individual which should make the government of the United States get up a great pageant on his account. . . . It is the people and not the government that ought to receive him." He went on to point out that significant official displays of recognition in the past had been reserved only for larger-than-life characters like George Washington or the Marquis de Lafayette, heroes who were "connected to the Revolution which gave us the liberties we enjoy." While Dawson stated several times that he held great personal admiration for Kossuth, the message was clear: Kossuth had not done anything for the United States other than embody in the minds of some the ideals of liberty and freedom, which were compatible with the American mission but incompatible with the way of life in the slaveholding South.[49]

Maintaining his reputation as a man who "never loses an opportunity for a sly hit at his opponent," John P. Hale of Massachusetts further complicated matters by suggesting an amendment to the Kossuth resolution designed to promote the abolitionist point of view. Hale was always tightly focused on the slavery issue, and getting involved in the discussion in this case was also irresistible because his amendment put Foote on the hot seat. Though not mentioning the South specifically, Hale's amendment was a lightly veiled censure of the region's slavocracy. He proposed that, in addition to welcoming Kossuth, the resolution should also assure Kossuth "of the sympathy of the Congress and the people of the United States with the victims of oppression everywhere, and that their earnest desire is that the time may speedily arrive when the rights of man shall be universally recognized and respected by every people and government of the world."

Foote was caught off guard but recovered quickly, immediately seeing that the amendment for what it was. He did his best to steer the course of the debate away from slavery, but it was useless as long as Hale was involved in the conversation. Still, Foote went on the attack. He tried to couch Hale and his friends as villains, political opportunists who would sully the cause of liberty by trying to press their own suspect agenda. Sympathy for Kossuth and his comrades was just as strong in the South as it was in the North, Foote claimed, and southern sympathy would remain strong despite the fact that "individuals, inimical of our own domestic institution, think proper to profess a peculiar sort of abolition sympathy for the heroic defenders of freedom on Hungarian soil." He went on to again defend slavery and the South, dismissing criticism of the region as the product of "fanaticism and demagoguery" in the North.

Though Foote had allies in the room, his bluster about the failings of abolitionists in the North could not overcome the reality that he was in an untenable position. Southern conservatives, who Foote did not want to alienate, were against the original resolution and certainly recoiled at the Hale amendment. Many northerners, in turn, would not support Foote without some type of statement promoting universal freedom. As for Hale himself, he watched with satisfaction as, for one of the few times in his life on the public stage, Henry Foote backed down. He admitted defeat and withdrew the resolution.[50]

Foote's experience with the Kossuth resolution was relatively minor in the grand scheme of American foreign policy, but it was significant in that it reflected what was going on in Congress at the time with regard to the slavery issue. Slavery affected debate not only on U.S. domestic policy but also on foreign policy, even on small issues. In the case of Foote's resolution, Congress could not come to an agreement on a simple expression of praise for the concepts of liberty and freedom, two primary components upon which the country was supposedly founded, because the slavery issue got in the way. Without the slavery issue, the resolution was little more than a formality. Northerners and Southerners alike would have favored it, or something similar to it, without giving the matter much thought. Politicians from both sections likely would have made lofty speeches supporting the measure, if for no other reason than to attach themselves rhetorically to the concepts of freedom and liberty, claiming that their support for Kossuth represented support for the ideals that America's own founding fathers held dear. However, with slavery in the equation, none of this was possible. Americans in the North and the South agreed wholeheartedly that freedom was something to be cherished, but they could not agree on the definition of the word.

The problem was fundamental and, by the time Foote entered the Senate, impossible to ignore. As the abolition movement gained traction in the North, its members sought to define freedom in *universal* terms, which would always alienate the southern political community as long as their region held slaves. In turn, politicians from the South were averse to being reminded that freedom, democracy, and slavery could not comfortably coexist, no matter how much energy they expended trying to claim otherwise. The words and concepts of *freedom* and *slavery* would not reconcile, and therefore northern and southern politicians could not reconcile with one another once those issues were part of any discussion.

Henry Foote's confrontational personality led him into many Senate debates, but it also made him enemies. He did not seem to recognize that the traits that had worked to his advantage as he sought high office actually hindered his abilities as a lawmaker. As a campaigner, he throttled his opponents to the point of humiliation, and he sometimes picked fights for the simple reason that he enjoyed the contest. He tried to ridicule and insult his rivals and to anger them to the point where they would lose control. While these traits excited voters and drew many to him, they did not translate well to the floor of the Senate. In Washington, the most effective lawmakers were those who knew which fights to pick, and when to pick them, and those who could win an argument without completely alienating an opponent. Creating fights for no reason, or trying to participate in every fight that came up, were counterproductive courses of action. Issues coming before the Senate were perpetually wide ranging, and an opponent on one issue might end up being an ally on another, as long as those involved maintained a certain degree of decorum. The Senate was a small club of men with huge egos, and its members had to find a way to work together on a regular basis. They had to get along with one another, at least up to a point, in order to get anything done. On the campaign trail, Foote's interaction with a debate opponent was relatively brief, while in Washington, interactions with his fellow senators were ongoing. "His propensity for the use of invective and sarcasm," one scholar who studied Foote's speeches later observed, "often led to breaches of Senate decorum and to personal difficulties with several senators." In a climate where sectional tensions over the slavery issue already had senators from the North and the South on edge, Foote's lambasting could be even more explosive, creating a spectacle that other senators did not want to see or be part of.[51]

While in Washington, Foote did not limit his opponents to fellow members of Congress. In early 1849, he involved himself in what most observers at the time thought was a needless dispute with John McLean, an associate justice on the United States Supreme Court. Born in New Jersey and raised in Ohio, McLean was a veteran politician who had seen it all by the time Foote chose to tangle with him. McLean served in the cabinets of James Monroe and John Quincy Adams and was appointed to the Supreme Court by Andrew Jackson in 1829. He was also an outspoken abolitionist who routinely made political pronouncements from the bench and elsewhere, a practice that some deemed unethical for a supposedly impartial judge. As a result, many called McLean "the politician on the Supreme Court," and it was his direct involvement in political matters that led Foote to challenge him.

In 1848, McLean unsuccessfully sought the Whig nomination for president and, in doing so, penned numerous letters to newspapers, stating his positions on issues of the day. One issue that he paid particular attention to was the Mexican War. Southerners were in favor of the war as a vehicle for the expansion of slavery, while antislavery Whigs in the North criticized the conflict for the same reason. McLean wrote inflammatory letters on the subject that were printed and reprinted in newspapers across the country. He stated his belief that the "miserable war with Mexico" was "unnecessarily and unconstitutionally commenced," and that Congress should immediately stop funding it. The letters drew fire from southerners, who argued that it was unethical for a Supreme Court justice to comment on the constitutionality of an issue outside the context of a case, particularly if he did so in an attempt to promote his own political agenda.[52]

Henry Foote had already attacked the Supreme Court as an institution by the time he tangled with McLean. The previous year, he had given speeches in the Senate critical of lifetime appointments and the notion that the court could declare unconstitutional a law passed by Congress. His specific problem with McLean developed as a bill granting franking privileges to Supreme Court justices came under discussion. As debate began on the normally mundane issue, Foote suddenly launched into a full-fledged rhetorical diatribe against McLean, stating that he did not want Congress to allow free postage to a justice who had written letters to newspapers critical of the Mexican War and the slaveholding South. The attack was personal, and to the point. He called McLean a "political letter-writer" and criminal who was "unworthy to preside in the most obscure court," and he suggested that the justice "owes to the country a solemn apology for the violation of public decency which he has committed. . . . and for the deep dishonor which he has brought upon our noble institutions." Foote's attack launched a newspaper battle, during which McLean defended himself, stating simply that "as a citizen, I claim the right and will exercise it, of forming and expressing my opinion on public matters."

In the Senate, Foote would not let the matter rest, and on January 23, 1849, he rose to attack McLean again, this time by reading aloud long passages from letters supposedly written by McLean. As time wore on, even southern senators who disliked the justice grew weary of Foote's tirade, believing that it was more personal than official in nature and therefore was not worthy of public debate. "I do hope my friend from Mississippi will postpone his remarks," an exasperated Senator William R. King of Alabama interrupted at one point, "as there is public business that needs attention, and I do not perceive that the debate now proceeding is in order."[53]

Foote's tirade against McLean accomplished little other than to underscore the senator's reputation as a loose cannon. It also caught the attention of northern newspaper editors and the Whig press in general, who condemned the Mississippian in no uncertain terms. The Philadelphia *North American* reported Foote's display as "an exhibition which called out a general expression of derision from the chamber. . . . He has humiliated the Senate and depreciated his personal character," while, in Washington, the *National Era* condemned the "wanton and indecent" attack on McLean as "gross and unbecoming." Across the Potomac River, in northern Virginia, the *Alexandria Gazette* took Foote to task as a hypocrite who himself routinely gave speeches on the Senate floor merely for political effect. "Mr. Foote certainly achieved an unenviable notoriety," the newspaper stated. "He has done more than any other man to bring his own station into disrepute by making electioneering speeches in the Senate, and by indulging in violent invective."[54]

Foote eventually stopped his attacks on McLean, but not before he wrote letters to Democratic newspapers back in Mississippi, defending his own conduct and pointing out that McLean was an abolitionist and therefore deserved whatever treatment he had received. Foote may have realized that he had embarrassed himself by attacking McLean with such ferocity, as many years later he did not mention the incident in his self-serving autobiography *Casket of Reminiscences*. As for McLean, he remained on the Supreme Court until his death, in 1861, four years after he was one of the two dissenting voices in the landmark proslavery decision *Dred Scott v. Sanford* (1857).

Embarrassed by his exchanges with McLean or not, Foote never let up. He knew that he had come to the U.S. Senate at a pivotal time, and he wanted desperately to make history. As the slavery debate drove the country apart, and as domestic issues as delicate as they were monumental dominated discussions in Washington, Foote made his voice heard time and again. He made many salient points on the Senate floor but continued to stir up controversy. The Mexican War, the cession of Mexican territory to the United States at the war's end, and the question of who controlled the Oregon country were among the primary issues of the day, as was the status of slavery in Washington, DC. Arguments between northerners and southerners never seemed to end as the abolition movement grew stronger in the North and, in the South, more radical proslavery politicians rose to prominence. Foote reveled in the drama, strong-arming himself into almost every important debate, never missing an opportunity to grandstand. He drew some to his side but disgusted others in an ongoing attempt to make sure that his voice was heard above the fray.

In the spring of 1848, Foote and Hale had yet another sharp exchange on the Senate floor, over resolutions thanking generals Winfield Scott and Zachary Taylor for their service during the Mexican War. Hale spoke out against the plaudits because he did not feel that he could vote to officially thank the men for service in a war that he believed was immoral, unnecessary, and fought only at the behest of southerners who hoped to expand slavery by acquiring Mexican land. "I will not be a hypocrite," Hale said. "I will not thank officers for the agency which they have had in producing results that I loathe." He went on to denounce the war, as most abolitionists of the period did, calling it "a war of robbery . . . unconstitutional and unjust."

Senators from the slaveholding states were incensed, viewing any disparaging comments about the war as an attack on slavery and the South. Foote could not hold back, challenging Hale with missionary zeal, disparaging him as a fanatic who represented only a "small, unprincipled faction in New England." The Mississippian went on to question his fellow senator's patriotism in the harshest terms possible. "I speak but the language of history when I say," Foote bellowed in one great flourish, "that in no age since civilization began, has there been any name for any man who opposed his country either in thought, word, or deed, when in arms for her own defense, except traitor. That is the name by which the Senator would be known if he dared to act out the sentiments of his heart." Knowing that to get angry would play into Foote's hands, Hale responded calmly, denying the claims as his fellow senator continued to push. Foote went overboard in another long rant, praising the war and denouncing Hale, until Kentucky senator John J. Crittenden finally urged him to stop so that other Senate business could proceed. In the end, separate measures commending Scott and Taylor passed the Senate, with Hale, true to his convictions, casting the lone dissenting vote on each.[55]

In their most publicized exchange, Hale and Foote tangled again over a bill related to the status of slavery in Washington, DC. The issue was highly symbolic and emotionally charged. Abolitionists argued that the institution of slavery was reprehensible and therefore had no place in the nation's capital, a position with which slave owners in the South naturally disagreed. Slavery, southerners argued, was not a southern institution but a *national* institution that contributed greatly to the national economy and was protected by the Constitution. As a result, it should occupy a prominent place in Washington and should be promoted there rather than banned.

The catalyst for confrontation between Foote and Hale was a bill that Hale introduced, related to the protection of private property in the District of Columbia. The previous week, the slavery issue had almost torn Washington apart. Proslavery agitators had rioted in the streets in response to the escape attempt by more than seventy slaves aboard the *Pearl*. The rioters believed that the incident, organized by antislavery activists, was part of a broader abolitionist conspiracy in the capital, and they threatened to destroy the offices of the *National Era,* a prominent antislavery newspaper operating in the city. City officials, backed by federal authorities, eventually restored order, but the atmosphere in Washington remained tense. In the Senate, Hale used the fallout from the riot as an excuse to introduce a bill to make the municipal authorities in Washington financially responsible for any damage done to private property by a mob. Hale claimed that he was only interested in protecting the offices of the *National Era* and other antislavery publications from harm, but southern ideologues were fierce in their opposition. They saw Hale's legislation as an attempt to protect an abolitionist press that was sympathetic to the slaves who had attempted to escape, and any abolitionists who had helped them.[56]

John C. Calhoun and Jefferson Davis both voiced their disagreement with the measure, but it was Foote who blasted Hale with the greatest force. Foote argued that any newspaper that sympathized with escaped slaves was actually giving those slaves aid and comfort and was complicit with "committing grand larceny." By association, any bill to protect these newspapers did nothing but promote "slave-stealing," and it was a slap in the face to southerners. "The attempt to legislate directly on the subject in the national councils is at war with the Constitution," Foote said, "repugnant to all the principles of good faith, and violative of all sentiments of patriotism." He questioned Hale's integrity and honesty, argued that northerners should not meddle with "local concerns" in the slaveholding states, and stated that Hale was acting to protect his "friends, the blacks—the slaves of the District of Columbia." Building toward a crescendo, he finally accused the New Hampshire senator of promoting policies that would tear the nation apart and lead to violence and bloodshed. "The senator from New Hampshire is evidently attempting to get up a sort of civil war in this country," Foote claimed, "and is evidently filled with the spirit of insurrection. . . . Let him buckle on his armor, let him unsheath his sword!"[57]

Hale, of course, denied doing or saying anything incendiary, but it was not so much his words as his attitude that eventually allowed him to get the best of Foote. No matter what Foote did or said, Hale kept a poker face and used his own brand of sarcasm both as a shield against Foote's tirades and as a weapon. "The sneer of the gentleman does not affect me," Hale said of Foote. "I recognize every member of the human family as a brother; and if it was done by human beings, it was done by my brethren." Hale kept his head as Foote hurled more criticism toward him, refusing to take the bait and get into a full-fledged argument with the Mississippian on the Senate floor. Finally, Foote had had enough. Frustrated, he lashed out at his fellow senator in what some at the time regarded as a death threat. He said that if Hale "really wishes glory, and to be regarded as the great liberator of blacks," he should visit Mississippi. "I invite him [there]," Foote continued, "and will tell him beforehand, in all honesty, that he could not go ten miles into the interior before he would grace one of the tallest trees in the forest with a rope around his neck, with the approbation of every virtuous and patriotic citizen, and that, if necessary, I should myself assist in the operation."[58]

Henry Foote had finally gone too far. His comments drew immediate condemnation from other members of the Senate, northerners and southerners alike. The direct threat broke decorum and was another example of how the tactics that Foote used to berate opponents on the campaign trail did not translate well to the floor of the U.S. Senate. It was now Foote who was out of control, and his fellow solons did not like it. While others in the Senate certainly had volatile tempers, the ferocity of Foote's attack on Hale, and particularly the threat to Hale's life, was viewed as unnecessary. His verbose pronouncements on "slave-stealing" were seen as self-serving, and while southern senators may have agreed with Foote in principle, they also knew the value of keeping the facade of gentlemanly politeness intact on the Senate floor. Feigned courtesy and effusive displays of respect among the senators sometimes served as the grease that allowed the lawmaking wheels to turn slowly without ever coming to a complete stop. Poorly timed or overextended displays of hubris tended to damage the process. "This gentleman is receiving more kicks than kisses at the present time," one northern newspaper said of Foote, not long after the incident with Hale, "notwithstanding the noble aspirations avowed by him a few days since to attain the dignity of hangman. Even his own friends give him the cold shoulder."[59]

Foote's attack on Hale was widely reported in the press, and northern newspapers weighed in, vilifying Foote as a "slavery crusader" and deriding him as "Hangman Foote," a nickname that would stay with him for years. The *Boston Courier* opined, "The renowned Mississippi senator, commonly known as 'hangman' Foote . . . is the most mischievous and wrong headed agitator in either house. . . . a reckless, conceited, noisy demagogue," while a Vermont editor called the Mississippian a "supremely contemptible" man whose brain was a "natural and ever-flowing fountain of gas." Likewise, the *United States Democratic Review,* in New York, called Foote a "senseless demagogue," described his diatribe against Hale as a "disgusting rant," and accused the Mississippian of using "language and sentiments which the most abandoned leader of a street mob would hesitate in this country to utter."[60]

The hubbub hurt Foote politically, and he knew it. It branded him in many northern circles as a southern radical and drew the ire of some southerners who believed his outbursts were too inflammatory and too frequent. Foote immediately realized he had made a mistake, and he was still expressing regret more than two decades later in his memoirs, where he described his tirade against the New Hampshire senator as "one of the most fumy, rabid, and insulting speeches that has ever dishonored a grave and dignified parliamentary body."

He described his own language as "stupid" and irresponsible and later stated, "I would have really given worlds to recall all the nonsense I had uttered. In less than forty-eight hours I received hundreds of anonymous letters, filled with the most caustic revilement, and others inclosing the most hideous caricatures of a person whom these same caricatures denominated 'Hangman Foote.'"[61]

Foote's disputes with fellow senators and his general propensity to comment loudly on almost every subject that came up on the Senate floor damaged his credibility. He was seen by many of his colleagues as too impulsive, too easily excitable, too quick to turn a political debate personal, and too long-winded. One observer of the period, abolitionist author and journalist Sara Jane Lippincott, wrote of the Mississippi senator, 'He is a most restless statesman. . . . is on his feet with every opportunity, pouring forth 'burning fluids' of speeches and inflammable gasses of southern democracy." A correspondent from the *Detroit Advertiser* was even less charitable when he wrote that "Foote's rising to speak has become a signal for a general evacuation of desks and galleries [in the Senate]." Despite his critics, Foote would not be silenced, and he continued to assume, according to one observer, "an active and conspicuous position in regard to all the important question of the period." He also continued to get into fights with colleagues, usually verbal but occasionally physical.[62]

In December of 1848, Foote was one of a number of southern senators and representatives stressing regional unity in reaction to the Wilmot Proviso and in the face of growing pressure to organize western territories. Early in the month, President James K. Polk urged Congress to settle the slavery issue out West, either by passing legislation extending the Missouri Compromise Line to the Pacific or by authorizing popular sovereignty as the best course of action. Residents of New Mexico stirred the pot on December 13 by submitting a petition to Congress requesting "the speedy organization by law of a territorial civil government." The petition went on to stress, "We do not desire to have domestic slavery within our borders, and until the time shall arrive for our admission to the Union as a State, we desire to be protected by Congress against their introduction amongst us."

Not long afterwards, representative Daniel Gott of New York introduced in the House of Representatives a resolution prohibiting the slave trade in the District of Columbia. In addition to the content of the resolution, southerners were particularly angered by Gott's contention that slavery "was contrary to natural justice and the fundamental principles of our own political system, notoriously a reproach to our country throughout Christendom." Gott's reso-lution sparked action from some members of the southern bloc, led by John C. Calhoun. After what Henry Foote later described as "fierce and acrimonious discussions" in Congress, the southerners decided to organize a meeting for the purpose of charting a unified, singular course for all of the slaveholding states.[63]

The meeting would not unite all of the southerners. Of the 121 represen-tatives from the slaveholding states, only seventy attended the caucus. A few prominent Democrats and most of the Whigs from the southern delegations chose not to show up, many believing that the exercise was really an attempt by Calhoun to promote a southern political party and his own well-chronicled views on nullification and secession. Remaining fiercely loyal to Calhoun, Foote was among those who organized and promoted the meeting, which was held in the Senate chamber on December 22. After much discussion, the as-sembly formed a committee to issue a collective position to the people of the South. In addition to Foote and Calhoun, the committee included John M. Clayton of Delaware, John G. Chapman of Maryland, Thomas H. Bayly of Virginia, Abraham W. Venable of North Carolina, Edward C. Cabell of Florida, William R. D. King of Alabama, Solomon W. Downs of Louisiana, Thomas J. Rusk of Texas, William K. Sebastian of Arkansas, David R. Atchison of Missouri, Alexander Stephens of Georgia, Charles S. Morehead of Ken-tucky, and Meredith P. Gentry of Tennessee. In reality, the establishment of a committee was merely a formality, as Calhoun would write the address and deliver it himself a few weeks later.[64]

While Foote's tirades against John P. Hale and others branded him as a loose cannon, they also helped establish the Mississippian's reputation among south-erners and northerners alike as one of the most radical southern firebrands. Assessing the nature of the southern delegates who attended the meeting, John Henry Lumpkin wrote to fellow Georgian Robert Toombs, "They are all men of calmness and deliberation, except for Venable, Calhoun, and Foote. I cannot tell you anything as to the probable course they might think proper to pursue."

The day after the meeting, Foote took it upon himself to go see President James K. Polk and report what had happened. Polk listened politely as the Mis-sissippian outlined the position of those who attended the meeting, stating that their desire was to "assert and maintain the constitutional rights of the south-ern states" with regard to issues related to slavery. In reply, Polk said that he did not believe that the nonslaveholding states would press the slavery debate to the point where it would threaten the Union. "I expressed the hope to [Foote]," Polk wrote later in his diary, "that the threatened interference from the North with the delicate subject of slavery would not be pressed to extremities."[65]

The address that Calhoun produced, titled simply "Address of the Southern Delegates in Congress to their Constituents," outlined the perceived historical abuses that the institution of slavery had suffered at the hand of northern politicians. The South Carolinian stressed the need for southern unity and warned southern whites in emotional terms that an unchecked abolition movement would end civilization as they knew it. If the slaves were freed, he wrote, they would "become the principal recipients of federal offices and patronage, and would, in consequence, be raised above the whites of the South in the political and social scale." He went on to state that emancipation would expose southern whites to "degradation greater than has ever yet fallen to the lot of a free and enlightened people," and that the South itself would "become the permanent abode of disorder, anarchy, poverty, misery, and wretchedness." Calhoun delivered the address in Congress on January 22, 1849, and it helped set the parameters for the proslavery argument for the next twelve years, until the Civil War. At the time, however, it did not bring the South together as he hoped. Only forty-six southern congressmen signed off on the address, while others saw it as far too inflammatory. The entire Mississippi delegation signed the document, including Henry Foote, but within a year Foote would break with his fellow Mississippians and with Calhoun himself.[66]

Before the end of the 30th Congress, Foote had another well-publicized row, this time with Senator Simon Cameron of Pennsylvania. The dispute grew out of the tension over the slavery issue, which had developed as lawmakers in Washington struggled to organize the territory that the United States had recently acquired as a result of the Mexican War. As the session drew to close, the Senate was gridlocked over the future of slavery in the Mexican Cession. Foreshadowing things to come, Stephen Douglas of Illinois introduced a compromise measure that would have decided the issue by using popular sovereignty, the idea that, instead of a federal mandate being involved, the people living in a specific territory or state should have the right to decide whether they would accept slavery. The proposal drew heavy fire from both northern abolitionists, who wanted slavery completely forbidden in the West, and proslavery southerners, who wanted the institution to spread.

On March 3, 1849—the last day of the session—the debate became heated and somewhat disorganized as tempers flared. Foote was active in the proceedings all day and into the evening. After midnight, in hopes of blocking any abolitionist agenda on the western territories that might gain traction, Foote made the odd argument that, constitutionally, the Senate session had officially ended at midnight and therefore the Senate should be adjourned. He claimed that any further debate on any issue was extralegal and that the official end of the session also meant that the terms of office of one-third of the Senate members had expired.

Though a few members agreed with Foote, most senators believed that there was no issue because the debates had begun before midnight and therefore they should be allowed to continue as long as needed. They also resented Foote for introducing into the discussion what they viewed as a needless complication, and for unnecessarily adding to the mayhem on the Senate floor. Even after his motion to adjourn the Senate failed, Foote would not let the issue rest. He continued to argue the point, generating groans, catcalls, and hisses from some of his colleagues as the Senate's presiding officer repeatedly declared him out of order. "I pronounce we are no longer a Senate," Foote said, "I care not who says the reverse. . . . The day expires at midnight!"

At one point during the proceedings, Senator Cameron of Pennsylvania, in an obvious reference to Foote, protested the increased lack of decorum in the Senate chamber. Foote took offense and the two men exchanged sharp words, with Foote claiming that Cameron had no right to speak at all because his term of office had expired at midnight. Then, according to amused Texas senator Sam Houston, who hated Foote, "The eloquent and impassioned gentlemen got into each other's hair." The *Congressional Globe* published a diplomatically worded description of the encounter, stating, "Other words were uttered by both the Senators from Pennsylvania and Mississippi, and something approaching a personal collision ensued."

Foote approach Cameron, wagging a finger in his face and continuing to call him "other opprobrious names," and the Pennsylvanian responded by hitting Foote in the face. A tussle ensued, and other senators had to pull the two men apart. The incident passed and was quickly forgotten, although one newspaper later reported that Cameron had expected Foote to challenge him to a duel and that the Pennsylvanian had asked Foote's enemy Jefferson Davis to serve as his second, should the duel take place. Davis reportedly refused, telling Cameron, "I cannot agree to that, because I expect to kill that scoundrel myself some day."[67]

HENRY STUART FOOTE. This photograph was taken by Matthew Brady around the time Foote entered the United States Senate. It features the balding Foote wearing a dark hairpiece. (Beinecke Rare Book and Manuscript Library, Yale University.)

HENRY STUART FOOTE. This photograph was taken around the time Foote entered the Confederate Congress in 1861. (Library of Congress.)

SEARGENT SMITH PRENTISS (1808–1850). Foote fought two duels with Prentiss, and both survived to later become friends. (Courtesy of the Archives and Records Division, Mississippi Department of Archives and History.)

ROBERT J. WALKER (1801–1869). Walker was Mississippi's leading Jacksonian during the 1830s, and Foote was quick to attach himself to Walker's coattails.
(Library of Congress.)

MIRABEAU LAMAR (1798–1859). Second president of the Republic of Texas.
Foote briefly attached himself to Lamar's regime while in Texas, and he wrote a
massive history of Texas at Lamar's request. (From Miabeau B. Lamar,
Verse Memorials [New York: W. P. Fetridge, 1857].)

JEFFERSON DAVIS (1808–1889). Henry Foote's bitter rival. Foote served in the United
States Senate with Davis and beat him in the 1851 Mississippi gubernatorial race.
The two men were mortal political enemies. (Library of Congress.)

JOHN ANTHONY QUITMAN (1798–1858). Although their mutual dislike for Jefferson Davis sometimes drew them together, Quitman and Foote had a tenuous relationship. (Library of Congress.)

JOHN P. HALE (1806–1873) of New Hampshire, one of Foote's most prominent adversaries on the Senate floor. (Library of Congress.)

SOLON BORLAND (1808–1864) of Arkansas. Borland attacked Foote on the streets of Washington, DC, after Foote broke with John C. Calhoun and other southerners during the compromise debates. (Library of Congress.)

THOMAS HART BENTON (1782–1858) of Missouri. Foote pulled a pistol on Benton on the floor of the U.S. Senate. (Library of Congress.)

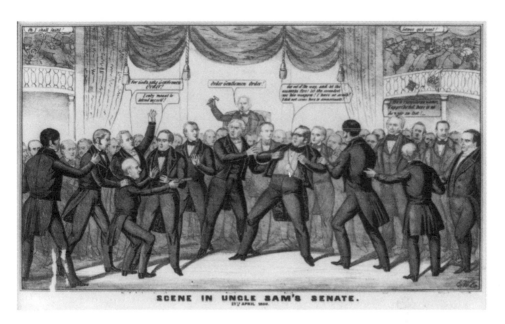

Political cartoon depicting the altercation between Foote and Benton on the Senate floor. (Library of Congress.)

Satirical political cartoon poking fun at the stormy relationship between
Foote and Benton. (Library of Congress.)

Published drawing depicting the major participants in the debates that produced the Compromise of 1850. The group includes Clay, Calhoun, and Douglas, among others. Foote is standing at the far right. (Library of Congress.)

WILLIAM LEWIS SHARKEY (1798–1873). Sharkey was one of Foote's closest unionist allies in Mississippi. (Dunbar Rowland, *The Official and Statistical Register of the State of Mississippi* [Madison, WI: Democrat Printing Company, 1908].)

Office U. S. Military Telegraph,
WAR DEPARTMENT.

The following Telegram received at Washington, 6¹⁰ P. M. Jany 16 ____ 1865

From City Point Va ____ Jany 16 ____ 1865

Hon A Lincoln

The following is obtained from todays
Richmond Dispatch —

"Hon I. I. Foote of Tennessee is still at
Fredericksburgh The House of representatives
not having yet decided what action they will
take in his Case. Persons who came down from
Fredericksburgh yesterday state that Mr Foote
was very indignant that he should have been
arrested and demanded to be brought to Richmond
immediately and when this was refused him he
wrote to Judge Halyburton petitioning for a
writ of habeas Corpus"

U. S. Grant
Lieut Genl

So cal
40054

Telegram from General Ulysses S. Grant to President Lincoln concerning
Henry Foote's whereabouts and some of the fallout from Foote's unofficial
"peace mission" toward the end of the Civil War. (National Archives.)

The New Orleans Mint, where Foote held his final government position.
The photograph was taken about 1900. (Library of Congress.)

HENRY S. FOOTE

This photograph was taken during Foote's later years, after he had begun sporting a long beard. (Courtesy of the Archives and Records Division, Mississippi Department of Archives and History.)

Portrait of Henry Stuart Foote that currently hangs with those of other past state leaders in the Mississippi capitol building in Jackson. The oil painting was donated to the state by Foote's family in 1903. (Ben Wynne.)

Compromise

I am for the Constitution and its guarantees. I am for the Union.
—Henry Stuart Foote, March 5, 1850

DESPITE HIS POLARIZING PERSONALITY and growing reputation in the Senate as a blowhard, there were some principles that Henry Stuart Foote held dear. He considered himself a loyal southerner and never passed up an opportunity to defend the region. As such he was also an unwavering proponent of slavery. However, as arguments related to the slavery question were tearing the country apart, Foote also maintained a devotion to the Union. At a time when southern agitation was increasing and some southern politicians were ready to explore secession as a means of settling quarrels with their northern brethren, Foote stood fast. While he was committed to the South and slavery, Foote believed that the Union should be preserved at all costs, and that any attempt to disrupt the compact of states was tantamount to treason. "I had long before this period become satisfied of the absurdity as well as of the criminality of all attempts to break up the Federal Union," he later wrote. "There is no safety to States or people save under the national flag." Foote believed that the slavery issue should not split the country politically, and he would be among those in the Senate who worked to forge some type of compromise between northerners and southerners when the 31st Congress convened in regular session, in March of 1849. "Never in my life, I assure you," the Mississippian wrote to Virginia's Henry A. Wise, shortly before the session, "have I felt more sorely oppressed with doubt and despondency, or considered the Union itself in more danger than I do at this moment."[1]

Ironically, while Foote's fight for compromise represented a high point of his career as a Washington politician, his dedication to preserving the Union also marked the beginning of the end of his career as a United States senator. As a senator, Foote never wavered in his hopes that the country would remain whole, even after it became obvious that, in doing so, he was inflicting upon himself political wounds back home in Mississippi. His stand made him one of the most outspoken southern unionists of the antebellum period.

Efforts to settle the great questions dividing the North and the South began as the first session of the 31st Congress convened, with Foote immediately making his voice heard. The tone of the session was partially set early on, in what became known as the "Father Mathew debate." Theobald Mathew was a well-known Irish Catholic temperance crusader who had persuaded hundreds of thousands of his countrymen to take the "pledge," promising that they would no longer consume strong drink. In July of 1849, the "Apostle of Temperance," or simply Father Mathew, as he was called, brought his message to the United States, arriving first in New York and then visiting Boston. He eventually went to Washington, where Vice President Millard Fillmore welcomed him and President Zachary Taylor invited him to dine at the White House. Senator Isaac P. Walker of Wisconsin introduced a resolution to invite Mathew to visit and sit within the bar of the Senate. The request was somewhat unusual in that the only foreigner to have ever received such an honor was Lafayette. Still, extending the privilege to Mathew was a technical courtesy that likely would not have created a stir had slavery not come to dominate Senate discourse on almost every subject.

While in the United States, Mathew tried to sidestep the slavery issue. He knew that voicing an opinion on the subject one way or the other would alienate large numbers of Americans and hinder his efforts to disseminate his temperance message. Regardless, he was dragged into the fray. Many southern politicians viewed Mathew's past association with Irish politician Daniel O'Connell, an outspoken critic of slavery, as a red flag, and they were also suspicious of Mathew because, in Boston, the priest had met with abolitionist leader William Lloyd Garrison. When they asked Mathew about his stance on the slavery question, he refused to reply, which some southerners viewed as a rebuke to the institution. According to one northern newspaper, southern resistance to Walker's request was absurd, unnecessary, and the result of "the extreme sensitiveness of some southern men upon everything which may have the most remote bearing upon the system of slavery."[2]

From the outset, the resolution to invite Mathew to the Senate met with strong opposition. Jeremiah Clemens of Alabama, who accused the priest of being in league with those who sought to "carry on a warfare against the institutions of the South," spoke up first, with Jefferson Davis also weighing in. "My first duty, my nearest ties, are at home," Davis said, "and I will say of the horde of abolitionists, foreign and domestic, that if I had the power to exclude them all from this chamber, I would not hesitate a moment to do it." Others favored recognizing Mathew and argued that his temperance work had nothing to do with slavery. Henry Clay of Kentucky argued that coupling the two issues was "imprudent and unwise," and Lewis Cass of Michigan agreed, stating, "I know nothing of the opinions of Father Mathew on the subject of slavery, nor do I seek to know them. . . . I deprecate the introduction of this topic on the present occasion."

Among those who were particularly vocal was New York's William Seward, who would later become Abraham Lincoln's secretary of state. Seward, an abolitionist, took the opportunity to use the debate to promote his views against slavery while voicing his support for Mathew. He called the priest a "benefactor of mankind" and told his senatorial brethren that "if slavery be an error, if it be a crime, if it be a sin, we deplore its existence among us and deny the responsibility of its introduction here." Seward said that he believed that the resolution should be unanimously accepted by the Senate and that he was proud to pay homage to a man "who exhibits not more a devotion to virtue than to the rights on man." The New Yorker's insinuation that slavery was a sin rankled his southern colleagues and brought Henry Foote into the debate with full force.[3]

While other southerners sternly criticized Seward, Foote launched a full-scale attack, accusing him of pandering to the Irish vote in New York through a "precious scheme of demagogical deception" and of ignoring his constitutional duties as a senator. In doing so, Foote highlighted again the traditional southern argument that slavery was protected by the country's founding document. He said that Seward "must have become suddenly oblivious to his official oath, which binds him to support the Constitution of the United States, whose sacred provisions guaranty perpetually protection to slavery against all foes." The attack on Seward turned extremely personal. Speaking of "the honorable senator from New York and his abolition associates here and everywhere," Foote growled that "whatever they touch they defile" and that "contact with them and their accursed cause is rank pollution." The attack on Seward was so vicious that it drew in other senators, not so much to defend Seward as to once again complain about the "ungentlemanly" course of the debate. During his tirade, Foote praised Mathew's temperance stance and the general idea of honoring him in some way, but the senator eventually voted against the resolution. In the end, the resolution passed by a 2 to 1 margin.[4]

Foote's lambasting of William Seward was the product of multiple factors. Foote was aware that whatever he said on the floor of the United States Senate would be published in newspapers all over the country, including in his native Mississippi. He was also aware that anxiety among Mississippi whites over the slavery issue was running high, and he wanted to continue posturing himself as a champion of the slavery cause. His speeches in Congress were the basis for many of his speeches before the public back in Mississippi. He would quote from them frequently so that no one could question his dedication to the institution.

Moreover, when the Mathew issue came up, Jefferson Davis was one of the first southerners to criticize Seward's remarks related to slavery. In addition to the personal animosity that he felt toward the man, Foote saw himself locked in a perpetual battle with Davis over who would emerge as the chief political spokesman for the state of Mississippi. Foote could not let Davis's remarks pass without comment, and he hoped to mute Davis's criticism of Seward by essentially drowning it out. Foote's goal was to speak louder, longer, and with more ferocity than Davis, in hopes of drawing more attention to himself in his home state and throughout the South in general.

Emily Baldwin, the wife of Connecticut senator Roger Sherman Baldwin, was in the gallery and witnessed the Mississippian's tirade against Seward. According to her account, Foote "rose for about an hour and with the most violent gestures and manner, abused and ridiculed Seward. . . . I expected every moment that he would be called to order, and yet one could not help laughing— some of his hits were so good." Seward, who had a habit of never responding directly to criticism on the Senate floor, did not seem to mind the personal attacks and understood that much of the Mississippian's bluster was theatrical in nature. Foote, of course, knew this as well, and he and Seward eventually became somewhat friendly behind the scenes.[5]

By 1850, the slavery issue had slowed to a crawl the legislative processes in Washington and impeded progress on a number of important issues that needed attention. In the wake of the Gold Rush, California was ready for statehood, and the additional territory acquired from Mexico as a result of the Mexican War needed to be organized. The status of slavery in the nation's capital, a highly emotional and symbolic issue, was still in play, as was the issue of whether there should be a strong fugitive slave law. Open hostility continued to pepper debates on the House and Senate floors as the national legislature struggled to do its job. The staunch abolitionists on one end of the political spectrum and the proslavery ideologues on the other began shouting louder and louder, making it difficult to establish any common ground between the northern and southern states, and some southerners were already advocating secession. Future president James Buchanan wrote at the time, "The blessed union of these states is now in greater danger than it has ever been since the adoption of the federal Constitution," while Jefferson Davis lamented that the 31st Congress "might be the last of our government." Of the era, Foote later commented that "the contest between the friends of peace and those whose conduct was at this period threatening to disturb the public repose, was now fairly in progress."[6] While Foote never abandoned his aggressive and many times obnoxious methods of getting things done, he eventually broke with his southern brethren and became a voice for compromise. He participated in all of the debates of the period and was a significant presence during the entire process.

Foote wasted no time in getting started. He greased the wheels of debate early in the 31st Congress by advancing a comprehensive bill to organize the American West. The "Bill to Provide for the Organization of the Territorial Governments of California, Deseret, and New Mexico, and to Enable the People of Jacinto, with the Consent of the State of Texas, to Form a Constitution and State Government, and for the Admission of Such State into the Union upon an Equal Footing with the Original States, in All Respects Whatever" was introduced on January 16, 1850. The legislation would set up territorial governments in California, New Mexico, and Deseret (much of what would eventually become the Utah Territory), with no specific references to slavery one way or the other, and allow for the division of Texas into two slaveholding states, Texas and Jacinto. The idea of a new slave state being carved out of Texas and no restriction being placed on the institution in the territories appealed to many southerners but drew opposition from the North. William Seward complicated matters by immediately proposing an amendment to Foote's bill that would have placed restrictions on slavery in the territories.

Even before the particulars of the bill were discussed, conflict arose over which committee would be the first to hear the bill. Southerners thought it should go before the Senate Judiciary Committee, chaired by South Carolina firebrand Andrew P. Butler. Northerners, whose goal was to kill the bill, hoped it would be given to the Senate Committee on Territories, chaired by Illinois senator Stephen Douglas, who opposed the plan. Debate on the committee issue went on for some time, with Foote repeating over and over again his belief that the matter belonged under Butler's charge. Butler himself chimed in, expressing the southern point of view—primarily that a host of legal issues needed to be sorted out before the federal government could create new territories and states—as did Alabama's William R. King and Georgia's John M. Berrien. Douglas stood his ground, insisting that the proposal come before his committee.

Much to Foote's irritation, the Senate voted along sectional lines with Douglas. Twenty-five northerners voted to send the bill to the Committee on Territories, with twenty-two southerners voting against the motion. The vote effectively killed Foote's bill, but he did not let the defeat slow him down. In fact, death of the legislation that he sponsored seemed to energize him and make him even more determined to cause a stir. As a result, he plunged headlong into the political fracas that eventually produced the Compromise of 1850.[7]

The debates that produced the Compromise of 1850 represented the swan song for three aged titans of the United States Senate, Henry Clay of Kentucky, Daniel Webster of Massachusetts, and John C. Calhoun of South Carolina. The drama began in earnest on January 29, 1850, when Clay presented to his colleagues compromise measures that he hoped would calm the passions of northerners and southerners and reconcile all of the issues related to slavery and the West that were dividing the nation. "I hold in my hand resolutions which I desire to submit to the consideration of this body," he told his fellow senators. "Taken together, in combination, they propose an amicable arrangement of all questions in controversy between the free and the slave states." Everyone in the room—senators, staff and spectators, northerners and southerners—knew that Clay's actions represented the beginning of a substantive and monumental discussion about the future of the United States. As Clay finished, an electric atmosphere prevailed in the capitol, with one newspaperman from Baltimore describing the proceedings as "one of the glorious days of the Senate." In the end, of course, the compromise that Congress cobbled together during the period did not create a lasting peace and only postponed the inevitable.[8]

By 1850, it was almost impossible to find common ground between politicians from the slaveholding states and those from the free states. The process of passing laws slowed almost to a halt as southerners circled the wagons in defense of slavery and some northerners began pressing an abolitionist agenda. While it seemed that every significant piece of legislation before Congress was tied in one way or another to the slavery debate, there were only a few foundational issues that were the greatest impediment to progress. These involved the status and statehood of California, the organization of remaining territory that had been part of the Mexican Cession, the boundaries of Texas, the status of slavery in the District of Columbia, and whether Congress would create a stronger fugitive slave law. The seventy-two-year-old Clay hoped his compromise plan would settle all of these issues. "He was sincerely anxious to settle all these questions," Foote later recalled, "and was fully resolved to leave none of them open, if he could avoid it."[9]

In the Senate, Clay proposed several bills, including separate proposals to bring California into the Union as a free state, to place no federal restrictions on slavery in other territories acquired from Mexico as a result of the Mexican War, to abolish the slave trade but not slavery in the District of Columbia, to strengthen the fugitive slave law, and to set the boundaries of Texas. Slavery was a unique issue that transcended political parties and excited popular discourse in a way that nothing else could. Unlike other issues, which generally involved Whigs and Democrats taking positions opposite each other based on party doctrine, the slavery debate made compromise difficult because it created four rather than two factions in the Senate, whose members needed to be appeased. These included northern Whigs, most of whom wanted slavery excluded from the entire West; Democrats from the South, most of whom were vehement in their opinion that slavery should spread into at least part of the West; most northern Democrats and some southern Democrats, who favored compromise through popular sovereignty; and most southern Whigs and a small number of northern Whigs, who favored peace and were open to the popular sovereignty concept. In short, there were too many points of view to easily reconcile. Southerners, in particular, were suspicious of any type of compromise as their fears of northern conspiracies to end slavery grew.[10]

When debates over Clay's proposals for compromise began in earnest, they immediately energized Foote. He knew that the 31st Congress was making history and he wanted a prominent place in the narrative. Foote began pestering Clay and others with suggestions related to the compromise effort, making address after address on the floor of the Senate. With a focused, ego-driven tenacity, Foote seemed to comment on everything, and it became impossible not to notice his presence on the Senate floor. While he would embrace the idea of compromise, Foote always postured himself as a protector of southern rights as they related to slavery.

Among Clay's proposals for compromise was a bill to bring California into the union as a free state, and many, including Clay, believed that the California bill should be the first bill addressed. Foote and other southerners objected, claiming that the status of California could only be discussed as it related to the other major issues. Foote argued that the California bill should be bundled with Clay's other proposals, some of which made concessions to the South. The status of slavery in California, Foote claimed, would set the tone for the rest of the debate, and if California entered the Union first as a free state, northerners would then have less incentive to compromise on anything else. This could spark a secession movement in the southern states that would disrupt the Union. Foote believed that as long as the status of slavery in California was undecided, the South had leverage to push for concessions on other issues. "I must say, and say it most seriously," Foote told his fellow senators, "that if California is admitted to the Union, except with some liberal and equitable plan of pacification and compromise, the vessel of state will have certainly sprung a new leak, and she will suddenly go down."[11]

Foote's colleagues in the Mississippi delegation agreed that the admission of a free California without "adjustments" on other issues would be a terrific blow to the southern cause. As debates on the subject began, all the Mississippians, including Foote, signed a letter to recently elected Mississippi governor John A. Quitman voicing their concerns. State newspapers published the letter and the Democratic-controlled legislature responded with official instructions for the delegation. "The senators and the representatives in Congress," the edict read, "should, to the extent of their abilities, resist the admission of California by all honorable and constitutional means." This helped Foote and the others as they argued against California's admission. It created the appearance that their opposition was not personal or partisan but the product of a much nobler effort to advance the opinions of the people they represented back home. The people had spoken through the legislature, Foote and others argued, and to ignore their wants would be both a political and a moral sin.[12]

During discussions about California, Foote also provoked Clay to make one of the most notable declarations of his Senate career. As Clay resisted the notion of linking the California statehood bill with other legislation, Foote prodded the "Great Compromiser" by reminded him that he represented a slave state and should therefore take a more southern point of view. Respectful of, but unintimidated by, Clay's status as a true national leader, Foote pressed the point that adding California as a free state without linking it directly to concessions for the slaveholding states would "strengthen the North at the expense of the South" and therefore give the North more leverage in future negotiations. Foote wondered aloud how "a senator from the state of Kentucky, within whose limits the system of domestic slavery exists, can reconcile it to his own sense of justice . . . to increase the number of adversary votes against (the South) upon all pending questions, without first receiving some compensation therefor." Clay was obviously irritated as he rose and responded famously, "I know no South, no North, no East, no West to which I owe an allegiance. I owe allegiance to two sovereignties, and only two; one is to the sovereignty of this Union, and the other is to the sovereignty of the State of Kentucky." The debate did not stop there, and Foote continued to promote the idea that the California issue alone should not be the sole focus of discussion. He also tried to cultivate an alliance with Clay, even though at the time there was friction between the two men over the California issue.[13]

John C. Calhoun was, like Clay, almost used up as he composed an address that outlined his view of the crisis. In a polarizing speech that opened up the slavery debate in full force, Calhoun argued for a constitutional amendment protecting slavery and stated that if slavery was not protected, southern states likely would leave the Union. Too weak to read the speech himself, he called on his friend James Mason of Virginia to deliver it in the Senate. Calhoun's speech left no room for compromise or negotiation. He noted that the time for talk had come and gone and that there should immediately "be an open and manly avowal on all sides as to what is intended to be done." If the protection of southern rights related to slavery were not guaranteed through, among other things, a constitutional amendment, then the slaveholding and nonslaveholding states should part in peace. "If you are unwilling we should part in peace," he told the northerners, "tell us so; and we shall know what to do when you reduce the question to submission or resistance." The message was clear: should the North continue to threaten the existence of slavery in the South, then the slaveholding states should leave the Union, by force if necessary.[14]

Calhoun's speech in response to Clay's compromise measures had a great effect on Henry Foote. Foote had always considered himself part of the "very ultra southern cast" that Calhoun led in the Senate. He supported Calhoun and certainly saw eye to eye with the South Carolinian with regard to the protection of slavery. "I respect Mr. Calhoun very highly," Foote wrote to a friend during the period, "and believe that few better, purer and more patriotic men have ever lived on this earth." But the Mississippian felt that he could no longer support the extremism in the southern bloc that Calhoun represented. Foote was for the protection of slavery, but he also supported the preservation of the Union. He wanted compromise and believed that Calhoun's address contained "the most menacing positions," which, if acted upon by the South as a whole, left no more room for discussions.[15]

Though Calhoun's speech helped lead to Foote's change of heart, there were other factors in play. While Foote seemed to have a sincere dedication to the Union and realized that the southern extremists with whom he aligned himself promoted ideas that made compromise unlikely, he also fancied himself an excellent judge of public opinion. He viewed the southern hard-liners as more radical in general than the constituents they represented. This was certainly the case in parts of Foote's home state of Mississippi, where some residents did not seem overly concerned with the status of slavery in California. On March 9, 1850, what one newspaper described as a "Mighty Rally for the Union" was held in Natchez, at the courthouse where Foote had argued many cases. More than three hundred local citizens, including some of the region's wealthiest slaveholders, met to reaffirm their allegiance to the Union and to declare that the admission of California as a free state alone was not a reason to advance a plan for secession. According to the *Natchez Courier*, everyone approached the gathering "with an earnest solemnity depicted upon their features indicative of the great fact that they had heard the Union of their beloved country threatened by rash and bitter demagogues." Similar meetings were held at the time in Jackson and in Canton.[16]

Foote also had an important pro-compromise ally in Mississippi, William L. Sharkey, the state's longtime chief justice. Foote's friendly relationship with Sharkey went back years, to 1835, when Foote helped the chief justice rescue his cousin Patrick during the slave insurrection scare in central Mississippi.

By the end of the 1840s, Foote and Sharkey were being drawn even closer together as each recognized an emerging common enemy—the radical, or states' rights, wing of the Democratic Party. A talented politician, Sharkey had quietly risen to become one of Mississippi's most influential figures. He was a Whig, but he was also popular with many Democrats and was seen as a levelheaded politician who could be trusted during a crisis. Sharkey made few true political enemies during his career because he remained in the judicial branch of government, operating with subtlety behind the scenes and remaining above the fray during openly partisan warfare. He also had a talent for straddling the fence and quietly coming down from his perch on the popular side of most issues at precisely the right time. As Mississippi politicians debated the merits of a national compromise over the slavery issue, Sharkey worked to promote a more moderate position for the state. "If a compromise can be adopted," he wrote to Foote during the summer of 1850, "our honor at least will be safe." In June, Sharkey was elected president of the Nashville Convention, a meeting originally called to promote unity among the slaveholding states. There, he pushed a more moderate agenda and was able to muffle some of the more radical voices among the delegates.[17]

Foote's new direction was not just a temporary shift of thought brought on by his reading of public opinion. Nor was it simply the result of a loss of confidence in Calhoun. It was a philosophical and foundational change of direction that would drive his professional career for the foreseeable future and end up being his most lasting political legacy. His choice to attach himself to the cause of the Union was one of the most important decisions of his life. In breaking with Calhoun and other states' rights ideologues, he was carving out a new place for himself and abandoning what at the time was the safer course of maintaining a states' rights stance in a climate of increasing uncertainty. His would be a more difficult position to maintain over time, and pressure would almost immediately mount for him to come back to the fold of southern Democrats who preached that the northern states and the federal government were a great threat to the southern way of life.

To his credit, as the pressure mounted, Foote never wavered, never gave in to political expedience. Instead, he began building his own organization based on the Union principles that he held dear. Always aware of what was going on in his home state, Foote knew that pro-Union sentiment ran high among many Mississippi Whigs like Sharkey and among some state Democrats, and the senator would soon attempt to build his own coalition in Mississippi by drawing voters from these groups.

Foote wasted no time in informing his fellow senators of his shift to a more national than regional outlook. The day after Calhoun's address, Foote rose on the floor of the Senate to criticize the old man and pledge his own loyalty to the Union. "I have resolved to waste no time," he said, "in entering my protest against such parts of the speech of the honorable senator from South Carolina as I deem likely to injure, instead of benefit the cause in behalf of which it was delivered." In characteristically extended remarks, he said that he believed Calhoun was promoting a dangerous and unnecessary course and that the South Carolinian's speech did not reflect the opinions of other southern senators. He termed Calhoun's demands "decidedly objectionable" and was particularly hostile to the notion that the Constitution needed amending to ensure the protection of southern institutions. He said that it was "unjust" to paint all northerners as anti-southern and pointed out that the South had many friends among northern Democrats and even some northern Whigs. When Calhoun, enfeebled by age and unable to match Foote's energy on the Senate floor, challenged the Mississippian on some of his points, Foote did not back down, maintaining that compromise was the only option and that Calhoun's speech was counterproductive. "I am quite satisfied for the present with the existing Constitution as framed by our wise and patriotic forefathers," Foote said. "I am for the Constitution and its guarantees. I am for the Union, as provided for and delineated in that sacred instrument."

With that, Foote became one of the South's most outspoken unionists in Washington at a time when many people felt that the Union was coming apart. He had directly challenged the leader of the southern states' rights movement and would soon drive him from the field. Calhoun could not match Foote in debate, and the exchange between the two men apparently upset the South Carolinian to the point that it affected his already fragile health. While it was obvious to most observers that Calhoun was in rapid decline, some would later accuse Foote of hastening the old man's death. In a letter to his sister during the period, John C. Calhoun Jr. seemed to place the blame for his father's failing health at least in part on Foote and Lewis Cass. "I reached Washington on the 28th of February, and found father much better than I expected to see him," the younger Calhoun wrote. "He continued perceptibly to improve, until he was provoked by senators Cass and Foote, to enter into an exciting debate, which was entirely too great a shock for the weak state of his physical system. . . . For the first time in my life, I heard him speak despondingly about himself." Calhoun died a month later.[18]

Three days after Calhoun gave his address, Daniel Webster of Massachusetts responded with what became known as the Seventh of March speech. Another member of the old guard, Webster was one of the North's primary spokesmen, and his address was eagerly anticipated by much of the general public. In a move that many northern abolitionists viewed as a betrayal, Webster pressed for compromise with the South, even endorsing Clay's compromise proposal that called for a stricter fugitive slave law. "Daniel Webster has openly repudiated Massachusetts," the editor of the Worcester *Massachusetts Spy* wrote on March 11. "He has also repudiated the whole North, and as such let us ever henceforth consider him a traitor to free sentiment of the whole country."

As Foote listened to the address, it confirmed to him that he had made the right choice in opposing Calhoun and promoting compromise. Webster's willingness to give concessions to the South on the slavery issue made it apparent that, one way or another, there was a great likelihood that some type of compromise eventually would be struck. Foote called the Webster's speech "a comprehensive and practical plan of pacification and settlement" and said that, with it, "the door of compromise had been at last opened in the most formal manner by a northern man." Foote was already friendly with Webster, and he would now be able to ally himself with both Webster and Clay in support of compromise.[19]

And then there was Jefferson Davis. Foote was always aware of what Davis was up to and always made a point of chiming in whenever his fellow Mississippian discussed legislation on the Senate floor. Sometimes Foote had something relevant to contribute to the discussion, but many times he spoke up just because he knew that the mere sound of his voice irritated Davis. Foote and Davis still hated each other, and Foote took pleasure in needling Davis whenever the opportunity presented itself. Foote also knew that Davis was positioning himself to become one of the primary spokesmen for the southern cause, filling the void left as Calhoun withered away and eventually died, on March 31, 1850.

Davis served on the Senate committee charged with arranging Calhoun's funeral, and he accompanied the old man's body back to South Carolina for burial. He also gave an emotional eulogy on the Senate floor, honoring Calhoun for his lifetime dedication to preserving the rights of the slaveholding states. This gave Davis a good deal of positive publicity in Mississippi and in the rest of the South, much to the chagrin of Henry Foote. Foote wanted to be his state's primary political spokesman, and to do this he had to take positions that would contrast with those of Davis, giving his Mississippi constituents two distinct choices. If Davis was for something, Foote believed he needed to be against it, using the strongest rhetoric possible. As a result, as the compromise debates began to dominate Senate discussions, Davis became one of the leading opponents of many of Clay's proposals and, in contrast, Foote positioned himself as the Deep South's leading supporter of a settlement. This did two things for Foote. First, it set him apart from Davis in a clear and distinct way. Foote also believed that public sentiment in Mississippi leaned toward a settlement of some type and that, as a result, he would eventually come down on the winning side of the issue.

Once the compromise debate began, a great intensity seemed to animate the chamber, and Davis and Foote were in the middle of the storm. Swedish writer Fredrika Bremer, who had come to the United States during the period to study American democracy, observed both men speak during the height of the compromise tension in Congress. She later wrote that Davis was "a young man of handsome person and inflammable temperament, who talks violently of southern rights," while Foote was "also a fiery man. . . . He stands for the Union, and his most brilliant moments are when he hurls himself into a violent, dithyrambic against all and each who threaten it."[20]

Foote's defection from the ranks of the hard-line states' rights ideologues to the side of compromise did not endear him to some of his fellow southern senators, and in one case it led to a physical confrontation on the streets of the nation's capital. On Thursday evening, March 14, 1850, Foote happened to meet Arkansas senator Solon Borland walking near the downtown offices of the *National Intelligencer* newspaper. Born in Virginia, like Foote, the thirty-eight-year-old Borland was a newspaper editor and physician who had served as a cavalryman during the Mexican War. Several slightly different versions of their encounter made the rounds after the fact, but apparently Borland had been offended by Foote's remarks to Calhoun on the Senate floor. He accused Foote of abandoning the southern cause and the two men began a heated exchange. Foote reportedly called Borland a "miserable tool of Calhoun" and Borland responded by striking Foote in the head, cutting him with his ring and causing a wound that bled profusely. Bystanders separated the men, and a stunned Foote was taken into the *Intelligencer* offices to have his injury tended. The incident caused a minor stir in the national press and was reported widely. Rumors of an impending duel circulated for a time but nothing ever materialized, and some reports claimed that Borland later apologized to Foote and the two men repaired their relationship.[21]

Desperate to be a major player in the compromise debates, Foote advanced a proposal to create a Senate committee to author legislation related to Clay's compromise items, a committee that came to be called the Committee of Thirteen. Years later, Foote maintained that the idea for a special committee originated with influential newspaper publisher Thomas Ritchie and Virginia representative Thomas H. Bayly, who brought it to Foote in hopes that he would take it to the Senate. According to Foote, he and Bayly then approached Clay, asking if he would offer the appropriate resolutions to create the committee. Clay listened but was not initially supportive. Foote told the Kentuckian that by advancing each compromise proposal separately, he was "throwing into the hands of his adversaries all the trump cards in the pack." The measures could only pass, Foote argued, if all the proposals were bundled into a single package rather than being treated separately, and that a committee was needed to facilitate the process.

In the end, Foote wore Clay down and the old man gave in. He told Foote that he was willing to accept the creation of the committee, and would even be willing to serve as the committee's chair, but he did not want to personally present the resolutions creating the committee. In turn, Foote said that he would be willing to help create the committee but did not want to serve on it. According to Foote, "[Clay] stated that, for various reasons . . . he would prefer that the resolutions proposing the committee of thirteen should be brought forward in the Senate by some other individual. I afterward agreed to offer it, on the express condition that I not be made a member of it." Foote was more than willing to introduce the proposal because he knew that it would garner him a great deal of attention and place him at the center of yet another volatile debate. Foote also hoped that he could help organize a committee that would be friendly to the concept of bundling all of Clay's proposals together in one massive compromise bill and would help steer the bill through Congress.[22]

During what seemed like endless discussions, Foote was relentless in promoting the special committee to his fellow senators, and he finally found enough colleagues willing to support the idea. He was able to convince some that it would be the first step toward a lasting compromise; others, he simply wore down until they were willing to agree with him just to shut him up. In the end, the Committee of Thirteen—nicknamed by some the "Foote committee" because of his role in its creation—included six southerners, six northerners, and Clay, serving as chair. The members were John Bell (Tennessee), John M. Berrien (Georgia), Clay (Kentucky), Solomon W. Downs (Louisiana), William R. King (Alabama), Willie P. Mangum (North Carolina), James M. Mason (Virginia), Jesse D. Bright (Indiana), Lewis Cass (Michigan), James Cooper (Pennsylvania), Daniel S. Dickinson (New York), Samuel S. Phelps (Vermont), and Webster (Massachusetts).

As Foote had hoped, the committee eventually recommended the bundling together of Clay's proposals, with critics calling the finished product the Omnibus Bill. While many in the Democratic press denounced Foote as a grandstander, he garnered high praise in some of the country's Whig organs. "The South seems to be triumphant," a correspondent from the *New York Evening Express* wrote. "Senator Foote seems to have carried the Senate by storm in favor of his compromise committee of thirteen." Back in Mississippi, the Natchez *Free Trader* also praised Foote, stating, "The appointment of the Foote committee seems to be regarded as a judicious measure. . . . Mr. Foote deserves, and receives, high commendation for his zeal and ability."[23]

The day before the Senate created the Committee of Thirteen, Foote had an altercation with fellow senator Thomas Hart Benton of Missouri, in a scene that would go down in the annals of Senate history. The incident was the culmination of a verbal sparring match that had been going on between the two men for more than a month. Benton was a tough character who, back in 1813, had shot Andrew Jackson in the arm during a duel. He was a veteran of the U.S. Senate, first elected in 1821, and as an elder statesman he thought very little of Foote's debate theatrics. As he aged, Benton had also alienated himself from other Democrats in the slaveholding states by taking positions against slavery's expansion. "My personal sentiments, then, are against the institution of slavery," Benton said in an 1849 speech, "and against its introduction into places where it does not exist." Foote knew that by backing compromise with the North, he risked being labeled by southerners as "soft" on abolition. As a result, he was always quick to exploit any opportunity to promote his proslavery credentials. A sharp verbal attack on Benton likely would garner Foote positive publicity in the South and, in the Mississippian's view, he needed to strike while the iron was hot.

At one point during Senate debates on the status of slavery in California, Foote accused Benton of "whining" and referenced an incident from Benton's early life, when, as a young student, Benton was expelled from the University of North Carolina for stealing. "There are certain stains," Foote said, "which have most hideously blemished the character of the honorable Senator from Missouri, since the days of his early manhood." In a very sarcastic manner, Foote then inferred that Benton was a coward. In response, Benton remained relatively calm but spoke up to warn his fellow senators that he would "protect [himself], cost what it may," from future attacks if Senate leaders did not rein Foote in. This lack of direct response likely irritated Foote, who was trying to provoke Benton into losing control. The Mississippian's ego thrived on attention, and Benton knew that he would hurt Foote more by ignoring him than by engaging him. The incident passed but the tensions between the two men did not go away.[24]

A month later, Benton was one of the leading opponents of Foote's special compromise committee. He hated the idea from the start and had done everything in his power to block it. At the same time, he continued to press the Senate to take up the question of slavery in California first, as a separate issue, something that Foote and other southerners were against. The harder Foote pushed for the committee, the harder Benton pushed back, until finally there was a major unraveling of decorum on the Senate floor. Though he was from a slave state, Benton believed that southern hotheads of the Deep South cotton states (including Foote) had created the present crisis, using emotionally charged rhetoric to frighten their constituents and convince them that, absent dramatic action, the demise of slavery was at hand. As there were no proposals to end slavery being discussed, Benton argued that the great crisis over slavery's demise had been manufactured by southern politicians to advance their political careers. "There is no design in the Congress of the United States to encroach upon the rights of the South," Benton claimed on the Senate floor, "nor to aggress upon the South, nor to oppress them upon the subject of their institutions."

By this time, Foote had had enough of Benton and went on the attack. After claiming that "I shall not be personal," Foote launched into a personal diatribe against the senator from Missouri, at which point Benton finally lost his temper, rose from his seat, and began making his way toward Foote. As he saw Benton approaching, Foote took several steps backwards, reached into his jacket, and pulled out a loaded revolver, which he pointed at Benton. The Senate erupted as members sprang to their feet, shouting at both men. According to one newspaper report, "The scene which ensued is indescribable. Loud calls for the Sergeant-at-Arms were made and cries of order resounded from all sides of the chamber. Many persons rushed from the gallery out of the chamber in apprehension of a general melee." Benton ripped open his jacket and shirt, exposing his chest, and began bellowing at the top of his lungs, "Stand out of the way. I have no pistols . . . Stand out of the way and let the assassin fire!"

Benton's friend Senator Henry Dodge of Wisconsin reached out and restrained the unintimidated Missourian, keeping him from reaching Foote as the Mississippian shouted that, in drawing the gun, he was merely defending himself. Senator Daniel Dickerson, a New York Democrat, appealed to Foote to surrender the weapon, which he did. Dickerson took the gun and locked it in his own desk as Vice President Millard Fillmore, the Senate's presiding officer, banged the gavel again and again in an attempt to restore order. Once things settled down, the Senate appointed a committee to investigate the fracas, but nothing was ever pursued, and Foote and Benton remained mortal enemies. Foote later issued a veiled threat that he would one day "write a little book in which Mr. Benton would figure very largely." Hearing this, Benton supposedly laughed and replied sarcastically that he would one day "write a very large book in which [Foote] should not figure at all."

Many northern papers condemned Foote and the fight in general, while southern newspapers were more charitable toward the Mississippi senator. In reporting its version of events, the *Richmond Enquirer* referred to him as a "gallant champion of the South," while in Auburn, New York, the local newspaper called him a "blustering coward." In Mississippi, the reviews of Foote broke along partisan lines. Whig newspapers were careful not to defend Benton, instead blaming both men for "mutual misconduct." Predictably, the Democratic press praised Foote's commitment to southern institutions and his "faithfulness and patriotism."[25]

The creation of Foote's Committee of Thirteen sparked yet another firestorm of debate in the Senate, particularly after the committee submitted its report. Among other things, the committee recommended bringing California into the Union as a free state, with no restrictions on slavery in other territory acquired from Mexico; abolishing the slave trade but not slavery in the District of Columbia; and passage of a more effective fugitive slave law. Southern stalwarts were against provisions in the compromise that did not call for the protection of slavery everywhere, while many northerners believed that it did not do nearly enough to curtail the institution. During discussions, a reporter from a Milwaukee, Wisconsin, newspaper wrote that the omnibus compromise bill "is not a compromise, unless the word has lost its ancient meaning in this age of progress."

As the issues were bandied about on the Senate floor and in the press, Foote became a target for criticism by northerners and southerners who were against the compromise. On the Senate floor, Clemens of Alabama chastised Foote as a hypocrite, pointing out that the Mississippian had only recently "constituted himself the advance guard of the grand compromise army," after forcefully arguing for many months for Calhoun's pro-southern agenda. Likewise, the *New York Times* believed Foote's history as a Deep South ideologue was inconsistent with his sudden willingness to compromise with northerners. "When [Foote] was most ardent in behalf of the integrity of the commonwealth," the newspaper told its readers, "he was equally ardent in his attachment to slavery, rating abolition as the first of political sins." In Jackson, the *Mississippian,* a prominent Democratic newspaper that Foote once co-owned, told its readers, "The course taken by Mr. Foote, in supporting the compromise bill, does not meet with the sanction of our people. . . . It is with deep regret that we find opposed to us, a man we have always regarded with the warmest feelings of friendship."[26]

Undeterred by criticism, Foote argued for the committee's recommendations to be adopted, while also claiming that he had not turned his back on the South, and especially not on the institution of slavery. His constitutional position rested on the ideas that the Union was perpetual and must be preserved at all costs and that the Constitution, as developed by the founders, provided a framework for the orderly solution of any political problems that developed among the states. "It is not a new Constitution, nor an amended Constitution, for which I have been all along contending," he argued on the Senate floor, "not such a Union as may be hereafter provided by the wisdom of the present generation, but the grand old Union, the fruit of the sage counsels of our immortal ancestors."

He was particularly pointed in an exchange on the Senate floor with Andrew Butler of South Carolina. Rumors were rampant that the South Carolina delegation had given up on interstate diplomacy regarding the slavery issue and was actively promoting secession in their state. Foote dismissed secession as "too absurd to deserve serious consideration" and went on to call two of the Palmetto state's most prominent political voices, Robert Barnwell Rhett and Maxey Gregg, "traitorous demagogues" for attempting to push their state in that direction. For Foote, secession was not a constitutional right, though he did believe that it was an available alternative as a "revolutionary act" to remedy "intolerable oppression."[27]

While Foote believed that the Union was perpetual, and that states had no right to "at pleasure secede from the Union," he did believe that a genuine threat to the institution of slavery amounted to an intolerable oppression and that the southern states could act accordingly. Using standard southern arguments of the day, Foote claimed that slavery was recognized and therefore protected by the Constitution via the so-called Three-Fifths Compromise, and that because American slavery predated the Constitution, those states with slaves never would have entered the Union if they had believed they would be penalized for allowing the institution. "The Constitution did not create property in slaves," he said. "Such rights existed anterior to, and above, the Constitution. As slaves were owned in many of the states, they would not, of course, have entered into the [Union] on such terms that would weaken the right of the owner to his slaves." He tried to sell the concept of compromise to his fellow southerners by emphasizing that special protections for slavery *already existed.* He told them that, since the Constitution automatically protected the institution anywhere in the United States, slavery did not need to be a major part of the compromise discussions. Following that line of thinking, any legislation formulated by Congress related to slavery was tantamount to questioning the general constitutionality of slavery and therefore it should not be allowed. The right to hold slaves, he said, was "a fixed principle, inseparable from the other provisions of the Constitution," and, as a result, calling for any legislation on the subject, either to restrict or protect slavery, "plainly calls into question the [constitutional] rights of the owner of slaves." As always, Foote went out of his way to trumpet his support for slavery to fend off charges by his southern critics that he was soft on abolition.[28]

Foote never wavered in his want for compromise, and as time wore on he grew more confident that some sort of compromise eventually would become the law of the land. He saw compromise as the only way to keep the Union whole, but he also wanted to end up on the winning side of history. He knew that his southern colleagues in the Senate were hostile to the proposals before them, but he also knew that he had many pro-compromise allies at the national level. Many of the Senate's most powerful leaders, including Henry Clay, Daniel Webster, Stephen Douglas, and Lewis Cass, were for compromise, as was Vice President Millard Fillmore.

On May 21, 1850, at Foote's request, former president John Tyler wrote a long letter promoting an amicable settlement of the current situation. Less than a month later, Foote was cheered to hear that southern delegates to the Nashville Convention, chaired by his friend and fellow unionist William L. Sharkey, had beaten back more radical elements within their ranks who thought that the southern states should secede. Led by Sharkey and other moderates, the convention condemned Clay's Omnibus Bill and reaffirmed the importance of slavery, but it also left the door open for more discussions by suggesting that the Missouri Compromise Line should be extended to the Pacific Ocean. This was a more moderate position than had been anticipated, since the convention was originally conceived as a great stand for southern unity against any encroachment—either real or perceived—on the South's "greatest domestic institution." In short, the convention's willingness to make any suggestions for compromise was a sign that at least some southerners were still willing to talk. Sharkey wrote to Foote, just days after the convention adjourned, regarding the pending compromise efforts and advised that "it would have been folly to have insisted on what you and I regard as strictly Southern rights. Nothing would have been obtained by that course."[29]

Compromise would indeed be adopted, but only after a few more dramatic twists and turns in Congress. On July 31, 1850, the Senate rejected Clay's so-called Omnibus Bill, which Foote had promoted, but this did not kill off the compromise. The individual components of the bill were broken up into separate pieces of legislation that would be voted on separately, giving senators more flexibility with regard to what parts of the compromise they could vote for or against. Debates continued, but Clay no longer led them, due to his declining health. Instead, Stephen Douglas of Illinois picked up the pieces and began to assert himself as leader of the compromise effort. Foote remained active, which led him into direct conflict with his archenemy Jefferson Davis. Foote, kept pressing for compromise, insisting that it was what the majority of the American people wanted, while Davis held fast that the protection of southern rights was paramount. For Foote, of course, Davis was no run-of-the-mill southerner that needed convincing. He was a rival from Foote's home state, and anything Davis said could have repercussions back home.

Though they were longtime opponents, the heart of the Foote–Davis struggle in 1850 was the question of who spoke for Mississippi. Davis, who by nature was aloof, assumed that he spoke for his state, and his strategy with regard to Foote was to simply ignore him or to patronize him as if his word carried no weight. Naturally, this enraged Foote, who was very difficult to ignore, and he started pressing the point in the Senate that he, rather than Davis, spoke for his people. After a terse exchange with Davis on the Senate floor related to California statehood, Foote argued that his efforts to aid the cause of compromise were part of his "sacred duty as a representative of the state of Mississippi" and that "my constituents feel interested in the settlement of this question. It is one of great national importance to them and the whole Union." He later quantified that most Mississippians and most southerners in general were not flying the "black flag of disunion," and that "nine-tenths of the enlightened freemen of the State of Mississippi are now, and have been all along, cordially in favor of this much abused plan of adjustment." Davis, who usually declined to rise to the bait where Foote was concerned, could no longer hold his tongue. "I have heretofore declined to state by vulgar fractions the opinions of the State which I represent. I do not intend to do so now," Davis said in response. "I have heretofore stated that I believed I represented the opinions of my constituents in opposing these measures. I am firm in that belief. But I do not intend to argue with my colleague about his opinions. I am well assured he will find no nine-tenths in any one county, still less in the State of Mississippi, favoring his course on these measures." Foote let the issue drop at that point, but the exchange was quite satisfying for him in that he had forced a response from Davis and obviously had gotten under his skin.[30]

While Foote had backed the Omnibus Bill, he continued to promote compromise after the bill was broken up into individual components. He also used the situation to his benefit. His efforts to promote compromise left him perpetually sensitive to being portrayed to his Mississippi constituents as soft on abolition, and like other senators, he was now free to vote for some parts of the compromise and not for others, in a way that might help him politically. For instance, when debates began on the critical California statehood bill, Foote began proposing amendments that he probably knew would be defeated. These included efforts to split California and create an extra territory that would presumably allow slaves within its borders. Once his amendments failed, he made a great show of voting with his southern colleagues against the California statehood bill, which passed on August 13 by a significant 34 to 18 margin.

The drama continued the next day, when southern senators submitted a written protest against the admission of California as a free state. Foote refused to sign the protest, claiming that once the statehood bill had passed, it was the law of the land and no protest would change that. He then suggested that those who continued to resist the admission of California—the same senators with whom he had voted the previous day—were extremists hell-bent on destroying the Union for their own purposes. "If California be admitted," he said on the Senate floor, "I shall never counsel resistance [to California's admission], and I shall be prepared to rebuke resistance, to denounce secessionists, and to make every kind of opposition to those men who shall dare to raise their arms against the government." Thus Henry Foote could tell his constituents at the state level that he had voted against the admission of California as a free state, but at the national level he could maintain his position as a unionist and continue to distance himself from his more hotheaded southern brethren.[31]

Foote was also able to use debates over the status of slavery in Washington, DC, to his advantage. He needed no prodding when, at one point, William Seward began pressing for an end to slavery and the slave trade in the nation's capital. In response, Foote quickly rose and gave an impassioned speech as both a proslavery ideologue and a champion of compromise. "No man in the world," he bellowed, "can doubt that any attempt now, on the part of the Congress of the United States, to abolish slavery in the District of Columbia, if successful would dissolve the Union." It was classic Henry Foote rhetoric. Less than a month after berating South Carolina's political leadership as "traitorous demagogues" for promoting secession as a way to gain leverage in the slavery debate, he was reversing himself. No one from the South was endangering the Union, he now made clear; it was those northerners who insisted on placing harsh restrictions on slavery. If the secession of the southern states ever became a reality, it would not be because the South chose the course voluntarily. It would be a natural and inevitable reaction to "intolerable oppression" of the slaveholding states by northern interests. Freeing the South from any responsibility if secession were to become a reality would play well in many southern newspapers and again help to reinforce his position as a defender of slavery.[32]

In the end, the compromise measures passed as individual pieces of legislation. California entered the Union as a free state, and Congress created the Utah and New Mexico territories with no restrictions on slavery. In Washington, DC, the slave trade, but not slavery, was abolished. The boundaries of Texas were set, and a stronger fugitive slave law went into effect. In general, northern Democrats voted as a bloc with Whigs and a few southern Democrats to pass the provisions, while almost every southern Democrat was opposed. Additional help with the process came from President Millard Fillmore, who supported the compromise settlement, and from powerful business interests in the North that sought an end to all the sectional bickering and pressured northern representatives accordingly.

By September 20, 1850, Fillmore had signed all the bills. The settlement kept the Union intact, at least temporarily, and Foote, among others, jockeyed for position in seeking credit for carrying out the process. While Stephen Douglas and Henry Clay received the lion's share of accolades for the settlement, Foote made sure that no one forgot his early role in the proceedings. In a speech that featured a great deal of bravado and little humility, Foote claimed that the compromise settlement would not have passed without his initial pressing for all of the separate parts to be combined in one bill: "Although these bills did pass separately, I maintain and shall ever maintain, that but for the fact of their being combined by the committee originally, and being blended here in discussion, and being united in the public mind; but for there having been a general understanding in both houses of Congress, at the time of the passage of these bills, that each of them should pass as a part of a scheme of adjustment, most of them would have never passed in any form."[33]

Henry Foote may have been quick to pat himself on the back for helping with the compromise settlement, but others at the time also recognized his contributions. Clay wrote that he believed "public gratitude is eminently due" to Foote as well as to those who served on the Committee of Thirteen. "He is an ardent, able and enlightened patriot," Clay said of Foote, who "no one has surpassed . . . in firm devotion to the Union." In Washington, DC, the *National Era* called Foote "the most zealous, the most indefatigable, the most efficient advocate of the Compromise bill," and in Virginia, the *Alexandria Gazette* praised him for "his manly and patriotic course during the late agitation."

There was certainly a groundswell of support for Foote and others, from those in Washington and the surrounding area, immediately following passage of the compromise legislation. Huge celebrations in the District of Columbia took place as "the people of all parties and sections are rejoicing over the passage of these measures, and the settlement of these vexed and dangerous sectional questions." According to press reports "bells were rung, a hundred guns were fired and rockets discharged; the people turned out in large numbers and, with a band of music, repaired to the residences of [Lewis] Cass, [Daniel] Dickinson, [Henry] Foote, [Stephen] Douglas, [Sam] Houston and [Daniel] Webster and called them out." During the period, Foote was the guest of honor at a dinner party in Warrenton, Virginia, where he had studied law as a young man. He was toasted as a returning hero by a crowd of around seventy people. "Virginia welcomes her native son," the *Alexandria Gazette* reported. "Nobly has he vindicated her rights by battling for the Union."[34]

With regard to the press, Foote received generally better treatment from northern Democratic newspapers and from Whig organs nationally. The South's Democratic press was quick to condemn him. "The unenviable position which Senator Foote holds as a traitor to the South is faithfully and strongly delineated," one South Carolina journalist opined. "He has outraged and insulted the feelings of a people who confided their integrity and honor to his keeping. . . . .He has basely deserted his post." The *Tallahassee Floridian and Journal* called Foote a "jackass," while in his home state, the *Mississippian* reported on "Foote and his Yankee friends," stating that "Foote is deluded if he believes that his course will be sustained by any respectable number of individuals." At a banquet in his home state, South Carolina representative William F. Colcock likened Clay and Foote to characters in a freak show, stating, during a racially charged toast, that the pair belonged in P. T. Barnum's New York museum, "in his cabinet of rare monsters, near the spotted negro." In Mississippi, almost the entire Democratic Party political community lined up against the compromise settlement, including the rest of the state's congressional delegation, the governor, and most of the state legislature. "It had been my fortune to stand alone in Congress in 1850," Foote later wrote. "All my five colleagues in both houses were zealously opposed to these [compromise] measures. . . . The governor of the state . . . was in close alliance with them, as were more than two thirds of the legislature and a large proportion of the public officers in the state."[35]

While the compromise measures passed, Foote had one more fight— literally a physical confrontation—left in him before the Senate adjourned. In late September, newly minted California senator John C. Fremont proposed "a bill to make temporary provision for the working and discovery of gold mines and placers in California, and for preserving order in the gold mining districts." The legislation was designed to regulate activities in the goldfields and required miners to pay a small tax on the claims that they worked. Before entering the Senate, Fremont had made a name for himself as a military officer and western explorer, and he was the son-in-law of Foote's nemesis Thomas Hart Benton. Why Foote chose to pick a fight with Fremont remains a mystery, but Freemont's relationship with Benton and the fact that Fremont was a Free Soil Democrat opposed to slavery were likely factors.

Foote rose to speak against Fremont's bill, claiming in no uncertain terms that the legislation was designed not for the public good but to line its author's pockets with profits from the goldfields. Fremont naturally took offense. "Mr. Foote directly accused Mr. Fremont of seeking and urging legislation over the gold fields in California for his own private interest and benefit," one newspaper reported. "This Mr. Fremont warmly repelled, and the two soon became involved in a personal struggle and fight." Fremont verbally accosted Foote in the Senate cloakroom, saying, among other things, that the Mississippian was no gentleman, to which Foote responded by punching Fremont in the face. Fremont returned the blow and the two men fell into a clinch. Senator John H. Clarke of Rhode Island eventually got between the two men and broke up the fracas.[36]

Foote's tussle with Fremont amounted to a parting shot to his enemies in the Senate. He soon would leave Washington and return to Mississippi to defend his position on the compromise. Foote's commitment to the Union and the compromise effort wounded him politically in the South, and especially in his home state. Most of Mississippi's Democratic politicians condemned the compromise, and Foote made himself a party outcast by going against the grain. That said, his work on the compromise would become, for all practical purposes, his most enduring legacy in government service. Foote was indeed as many saw him: a hot-tempered blowhard who reveled in the sound of his own voice. He picked fights, held grudges, and burned bridges like no other man in the Senate.

Yet he could also stick by a principle, as he showed during the compromise debates. He was the most vocal southern Democrat to champion the compromise settlement, and even after it became apparent that the compromise was not popular in the South or in his home state, he never wavered. He maintained his position even after it became apparent that his support for the compromise would damage him politically and likely cause him to lose his Senate seat. He held his ground and ignored all of the pressures to conform. "He has just come through a gallant campaign," the sympathetic New Orleans *Daily Picayune* wrote of Foote after the compromise measures passed, "which, whether he survives or falls politically . . . has won him wide and enduring fame, and will mark him as one of the truest and bravest friends of the Union."[37]

Governor Foote

Foote is a peculiar man. Always was. He never yet delivered a discourse of
speech that he did not follow with one twice as long to explain it.
—*Free Trader*, January 10, 1854

DURING THE DEBATES RELATED to the Compromise of 1850, Henry Foote
went out on a limb in support of legislation that many other southern Democrats found unpalatable. However, a great deal of Foote's posturing during the
period was tied to what he believed his constituents in Mississippi wanted to
hear. Foote wanted to maintain a national reputation, but he was always conscious of the fact that his political base was in his home state. In Mississippi,
the compromise pitted Foote against many of the state's other political leaders
in his own Democratic Party. The compromise debates, centered as they were
around the future of slavery, frightened many white Mississippians by making
them aware of a growing abolitionist agenda in the North. As a result, while
most Mississippi whites still viewed secession as a dangerous proposition, they
were more open to states' rights rhetoric than ever before. The state's Democratic political establishment fanned the flames of fear by using provocative
language that cast the abolitionists as the enemy in a titanic struggle over the
future of slavery in the country. The South was under siege, they maintained,
and it was time for southern whites to band together to protect their own interests, even if that meant leaving the Union. "Mississippi was in a blaze from
east to west, and from north to south," one of Foote's political friends, Reuben
Davis, later recalled. "The issue involved the exact relation of the states to the
general government, and the right of secession. Public feeling was intensified
by the danger of emancipation."[1]

While Henry Foote was busy debating the merits of compromise in the Senate, John A. Quitman was taking advantage of the fear and trepidation among Mississippi's electorate to advance his own political fortunes. In 1849, the Mexican War hero received the Democratic nomination for governor as a strong states' rights advocate. He campaigned on a platform that promoted the federal government as an enemy and any compromise with northerners as a surrender. The Whig Party, which was in decline in Mississippi as well as nationally, ran former state legislator Luke Lea. While some individual Whigs retained their political influence in the state, their party as a whole was showing signs of strain.

Quitman defeated Lea in November, garnering 59 percent of the popular vote, and took office in January of 1850. The new governor devoted more than three-quarters of his inaugural address to federal–state relations. He branded abolitionism as an abomination, claiming that representatives from the free states had embarked on a "systematic and deliberate crusade" against southern rights that placed the Union in jeopardy. "We have a right to the quiet enjoyment of our slave property," he said. "We cannot and will no longer permit that right to be disturbed." Quitman said that the state should resist any type of settlement measure, and under his leadership, Mississippi's mainstream Democratic leaders became more radical in their thinking. With the adoption of the compromise measures in Congress, debate and political comment on slavery and secession in the state reached a fever pitch.[2]

After the compromise measures became law, Henry Foote made plans for his own political future. His next move was based on several premises. First, because he had alienated much of the Mississippi legislature through his support of the compromise, prospects for his reelection to the Senate seemed dim. Second, he believed that Mississippi voters were not nearly as radical in their thinking as Mississippi's Democratic leadership. Foote surmised that while crowds might cheer for a Democrat like Quitman who pledged to defend slavery and the "southern way of life" to the bitter end, they also feared the great unknown that secession represented. There were also Mississippi's Whigs to consider. They generally favored the compromise and they voted in significant numbers, despite the fact that their state party infrastructure was crumbling. Finally, Foote believed that he could rally a majority of Mississippians to his side through the sheer force of his will. He believed that he could talk anyone into anything and that he could convince a majority of his state's voters to accept his view if he could only find the time to give enough speeches.

His confidence was part of his personality, but the senator also realized the difference between a strictly political battle and a contest for public opinion. Foote knew that while the governor and the rest of Mississippi's congressional delegation opposed the compromise on political grounds, many of their more moderate constituents had grown weary of sectional bickering and were willing to accept the legislation as a vehicle for relief. "Take my word for it," William Sharkey, Mississippi's most prominent Whig, advised Foote, "conservative men will approve your course. Whigs generally approve it, and most moderate men of your own party."[3]

With all this in mind, Foote returned to Mississippi in the fall of 1850 with a clear strategy. He believed that if he could paint his opponents as radical secessionists bent on splitting the Union, he could build a strong coalition of Whig voters and moderate Democrats committed to keeping the Union whole. He launched an extensive speaking tour around the state, talking to as many people as possible. "Foote avowed his determination to speak in every county in the state," one newspaper reported, "and challenged any man to meet him."[4]

Like Foote, Mississippi Whigs saw an opportunity to make political hay out of the unprecedented sectional tension. Since Quitman's election as governor, their party had floundered, without a cohesive issue to call its own. To promote their cause, they needed a strong voice, someone with undeniable pro-slavery credentials. As natural enemies of the Democratic mainstream, many Mississippi Whigs suddenly began to rally around Foote—whom they had previously criticized—by condemning secession and promoting the protection of the Union as their primary cause. This was the issue that they believed might give them significant leverage against the Democrats.

The new alliance between Mississippi Whigs and Foote was uneasy, to say the least, but at the time it made good political sense for all concerned. The Whigs praised Foote's stand on the compromise and dutifully linked the state's Democratic Party with despicable schemes to break up the United States. In late 1850, a pamphlet framing their argument began circulating in Mississippi. "The issue is Union or Disunion," it read. "No subtlety of argument or speech, no special array of words, no ingenious or metaphysical terms can long cover the designs of those . . . abetting schemes and movements, which look, in their consequences, [like] nothing less than actual secession or dissolution of the

Union." The text of the pamphlet was later published in the *American Whig Review*.[5]

As Foote promoted the Union and himself, the rest of the state's congressional delegation returned to Mississippi to advance the opposite point of view. Soon after the final compromise measure passed, Jefferson Davis wrote that the legislation amounted to "an alienation of the [southern] people from the yet revered Union of our fathers" and a "perversion of the Constitution from its intent and spirit." Rather than advocating immediate secession, Davis promoted the idea of coordinated action among all the slaveholding states. "The States thus united should," he declared, "demand of the other States such guarantees as would secure to them the safety, the tranquility which the Union was designed to confer." Albert Gallatin Brown, a former governor who represented Mississippi's Fourth Congressional District in the House of Representatives, was much less reserved in his public statements, crying out before a gathering in Jackson, "So help me God, I am for resistance; and my advice to you is that of Cromwell to his colleagues, 'Pray to God and keep your powder dry.'"

Virtually all of Mississippi's Democratic press railed against the compromise, and some newspapers openly promoted secession. One of the state's leading party organs, the Jackson *Mississippian,* the newspaper that Foote had once co-owned, advised its readers that "the acts of the present Congress . . . are each part of a grand system of measures devised for, and tending to the abolition of slavery in the states. . . . Must the South submit in patient silence to those wrongs which all men know, and all men feel, have been inflicted upon her?" The *Woodville Republican* was more blunt, stating that, because of political treachery, "we must and will secede from this Union!"[6]

Foote was well received in many places as he moved from town to town—treated in some locales as a conquering hero—but he also encountered a great deal of hostility from crowds that were sympathetic to the states' rights argument. After a speech in Canton, Mississippi, Foote was hung in effigy, and the same thing happened in Holly Springs not long afterward, with members of the crowd referring to the senator as "the South's Judas." Much of Democratic press was also quick to denounce Foote in the harshest terms. The Natchez *Free Trader* turned on Foote, predicting that he "will be met wherever he goes by an incensed people whose will he has so contemptuously set aside," and throughout the state there were calls for the senator to resign. One editor likened Foote to Benedict Arnold and wrote that when the state legislature next met, its first order of business should be to "condemn the course of Senator Foote on all the southern questions that have come up this session of Congress." Rumors circulated that Foote ultimately would be forced out and that either Quitman or Roger Burton, a Vicksburg politician who also favored secession, would be chosen to replace him.[7]

From the governor's mansion in Jackson, Quitman continued his fierce opposition to the compromise, and he issued the call for a special session of the legislature to "take into consideration the alarming state of our public affairs, and, if possible, avert the evils which impend over us." The governor had little confidence in coordinated southern action. He viewed withdrawal from the Union as his state's most honorable course, and he hoped the legislature would validate his position. As the state's Democrats split into radical and moderate wings over national issues, Quitman became the acknowledged leader of the radical wing. Unlike his more moderate counterparts within the party, the fiery Quitman saw secession as a necessity rather than a last resort. Before the special session met, he confided in South Carolina governor Whitemarsh Seabrook that "my view of state action will look toward secession," and Seabrook in turn pledged that his state would follow Mississippi's lead.[8] Democrats, many of whom won their seats in 1849 as sectional tensions were peaking, dominated the special session that convened on November 18, 1850. The legislature applauded Quitman's stance that the state should "assert her sovereignty" but, despite a great deal of harsh talk, stopped short of immediate action. It called for a convention of delegates to be elected in September 1851 and seated the following November to take a definitive stand on Mississippi's relationship to the Union.[9]

The legislature also reviewed the conduct of the state's congressional delegation during the compromise debates. Democrats advanced resolutions praising opponents of the settlement and also censured Foote for the path that he chose. They accused him of "disregarding the interests and will of the people of Mississippi" through his support for the compromise and of conspiring with others to deny the southern states their rights under the Constitution. In the House, the vote to censure was 50 for and 37 against, while members of the Senate condemned Foote by a vote of 23 to 8. Foote characteristically dismissed the rebuke, but he could not ignore the fact that he had only a limited number of friends in the state legislature, making it highly unlikely that he would win reelection to the U.S. Senate in the future, unless some extraordinary event took place. "I have no feeling at all relative to the proceedings [of the legislature]," he said. "The gentlemen who compose it are doubtlessly very respectable gentlemen, but I think they are little acquainted with public sentiment, and before the next autumn they will find these resolutions were wholly unnecessary and undeserved." From that point on, Foote put all of his energies, and his faith, in his own ability to connect directly with large numbers of Mississippi voters. As a result, his assessment of "public sentiment" in Mississippi would prove somewhat prophetic.[10]

Just as it ushered in the final turbulent decade of national debate on the slavery question, the Compromise of 1850 reshaped Mississippi's political landscape. The legislation created a concrete issue of great substance that politicians could debate, or the general population could discuss, in easily understood terms. As a result, two opposing camps emerged to fight for political supremacy in the state, both of which claimed allegiance to the Constitution and tirelessly evoked the mandates of the founding fathers in their discourse. The state's existing Democratic apparatus, including a few Whigs and a number of recently formed states' rights organizations, represented the first group, which was growing more radical with each passing day. An intense hatred of what they believed the compromise represented fueled their rhetoric as they sought to link the settlement with an assault on slavery, southern liberty, and the Constitution itself. They said that the compromise was a perversion of the principles that had fueled the American Revolution and an insult to the legacy of the men who struggled at such great risk to create the United States. Despite claims to the contrary, however, the State Rights Democrats, or the "State Rights Party," as some called it, often found it difficult to diffuse charges that they were simply disunionists.

On the other side, the vast majority of the state's Whigs and a number of conservative Democrats rallied around Foote. They promoted the compromise as a final solution to sectional troubles and adopted "Union Party" as their official political moniker. This coalition would serve as Foote's new political power base in his state, and Foote would style himself as a "Union Democrat." On November 20, 1850, two days after the legislature convened, 1,500 unionists met at the capitol building in Jackson for what was the first major gathering of the Union Party in Mississippi. Foote addressed the boisterous group, which subsequently passed resolutions that pledged loyalty to the Union, denounced Quitman's conduct as treasonous, and called for a Union Party convention to meet the following May to nominate candidates for state and local offices. The group also announced that ample evidence existed of an organized plot by "agitators, disorganizers, and disunionists of the South" to destroy the Union and organize a southern confederacy. According to rumor, Quitman was set to become president of the new southern nation. "Senator Foote spoke at the capital hall, which was thronged," one newspaper reported. "The enthusiasm of the large audience was unbounded, and whenever the senator had occasion to use the word 'Union' universal shouts of applause broke forth."[11]

Of the two new parties that were forming, Foote's Union Party coalition was the most volatile. While the Whigs eventually rallied around the senator and the Union, they were never completely comfortable with Foote as their standard-bearer. He had spent most of his career promoting a Democratic agenda and criticizing Whig candidates, and it was obvious to most concerned that his new association with Whig loyalists was more a marriage of convenience than a coming together of ideological kinsmen. In early September, before the dust had settled from the compromise debates, an editorial in the *Vicksburg Whig* summed up the situation. While supporting Foote for his stand for compromise, the editors at the newspaper also made it clear that they had a hard time trusting him. "Upon the single question of the compromise we have given our best support to Senator Foote," it read, "[but] it will be long, we fear, before we can have the opportunity of agreeing on other subjects with our chivalrous senator." Almost three months later, in the wake of the Union Party meeting in Jackson, the unusual coupling of Foote and the Whigs remained tenuous. "We are twitted because we are now paying honor to Senator Foote," editors of another major Whig newspaper, the *Natchez Courier* stated on November 22, 1850, "but he has the right to speak for the Union men of Mississippi. We honor him as a Union man."[12]

Despite the chaos, by the beginning of 1851 the immediate parameters of Mississippi's political universe were set, at least for the next election cycle. Both the State Rights Democrats and the Union Party had established central and local organizations, and the primary issue of the campaign was clear. One side believed that the Union was supreme, no matter what issues or events were in play at any given time, while the other side claimed that southern rights were under siege and that secession might be the only remedy for the situation. In the words of antebellum humorist and political commentator Joseph B. Cobb, himself a Mississippian, "Former party distinctions [in Mississippi] are now very much merged in that of Unionists & real though not avowed disunion-ists." Foote's fierce personality and partisanship served as the glue that helped hold the Union Party together, while the more dignified guidance of estab-lished Whig leaders helped put a calmer face on the enterprise. The party also had the support of the federal administration and a growing network of Union concerns in other southern states. The states' rights coalition had the advantage of established public leaders such as Davis and Quitman, whom voters had grown accustomed to following. It also operated through the well-established machinery of the Democratic Party, which had long dominated the state and with which the majority of the state's voters identified.[13]

After the Union rally in Jackson, Foote left the state to continue his speak-ing tour. In New Orleans, he addressed a raucous pro-Union crowd that was "jammed from pit to dome" into the Saint Charles Theater. The senator de-fended his position on all facets of the compromise and promised to one day write a book about the compromise debates in which he would, in great detail, identify the "patriots and the traitors" involved in the compromise process. He also told the crowd that he would "live and die under the American flag" and never waver in his support of the national interest. "The address was frequently interrupted by hearty applause," the New Orleans *Daily Picayune* reported, "and at its conclusion three cheers for Foote and the Union were given."

After the gathering, the senator left New Orleans on the steamship *Pacific*, bound for New York. Soon after his arrival there, he met with the mayor and then gave an address before a pro-Union crowd outside city hall. He once again chastised southern radicals who pressed for rash action, but he also criticized the abolition movement as equally extreme. "The abolition party, too, was severely dealt with," one reporter covering Foote's speech wrote. "As for the South, Mr. Foote said there would be no disunion there if the North would do its duty." Foote went on to claim that the secession movement was in decline in the Deep South and that his home state of Mississippi would never press for seces-sion, "as surely as God reigneth." While the speech was met with "great cheer-ing" from the crowd, Foote's assessment of the southern political climate was at best optimistic and at worst delusional. In truth, opposition to the compro-mise was far from dead in the South, and many political leaders in Mississippi and other southern states still viewed secession as a viable course of action.[14]

After his New York visit, Foote went to Washington for several days and then accepted an invitation to speak in Philadelphia. The event, titled "Lectures on Popular Subjects," was part political meeting and part fund-raising event, with Foote sharing the stage with his old nemesis Sam Houston of Texas and Whig congressman Henry W. Hilliard of Alabama, one of that state's more prominent Union voices. Spectators paid fifty cents each to hear the southerners speak, with proceeds going into a fund to rebuild a local church that had been destroyed by a tornado the previous year.

The gathering was held at the Musical Fund Hall on Locust Street. Houston spoke about life on the Texas frontier, while Hilliard spoke on his philosophy of government and the "indissoluble" nature of the United States. Foote titled his presentation "A Lecture on the Value of the American Union," and it lasted around an hour. "Citizens of Philadelphia! Fellow Country-men!" the senator crowed, with his usual theatrics, "in obedience to your gracious invitation, I come hither from the Capitol of the Republic, and from scenes of excitement and toil, to hold a frank and patriotic commune with you." The speech placed the nature of the Union in historical context and naturally was tailored to promote the compromise settlement as well as Foote's role in it. He defended slavery and sent a clear message that further tampering with the institution was the only thing that could disrupt the relationship between the slaveholding and nonslaveholding states. "We desire to give permanency to those peaceful and kindly relations which are now happily springing into new vitality among us," he said, "and to banish forever from our midst those hideous evils with which we have been so fearfully menaced for many months past."[15]

Back in Mississippi, things seemed to be slowly breaking Foote's way. Though the states' rights coalition was seemingly more stable from an organizational standpoint, fissures were developing as a result of external events. Significant unionist activity in other states, particularly Georgia, made it apparent that cooperative southern action against the compromise was no longer an option. If Mississippi chose to resist the compromise, it would stand alone, or at best in partnership with South Carolina, where radical sentiments prevailed.[16] While independent action still appealed to some in the coalition, the majority of moderates were not willing to set such a dangerous course. Even the most vocal opponents of the compromise began tempering their rhetoric, stressing that while the national legislation still threatened southern rights, the state should not act rashly.

To confuse matters even further, during the same period an unrelated federal investigation involving Governor Quitman came to a head. The matter concerned an unsuccessful filibustering expedition to liberate Cuba from Spanish rule, which Quitman had supposedly helped promote from the governor's mansion, in March of 1850. He was accused of helping Venezuelan filibusterer Narciso López recruit men and obtain supplies for the effort and, as a result, was one of sixteen men indicted for violating the federal Neutrality Act of 1817. While a lack of evidence eventually led to a dismissal of the charges, the governor resigned his office in February 1851, and Democrat John I. Guion, president of the Senate, became acting chief executive. The incident was a distraction, but rather than silencing Quitman politically, it increased his popularity among radicals, who viewed the governor's vindication as a triumph of state concerns over national interference.[17]

Meanwhile, unionists around the state continued to organize. One gathering of Issaquena County unionists captured the tone of the new party's arguments against State Rights Democrats when it passed a resolution stating, "The spirit of disunion and anarchy is abroad in the land, prompted by a lust of office," promoted for "unholy purposes" by "artful demagogues." The keynote speaker at a meeting in Lowndes County assured the assembled crowd that "the Union of Washington and Jackson will be preserved in its integrity," while the state's major Union newspaper, the Jackson *Flag of the Union,* linked current controversies with the Nullification Crisis of the 1830s. "In 1832 and '33," it told its readers, "the friends of the Union were firmly united in defense of the government . . . and so they are now!" While unionist rhetoric was predictable, it was also laced with irony. The "friends of the Union" during the Nullification Crisis, who midcentury unionists quoted extensively, were for the most part Jacksonians whose political enemies formed the Whig Party. The unionists of 1850, however, were primarily Whigs who, as a matter of political expedience, used gushing references to Jackson in their speeches and resolutions.[18]

After Congress adjourned in March of 1851, Foote returned to Mississippi to continue promoting his position on the compromise and the Union. He embarked on an ambitious speaking tour during the month of April, and as he canvassed the state, Whig newspapers began promoting the idea that he should leave the Senate and run for governor in the upcoming election cycle, on the Union ticket. For many Whigs, the idea was irresistible. Most expected Quitman to try to regain the seat, and a Foote–Quitman race would pit the state's most visible Union man against the state's leading radical, neatly framing the election in terms of "Union vs. Disunion." Quitman called accepting the compromise measures "submission" and "surrender" and was on record again and again as favoring secession. As the *Natchez Courier* correctly editorialized, "With these two candidates there would be no mistaking the issue." For the Whigs, Foote and his new Union Party also represented their best chance for winning, despite the fact that he technically was not one of them. Foote could draw crowds, and he was a much better stump speaker than Quitman. The senator was energetic, a known commodity, and traditionally at his best on the campaign trail.[19]

Foote liked the idea of running for governor because it represented a potential solution to his most serious political problem. Foote's Senate term would end soon, and as he had just been censured by the Mississippi legislature, the chances of that body selecting him for another term were slim. In fact, Foote's enemies were already planning a campaign to replace him and looked forward with relish to the day when they could put the irascible senator out to pasture. For Foote, having the Senate seat taken away in such a manner meant humiliation. It would empower his enemies and likely create a scenario that would make it difficult for him to ever again hold public office.

As a result, Foote conceived a plan that he hoped would save his political career. He would accept the Whig offer to run for governor on the Union ticket. He would then return to Mississippi to do what he did best: work the crowds of his home state and win support for himself through his inexhaustible enthusiasm for political debate and his antics on stage. If elected, he would then be in a position to strengthen his Union coalition of Whigs and disaffected Democrats and help pro-Union men win election to Mississippi's House and Senate. Once his term as governor was up, he reasoned that a more sympathetic legislature might send him to Washington again. The whole plan depended on his calculation that the general public in Mississippi would increasingly turn against the concept of secession and, as time passed, embrace the idea that their security lay within the Union. Foote's enormous ego was also a driving force in his decision to run for governor. Never doubting his own powers of persuasion, he seemed to believe that if he took his case directly to the people and spoke to them face-to-face, he could hold any office that he might want to pursue.

On May 5, 1851, the Union Party convention met in Jackson to nominate candidates for state offices. According to one account, the gathering found "old veteran Whigs—or those who were formerly so—and Democrats—not only forgetting, but declaring that they were no longer Whigs and Democrats." Foote addressed the convention and accepted the new party's nomination for governor. He spoke of the dangers of secession and the great responsibility that the Union ticket held as stewards of the founding fathers' legacy.

Now staunchly behind the Union cause, the Whig press praised their new standard-bearer's acceptance speech. After hearing the address, one correspondent from Vicksburg reported that Foote "manfully vindicated the wisdom, justice, and patriotism of the compromise measures—crushing with herculean power the base schemes of disorganized secessionists." In Jackson, the *Flag of the Union* urged its readers to "throw aside old party prejudices and party leaders, and under the lead of the gallant Foote aid in the overthrow of those who would plunge our happy country into civil war and ruin." Conversely, within several days, Democratic editors turned their full wrath on the Union Party candidate, disparaging him as "traitor Foote" and "the great Mississippi humbug" and referring to his new organization as the "Northern Union Whig Abolition Foote party." In Foote's home county, one newspaper argued that "Foote must be killed off, put down, and of course politically buried."[20]

After the Union convention adjourned, Foote took to the stump, characteristically relentless, traversing the state and speaking in a different town almost daily during the summer. The timing of their convention gave the unionists an advantage over their rivals, who did not meet until mid-June, and Foote wanted to take full advantage.

While the Union Party fell in line behind Foote, the gathering of State Rights Democrats the following month reflected disunity within their party. A general division existed between radicals who pushed for Quitman's reelection and moderates who promoted other candidates for governor, including Jefferson Davis. Moderates realized that while many Mississippians disliked the compromise measures, they were increasingly willing to accept them and to continue the struggle for states' rights and the protection of slavery within the Union. Like many of his political friends, Jefferson Davis judged that Quitman and his associates were "plucking the fruit before it is ripe" by pressing "secession before submission." While Quitman was favored to win the nomination, many delegates opposed him for his inflexibility and doubted whether he could win the general election. Still, they were more afraid of an open rift within their party that would give the election to the unionists on a silver platter and perhaps hurt Democratic candidates who were running for the legislature. At one time, the convention's nominating committee brokered a proposal that involved Davis resigning his Senate seat to run for governor and, if elected, appointing Quitman to fill the vacancy. "I offered no objection to this arrangement," Davis later recalled, "but left it to General Quitman to decide." Quitman refused the deal and received the nomination for governor.

Though the party—officially named the Democratic State Rights Party by the convention—publicly announced that it opposed withdrawal from the Union under present circumstances, the record and past rhetoric of the party's nominee firmly established secession as a primary issue of the campaign. Unionists around the state were ecstatic. "I always told you that Mississippi was one of the most reliable Union States," a confident Foote wrote to fellow unionist Howell Cobb, who would soon become governor of Georgia. "We will prove this to be literally true in September. Quitman and Quitmanism are dead in Mississippi forever."[21]

Quitman and Foote scheduled a grueling series of forty-eight joint debates, beginning on July 7 in Yazoo City. While the candidates had a history and were certainly not the best of friends, they had kept their relationship reasonably cordial while Foote was in the Senate. This changed quickly as the tour commenced and Foote seemingly turned the campaign into a personal vendetta. Foote never failed to exploit his superior speaking skills, and he did his best to humiliate Quitman in the process. According to Reuben Davis, a Foote friend but Quitman ally, "It was most unfortunate for Quitman, whose style of speaking was poor and flat, that he was obliged to encounter Foote, whose gorgeous imagery, and splendid diction carried everything before him." The men discussed the compromise measures in detail, but more often than not the appearances degenerated into personal attacks in which Foote routinely breached debate etiquette and "assailed Quitman and his friends in a most merciless manner." On one occasion, Foote made sport of Quitman's voice, mocking his hoarse, sore throat until the audience laughed at the former governor as he tried to speak. At times, the tension between the candidates spilled over into the crowds. Just two days into the tour, at Lexington, in Holmes County, partisans for both men brawled and brandished pistols at one another. At another stop, Quitman finally suggested to Foote that they might retire to some nearby woods to personally settle their differences.[22]

The joint tour was memorable but short-lived. On July 17, at Polkville, in Panola County, an onstage argument ensued over remarks by Foote concerning the federal charges that had led to Quitman's resignation. The conflict continued during the debate the next day, in Sledgeville, until Quitman finally raged that Foote's statements regarding the matter were "false and cowardly, scandalous and ungentlemanly." The men exchanged more words and Foote rushed Quitman, knocking him off balance with a glancing blow. Before onlookers could separate the candidates, Quitman responded with a punch that reportedly left Foote with a large bruise on his forehead. The fight discredited both men, but in a way it worked to Quitman's advantage in that it gave him an excuse to terminate the joint appearances. Soon after the altercation, he announced his own speaking schedule. Foote continued to fill the previously announced dates, boasting that he had "whipped Quitman and driven him from the field."[23]

As the separate canvasses began, the strength of the State Rights Party ebbed. At meetings resplendent with fluttering American flags, patriotic banners, and portraits of George Washington, unionists assailed their opponents as enemies of the Constitution. Foote was the perfect spokesman for the cause, assuring listeners that he and his party stood for "the rights of the South, liberty and Union, now and forever, one and inseparable." Just as many State Rights Democrats feared, Quitman's extremism could not be effectively defended. State Rights newspapers had few answers to the charges that their candidate was a secessionist. They could do little more than call Foote a traitor to the state and disparage the Union Party as some type of "Whig trick" backed by "fourth-rate politicians." The political climate had changed significantly in the months since Quitman and the state legislature had called for a special state convention to "avert the evils that impend over us." Unionism had taken hold in many parts of the state, and Quitman's bid to recapture the governor's chair had turned into a disaster.

In September, the selection of delegates to the special convention took place in what amounted to a preliminary referendum on the upcoming gubernatorial contest. Members of the convention would be charged with "taking action with reference to the Compromise schemes of the last Congress," and in most local races, avowed unionists and State Rights Democrats vied for seats. In a sweeping triumph, Union Party candidates carried the day by a collective statewide margin of 28,402 to 21,241, losing only sixteen counties. For Quitman, the defeat was devastating and filled with irony, as he had called for the special convention in the first place in hopes that the delegates would embrace radical action. Succumbing to the inevitable, he withdrew from the governor's race on September 6, leaving his party in a shambles. In an open address, he stated that while his personal beliefs had not changed, "as a State Rights man, and a Democrat, I bow in respectful submission to the apparent will of the people."

Quitman's withdrawal was reported, but rarely discussed in detail, in the Democratic press, and even the most partisan newspapers had little choice but to concede the shift in public sentiment. In Jackson, the powerful *Mississippian* realized that the election of convention delegates had abruptly decided the question of resistance to or acceptance of the compromise. "The scattered returns of the election," the newspaper's editor wrote glumly, "indicate the decision of the people in favor of acquiescence [to the compromise measures]. . . . We pledge ourselves to abide by their decision. This pledge we are prepared, in good faith, to redeem."[24]

While the convention election temporarily decided the compromise debate in Mississippi, the State Rights Democrats still needed a candidate for governor. Immediately after Quitman left the race, party operatives met to discuss filling the vacancy. The men mentioned a number of candidates but quickly settled on Jefferson Davis, who at the time was at his home in Warren County, nursing a fever and a badly inflamed eye. The offer placed the senator in a personal and political dilemma. He had never been intensely interested in the office, he was ill, and it was apparent that Foote would now probably win the election regardless of the opponent. To make matters worse, Davis felt compelled to follow the convention of resigning his Senate seat to run for state office, although Foote had not done so. Nevertheless, he was a party man and his party was in dire need of his name and his voice. Davis accepted the offer, despite having good reason to turn it down. He resigned his Senate seat and placed himself in a political contest which he thought was probably unwinnable, against an opponent that he thoroughly detested.[25]

While the State Rights Party cause seemed lost, Ethelbert Barksdale, a prominent Democrat and editor of the *Mississippian,* penned a letter to Davis, on September 19, stating his belief that the situation might not be as grim as it appeared. Barksdale pointed out that there were about sixty thousand voters in the state, and therefore the Union ticket had failed to achieve a plurality of the total electorate in the recent election. He believed that thousands of Democrats who had lost interest in sectional questions, and as a result failed to turn out to vote for convention delegates, would appear at the polls to cast votes for governor. In addition, he told Davis that "there are many Democrats who voted for the Union ticket, and would not sustain Gen. Quitman, [who] will give you a hearty support." While Barksdale's letter seemed overly optimistic, his point was valid. Many Democrats who had been wary of Quitman's extreme views readily accepted Davis as "the man for the crisis."[26]

Because of his illness, Davis could not actively canvas until mid-October, and even then he made only a few public appearances. His name alone, however, was enough to revitalize the State Rights press. In his speeches and published correspondence, Davis continued to chart a relatively moderate course. He viewed withdrawal from the Union as a last resort but warned his audiences that "to secure the rights of the State and perpetuate the Union, I have believed it indispensable that the Constitution should be strictly construed . . . that the federal agent should be 'bound by the chains of the Constitution.'"[27]

Oddly enough, Foote continued to lambaste State Rights Democrats as secessionists but rarely inflicted personal attacks on his former Senate colleague during the final weeks of the campaign. One explanation for this uncharacteristic behavior may be that Foote believed he already had the race in hand. While Foote certainly hated his former Senate colleague, Davis was still a war hero and was respected by many people in the state, especially moderate Democratic voters whom Foote himself might want to court in the next election cycle. Should he attack Davis personally—and with excessive vitriol, as was his way—Foote risked alienating those voters. If he believed that he already had the race won, Foote likely saw no reason to take the risk, regardless of his feelings for his rival.

Mississippians went to the polls on November 3 and 4, 1851. As Barksdale had predicted, the turnout was significantly higher than it had been the previous September. An additional eight thousand voters, most of whom were Democrats, cast ballots for governor. According to one observer, the high turnout was a direct result of Davis's candidacy. "He was stronger in Mississippi not only than any man, but than any principle," a Democrat later wrote. "His name was a magic sound in the ears of all the ranks." In the end, Foote garnered 29,358 votes to Davis's 28,359.[28] In the span of a few weeks, with only limited campaigning, Davis had risen from his sickbed to pull the State Rights Democrats to within just less than a thousand votes of their adversaries.

The election results, in one way, were a vindication for Foote, in that he won, but they also signaled trouble for the governor-elect in the future. In the September election for convention delegates, the Union Party had carried the day with 57.2 percent of the total vote, but Foote was able to garner only 50.8 percent of the vote in the governor's race. Foote's victory was far from a mandate and, in reality, Davis might have won the race had he had more time to campaign. Though Foote did not know it yet, the coalition that had helped him win was not sustainable. His victory was in large part a product of circumstance. He had been in the right place at the right time, when the secession issue was ripe for exploitation and the ranks of his opponents were divided. After being elected, Foote found himself living on borrowed time, politically. States' rights advocates were already reorganizing for the next election cycle, and over the next few years national events would play into the hands of those with a secession agenda.

Ironically, it would be Davis, more than Foote, who benefitted from the election. Because he entered the governor's race at great personal sacrifice, the Mexican War hero enhanced his already stellar reputation within the Democratic Party, and the political winds in Mississippi would soon shift again as a result of other factors. "I regard your future political sky as being without a cloud," a friend wrote Davis, a few days after the election, "and your course will be necessarily onwards and upwards, until you reach the Presidency."[29]

Despite the narrowness of Foote's victory, the statewide political races of 1851 represented a triumph for Mississippi unionism. "The result is sufficient," the Jackson *Flag of the Union* reported, on November 14. "Our chief standard bearer, General Foote, against whom all the heavy artillery of the secession party was brought to bear, as well as all the small arms of their guerrilla skirmishers, has been most gloriously sustained." The Union Party captured the governorship, sent sixty-three out of ninety-eight members to the state House of Representatives, and won three of the four congressional seats, though it failed to capture the Mississippi Senate. The election repudiated radical action, albeit for only a while, and forced John A. Quitman into temporary political retirement. On November 10, 1851, the convention that Quitman had hoped would usher Mississippi out of the Union met in Jackson. The gathering passed a number of resolutions accepting the compromise settlement, pledging loyalty to the Union, and insisting that "the asserted right of secession from the Union on the part of a State or States is utterly unsanctionable by the Federal Constitution, which was framed to 'establish,' and not destroy the Union of the States."[30]

A few days after celebrating his victory, Foote left Mississippi for New Orleans, where he gave a quick address on the Union cause. He was well received there and passed the night of November 16 at the fashionable Verandah Hotel on Saint Charles Street. "The Hon. Henry S. Foote arrived in our city yesterday," the pro-Union New Orleans *Daily Picayune* reported. "He is enjoying excellent health. He will leave for Washington City today. He has been doing yeomen service in a glorious cause, and deserves the congratulation he receives wherever he goes." Foote left New Orleans and headed back to the nation's capital to finish up his Senate business and meet with friends and allies. On the way, he stopped in Montgomery, Alabama, where he gave a speech about his future political expectations for his home state. According to newspaper reports, he told the crowd that he believed "that the fixed policy of Mississippi was the maintenance of a Union organization which . . . was indispensably necessary to keep the fire-eating schismatics [secessionists] in check."

Once back in Washington, by the end of November, Foote accepted praise from pro-Union politicians who had been keeping up with the Mississippi governor's race, and he also got to work reestablishing himself within national Democratic circles. Tired of being labeled a Whig by his enemies, Foote gave a pro-Union speech on "the duties of the Democratic Party" at a large gathering of the Jackson Democratic Association. Despite the fact that he had been elected governor of Mississippi with the support of state Whigs and only a limited number of Democrats, he clarified to the crowd in Washington that he remained "a consistent, unwavering Democrat." Foote wanted to make clear his party loyalties because he hoped to return to the Senate one day as a Democrat. Ironically, in the long run, this quick pronouncement, made so soon after many Mississippi Whigs had helped him get elected, probably alienated more supporters than it drew to him.[31]

Foote's swan song in the U.S. Senate lasted from December 1, 1851, when the first session of the 32nd Congress convened, until he left for Mississippi later in the month. The fact that he soon would be leaving the Senate did not seem to slow him down at all with regard to introducing onto the Senate floor highly charged rhetoric. If anything, his election as governor seemed to embolden him with a determination that his last days in Washington would be some of his loudest. Almost immediately, Foote introduced a joint resolution dealing with Hungarian patriot Louis Kossuth's pending visit to the United

States. Foote, who months before had expressed support for Kossuth and the Hungarian cause on the Senate floor, wanted a joint committee formed "to make suitable arrangements for the reception of Louis Kossuth, governor of Hungary, on his arrival in the United States, and to communicate to him the assurances of the profound respect entertained for him by the people of the United States." Foote's proposal reignited an old debate related to any sort of official recognition of Kossuth, because some interpreted the Hungarian's commitment to universal liberty as support for the abolition movement in the United States. Foote's resolution never made it to a vote, but it touched off several days of terse discussions that, at the time, seemed unnecessary.

Foote also stirred the compromise pot again, on December 18, by introducing legislation declaring the compromise measures "to be a definitive settlement of the questions growing out of domestic slavery." Foote claimed the legislation was needed to add another layer of finality to the settlement so that in the future it would not be "subject to repeal or modification." In reality, there was no way to guarantee that any legislation passed by Congress would never be modified. Foote knew this but felt compelled, during his remarks, to repeat at great length his opinions on the compromise and to chastise those who had worked against its passage. As with the Kossuth resolution, the legislation dealing with the compromise never reached a vote but took up a great deal of the Senate's time for no apparent reason. That said, the principle of accepting the compromise as a final solution to sectional issues did resurface in the 1852 national Democratic platform. All in all, Foote's last three weeks in the Senate were unstatesmanlike, to say the least, and seemed to confirm everything that his enemies said about him. "[He is] a flashy fellow," one journalist wrote of the Mississippian at the time, "all impulse, nothing mature."[32]

Foote left the Senate floor on December 19, never to return, and spent the next few days making the rounds to visit friends, and even a few foes, before departing Washington. "The distinguished Senator [Foote] has at length taken leave of the Senate," the *Alexandria Gazette* reported. "There was much doubt in the minds of certain of his peers—so numerous were his leave takings and farewells—whether his intention really was to leave at all." Senator John Barney of Maryland hosted a farewell dinner for Foote with an impressive guest list that included much of the cabinet as well as numerous senators and congressmen. Liquor flowed freely, and a highlight of the festivities occurred when

Daniel Webster toasted the Mississippian with a humorous poem especially composed for the occasion.[33]

Even before Foote left Washington, speculation about his future and about a long-term plan that he had apparently formulated began appearing in the press. Mississippi's political environment had become somewhat complicated because Jefferson Davis had resigned his Senate seat to run for governor and Foote would have to do so before assuming his new position. This left two unexpired Senate terms—Foote's term, which expired in just over a year, and Davis's term, which ended in 1856—for the state legislature to fill. After they selected men for these vacancies, Mississippi legislators would then have to hold another, separate election to fill the old Foote seat for a full six-year term, set to begin early 1853. Fresh from his victory over Quitman, Foote daydreamed that he might win election to fill the old Davis seat for the next three years, or that after legislators filled the unexpired terms, they would elect him to his old seat for another full term, at which time he would return triumphantly to Washington. Despite the fact that State Rights Democrats still controlled the Mississippi Senate, Foote believed that he could make this happen, and he told many people about his plan.

During this period, the New Orleans *Daily Picayune* informed its readers that "Senator Foote today announced his intention of retiring from the Senate, and at the same time made the somewhat singular announcement that he intended to return to the Senate again next fall," while, in Boston, the *Evening Transcript* reported that "the senator anticipates re-election in place of Jefferson Davis, when he will resign the governorship and return in a few weeks." Before leaving for Mississippi, Foote visited New York long enough for a journalist from the *Albany Journal* to write that "Foote will leave here on Monday when, should the legislature elect him to replace Jefferson Davis, which he believes they will, he will resign as governor and return to Washington." Back in Mississippi, the Democratic press also reported Foote's plan, which in reality was a pipe dream. "[Foote] speaks very confidently about being returned to the Senate of the United States by the legislature," the *Vicksburg Sentinel* reported in late December. "No doubt he seems to have on that score."[34]

Foote arrived in Jackson, Mississippi, during the first week of January 1852, and on January 8 he resigned his Senate seat. Two days later, he was inaugurated at the state capitol as Mississippi's governor "in the presence of the two houses of the legislature, and a large audience." His inaugural address included yet another long, detailed rehashing of the issues surrounding the Compromise of 1850. He called the compromise the "termination of a fiercely contested political struggle" and made the wildly exaggerated claim that "in our beloved state not a single voice can now be heard in opposition to the [compromise] measures." He also claimed that passage of the measures had ended forever the friction created between the northern and southern states over slavery and that his election as governor signaled the state's approval of the settlement. None of these statements were really true. Foote's Union Party had won the gubernatorial election by a small margin, indicating that there were indeed a good many voices within the state that questioned the compromise. And, of course, the compromise did not end the problems between the North and the South. Only toward the end of his address did Foote discuss state matters, pledging to support "various schemes of internal improvement" and a "practicable system of popular education."[35]

Though flush with victory in the weeks following the election, unionists around the state would have little time to savor their triumph. Foote's victory represented both the high point of unionism in antebellum Mississippi and, as such, the beginning of its decline. In his inaugural address, the new governor reasserted his dedication to the Union but offered little in terms of a domestic agenda. He had constructed a successful gubernatorial campaign around the secession issue, but once the issue was settled, albeit temporarily, he had no political foundation on which to build. Unionists held the House of Representatives, but vindictive State Rights Democrats still firmly controlled the Senate, and the governor had only a limited number of close allies in either chamber. Many Whigs in the Union coalition still distrusted him because he was at heart a Democrat, and most mainstream Democrats hated him because he had abandoned their cause and viciously attacked their stalwarts.

While he continued to view his election as governor as a mandate, Henry Foote was in truth a man without a party, and charges that his coalition was nothing more than "whiggery in the garb of Union" were based in fact. In many ways, the Union Party was indeed a "Whig trick," as many Democrats claimed. The party drew its strength from the old Whig strongholds along Mississippi's major rivers, and most of its leaders had been prominent Whigs for years. The secession issue and a cosmetic name change had merely given a brief reprieve to a mortally wounded party that would be nothing more than a memory by the close of the decade. Astute State Rights Democrats were only temporarily discouraged by the November returns. Most believed that Davis would have defeated Foote, had Davis been able to carry out a full campaign. As Foote's coalition crumbled, mainstream Democrats continued building their coalition around the states' rights doctrine.[36]

The year 1852 was one of political confusion in Mississippi, with the most pressing issue before the state legislature being the election of United States senators to fill the seats vacated by Foote and Davis. Foote pushed for the legislature to quickly fill the unexpired positions and at the same time elect a senator to his old seat for the next full term, which began in early 1853. Hoping to take advantage of the strong unionist presence in the House of Representatives, Foote wanted to either be chosen to finish Davis's term or elected to fill his old seat for the full term. State Rights Democrats in the Senate blocked Foote's wishes and the end result was a compromise. The legislature, in joint session, chose Whig Walter Brooke and Union Democrat Stephen D. Adams to fill the unexpired terms, with Brooke's selection being linked to his pledge to support the 1852 Democratic presidential nominee. State Rights Democrats were willing to make a deal with the Whigs in the legislature, giving them one seat and appointing a Union Democrat to the other, in return for no action on the full-term seat that Foote coveted. The fact that the Whigs were willing to deal with the State Rights Democrats and leave Foote out of the equation was also an ominous sign for the governor. At the time, keeping the Senate seat away from Foote seemed to be something that most Democrats and at least a few Whigs could agree on, another indication that Foote's coalition was in trouble.

As a result of all this activity, the legislature made little progress with proposals for congressional redistricting, made necessary by the 1850 census. Disharmony was the order of the day in a statehouse divided into what many referred to as the Foote House and the Davis Senate. The split in the legislature was indicated early in Foote's administration, in votes taken on a resolution to rescind the censure of the governor, which had been handed down when he was a United States senator. With votes cast along party lines, the measure passed in the House, 52 to 26, but was voted down in the Senate, 18 to 10.[37]

Stalling on various issues by the mainstream Democrats was part of a political strategy designed to revitalize their party and neutralize Foote. The threat of secession had created the Union Party, and Foote could never have put together his coalition without it. As the threat faded, however, Democrats hoped to reunite their ranks during the next election season for a more traditional "Democrats vs. Whigs" campaign. Most Union Democrats eventually returned to the fold, with apparently little stigma attached to their support of Foote. In reality, they had little choice; the only alternative was to join the Whig ranks permanently as a vocal but outnumbered minority. One Democratic newspaper stated accurately that "the [1852 presidential] canvass cannot fail to be a sifting process among politicians, it will separate the tares from the wheat. . . . The Union party organization in this State must become extinct under such an ordeal. Then let us wait a while to see where men stand."[38]

Many in Foote's coalition had been loyal to the Union cause but not necessarily to Foote himself, so once the Union seemed safe, Foote's personal support began to decline. As a result, he accomplished little as governor, in terms of legislation, and his influence as the state's chief executive was weak from the outset. During his term, he gave speeches on general issues related to internal improvements, railroad building, public education, and the status of Mississippi swampland, but in general he seemed disinterested in the nuts and bolts of governing. He made abstract pronouncements about things that should be done but offered few concrete plans of action. His disinterest in advancing legislation may have stemmed from the fact that any measures he promoted had little chance of passing, with his enemies firmly in control of the Senate. In short, Foote may have seen the fight to promote a strong domestic agenda as not worth fighting.

During Foote's term as governor, state Democrats focused tightly on trying to reestablish old political lines. They employed a relatively simple strategy, appealing to national party loyalty and the advancement of national Democratic candidates. Not long after Foote's victory, they put out the call for a joint convention of both State Rights and Union Democrats, ostensibly to select delegates to the national convention in Baltimore, but also to mend fences. In Jackson, the state's primary State Rights newspaper, the *Mississippian*, urged Democrats of both factions to unite and "come up in all their strength and numbers, and make ready for the great contest which is to be fought between themselves and federal Whiggery in 1852." Many Union Democrats accepted the invitation to reunite the party, and the Democratic press disparaged those who did not as being "satisfied to remain as a scouting party attached to the old whig army. . . . a guerrilla band making predatory excursions on the domains of former friends and associates." Soon, important Union Party newspapers around the state—those that had not been Whig organs before the Union Party's creation—fell in line in the effort to promote the Democratic agenda.[39]

Meanwhile, Whigs recognized the growing threat but were unable to do anything about it. The Whig press begged Union Democrats not to break ranks and to return to a reunited Democratic Party, claiming that no matter what they promised at present, State Rights Democrats were extremists who could not be trusted. National events also worked against the Whigs. The upcoming 1852 presidential election season, coupled with the passing of the most recent sectional crisis, promoted traditional party realignment behind national candidates. For Mississippi Whigs as well as for Whigs throughout the South, the compromise settlement posed yet another problem in that many of their more extreme northern brethren opposed the tenets of the compromise dealing with the Fugitive Slave Act. The act, which gave the federal government responsibility for apprehending and returning slaves who had escaped to free states, was highly symbolic in the South. It legitimized national acceptance of their peculiar institution and, in so doing, enhanced the South's image of itself as an important part of the federal union. It was also the part of the compromise that, more than any other, antagonized abolitionist elements within the ranks of northern Whigs. Southern Whigs were particularly alarmed when, in 1852, their party nominated Winfield Scott for president over Millard Fillmore, who had vigorously pledged to enforce the Fugitive Slave Act. While Scott was a southern-born war hero, his lukewarm support of new fugitive slave laws branded him as suspect in the minds of many southerners, as did the fact that he was the preferred candidate of antislavery northerners.

In short, by opposing the Fugitive Slave Act, northern Whigs left southern Whigs with a heavily depleted arsenal for use in their state's slavery-based political wars. Tensions between the northern and southern Whigs were heightened when a number of prominent northern Whigs led efforts to rescue fugitive slaves during the early 1850s. Because they could not disassociate themselves from the onus of abolitionism in their national party, many southern Whigs were left with the choice of aligning themselves with the Democrats or sitting out the upcoming presidential campaign altogether. In contrast, the Democrats settled on a presidential candidate who helped foster unity in their ranks. They nominated New Hampshire governor Franklin Pierce, a northerner with southern sympathies, and he proved to be an effective compromise candidate that Democrats from both sections could rally behind.[40]

The choice of Pierce as the national Democratic nominee for president was another blow to Foote, who had supported Lewis Cass of Michigan for the position. Foote and Cass worked well together in the Senate, and Cass had supported the compromise settlement. During this period, and afterwards, Foote was always effusive in his praise for the man he called "my venerated friend from Michigan," and years later he wrote that he would "forever feel proud of having zealously sustained [Cass] in the presidential contest." Mississippi's governor thought that Pierce was weak, but what horrified Foote the most was the fact that Pierce and Jefferson Davis were close friends. If Pierce were elected, Davis would become part of the new president's inner circle, enhancing Davis's reputation and giving him even more political leverage in Mississippi. Foote still hated Davis, but he had no choice but to support Pierce when he received the nomination. To do otherwise would have made it much easier for Foote's enemies to label him as a Whig at a time when the Whig Party was falling apart. It was a no-win situation for Foote, who would have to sit back and feign support as the close friend of his greatest political enemy was elected to the highest office in the land.[41]

Mississippi Whigs did not give up without a fight, but their appeals to unionism had little effect as Foote's old coalition of mainstream Whigs and Union Democrats unraveled. The compromise settlement had temporarily diffused the sectional crisis and rendered moot any question of whether southern states would leave the Union. With the issue settled, both wings of the Democratic Party, especially State Rights Democrats, could claim loyalty to the American Constitution. Confident that the Union was safe, Mississippi's electorate could be swayed by states' rights arguments, because such arguments traditionally lost their appeal only when taken to the extreme. State Rights Democrats may have opposed the compromise on principle, but in finally accepting it as a political reality they consolidated Democratic strength in Mississippi by taking the sting out of charges that they were secessionists. With this radical taint removed, both wings of the party could unite and turn their full attention to defeating the Whigs, who remained vulnerable because of the antislavery elements in their party's northern wing. One of the final nails in the coffin of the Union coalition that had carried the 1851 state elections was reluctantly driven in by none other than Foote himself. Still titular head of the Union Party in Mississippi, he weakened it considerably when he joined mainstream Democrats in support of Pierce. Pierce won the presidency and carried Mississippi with 26,876 votes to Scott's 17,548.[42]

The 1852 presidential election helped seal the fate of the Whig Party as a national political entity, and it established Democratic dominance in Mississippi for the rest of the decade. In the future, opposition candidates in various guises would challenge Democrats for state offices, but with little success. Over the next several years, many major political battles in the state would involve factional struggles within the Democratic structure, or local, personality-based conflicts in which party labels meant little. The Democratic victory of 1852 also established the parameters for the political jousts that would take place in the years preceding the Civil War.

For Mississippi Democrats, the states' rights argument was irresistible, particularly in the face of national events that continued to widen the gulf between North and South. Mississippi's economy was firmly affixed to slavery, and each year the state was among the leading cotton producers in the nation. Wealthy planters held allegiance to slavery as a central pillar of their economic status, and because the cotton economy touched vast numbers of nonslaveholders in some form or fashion, simpler white farmers supported the institution as well. Poorer whites also feared abolitionism on social grounds. Freedom for slaves, they were told again and again, would bring competition from free blacks for land and in the labor market. Just as wealthier Mississippians reaped profits from slavery, poorer whites defined their status as a function of the institution. Through the rest of the decade the Democratic press never failed to remind struggling white farmers, most of whom owned no slaves, that "when menial labor has to be done by the poor whites, as is the case in the governments of Europe and in many of the free States, they cease to be freemen."[43] This was highly potent rhetoric when aimed at a population that possessed little more than their self-identity as independent white property holders.

The 1852 election results effectively rendered Foote a lame duck. Jefferson Davis and his allies controlled the Mississippi Democratic Party and they were certainly not going to give Foote a seat at the table. In the nation's capital, one sympathetic newspaper opined, "Mr. Foote, who was perhaps more effective than any other man in Congress in carrying through the Compromise bills, at last finds himself, for that very reason, in a minority of the Democratic Party in his own state, his political prospect, at the present, all blighted." Union

Democrats who helped Foote win the election were deserting him in droves to rejoin their party's mainstream, and it seemed that some Whigs who had been part of the Union Party coalition were tired of Foote's rhetoric and overbearing behavior.

The election also ended one of Foote's pipe dreams: that the national Democratic Party would adopt a strong pro-Union platform in 1852 and that he might even secure a spot as the party's vice presidential nominee. To add insult to injury, Pierce, after his election, appointed Jefferson Davis secretary of war in the new administration. More than two decades later, Foote was still bitter about the whole situation. "Surely there was nothing in Mr. Pierce's abilities or habits of life," Foote wrote in 1874, "to cause the public attention to be fixed upon him as a suitable person to mount the car of state at a moment so critical." He claimed that he had only given Pierce "cold and reluctant support" because he had no other choice and that he had, in truth, considered the Pierce administration "sublimely ridiculous."[44]

Though Foote failed in efforts to promote a legislative agenda while governor, he was far from silent, and he remained a bombastic presence as he carried out the many ceremonial duties required of the governor. In March of 1852, Hungarian patriot Louis Kossuth visited Mississippi while on a goodwill and fund-raising tour of the United States. Foote had always spoken highly of Kossuth while in the Senate, and Kossuth apparently felt a "duty of gratitude" to call on Foote and thank the Mississippi governor for his past support. Kossuth and his party, which included his wife, Terézia, arrived at Vicksburg on March 22, aboard the steamer *Aleck Scott,* and then traveled by rail to Jackson. An enthusiastic crowd met the Hungarian leader, although members of the state's Democratic press were not impressed with the visit. They disparaged Kossuth for his alleged ties to abolitionists in the North and for his association with "causes fraught with especial dangers for us in the South." They also criticized the governor for agreeing to play host to him.

Foote was unmoved by negative stories in the newspapers and was determined to make Kossuth's visit a success. "In the name of the sovereign people of Mississippi," Foote told Kossuth during a ceremony at the statehouse, "I bid you welcome to our capital, and pray that a bounteous Providence may vouchsafe to you and the sacred cause of which you are advocate." Kossuth reciprocated, paying personal tribute to Foote during a long and somewhat rambling speech. Later that evening, the Mississippi governor hosted a banquet in

Kossuth's honor. The next day, Kossuth and his party returned to Vicksburg, where they boarded a ship bound for New Orleans. Still operating more like an elected official with a mandate than a man without a political party, Foote never seemed concerned that Kossuth was a controversial visitor whose rhetoric about "universal liberty" threatened some in the slaveholding South.[45]

Later in the year, Foote caused a stir when he tried to appoint a U.S. senator to the full term that he had earlier tried to obtain for himself. Once the legislature failed to fill the seat, Foote claimed that it was his right to do so. The problem for the governor was that the seat in question was held by Walker Brooke and would not be officially vacant until March 4, 1853. Foote claimed the right to appoint a successor to Brooke even though there was no official vacancy. Foote chose Union Democrat Benjamin N. Kinyon to fill the seat, but a furor ensued as mainstream Democrats and some Whigs around the state claimed that Foote was overstepping his authority. The governor had the right to fill a sudden vacancy, such as a vacancy created when a senator dies in office and the legislature is not in session, but to most observers, Foote's attempt to appoint someone to a seat not yet vacant was unconstitutional. In Natchez, the *Mississippi Free Trader* told its readers, "A very simple fact settles the unconstitutionality of the present appointment of Mr. Kinyon, namely, that no vacancy has happened. The governor can make no prospective appointment." There was little doubt that Foote's appointment would not survive legal scrutiny, but Kinyon settled the controversy by turning down the position. The governor accepted defeat on the issue and the Senate seat remained vacant.[46]

In November of 1852, tragedy struck Foote's family in the form of a violent altercation between Foote's son-in-law Thomas D. Carneal and another man. Foote's oldest daughter, Jane, had recently married the twenty-nine-year-old Carneal, the son of a wealthy Washington County, Mississippi, planter, and the couple were expecting their first child. On November 8, Carneal was a passenger on the steamer *C. E. Watkins,* traveling on the Mississippi River with several other men, including Peter James, the sixty-five-year-old patriarch of a large family that also owned a plantation in Washington County. James was notorious for treating the slaves on his place very harshly, to the chagrin of some of the other planters in the region. The James plantation was near Greenville, Mississippi, on a stretch of river nicknamed the "Kentucky Bend" because of the large number of native Kentuckians, including James's family, who had settled in the area.

After the steamer docked at his plantation, James offered his fellow passengers a drink, but Carneal refused on the grounds that he would not drink with someone who treated his slaves so badly. James was insulted, and "high words ensued." Carneal eventually slapped James across the face and the old man retaliated by striking Carneal with a cane, causing a bloody gash in his forehead. Carneal then pulled out a knife and stabbed James, who staggered away from the boat dock and made his way to his home. James died there, but not before telling one of his sons what had happened. The son, in turn, grabbed a loaded double-barreled shotgun and went back to the dock, where he found Carneal sitting calmly on a bale of cotton. He leveled the weapon at Carneal and fired both barrels, killing Carneal instantly. As Carneal was the son-in-law of the governor, his death was widely reported in the press, with the *Vicksburg Sentinel* lamenting, "It is a sad affair and Carneal leaves behind, in addition to numerous friends, a most interesting and accomplished widow to bewail his tragic end."[47]

Foote received another controversial visitor in Jackson, toward the end of 1853. English Quaker and staunch abolitionist John Candler had come to America on a speaking tour, preaching against slavery. His tour took him into the Deep South, and in December of 1853 he called on Henry Foote at the state capitol. Foote took the opportunity to try to convert the abolitionist to the proslavery position by lecturing the Quaker on the "positive" aspects of the institution. "The governor is the most determined pro-slave advocate I ever saw," Candler reported in a letter not long afterwards. "He went on fluently and politely, urging the benefits of slavery as an institution; how it gave wealth to the nation, and the happiness to the slave. . . . He spoke of the province he governed as a very Eden to them, and of slavery as the panacea of all social evils." As he defended slavery, Foote apparently tried very hard to charm his guest, with the abolitionist later describing the governor as "a most gentlemanly man." Foote conceded that perhaps Mississippi's slave codes needed updating and that legislation was needed to prevent the separation of husbands from wives, and of young children from their parents, in the slave community. "The Northern abolitionists are men of mischief," Foote told Candler, "who would render the Union asunder." Foote and Candler dined together that evening and Candler left the next day.[48]

While the collapse of his Union Party coalition hampered Foote's effectiveness as governor, he was also distracted during much of his term by his own restless ambition. Desperate to return to the U.S. Senate and unable to manipulate the legislature, he decided to take his case directly to the people and openly campaign for the still vacant Senate seat. Believing in his own powers of persuasion, he was confident that he could sway a majority of the Mississippi electorate over to his side and that they, in turn, would pressure the legislature to send him back to Washington. It was essentially the same strategy that won him the governorship, and he saw no reason why it could not work again.

Foote tried to cobble together another coalition based on loyalty to the Union, but it was difficult. Many Union Democrats had returned to the Democratic Party proper and were in no mood to leave it again, and many Whigs had never fully trusted the governor even though they had supported him against Democratic candidates in the past. There were far fewer active members of the Union Party than there had been when Foote won the governorship, and fewer voters were willing to support what was now being called his "People's Union Party" ticket.

To make matters worse, Foote had painted himself into a corner from a purely political standpoint, and his position was untenable. On the one hand, he did not want to be viewed by Democratic voters as a tool of the Whig Party, but on the other, he needed significant Whig support if he hoped to win. When a few Whig newspapers began promoting the governor for the Senate seat, Foote quickly issued a statement that he was "inflexibly attached to the established principles and policy of the Democratic Party as a national organization" and that the Whig Party might want to nominate someone else. The statement alienated many potential Whig supporters and seemed to indicate that Foote was acting on the delusional premise that, if he could sway enough Democratic voters over to his side, he could reenter the ranks of mainstream Democrats and become their standard-bearer.[49]

Foote officially announced his campaign for the Senate in March of 1853, at Raymond, Mississippi. Using basically the same rhetoric that he had used while running for governor, Foote promoted the Union and recalled in meticulous detail his role in the Compromise of 1850. He courted Democratic voters and tried to mend fences within the Democratic Party—a task that proved impossible. "[Foote] announced himself as a candidate and stated the grounds on which he based his claims to the seat," one Democratic newspaper reported. "He referred particularly to his agency in the passage of the Compromise measures, which he lauded highly. He disclaimed any desire to renew the feuds in the Democratic ranks."

Some of the Whig press rallied around the governor, as did a small minority of Democratic organs still controlled by Union Democrats. In describing Foote and a full slate of pro-Union candidates running for various state offices, Whig editor Jason Niles wrote, in the *Kosciusko Chronicle*, "The candidates are all good men and true. No blot attaches to their names. They are all untainted with secessionism, are all popular well-tried Union men . . . [who] rallied around the Union flag in 1851 and bore it triumphantly aloft." In Marshall County, the *Holly Springs Guard*, a Union newspaper, praised Foote, exaggerating wildly that "the great mass of people are for Foote with immense enthusiasm and no mistake. Politicians are against him, not from political hostility or honest differences of opinion, but from personal malice, revenge and jealousy."[50]

Despite praise from a few newspapers, Foote's campaign was doomed from the start. The Union coalition that had triumphed in 1851 was almost gone. Foote had alienated too many voters, both Democrat and Whig, and the governor's campaign strategy of regurgitating old pro-Union rhetoric related to the Compromise of 1850 excited almost no one. Though Foote constantly denied it, Democrats told their voters as often as possible that Foote was really a Whig and that even most Whigs had grown tired of him.

The leading Democratic candidate for the Senate seat was former governor and current congressman Albert Gallatin Brown. A strong states' rights man, Brown was popular with the electorate and had been a political force in the state for years. Foote challenged Brown to a series of joint discussions of the issues, but Brown refuse to rise to the bait. A joint debate tour like the one Foote wanted would only give Foote more publicity at Brown's expense. Even after Foote threatened to follow him from place to place as he canvassed, Brown continued to ignore the governor. The Democratic press smelled blood in the water and furiously attacked Foote at every level, calling him every name imaginable and condemning his past demagoguery. In Jackson, the *Mississippian* called him an "agitator and untiring political trickster," while in Natchez the *Free Trader* was particularly vicious, comparing Foote's new campaign to a disinterred corpse.[51]

The elections for the state legislature in the fall of 1853 effectively ended the contest for the Senate seat. State Rights Democrats regained control of the Mississippi House of Representatives and retained the Senate, meaning that Foote had no chance of returning to Washington. In an attempt to save face, Foote withdrew from the campaign before the legislature voted, sending out a letter that numerous state newspapers printed and reprinted. "In thus retiring voluntarily from the arena," Foote wrote, "I gladly embrace the opportunity afforded me of declaring to you the cordial gratitude which I feel." He thanked his friends for their "generous and truly patriotic sympathy and support." He then went on to place blame for his defeat, recalling his "unjust" legislative censure and the manner in which he was attacked by mainstream Democrats for his role in the Compromise of 1850. He also blamed his loss, in part, on the new Democratic president Franklin Pierce and on Jefferson Davis, claiming that Pierce was ignorant of "the condition of affairs in our state" and that Davis's appointment in the Pierce administration "discouraged the friends of the Union and inspired our adversaries." The official vote took place on January 7, 1854. Brown won the seat with seventy-six votes, while Foote finished a distant second with twenty. With that vote, the Union cause in Mississippi officially gave up its ghost.[52]

To put it mildly, the loss of the Senate seat represented a negative turning point in the life of Henry Foote. He was finished in Mississippi and he knew it. "My political career is now fast coming to a close among you," he wrote in his concession statement.[53] Foote also became a truly embittered man. By most standards, his political descent was rapid and stark. Within three years he went from being a United States senator immersed in some of the most important national debates in America's history, to head of his own political movement and governor of his state, to a political outcast with a dwindling number of allies and no viable path to political redemption immediately available.

The loss of the Senate seat also seemed to mark the period when Foote's resentment and anger toward Jefferson Davis turned into an obsession. It was well known that the two men were enemies, but Foote let his hatred for the future Confederate president get the better of him. Like a child refusing to take responsibility for his own actions, Foote seemed to blame all of his failures on Davis and Davis alone. In an often petty and infantile manner, Foote would spend the rest of his life publicly criticizing his longtime rival in the press and in speeches, to the point that it damaged his own credibility.

Nowhere were Foote's resentments and insecurities on greater display than during the last days of his administration. Angry and bitter at the result of the legislative elections, he began making plans to leave the state of Mississippi for California. He had a number of political contacts there and believed that he might be able to get a new start in an exciting new state only a few years removed from the Gold Rush. He planned to move there with his family and establish a new political base that would eventually lead him back to the national stage. However, nothing in Henry Foote's personality would allow him to leave Mississippi quietly. He was too high-strung, too angry, and too enamored with the sound of his own voice to pass up the opportunity for one last tirade. Foote resigned the governorship a few days before his two-year term ended, and on January 3, 1854, gave a farewell speech to the legislature. It was a mean, undignified address based in self-aggrandizement and self-pity.

The beginning of the speech was somewhat traditional, with the outgoing governor making suggestions to the legislature regarding the state's future economic well-being, the future of public education, and the need to maintain and expand the state's infrastructure through the building of roads and railways. From there, Foote's tone turned nasty, and he devoted the last three-quarters of the address to pontificating on his own achievements and, in the words of one newspaper, making "some very caustic commentaries upon the political courses of his chief opponents, particularly of Jefferson Davis, the present Secretary of War." In summarizing the event, another editor called Foote's speech "an outpouring of long-pent wrath—an upheaving of bile accumulated during three years of bitter contest."[54]

Rather than retiring gracefully or striking a conciliatory tone that might have helped mend at least a few of the fences that he had destroyed over the previous few years, Foote went on the attack as if he were still campaigning. He defended his position on the compromise and condemned those who were against the settlement as "demagogues and factionalists." He said that he had no respect for the press or, as he put it, the "mercenary scribblers . . . who have been assailing me for years past with the coarsest revilement and the most vile calumnies." He then attacked reporters in general, stating, "I have never attached any particular importance to the efforts of this class of persons to do me injury. I seldom even glance at the absurdities they publish."

Foote's attack on Davis, whom he called "my late secession opponent for Gubernatorial honors," was particularly pointed. He said that Davis was nothing but a schemer whose lone goal was individual advancement, and he accused his fellow Mississippian and compromise opponent of having "unholy designs" on destroying the United States. Foote claimed that he and his followers were patriots and that, despite Davis's appointment to Pierce's cabinet, Davis was no friend to the country. "Let others enjoy, for the present," he said of Davis, "the dignity and emoluments of station, and bask in the sunshine of executive favor under a government which they have plotted to destroy." He called Davis's supporters a "squad of ultra-secession admirers" led by a man of suspect character, and he claimed that Davis should never have entered the 1851 governor's race in the first place. He finished his speech by pledging to continue the fight against "blind and unreasoning fanaticism," declaring once again his loyalty to the Union and the constitutional rights of the South.

The state's Democratic press was quick to condemn the governor's message and gloat over his downfall. In Jackson, Foote's former newspaper, the *Mississippian,* cheered his "expulsion from the office he has disgraced," crowing that the governor's "political prospects have been snuffed out."[55]

Foote's speech was a sad end to his stormy term as governor and a tarnished milestone in his two-decade-long journey through the twists and turns of southern and national politics. It was raw hubris run amok and a completely unnecessary public fit of temper. Had he couched his message in conciliatory terms and perhaps owned up to at least a few of his own past mistakes, he might have survived to fight more political battles in Mississippi. He still had some friends in the legislature, and perhaps over time he could have accumulated more if he had softened his rhetoric. He had many enemies in Mississippi politics, but he was also capable of drawing large numbers of voters to his side, as he had in the governor's race. But conciliatory language and softened rhetoric were foreign concepts to Henry Foote. He was a wonderful and effective speaker, but he routinely took things too far. He did not know when to draw back strategically, and rather than feint to the left or the right when appropriate, he plunged straight ahead at all times, too often employing the rhetorical bludgeon rather than the rapier.

His term as governor could only be considered a failure. He accomplished little in the face of a hostile legislature and a voting public increasingly sensitive to the slavery issue. He proved delusional in his belief that he could once again represent Mississippi in the United States Senate, and he seemed shocked when that dream was crushed. Most of his enemies bade good riddance to the governor once he announced his plans to leave the state, and most believed that his political career was finished. But giving up was also a foreign concept to Henry Foote, and, despite the defeat, he maintained his political energy and ambition. His political career had indeed peaked and was now in decline, but it was far from over.

7

California

I have come among you with no political aspirations to gratify,
no schemes of a merely partisan character to accomplish. . . .
I desire peace and friendship with all.
—Henry S. Foote, 1854

HENRY FOOTE LEFT MISSISSIPPI soon after concluding his final speech to
the state legislature. His resignation became official on January 5, 1854, and
within twenty-four hours he was gone. He did not even stay long enough to attend a small dinner in his honor organized by some of his old Union Democrat
and Whig friends, including William Sharkey. Foote planned to go to California alone and then send for his family after he was settled, and he wasted
no time.[1] He left Jackson and stopped briefly to make a speech to a small pro-
Union crowd in Summerville, South Carolina, then traveled to Washington,
DC. From there he would go to New York and board a steamer bound for
Panama. After crossing the isthmus, he would then board another ship that
would take him to San Francisco. The whole process would take several weeks.

In Washington, an average observer would never have known that Henry
Foote left Mississippi an angry, beaten man. He returned to the nation's capital
as if he were a conquering hero, calling on old friends and being called upon
to make political pronouncements. He checked into the National Hotel, at
Pennsylvania Avenue and Sixth Street—the famous hotel where Henry Clay
died in 1852—and held court, mingling with other Union Democrats, Whigs,
and, in general, anyone who did not favor the Pierce administration. Goaded
by his friends, Foote agreed to make a formal political address at the hotel,
on January 17, 1854. The event drew a friendly crowd of two hundred to three
hundred people, many of whom were old allies from the compromise debates.

For more than an hour, the Mississippian spoke on familiar themes, including "the Compromise measures of '50, National Democracy, the political orthodoxy of the inaugural address of President Pierce, and the glaring inconstancies of the administration." As usual, Foote's most biting remarks came at the expense of Jefferson Davis. The *Alexandria Gazette* reported on Foote's address two days later: "The Secretary of War [Davis] was also assailed most furiously. . . . The speech can be characterized by saying that its principle ingredients were gall and wormwood with a smart sprinkling of cayenne—it was Henry Stuart Foote all over." The newspaper went on to say that the audience "appeared to be delighted with the speech and applauded the orator's sarcastic hits against the President and his cabinet." Beaten or not, Henry Foote proved that he could still put on a show.[2]

Foote left Washington soon after the event and traveled to New York, where he booked passage on the *George Law*, a 280-foot sidewheel steamer owned by the U.S. Mail and Steamship Company. The ship made regular trips between New York and Panama, averaging one every month. He checked into the Saint Nicholas Hotel, a new thousand-room luxury hotel that had recently been built on Broadway. General John Ellis Wool was also a guest there, and he would be joining the former governor on his voyage to California. Ironically, Foote's nemesis, Secretary of War Jefferson Davis, had just appointed Wool to command the Department of the Pacific. Despite the appointment, Wool and Davis had a chilly relationship, which gave the general something in common with Foote that apparently sparked a friendship between the two men.

Never one to remain silent for too long, Foote gave another speech while in New York, this time at the Stuyvesant Institute, a library, museum, and lecture hall built on Broadway in the 1830s. Foote delivered basically the same address he had delivered in Washington. He spoke about the compromise and the unbreakable bonds of the federal union, condemned abolitionists as fanatics, criticized President Pierce, and took his customary shot at "the Secretary of War, not a very popular person, who I easily beat for governor." According to newspaper reports, Foote received "three hearty rounds of applause" and proved once again that he could draw and entertain a good crowd, whether in a small town or in the largest city in America. Before Foote and Wool left for Panama, local officials threw a party in their honor at the Saint Nicholas, where "there were good things to eat and drink and a few good things said." When word of the event reached Davis, he allegedly was angry that New York officials were honoring both his new appointee Wool and Foote at the same gathering.[3]

With Foote, Wool, and seven hundred other passengers on board, the *George Law* finally departed New York on January 20, 1854. While the former Mississippi governor had been well received in the city, he remained a controversial figure, and some were happy to see him go. "Alas that he could save the Union but not save himself," the *New York Tribune* stated sarcastically upon his departure. "We bid an affectionate adieu to the ex-senator until the next time he turns up. He will certainly be along soon with something supple."

The trip from New York to the port city of Aspinwall (now Colón), Panama, took about a week to complete. From there, Foote and others crossed the isthmus, over the course of a few days, by mule and railway, finally reaching Panama City, where they connected with another vessel for the trip to California. Foote boarded the *John L. Stephens,* a two-year-old steamer owned by the Pacific Mail Steamship Company, and left Panama City for San Francisco at ten a.m. on February 1. The ship arrived two weeks later, on the night of February 15. Before departing the vessel, a small contingent of the more well-heeled passengers organized an informal gathering to honor the captain, Robert Pearson, for delivering them safely. Serving as spokesman for the group, Foote presented Pearson with a small gift and a letter praising him as "an energetic and vigilant commander" and "a courteous, high-bred gentleman."[4]

Prior to organizing his trip west, Foote had communicated with a number of California politicians as part of a strategy to cleave to state's Democratic Party, and they were ready to welcome him. California was also the home of William Gwin, one of Foote's oldest political friends, who had come west from Mississippi and found success. Foote and Gwin had a long history that went back twenty years. Both men had been part of Robert Walker's political network in Mississippi during the Jacksonian era, and Foote had been especially close to Gwin's late brother, Samuel. William Gwin relocated to California in 1849, just before statehood, and was able to navigate the political waters there to such an extent that, along with John C. Fremont, he eventually won election as one of the state's first two senators. He served with Foote in the United States Senate and was in favor of the compromise settlement in 1850. Shortly after the former governor's arrival, the San Francisco *Placer Times and Transcript* reported, "We know that Mr. Foote has been an intimate personal friend of Dr. Gwin for a long number of years, perhaps one-third of his life, has served with him in the United States Senate, and brings with him to these shores most recent evidence of their warm attachment."

Gwin was a force in state Democratic politics, and Foote hoped to use the connection to his advantage. Though he would ultimately find it easier said than done, Foote hoped to do in California what he had attempted to do in Texas and what he had done with some success in Mississippi. He would move into a region that was just settling up politically, taking advantage of any growing pains or general chaos that prevailed to bully and bluster his way to prominence and, ultimately, public office. His primary goal was a return to the United States Senate, although he regularly denied this. California was accustomed to welcoming politicians from other parts of the country who were looking for a fresh start, and Foote initially received a warm welcome in San Francisco and good treatment from the press. "This distinguished statesman has come to make his home among us," one newspaper effusively reported. "His brilliant career in the U.S. Senate and his popular course as a prominent citizen of Mississippi, which placed him in the executive chair of that state, have made him known wherever American politics are read, and known too as a statesman and orator of a superior mold and intellect."[5]

In 1854, the Democratic Party in California was mired in chaos and intrigue. With only cursory competition from the Whig Party, the Democrats split into two factions. Senator Gwin led a wing that included many other southerners who had come west to seek or rehabilitate their political fortunes. This group was referred to in the press as the Chivalry branch. Former state senator and lieutenant governor David Broderick led the opposing faction. Like Gwin, Broderick had come to California and established himself shortly before statehood. He came from New York, and his faction included many politicians with northern origins who were averse to the institution of slavery.

Although there were serious difficulties within the party, based in sectionalism and the slavery issue, a major factor in the party's split was a dispute between Gwin and California governor John Bigler. At one point, Bigler went to Gwin to ask for assistance in securing an ambassadorship to Chile. Gwin refused, and a feud commenced that included Bigler appointing Broderick as chairman of the California Democratic Party. From there, Broderick was able to build a coalition that remained a minority in the party but was strong enough to muddy the water with regard to legislation, political appointments, and elections.

Foote had a long association with Gwin, but the former governor could never fit in with the Chivalry Democrats in California. Gwin led a faction of southerners, many of whom opposed the compromise settlement and resented Foote's part in it. Gwin was also close to Jefferson Davis, while the southern wing of California's Democratic Party was for the most part loyal to the Pierce administration. This meant that if Foote wanted to become a player in California Democratic politics, he would have to attach himself to the other side, which was an attractive option to him because Broderick's wing of the party did not like Pierce or Davis.

In the end, his hatred of Davis served as one of the two primary catalysts for Foote's association with Broderick's northerners, the other being the former governor's commitment to the Union. Aware of the testy relationship between the two Mississippians, Broderick saw Foote as a potentially useful ally and immediately began recruiting him. As chairman of the state Democratic Party, Broderick organized a reception for both General Wool and Foote shortly after their arrival. The event was supposed to be nonpolitical, but during testimonials and toasts, many of Broderick's friends criticized the Pierce administration. Even Wool got into the act by toasting the federal union in a manner that was interpreted by some as a slap at both the southerners in the Chivalry and Secretary of War Davis, who was an opponent of the compromise settlement. "I have not been influenced by any sectional feelings," the general said, in relation to his military service. "I have known but one country and that is the United States. . . . It was my attachment to the Union which induced me to offer my life as a sacrifice for my country. I have no attachment that would divert me from a faithful and just discharge of all the obligations due to the whole Union."

When it was Foote's turn to speak, he thanked his hosts for inviting him to the dinner, made a few comments criticizing the national administration, and then told everyone in the room a lie: "I have come among you with no political aspirations to gratify, no schemes of a merely partisan character to accomplish," he said. "I desire peace and friendship with all." Everyone in the room knew that Foote had not come to California just to practice law, and most realized that his public shunning of California politics was actually an announcement that he would one day pursue high office in the state.[6]

Despite his claims to the contrary, Foote planned to align himself with the northerners in the Broderick wing of California's Democratic Party. To the casual observer, this might have seemed odd as Foote was a southerner, a defender of slavery, and had a long-standing relationship with William Gwin. However, he also had a reputation as a staunch unionist whose support of the compromise had made him anathema to many Democrats from his home region. Many southerners in California also supported the Pierce administration and, more importantly, Foote's sworn enemy Jefferson Davis. As a result, Foote planned to use in California a version of the political blueprint that had won him the governor's race in Mississippi back in 1851. His goal was to become a dominant force in a coalition that consisted of Whigs, whose national organization was fading away, disaffected Democrats who distrusted the current national government, and office seekers from both parties who were looking for a home but lacked true political convictions. He envisioned, once again, a commitment to the Union as the glue that would hold the coalition together. "Taken all in all the Wool and Foote dinner was one of the most curious affairs that has come off in a long time," an observant correspondent from the *Alta California,* a San Francisco newspaper, wrote, the day after the event. "It requires a politician to understand it. . . . It may seem a little strange that Governor Foote should attach himself to that segment of the party which got up the dinner. But it is not so strange as it may seem. He was known at home as a Union man in opposition to secessionists. In fact for a long time he followed the profession as a Union saver." As for the Chivalry Democrats, they also understood what Foote was up to, and soon after the banquet, those newspapers in the state loyal to the southern wing of the party began referring to Foote in a derogatory manner as a "bolter" from the Democratic Party.[7]

It would take Foote a while to chart his exact course. In the meantime, he took steps to secure his financial well-being and to establish his new western household. Foote opened a law practice and soon was one of the defense attorneys in two high-profile filibustering cases. In the first, Henry P. Watkins, Henry Clay's nephew and a chief lieutenant of the famous filibusterer William Walker, was accused of conspiring with Walker to carry out military missions to Latin America in violation of U.S. neutrality laws. Foote's former shipmate, General Wool, placed Watkins under arrest and the case went to trial in March of 1854.[8] Watkins's lead attorney was Edmund Randolph, grandson and namesake of George Washington's attorney general and a member of one of Virginia's oldest families.

While Foote won many court cases during his career, he also had a talent for inserting himself into high-profile cases even if the odds of winning were low. There was a great deal of evidence against Watkins, but Foote knew that his name would appear over and over again in California newspapers even if the jury convicted his client. Furthermore, a high-profile case always meant a packed gallery, and Foote could never resist performing before a crowd.

The jury convicted Watkins after only five hours of deliberation, but not before Foote was able to put on a show. "The trial of Col. Watkins was concluded today," Sacramento's *Daily Democratic State Journal* reported. "Gov. Foote spoke four hours and made a most brilliant and powerful effort for the defense." Though convicted, Watkins received little more than a slap on the risk, considering that he had violated a significant federal law. He avoided jail time, and the judge ordered him to pay a $1,500 fine.

Not long afterwards, Foote was involved in the case of Guillaume Patrice Dillon. Dillon was an Irish-born diplomat who served as a French consul in San Francisco. In 1854, he was implicated in a scheme conceived by French adventurer Count Gaston de Raousset-Boulbon to colonize Sonora, Mexico. Raousset-Boulbon planned to recruit French nationals who had come to California during the Gold Rush into a mercenary army that would take Sonora by force and create a republic separate from Mexico. The Mexican consul in San Francisco, Don Luis del Valle, was also implicated in the plot. The authorities arrested Dillon in May of 1854 and released him after he posted a $10,000 bond. Foote defended Dillon during the trial, which resulted in a hung jury, allowing the French consul to go free.[9]

In early June, Foote formed a temporary legal partnership with political overtones with three younger men, William M. Stewart, Lewis Aldrich, and Watkins Leigh. Twenty-six-year-old Stewart had come west during the Gold Rush and was well on his way to becoming a successful mining lawyer. He had political aspirations and would one day represent Nevada in the United States Senate. At thirty-four, Louis Aldrich was an established attorney and district court judge, while Leigh, the youngest of the group, at twenty-three, was a newly minted attorney who had migrated from Virginia to California in 1852. He was from a prominent Virginia family, and his father had been a United States senator during the 1830s. The firm opened an office in San Francisco, on Market Street, in a building formerly used as a Masonic hall. Stewart later recalled in his memoirs that the firm "lasted about a year and did a good business." Indeed, over the next few months Foote and the others were involved in a number of highly publicized trials covered by the California press, and in 1855 the state paid the firm $20,000 in fees related to land claim cases.[10]

As he added to his personal fortune, Foote also worked to bring his family out West. His first order of business was to find a suitable location for a home. Though he practiced his profession in San Francisco, he did not want his wife and children living there, and he looked for a quiet place away from the hustle and bustle of the city. As had been the case in Mississippi, Foote would make sure that his family had a comfortable place to live, but his legal and political travels would keep him away from home much of the time. He chose the small settlement of Clinton—coincidentally, the name of the small village where he once lived in Mississippi—just across the bay and just east of Oakland. Founded in 1852, the town was beginning to attract many of the well-to-do from San Francisco and the surrounding area. One San Francisco newspaper called Clinton "the beautiful town over the bay," reporting that "Clinton is a favorite suburb of San Francisco and has already become the residence of many of our citizens."

Foote wasted no time establishing himself in the community. On July 4, he read the Declaration of Independence during an Independence Day ceremony in the town and mingled with local dignitaries at a "grand ball" later that evening at a local hotel. "A large number of our citizens were ferried across the bay and participated in the celebration of the Fourth [at Clinton]," the San Francisco *Daily Placer Times and Transcript* reported, two days later. "Gov. Foote and others were toasted and replied in patriotic terms. . . . The whole company were delighted with the entertainment of the day and evening, and retired in high gratification."[11]

Foote's wife and children were in California by Christmas of 1854, and they passed the holiday season in their new home. Over the course of the next year, three significant events—two joyful and one tragic—altered the Foote family forever. On May 31, 1855, Foote's daughter Annie married the former governor's law partner William Morris Stewart in a ceremony at the Foote home. It was the beginning of a successful union that lasted until Annie's death, in 1905. Less than two months later, on July 9, tragedy struck, when Foote's wife, Elizabeth, suddenly collapsed and died at age forty-five. Foote left no written testament about how he felt about losing his devoted wife of more than a quarter century, but the effects of her death must have been devastating, particularly since four of the Foote children were still minors. Two months after her mother's death, another Foote daughter, nineteen-year-old Virginia Cecilia, married Foote's other bachelor law partner, Lewis Aldrich, in another ceremony at the Foote home in Clinton.

Foote's two other daughters would also find husbands in California. In 1856, Jane married her second husband, J. West Martin, who later became the mayor of Oakland, and the following year Arabella married Clement F. Wood, a successful rancher and attorney. Foote's three sons, Henry, William, and Romilly, all later married and made their homes in the West as well.

The catalyst for Henry Foote's return to politics, in 1855, was the rise of the American Party, nicknamed the "Know-Nothings," in California. The Know-Nothing movement began in the East as an anti-Catholic, anti-immigrant movement dedicated to curbing the number of foreigners entering the United States. Members of the movement were alarmed at the large number of German and Irish Catholics who had recently entered the country, bringing with them a foreign culture and habits that many Americans did not understand and therefore feared. Hoping to consolidate support and gain national political influence, the Know-Nothings formed the American Party in 1854.

In California, the movement and subsequent political party evolved in a somewhat different manner. Due to the Gold Rush and California's status as a frontier state, California included among its voters many foreign-born citizens whom politicians did not want to alienate. As a result, the Know-Nothing movement in the state did not start as a purely nativist undertaking. It was more of a reform movement and a backlash against what many perceived as serious corruption in state politics and, especially, corruption among those who controlled San Francisco. Rather than shun Catholics, California Know-Nothings had Catholics in their ranks and initially veered away from the anti-Catholic agenda of their national organization. After Know-Nothing candidates dominated the city elections in San Francisco in 1854, the *Alta California* declared that, because of California's large foreign-born population, news of the movement's success "will much astonish the people of the Atlantic states." The newspaper went on to maintain, "We presume, however, that the 'Know Nothing' party owe their success here . . . more to their promise of reform than [to] the peculiar principle which is understood to be the basis of their [national] organization." However, this spirit of tolerance only went so far. As time passed, California Know-Nothings used more and more antiforeigner rhetoric, particularly against the families of Chinese immigrants, and eventually the presence of Catholics within their ranks caused friction.[12]

Foote watched the development of the Know-Nothing movement and judged it to be an opportunity. Still clinging to the Union principles that had helped him win election in Mississippi, and still possessing the ego that drove his need for public acceptance, Foote hoped to parlay the divisions in the California Democratic Party and the rise of the American Party into a ticket back to the United States Senate. Instead of cleaving to the northern wing of the state Democratic apparatus, he would make the American Party his own by assembling former Whigs, anti-administration Democrats, and any disaffected Democrats in general from the warring branches of the party into a new coalition based on an affinity for the federal union. As a result, he broke ranks with the leadership in the Broderick wing of the Democratic Party and charted his own course. He began making allies among the Know-Nothings and, as the movement grew, became more aggressive behind the scenes in support of the group. He was welcomed into the fledgling organization as a significant defector from the Democratic Party. In June of 1855, he acknowledged publicly for the first time that he was a member of the American Party, at a mass meeting held in Sacramento, in front of the Orleans Hotel.

Foote was in a somewhat precarious position as he rose to speak before the crowd, which numbered around 1,500. Aware that many labeled him an opportunist and that he had publicly declared that he was finished with politics, he wanted the assembly to know—or at least believe—that his motives for appearing were pure. As a result, many of his remarks were blatantly self-serving, though his audience did not seem to mind. When it came time for him to speak, the sympathetic *Sacramento Union* reported the next day, "there was no mistaking who the crowd wanted to hear now. Vociferous demands for 'Foote' . . . arose from the center and circumference of the dense multitude. Soon the massive white head peered above the platform, when tumultuous cheering greeted the venerable statesman."

Foote told the crowd that he had no choice but to reenter politics because, as a patriot, he could not sit idly by and watch "the fanatics of the North and the secessionists of the South in their unholy attempts to distract the peace of the country and to endanger the safety of the Republic." He claimed that the country was in imminent danger of splitting apart and that it could only be saved by uniting Whigs and those Democrats opposed to the current administration into a new political alliance "based on a love of the Union and under the flag of the American Party." He blamed men like William Seward and the "corruption and imbecility" of the Pierce regime for all of the country's ills.[13]

As expected, Democratic newspapers around the state began targeting Foote as a party traitor soon after the Mississippian made his appearance at the Know-Nothing gathering. They feigned surprise that Foote would engage in "a travelling crusade against the Democratic Party" and did their best to discredit him. They said that his haggard rhetoric was the result of his "ardent temperament and a misdirected judgment" and was nothing more than a weak and ineffective attempt to create a political future for himself. They disparaged the Know-Nothings in general as "thugs" and accused the national organization, and Foote by association, of being sympathetic to the abolition movement. Point by point, they refuted Foote's arguments that the Union was still in danger, and they belittled him at every opportunity, casting him as a used-up politician whose spotlight had dimmed considerably. "Verily can we exclaim," the editor of the *Daily Placer Times and Transcript* in San Francisco wrote at the time, "with all respect to Governor Foote, 'How the mighty have fallen!'"[14]

Regardless of the attacks, Foote was in full campaign mode during the summer of 1855, stumping for Know-Nothing candidates for the California legislature. Called "the great speaking gun" of his party, the former governor barnstormed from town to town in the way that only he could, day after day, speech after speech. It was a grueling pace reminiscent of his past campaigns in Mississippi. On the campaign trail, he seemed to never run out of energy. In succession during the summer, he appeared in Forest City, Camptonville, Yuba, Sacramento, Nevada, Marysville, Stockton, Auburn, Downieville, Mokelumne Hill, Sonora, and San Jose, debating Democrat and future governor John Weller at many of the stops. Contrary to his approach in other campaigns, Foote usually did not resort to personal attacks on his adversaries during debates, instead concentrating on the issues. This was probably because he did not want to burn too many bridges in a political environment that was still quite fluid. While others in the Know-Nothing movement also did their part, both friends and foes alike recognized Foote as an effective stump speaker, and even some Democratic newspapers paid him grudging tributes as a key party spokesman, once the 1855 election cycle was over.[15]

The state elections were a triumph for the Know-Nothings as the American Party captured the state legislature and saw their candidate, J. Neely Johnson, elected governor. It was also a triumph for Henry Foote in that it seemed to legitimize him in the rough-and-tumble world of California politics. Not long after his election, the new governor traveled to San Francisco for a rally at the Oriental Hotel, and he took Foote with him. Foote rode to the event in the governor's carriage, and following the governor's address, the Mississippian also gave a speech. Incredibly, in a relatively short time Foote had become one of the most high-profile members of California's fledgling American Party, and many began to believe that once the new Know-Nothing legislature went into session, its members would reward him with a seat in the United States Senate. This had been Foote's goal all along, and it looked as if it were about to be realized. And then everything began to unravel.[16]

Foote helped sow the seeds of his political downfall in California toward the end of the year, when he got into a needless quarrel with the editors of the *Sacramento Union,* one of the state's most important Know-Nothing newspapers. Many Know-Nothings in California were idealistic and had joined the movement in hopes of reforming state politics. After the American Party swept to power in 1855, these same people became disillusioned. They watched as party leaders jockeyed for position as the state's new power brokers, and they were particularly disgusted when several prominent members of the party, including Foote, began aggressively pursuing the state's open U.S. Senate seat. The *Union's* editors were disgusted with what they saw, describing the chase for the Senate seat as one of "depravity," the product of "profane, verdant and ridiculous pretensions and aspirations." Furthermore, the newspaper said, those directly involved as candidates were "migratory partisan quacks" rather than statesmen.

When he read this assessment, Foote was outraged. He demanded to know whether the newspaper was referring to him directly, and he claimed that, regardless of what anyone said, he was not a candidate for the position. In an effort to placate Foote at least somewhat, the editors responded that they were writing in generalities and were not referring to the former governor personally. As was his habit, Foote would not let the issue rest, and he continued to press the newspaper until the editors turned on him. The *Union* published another editorial, this time outlining the reasons why Foote should *not* be a United States senator representing California. The newspaper recounted Foote's past quarrels in the Senate, citing specifically his pulling a pistol on Thomas Hart Benton, as evidence that he did not have the personal discipline required to succeed in that body. It also took Foote to task for his personal quarrels with Jefferson Davis, claiming that the long-standing animosity between the two men would make it difficult for Foote to work effectively with the Pierce administration. Finally, the newspaper stated emphatically that Foote had not been in California long enough to represent the state in Washington, and that the seat should only go to someone who was a resident in 1849 or earlier.

While Foote eventually received the American Party nomination for the Senate, his quarrel with the *Union* made his path to the nomination more difficult. It empowered his rivals both inside and outside of the American Party and reminded a significant segment of the California electorate of his political deficiencies. In sum, it was yet another example of Foote's inability to keep his mouth shut at the appropriate moment, and of the ego-driven, sometimes self-destructive aspects of his personality.[17]

Foote traveled to Sacramento and took a room at the Orleans Hotel, the city's largest hotel and the center of state politics whenever California lawmakers were in town. The California legislature met on January 7, 1856, and ten days later the American Party held its first caucus to select a Senate candidate. Foote received the nomination for the Senate, but only after several contentious ballots. Know-Nothings with northern roots were hesitant to trust the former Mississippian because of his proslavery stance. They also knew the story of "Hangman Foote," who had once threatened to string up an abolitionist if he ever came to Mississippi. "The venerable gentleman," the *Weekly San Joaquin Republican* in Stockton, California, wrote of Foote, "in addition to being obnoxious to the Democratic Party, is equally objectionable to a large portion of the party whose principles he espouses." Despite the resistance, the former Mississippi governor mustered enough support to become the Know-Nothing's candidate. Afterwards, he addressed the caucus, pledging that he was no longer a Mississippian but a "true Californian," whose "interests, hopes and family" were tied to the state.

Once word of his nomination got out, Foote faced an onslaught of criticism from Democratic newspapers, which ridiculed his pledges to the federal union by pointing out Foote's former allegiance to John C. Calhoun and other southern fire-eaters. In Sacramento, the *Daily Democratic State Journal* feigned astonishment that "Gov. Foote, who had been a warm supporter of Mr. Calhoun, and classed amongst the most ultra of the secession school, suddenly metamorphorized [sic] into a Union man of the most approved pattern." Foote was nothing more than a cheap opportunist, the opposition press claimed, who had come west to use California rather than represent it, and, by association, the Know-Nothing movement in the state was nothing but a fraud. "Know-Nothingism is now Footeism," one editor clamored, "and nothing else."[18]

Despite opposition from Democrats and even a few members of his own organization, it seemed that Foote would easily become the state's next United States senator. The Know-Nothings controlled the governor's chair and both houses of the legislature and would surely be able to send their nominee to Washington. Many believed that Foote was about to accomplish a miraculous political comeback and that his loud and lively voice would soon be heard again in the halls of Congress.

Unfortunately for the former senator, it was not meant to be. The Democrats outmaneuvered Foote and his Know-Nothing friends on a technicality, muddying the water and making it impossible for anyone to win the seat. In order for the election to take place, both houses of the state legislature would have to vote to meet in joint session. The House, with its sizable Know-Nothing majority, voted to do so, but the vote stalled in the Senate. The Know-Nothings had only a one-vote majority (17 to 16) in the upper house, and the Democrats were determined to find a Know-Nothing who would join them to undermine Foote's candidacy.

They found their man in San Franciscan Wilson G. Flint. Originally from New Hampshire, Flint despised slavery and the southern slaveholding elite, and he did not want a proslavery man representing California in Washington. Encouraged by David Broderick, and true to his convictions, Know-Nothing Flint voted with sixteen Democrats to block the special session and therefore block the election. Despite extraordinary pressure from his Know-Nothing colleagues, Flint held his ground, and the U.S. Senate seat remained vacant for the next year. In that time, the Know-Nothing movement crumbled and Foote lost his chance at the national limelight. "Our readers will rejoice with us over the actions in the Senate," the Democratic *Marysville Express* reported afterwards. "The Democracy have done nobly, gloriously. They have shown themselves worthy of representing California by rescuing her from the foul stain of being misrepresented in the Senate of the United States."[19]

While he would write two more books, including a massive memoir, Henry Foote never disclosed in print how he felt about the defeat, but he likely was stunned and disappointed. The Senate seat had been in reach and had then been pulled away. It must have been a hard pill to swallow. As always, Foote regrouped, and he remained in California for another year, practicing law and hoping in vain that another major political opportunity would present itself. He also remained loyal to the Know-Nothings—at least for a while—and in August of 1856 he spoke at a state rally for the party's presidential nominee, Millard Fillmore. He was well received among the faithful as he "reviewed the life of Fillmore in a masterly manner, and paid him some of the most distinguished compliments, both politically and privately." The following month he gave another speech that was vintage Foote, promoting Fillmore but lambasting the Democratic nominee, James Buchanan, as someone who would continue Pierce's failed policies if elected president. "Gov. Foote arose," one newspaper reported. "He turned his guns on President Pierce and Jeff Davis. He made Buchanan responsible for everything that Pierce ever said or did. . . . The governor concluded by saving the Union two or three times over, and politely took leave of the audience." Foote canvassed relentlessly for Fillmore, and both the friendly and the hostile press reported his every move. In addition to critiquing his tirades against the Democrats, reporters also seemed to take pleasure in reminding the public of Foote's previous feud with Republican presidential candidate John C. Fremont while both men were in the Senate.[20]

In the end, Buchanan carried California and the state's Know-Nothing Party went into a rapid decline. Stung by defeat and not wanting to stay aboard a sinking ship, Foote concentrated on his law practice as he planned his next move. In early 1857, the American Party's national organization contacted him to enlist his aid in rounding up California delegates to the party's national convention, but he refused to help. In what could only be described as an extraordinary political pivot, he published a letter in the state's major newspapers, claiming that the Know-Nothing movement was dead and that he could "see no propriety in attempting to keep up the distinctive organization of that party in California or elsewhere." He went on to praise and offer his "hearty and true support" to the new Democratic administration, stating that "such a cabinet that Buchanan has formed, and such political views as are announced in the inaugural, should command universal confidence."

The letter again confirmed, in the minds of his critics, the claims that Foote was nothing more than a political opportunist and carpetbagger who had come west to improve his personal political fortunes. It was a point that was hard to argue against. Foote had almost returned to the Senate as a result of the Know-

Nothing movement but had quickly abandoned the American Party once he sensed that the party was in trouble. He had also spent considerable time and energy criticizing Buchanan and the Democrats during the presidential canvas, only to offer them effusive praise once they won the election. All this damaged his credibility in his new home. His California maneuverings were simply too transparent, and once he washed his hands of the Know-Nothings, he was effectively finished in the West as a politician. Mirroring his experience during his last years in Mississippi, he was certainly a man without a party in California. The American Party was collapsing, and the chances of either wing of the state Democratic Party accepting him back into the fold were slim. As for the new Republican Party, it was not an option; Foote could never align himself with an antislavery organization.

In July, Foote announced that he was going to Washington, DC, to attend the next session of the United States Supreme Court, giving everyone the impression that his visit to the nation's capital would be temporary. He left in early September, and within six weeks notices began appearing in San Francisco newspapers that the Foote home in Clinton was for sale. It was a clear sign that Henry Foote would not be returning from his trip back East.[21]

8

The Confederate

Mr. Foote is a man of decided talents, but excitable and suspicious,
and his tongue is more ready to wage war than his head.
—New Orleans *Daily Picayune,* April 28, 1865

RETRACING THE ROUTE that brought him to San Francisco, Henry Foote
took a ship to Panama and crossed the isthmus by rail. At Aspinwall, he and
four hundred fifty other passengers boarded the *Star of the West,* a mail steamer
originally built for Cornelius Vanderbilt, and, after brief stops in Havana and
Key West, arrived in New York on Sunday, October 4. As was customary, the
next night, Foote and some of the more prominent passengers threw a small
party for the ship's captain, A. G. Gray, and presented him with a silver goblet
and pitcher in appreciation of the safe voyage.

Foote quickly went to work trying to rebuild his reputation among Democrats, speaking to a small gathering of the party faithful in the city and then
leaving for Washington. Foote later wrote that he stayed in the capital long
enough to hear the latest news about the violence in "Bleeding Kansas" and
then headed south "to offset the fire-eaters." As sectional tensions were again
on the rise, Foote chose to return to Mississippi to gauge the political climate there. He had been away for more than three years, during which time
the compromise settlement had begun to unravel, and emotions related to the
future of the South were again running high. He thought that perhaps his
pro-Union message might again resonate among those who feared rash action.
Despite his recent setbacks, Foote remained loyal to the Union cause and concerned over the course that the nation had taken. "In common with thousands
of others," he later wrote, "I had now become seriously alarmed at the condition of the country. I knew well that a scheme for the destruction of the Union
had been long on foot in the South."

Before reaching Mississippi he gave a pro-Union address in Memphis, where he spoke directly to the Tennessee Know-Nothings in the crowd. According to one report, "Governor Foote advised the disbanding of the American organization, and indicated to his late brethren the expediency of joining hands with the Democratic Party." From there, the former governor traveled to Jackson, for a speech at the Mississippi capitol. He was well received by a small but friendly audience of Whigs and disaffected Democrats. Even with a diminished reputation, Foote still had followers in the state, and his unpredictability on the stump always allowed him to draw spectators who were simply curious to see what he might say or do.[1]

It did not take long for Foote—or even the most casual observer—to determine that he would never be able to rejoin Mississippi's Democratic Party in any relevant capacity. As the 1850s progressed, memories of the 1851 political triumph of his Union Party were a distant memory. In less than a decade, the Democratic Party had laid waste to its competition and, in the process, instilled in much of the electorate a distinct fear that their social and economic institutions were under siege as a result of the abolition movement. While most Mississippians still believed in the Union, many had also come to believe that, to one degree or another, an abolitionist conspiracy drove politics in the northern states. Democratic demagogues did their best to promote these notions, to the extent that they became completely intolerant of any form of dissent. Those who spoke too loudly against Democratic excesses risked being labeled as traitors to their homeland or as proponents of social race mixing, the ultimate southern taboo. Party leaders spoke more and more about secession, while a shrinking number of dissidents within the party tried in vain to sidestep the slavery issue and to paint their secessionist rivals as fanatics. Halting the rising secessionist tide would prove impossible, as anyone professing loyalty to the federal government risked being branded as disloyal to the South.

Henry Foote's pro-Union stance had been an asset for him in the state in 1851, but as the years passed it had become a serious liability. There were also more practical reasons why Foote was not welcome under the Democratic tent. He was still the sworn enemy of Jefferson Davis, the party's chief standard-bearer in the state, and he had alienated himself from other party leaders through his own stubbornness and his past hostile rhetoric. Foote's inability to stay in one place and follow a single course left him vulnerable to attacks from critics who claimed that he was never a "real" southern Democrat in the first place. They pointed to his alliance with northerners during the compromise debates of 1850, his political alliance with Whigs in the Union Party in 1851, and his dalliances with the Know-Nothing movement in California as evidence that he could not be trusted. Others were simply tired of his political shenanigans and theatrics.

Foote seemed rudderless during this period, conflicted about what to do next. Although his chances for reviving his political career in Mississippi were slim, he moved back to Vicksburg and established a law office. He also traveled through Tennessee quite a bit, spending time in Memphis and Nashville, along with Louisville, Kentucky, as he plotted his next course. One newspaper reported the rumor that the former governor planned to move back to Washington, DC, where, "free from the excitement of politics he can quietly attend to his profession in [front of] the Supreme Court." He mounted a very brief congressional campaign for a seat that included the Vicksburg district but withdrew when it became obvious that he had no chance of winning.

On one of his visits to Memphis, Foote met a local physician, Lunsford Pitts Yandell, who, in a letter to a relative, took the time to describe his impressions of the former governor, including comments on Foote's hairpiece and dyed facial hair. The description was brief, but it provides an interesting snapshot of Foote in his midfifties: "Gov. Foote is here. . . . He is a very common looking little man. . . . [He] looks as if he wears a corset and jumps about like a jaybird. He wears an immense black wig and has his whiskers dyed black, but on the back of his neck the short hair is as white as snow and his whiskers close to his face are white. The papers are very hard on him, one paper calls him the 'funny renowned and rejuvenated little renegade from Mississippi, the fallacious, the fantastic, the ineffable Foote.'"[2]

Foote apparently visited Nashville enough to find a new wife there, Rachel Smiley, a widow more than twenty-five years his junior. She had been married to Robert G. Smiley, a Nashville attorney, who died in 1854, and she had two children. She also had a sizeable amount of property in Nashville that had been left to her by her grandfather, a prominent Texas politician. The marriage took place in the Tennessee capital on June 14, 1859. Within a year, the Footes established a permanent household in Nashville and built a house on Rachel's property, which would one day become part of the campus of Vanderbilt University. The household included Foote's three teenage sons, William, Henry, and Romilly, who had come east with him from California, as well as Rachel's six-year-old son, Robert, and eight-year-old daughter, Louise, from her previous marriage. At the time he moved to Nashville, Foote owned four slaves.[3]

Foote's marriage—and perhaps his new wife's significant property holdings in the city—led him to leave Mississippi for good and relocate permanently to Nashville. Some believed that the move was purely political, marking a "resumption of his purpose to try to get into Congress from some place." In New Orleans, the editor of the *Daily Picayune* opined that Foote moved to Tennessee just to reenter politics and "that he should content himself out of public life is scarcely possible." Firing speculation about his motives was the fact that Foote's move fit a pattern that he had followed for decades. If he was not welcome or felt that he could not succeed politically in one place, he would simply move to another. After he burned bridges in one location, he just moved on. It was one of the reasons that he had never achieved long-term success. He was too restless and too volatile, always making more enemies than friends wherever he went, always forgetting that one element of statesmanship is the ability to at least occasionally entertain the opinions of others. Foote had all of the qualities that most good politicians of his era were supposed to have in order to get elected, which is why he was able to have some degree of success in multiple and diverse locations, but his influence was always fleeting. Still, Foote was a well-known man, and many people who had not done so before wanted to hear him speak. As one newspaper put it, he was still "pretty well known everywhere for his prominence in public life and politics." The Nashville capital became the staging ground for his political maneuverings, and he seemed determined to make the most of his new surroundings.[4]

As the presidential election of 1860 drew near, Foote took an active role in promoting the Democratic Party, and specifically the candidacy of Illinois senator Stephen Douglas. In September of 1859, he began canvassing for Douglas with a series of speeches that portrayed the Illinois senator as the last hope for keeping the Union together. Foote lauded Douglas's support of popular sovereignty as "the only constitutional and safe exposition of the subject of slavery" and, as usual, framed most of his arguments in terms of patriotic unionists versus traitorous secessionists. He condemned southern hotheads for threatening the stability of the Union and reminded audiences around the country that he and Douglas had worked together during the compromise debates of 1850.

Apparently, a good many Democrats outside the South were willing to forgive and forget Foote's association with the Know-Nothings. "Whatever Gov.

Foote's past political acts may have been," one correspondent from the *New York Herald* reported at the time, "he is now a devoted friend of the Union, and as such merits all men's support and respect." After an address in Saint Louis, a local correspondent wrote that "the applause bestowed among his many happy hits at secessionists and disunionists of whatever party bordered upon the frantic."[5]

Of course, Foote had his detractors, and they were legion. Many southern Democrats never forgave him for his pro-Union ramblings and his attacks on the Democratic establishment in the region. They continued to disparage him as an opportunist and tried their best to discredit him with the party faithful. Hoping to alienate him from protestants, some newspapers circulated rumors that Foote had taken an oath "to prescribe to the Catholic religion" after his association with the American Party ended. The claim angered Foote, who issued a series of denials in the press. Southern Democrats also charged Foote with being a traitor to the Democratic Party, as a result of his creation of the Mississippi Union Party, in 1851, and his more recent association with the Know-Nothings in California. They charged that the former Mississippi governor had abandoned the party, citing as proof his withering attacks on the Pierce administration. These were charges that Foote had trouble refuting, as he had indeed attacked the Pierce regime at every turn when Pierce occupied the White House.

Since he could not deny the accusations, Foote simply lied. In a long letter published in several southern newspapers, Foote made misleading statements and also took the opportunity to criticize his old enemy Davis. "I supported, and with singular zeal," he wrote, "the administration of Mr. Pierce long after he formed his ill-starred cabinet, and did not abandon him even after he had permitted one of his cabinet ministers (Davis) to utterly to crush out the Union organizations of the South." The letter could not have been further from the truth. Foote was an outspoken critic of Pierce from the outset, and his hatred of the Pierce administration only increased after the president appointed Davis as secretary of war.[6]

Foote's rhetoric in support of Douglas became even more pointed during the summer of 1860, after the presidential contest was set. By that time, the national Democratic Party was bitterly split into two factions. Northern Democrats nominated Douglas for president, while southerners advanced their own candidate, John C. Breckinridge of Kentucky. Southern Whigs and Know-

Nothings, along with a few dissatisfied Democrats, came together to form the Constitutional Union Party, nominating John Bell of Tennessee as an anti-secession candidate. At their convention, the Republicans nominated Abraham Lincoln of Illinois on a platform that included stopping the expansion of slavery into the West.

Though the Constitutional Union Party, with its dedication to keeping the country whole, was an ideological descendant of the Union movement that Foote had helped lead in the South in 1850–1851, he did not support the party in 1860. Foote hoped to once again become a player among national Democrats, and to cleave to a third party, regardless of its principles, would not accomplish that object. He argued that the best chance to preserve the Union lay with Douglas, an imposing national figure who was adept at brokering compromise. Still, Foote was sympathetic to Bell and his friends and on a number of occasions during the campaign commented that if Douglas lost and Bell won, the country would still be in safe hands.[7]

In his speeches and letters to various newspapers, Foote claimed that the Democratic Party was the only true "national" party and therefore Douglas was the only candidate who could bring the country together and save it from abolitionist extremism in the North and radical disunionists in the South. He referred to Douglas supporters as "Union-loving, traitor-hating patriots" and painted Breckinridge as a dangerous secessionist. He also tried to convince southerners that every vote for Breckinridge was a vote against the national Democratic Party and, in essence, a vote for Lincoln and the "Black Republicans," who were dedicated to ending slavery and the southern way of life as they knew it.

At a Douglas rally in Nashville, on July 7, 1860, Foote gave a lengthy address that summed up his position. He called the Breckinridge nomination a "rank secession scheme" and went on to speak directly to Breckinridge's Democratic supporters in Tennessee. "Because the Douglas and [vice presidential nominee Herschel] Johnson ticket constitutes the only available Democratic ticket now in the field, to abandon them is to abandon all hope of Democratic success in the present presidential contest; to withdraw votes from them is to strengthen Lincoln and increase the probability of his election, with all the dire consequences." It was the same pro-Union message that he had been advancing for a decade. Foote claimed that secession was inevitable if either Breckinridge or Lincoln won the election and that only a calm, reasonable course could stave off disaster. Major newspapers in Tennessee and elsewhere reprinted Foote's remarks, garnering him a good deal of attention from unionists in the Nashville area and beyond. "Gov. Foote made an able and eloquent speech for the candidates," one newspaper reported. "He reviewed the history of the Democratic Party, proved Douglas and Johnson to be the Democratic nominees, and denounced the secession ticket as sectional and irregular."[8]

In the weeks leading up to the election, Foote traveled a great deal, stumping for Douglas. In addition to canvassing Tennessee, he went to New York to meet with Democratic leaders and gave "a long and able address before a large audience" at a major Democratic gathering in Saratoga Springs. During the months of August and September, he participated in a series of joint appearances in Virginia with that state's longtime senator James M. Mason, who spoke for Breckinridge. In a three-hour speech at Staunton, Virginia, Foote harangued the Democratic leaders in the South who were in the Breckinridge camp. "He reviewed the acts, canvassed the schemes, discussed the purposes, weighed the arguments and analyzed the motives of those who were the chief managers in securing the nomination of Breckinridge," one sympathetic newspaper, the *Staunton Spectator*, stated after the event, "and drew as with a pencil of light, a picture of their dark and treasonable designs to destroy the palladium of our liberties." Returning to the Deep South, he gave a notable speech in Memphis and even canvassed briefly in Mississippi, a Breckinridge stronghold, on behalf of the national Democrats. True to his nature, Foote courted controversy and generated rumors and gossip wherever he went. At one point, a false story circulated in print that he was set to fight yet another duel, this time with his sworn enemy Jefferson Davis; in Tennessee, another false tale had Foote taking a controlling interest in the influential *Nashville Banner*.[9]

The election of Abraham Lincoln as president of the United States, in November of 1860, dramatically changed Foote's outlook on politics. He had spent the previous dozen years as one of America's most vocal unionists and had been part of the compromise debates of 1850 that ultimately kept the Union together and postponed the Civil War for a decade. He won the governorship of Mississippi in 1851 on a pro-Union platform, after much of Mississippi's political community had turned against him. He had promoted the Union during his stay in California and had done the same upon his return to Mississippi and Tennessee. But after the election of Lincoln, Henry Foote abandoned the principles he had fought for over the years and became a secessionist.

The move was one of political expedience, brought on by the fact that he believed that the Republican victory had decided the issue. Just a few weeks after Lincoln's election, South Carolina voted in convention to leave the Union, and throughout the month of January 1861, several other southern states, including Mississippi, followed suit. It was only a matter of time until Tennessee joined them and, like other ambitious unionists from around the South, Foote did not want to be viewed as anything other than a patriot when that time came. He knew and admired other southern unionists, such as Jeremiah Clemens of Alabama and Alexander Stephens of Georgia, who had already accepted the idea of secession, and he followed their lead.

Years later, Foote claimed in his memoirs that he abandoned his unionist principles not as a result of Lincoln's election alone but only after the military action at Fort Sumter, in April of 1861, and Lincoln's subsequent call for volunteer troops in the North. This was no doubt a literary ploy to revise his own history and make it look as though overwhelming, naked aggression on the part of the federal government had forced him into the decision. In truth, by the end of January 1861—well before the Confederates fired on Fort Sumter— Foote was preaching secession, in a move that yet again confirmed, in the minds of his critics, that the foundation of his political character was opportunism. At the time Foote became a secessionist, Tennessee had not yet voted to secede, and there were still many in the state who believed that secession was dangerous. He could have remained a pro-Union voice and been their champion, but he chose not to do so. After hearing that Foote had abandoned the Union cause, the *New York Daily Tribune*, a northern paper that had praised him in the past, gave a blunt assessment of the former senator, calling him "the greatest gas-bag in the South."[10]

Regardless of his motives, Foote dove headlong into Tennessee politics following the election of Lincoln. He was among a group of prominent citizens who called on Governor Isham Harris to organize a state convention to determine Tennessee's response to the Republican victory. At first, Foote counseled caution, although he believed that secession was probably unavoidable. "A Republican president, to be sure, has been elected," he pointed out to a friend at the time, "but there will be such a majority against him in both houses of Congress that he will be utterly powerless for mischief, however inclined he may be to commit aggressions upon our slaveholding rights." A month after the election, Foote still claimed that the secessionists in the Deep South were moving too quickly and that "secession, in any form that it might be proposed, will give us no relief from our present grievances." He predicted—correctly, as it turned out—that "wars of a most bloody and wasting character would be unavoidable" should the Union break apart.

Nonetheless, toward the end of January 1861, Foote completely changed course. Sensing the inevitable, he abruptly abandoned the Union principles that had defined his career for so long and leaped with gusto onto the secessionist bandwagon. Rather than decrying the dangers of disunion, he began giving fiery speeches on the evils of abolition and the threat that the Republicans posed to the South. Using inflammatory, racially charged rhetoric, he addressed a large meeting at the Tennessee state capitol on January 20, telling those assembled that Lincoln and his cohorts "are intensely radical and dangerous, and in favor of forcing the political and social equality of the negroes with the whites." Foote now claimed that the abolitionists had forever shattered the Union and that southern rights could only be maintained through the establishment of a separate republic. Trying to have it both ways, he stated that, while he was opposed to the "abstract right of secession," he was a staunch supporter of southern rights and "the right of revolution through the intervention and machinery of state government." Thrilled that the former unionist whose rhetorical abilities were legendary was now on board, secessionists in Nashville promoted Foote as one of their new champions. Glad to be wanted again, and sensing the chance for a political resurrection, Foote accepted the role.[11]

In early February, representatives from the seven states that had voted to secede from the Union up to that point—South Carolina, Mississippi, Florida, Alabama, Georgia, Louisiana, and Texas—met in Montgomery, Alabama, to form the southern Confederacy. In Tennessee, secession was a gradual process, as many residents were initially reluctant to take such the dramatic step. In general, the issue of whether Tennessee would leave the Union split the state into three geographical divisions. West Tennessee favored secession while East Tennessee was filled with adamant unionists. There were mixed sentiments in the central third of the state, where Foote lived. Governor Harris and the state legislature called for a public referendum on the secession question, and on February 9, 1861, Tennessee's citizens voted to remain in the Union, by a vote of 69,675 to 57,798.

The results were a setback for Governor Harris, who favored secession, and for men like Foote who also carried the secessionist torch. For the next two months, the former Mississippi governor and his friends continued to agitate during public appearances and through the newspapers. They disparaged the "Union shriekers" as "cowards and submissionists," traitors who were bent on capitulating to northern tyranny. The unionists, in turn, called the secessionists reckless demagogues who were intent on destroying the country to promote their own nefarious political agendas.

The issue of Tennessee leaving the Union was effectively settled the following April, when Fort Sumter, in South Carolina, surrendered to the Confederacy. The fall of the fort prompted President Lincoln to call for seventy-five thousand volunteer troops to meet the southern threat, after which Tennessee took action. Almost overnight, a groundswell of support for secession developed in the state, which included many who had previously condemned such action and pledged their wholehearted support to the Union. "The president's extraordinary proclamation [has] unleashed a tornado of excitement that seems likely to sweep us all away," Tennessee congressman and staunch unionist Horace Maynard wrote. "Men who had heretofore been cool, firm and Union loving have become wild." Fellow Tennessean Gideon Pillow, who, like Foote, had supported Douglas for president, wrote to Confederate secretary of war LeRoy Pope Walker, "The action of the tyrant Lincoln and the cry of war have stifled the Union shriekers, and we are now ready and anxious to place Tennessee under the protective aegis of the Confederate Constitution."[12]

Understanding the shift in public opinion, Isham Harris pushed again for secession, and on May 6 the state legislature passed the "Declaration of Independence and Ordinance Dissolving the Federal Relations Between the State of Tennessee and the United States of America." In addition to claiming independence for Tennessee, the declaration also provided for another referendum as a way to officially validate the state's exit from the Union. The new vote was scheduled for the next month, and representatives from the secession and Union camps once again began canvasing Tennessee in hopes that their viewpoints would prevail. Now one of Tennessee's more high-profile secessionists, Foote gave speech after speech urging his audiences to vote to uphold the legislature's actions.

In the subsequent election, held on June 8, approximately 105,000 Tennesseans voted in favor of secession, with only 47,000 voting against. The most dramatic swing in public opinion took place in previously divided Middle Tennessee, Foote's new stomping grounds, where secession won out by a wide margin. "We have thrown off the old government and taken shelter in another," the pro-secession *Daily Nashville Patriot* trumpeted to its readers, two days after the vote. "Let all conform to the new order of things, and stand together in opposition to a common enemy."[13]

Secession triumphed in Tennessee and the state joined the Confederacy, creating for Henry Foote one final opportunity to hold elected office. Foote's canvas promoting secession during the summer of 1861 had been very successful, and in a relatively short time it had established the former Mississippi governor as a political player in his newly adopted state. Hoping to strike while the iron was hot, Foote announced that he would be a candidate for the Confederate Congress, representing Tennessee's Fifth District, which included Nashville. Audiences were still drawn to him, and the sheer force of his personality on the stump remained strong. He still had the ability to draw a crowd and, as always, he believed that he could still talk anyone into anything. "The Hon. Henry S. Foote has, for a quarter century past, enjoyed a national reputation," one sympathetic newspaper told its readers, after Foote announced his candidacy. "Very few men of his day have filled a larger space in the public eye, or acquired a wider and more extended influence. He is one of the most remarkable men this country has produced."

Two other candidates entered the race. One was Nathan Green, a former state supreme court judge and law professor at Cumberland University, while the other was thirty-nine-year-old Robert Emmett Thompson, a lawyer and former member of the Tennessee House of Representatives. Of Foote's two opponents, Green was the more formidable candidate, but at age sixty-eight he was well past his prime. Foote later described him as "amiable and of a patriarchal character" and claimed that he "never heard the old judge utter a harsh word during the campaign." Compared to Foote's past races, the contest for the congressional seat was calm with regard to personal attacks. Rather than turning their wrath on one another, the candidates turned it on the United States government and Abraham Lincoln.

Although he was as fiery as ever when discussing "the success of the Confederate states in the momentous struggle now waging for independence and freedom," Foote was more subdued toward his rivals, perhaps because he knew that he was going to win. Regardless of his faults, few men could match Foote's stamina on the campaign trail as he moved from town to town giving speeches. His cause was likely aided by the general chaos of the times. While many voices struggled to be heard during the period, his was undoubtedly one of the loudest, and his talent for capturing attention, for better or for worse, served him well once again. In the end, his opponents were simply overmatched, and the Tennessee transplant won by a comfortable margin.[14]

Henry Foote's service to Tennessee in the Confederate Congress was at best erratic. At worst, it was evidence that he was coming unhinged. During his time in the body, the negative traits of his character rose to the surface for all to see. He was overbearing and aggressive at times when he should have been more reserved, and his conduct seemed almost completely driven by his hatred for Jefferson Davis. Foote's hostility toward Davis was well known, and some believed that the Tennessean's run for Congress was little more than a ploy to put him in position to continue his feud with the Confederate president. Entering Congress, Foote was an instant critic of Davis, and his verbal broadsides against the Davis administration became more frequent and bitter as time wore on. Foote even admitted, after the war, that "not a day passed while I occupied a seat in the Confederate Congress that was not more or less signalized by my vehement opposition to Mr. Davis."

As a Confederate congressman, Foote was a fish out of water, and it hampered his abilities to affect policy. Throughout his political life he was known for his devotion to the Union, and his dedication to keeping the Union whole had been unwavering. It was the issue that defined him. But as the secession movement picked up steam in Tennessee, he abandoned the Union cause. He became a disunionist and took advantage of the chaotic times to run for and win a congressional race. Once elected, however, he had no political foundation on which to build. He was no longer a Union man but had no history as a true secessionist. All he had was his voice and his pen, and he would overuse them both as the Civil War progressed.[15]

Congressman Foote was not the only member of his family to support the Confederate effort. His three sons enlisted in the Confederate army at the war's outset. Twenty-one-year-old Henry Stuart Foote Jr. initially joined a volunteer company, the "Sons of Erin," in Nashville, and then received a commission in the Confederate army as a second lieutenant.[16] Because of his political contacts, he was assigned to the staff of Major General John Porter McCown, a Tennessee native, and later served on the staff of Lieutenant General Simon Bolivar Buckner. Eighteen-year-old Romilly E. Foote joined a Tennessee artillery unit and later achieved the rank of major, serving on the staff of

General Bushrod Johnson. He was captured not long before the war's end and was paroled in Virginia. Henry Foote's youngest son, William, was only fifteen years old when he volunteered for a Tennessee infantry unit in December of 1861. Captured twice—once at Fort Donelson in Tennessee and a second time after being wounded at the Battle of Raymond, Mississippi—he was paroled on both occasions and served for the war's duration.[17]

Henry Foote was one of the most vocal members of the Confederate Congress, which was not a surprise to those who knew him. From the outset, he went on the offensive as a critic of the Davis administration, blaming Davis and his cabinet for every Confederate misstep. By late February of 1862, the southerners had already experienced significant setbacks in the western theater, most notably a defeat at the Battle of Mill Springs, Kentucky, and the loss of Fort Henry on the Tennessee River and Fort Donelson on the Cumberland. As a result, the Confederates were forced to abandon Kentucky and much of Tennessee, and on February 25 Nashville became the first Confederate capital to fall into Union hands. At the same time, the Federals were also making inroads on the North Carolina coast. They captured Roanoke Island on February 8 and were in the process of establishing a freedmen's colony there.

Foote was appalled by these developments, in addition to feeling the full force of the war on a personal level. His son William was captured at Fort Donelson, and Nashville, the Foote's adopted home, was now under Union occupation. He blamed Davis for all these things and lashed out at the Davis administration and its war strategy. On the House floor, he demanded a congressional inquiry "into the causes of the recent disasters which have befallen the armies of the Confederate states in the states of North Carolina, Kentucky and Tennessee," and with equal fervor he argued that the Confederacy's "defensive strategy" should be abandoned and that the government should "impart all possible activity to our military forces everywhere, and to assail the forces of the enemy wherever they are to be found." When Foote said "the government," he actually meant Davis, and the inference was that Davis was responsible for the Confederate defeats because he had somehow held the Confederate military back, not allowing them to operate freely to repel the Yankee hordes.[18]

Foote was relentless. He demanded that the secretary of war, Davis confidant Judah P. Benjamin, forward to the House detailed reports on "the present condition of our armies in the field" and "the state of our defenses on the seaboard, along our rivers, and elsewhere." He was appointed chair of a committee established to investigate the losses of Fort Henry, Fort Donelson, and Nashville. Rather than undertaking a balanced inquiry, he used his position to try to discredit Davis and Benjamin, with questions focusing more on the conduct of the Confederate president and the War Department than on the activities of the military officers directly involved: Did the War Department withhold reinforcements or fail to deploy reinforcements properly? Did the "defensive strategy" conceived and carried out by the War Department restrict the free movement of Confederate troops and therefore contribute to the "calamities" in Kentucky and Tennessee? At Nashville, did commanding general Albert Sidney Johnston "proceed upon his own discretion or under instructions from the War Department in regard to surrendering the city into the hands of the enemy?" Under pressure from Foote, Benjamin was forced to defend himself, and by association defend Davis, stating repeatedly that Confederate commanders in the field were "never at any time restrained by instructions from the War Department."[19]

In addition to questioning Benjamin's wartime judgment, Foote lambasted the secretary of war during several inflammatory anti-Semitic rants on the floor of the Confederate Congress. Benjamin—the Confederacy's most prominent Jewish official—was the target of anti-Semitism throughout his tenure in the Confederate cabinet, but because of the secretary's close personal ties with Davis, Foote was quick to pounce and was exceedingly vicious. The criticism became even more pointed after Benjamin became secretary of state. Playing on fears generated by the instability of the Confederate economy, Foote placed the blame for the South's financial woes on the Jews, suggesting that some type of financial conspiracy was taking place and that Benjamin was part of it. A "swarm of Jews," Foote said, had entered the Confederacy through "mysterious means" and were now "scattered all over the country, under official protection, engaged in trade to the exclusion of our citizens." These Jewish interlopers, he went on to state, were "permitted in many cases to conduct illicit traffic with the enemy without much official examination into this part of their transaction." "Official protection" and "official examination" were thinly veiled references to Benjamin, as if the secretary were the leader of some type of nefarious Jewish cartel.

While Foote was certainly not the only anti-Semite in the Confederate government, he was one of the most vocal when it came to attacking the secretary. He hoped to play on prejudices within the Confederate citizenry to discredit Benjamin and, through association, Davis. Foote routinely referred to the secretary as "Judas Iscariot Benjamin" and the "Jewish puppeteer" behind the "Davis tyranny," and more than once identified him as "the sole cause of the calamities which have befallen the country." At one point, Foote went as far as proposing that the Confederate constitution should be amended to specify that no Jews should be allowed within twelve miles of the national capital. Even after the war's end, Foote continued to write about Benjamin's "fiendish character" and "heartless schemes of mischief," alleging that during his time in the Davis cabinet, Benjamin committed "more barefaced acts of corruption and profligacy than any single individual has ever been known to commit in the same space and time in any part of Christendom."[20]

Attacks on Benjamin and Davis occupied only part of Foote's time in Congress. As was his way, Foote spoke up constantly, proposed legislation (most of which failed to pass), and pontificated on various subjects. At times he seemed to forget that he had once been one of the South's most prominent unionists and that he had fought secession with vigor for most of the past decade. Where he had once promoted cooperation between the North and the South and had denounced secessionists for promoting self-serving, shadowy agendas, Foote now turned to standard Confederate rhetoric in his speeches and resolutions. A year into the struggle, much of his language echoed that of the men who had led the southern states out of the Union back in early 1861. "This unholy and sanguinary war," he wrote in March of 1862, "owes its accursed origin alone to Yankee cupidity and a semi-barbarous and insatiable lust for political domination." In contrast, he claimed, the Confederate states were peace-loving and asking for nothing from the North other than "to be let alone and to be permitted to enjoy in peace the invaluable right of self-government."

This language and interpretation of events went against everything that Foote had argued for, leading up to the war. Whereas he had once hailed the Union as sacred and perpetual, he now condemned it as "a source of continued injustice and oppression." While many southern unionists embraced the Confederate cause with a fervor as a matter of political expedience, once their states seceded, the change in Foote's behavior was particularly dramatic. His attachment to the Union cause had once seemed unbreakable, and he seemed to have a single-minded determination to cling to his agenda, no matter what the cost. Now he condemned the Union with the same ferocity that he had once defended it. The situation provided further proof that, by abandoning the

Union cause, the Tennessee congressman had broken the single tether that kept him politically grounded.[21]

Foote's other pronouncements while in the Confederate Congress usually involved either more gibing at Davis and his administration or transparent attempts to curry favor with the masses through overzealous praise of the Confederate cause. In both cases, it was clear that he still loved to hear himself speak. "Our soldiers are far superior to those of the enemy in courage, in energy, and in patient endurance of suffering and hardship," he stated with great pomposity, during one long-winded rant, "altogether superior to their selfish and mercenary foes." With a populist flair, he introduced legislation that was never destined to pass, requiring Confederate senators and congressmen to serve in the military whenever Congress was not in session. He was forever requesting reports from the president related to war strategy and never missed an opportunity to insinuate that Davis and his advisers were incompetent. At one point, he advanced a hollow resolution that the war "should be hereafter prosecuted with all proper vigor and enterprise" and that after driving federal forces out of the South, the Confederates should "carry the war to the enemy's country with a view of obtaining full indemnity for the past and security for the future." On the surface the resolution seemed like bravado, but the inference was that the Davis administration was not aggressively pursuing victory. Early on, Foote tried to get himself elected Speaker of the House, but he withdrew his name from consideration after it became apparent that he had little support.[22]

On another occasion, Foote promoted legislation condemning the Confederate secretary of the navy, Stephen Mallory. Mallory had previously served with Foote in the United States Senate, representing Florida, and like Foote he had resisted secession during the early 1850s. This mattered little; he was now part of the Davis administration, which made him fair game. To Foote, criticizing Mallory was tantamount to criticizing Davis, and Mallory was vulnerable as investigations into the fall of New Orleans were already under way in Congress. Foote was highly critical of Mallory and offered a resolution declaring that "S. R. Mallory, as Secretary of the Navy, does not possess the confidence of Congress or the country."

Mallory survived the scrutiny and served the Confederacy until the surrender. However, Foote's crusade against him angered Mallory's many supporters, including Confederate officer and engineer John Mercer Brooks. In his diary, Brooks called Foote "puffed up" and "ignorant of all that pertains to nobility of character" and went on to state that if Foote were to ever die, "the country would lose a slanderer and conceited ass." It was a sentiment shared by a growing number of people in Confederate circles who had dealings with the Tennessee congressman. "Foote never did know how to behave himself, and is of little benefit to the Confederacy" one newspaper correspondent from North Carolina wrote in 1863. "The Hon. H. S. Foote is a great bag of gas."[23]

Foote also seemed to rejoice in promoting the idea that there was rampant corruption within the ranks of the Confederate quartermaster corps. The quartermaster corps was often criticized on the floor of Congress and in the southern press. The criticism ranged widely, from reports of actual corruption to simple frustration related to a lack of supplies within the Confederacy. Regardless of the situation, quartermasters always made good targets for a congressman who craved seeing his name in the newspapers, and Henry Foote understood this. In August of 1862, he moved for the formation of a special committee to "investigate thoroughly the present condition of the departments of the Quartermaster-General and the Commissary-General, with the power to examine all accounts within those departments."

On the surface, the creation of such a committee seemed to be a logical check on individuals who dealt with government funds and supplies, but Foote also knew that if he could gain access to department files, he could pick them apart with a fine-tooth comb and potentially embarrass the Davis government with every discrepancy. The following year, Foote helped to launch a high-profile investigation of quartermaster D. H. Wood, a Virginian in charge of troop transport in the Richmond area. "Pass your eyes around and you will see these quartermasters and commissaries living in palatial wealth," Foote huffed with great hyperbole, "with their fine houses, driving fine horses, [and] dressing in the finest style." Foote lambasted Wood—insulting him in much the same manner that he publicly insulted his political opponents all of his life—describing the quartermaster as "formerly a horse trader . . . so poor that he could not get credit for a beefsteak," who had used his position in the government to accumulate "an immense fortune." The congressman eventually suggested that, because of corruption in the city and "a spirit of extortion manifested here which I hope to never encounter elsewhere," the Confederate capital should be moved out of Richmond.[24]

Foote's tirades were not limited to the civilian government. He was also quick to criticize Confederate military leaders, particularly those who had close relationships with Jefferson Davis. Conversely, he was always quick to praise those who did not get along with the Confederate president. Braxton Bragg made a perfect target for Foote's rhetorical barbs. Bragg's controversial military decisions and quarrels with subordinates had decimated morale in the Army of Tennessee's office corps during 1863, but despite receiving many complaints, Davis was hesitant to remove the general from command. Foote quickly joined the legion of Bragg critics in Congress who were calling for his head, stating that he had "never regarded him as capable of commanding a large army in the field." Foote went further, in a letter published in a Richmond newspaper in August of 1863, demanding that Davis replace Bragg because "no sane man can, with the history of [Bragg's] operations in Tennessee before him, for a moment believe him competent to command a large army."[25] Davis eventually replaced Bragg and brought him to the Confederate capital to serve as a military adviser.

Another target of Foote's wrath was Major General Thomas C. Hindman Jr., who in 1862 was appointed commander of the Trans-Mississippi District and charged with keeping federal troops out of Arkansas. In the discharge of these duties, he declared martial law in the state, a move that concerned many Confederate officials. Born in Knoxville, Tennessee, Hindman was a Mexican War veteran who moved to Mississippi and served in the state legislature during the 1850s before finally relocating to Arkansas. Foote knew the general well. During the 1851 Mississippi gubernatorial contest, Hindman had supported Davis and had been one of Foote's harshest critics. Still bitter, years later, Foote called Hindman "a most noisy and unscrupulous advocate of Jefferson Davis" and bragged in his memoirs that "I exposed all the enormity of this fiend in human form in open session of the Confederate Congress on more than one occasion."

Foote railed against Hindman and introduced a resolution that the House judiciary committee take action to "prevent abuses on the part of those entrusted by the president with the enforcement of martial law" and to determine what legal punishments "should be provided for so serious a violation of the rights of our citizens." As was the case with others whom the Tennessee congressman criticized, Hindman had his supporters, some of whom were sympathetic to the general primarily because it was Foote making the attack. In the *Arkansas Gazette,* owner C. C. Danley, who served with Hindman during the Mexican War, wrote that Foote's attacks were the "veriest humbuggery that was ever attempted" and that the general's critics were "fools, grumblers and enemies of the country."[26]

Foote attacked others whom he perceived as Davis allies, such as Christopher Memminger, the Confederate secretary of the treasury, and General Earl Van Dorn, who at one point declared martial law in Vicksburg. Beginning in late 1863, however, he began more pointed verbal assaults on the president himself. In a speech related to expanding Confederate conscription laws, Foote attacked Davis for abandoning states' rights principles, suggesting that the president wanted take dictatorial control over the army to promote "a huge and overwhelming military despotism." He criticized Davis's "unreasonable partialities and prejudices" and said that the president had a "dangerous capacity for mischief." He denounced Davis as "the author of all the [South's] calamities" and charged him with "exerting a malignant influence wherever he has visited the troops."

Other Confederate congressmen certainly disparaged Davis and complained about some of his decisions, but few were as long-winded as Foote. Open sighs greeted Foote every time he stood up in the chamber to speak, and, to make matters worse, reports of Foote's tirades against Davis were filtering into the North, giving the impression that the Confederate government was in disarray. "Northern newspapers are delighted with Mr. Foote's denunciation of President Davis, the heads of departments, sub-officials, etc.," one North Carolina editor opined, "and on their faith in his oratorical displays, profess to regard the Confederate cause as desperately bad. . . . Thus have we been made to suffer the indiscretion, the vanity and wickedness of our own people."

Foote also claimed that inefficiency and corruption within the Confederate government had led to supply shortages and that many Union troops were starving in Confederate prison camps as a result. These charges also made their way north, enraging thousands of citizens. At one point, Foote's wife was indirectly drawn into the feud between her husband and the Confederate president. Some of her correspondence was intercepted and ended up being printed in northern newspapers. In one letter, Mrs. Foote wrote of Davis's wife, Varina, "[She is] not pretty, but a fine-looking woman.—dresses badly, in no taste. She is not much liked here, and is said to control 'Jeffie' as she calls her husband. She has several children. She takes little notice of them, they go about with their clothes tossed on in any way and every style."[27]

In addition to his political comings and goings, evidence suggests that

Foote may have been involved in a gold, silver, and currency speculation scheme that could have compromised him as a southern official, even though it probably never made him any money. The story began with Gazaway Bugg Lamar, member of the wealthy and influential Lamar family, which included his cousins Mirabeau Lamar, the former Texas president, and prominent Mississippi politician L. Q. C. Lamar. In 1863, Gazaway Lamar organized the Importing and Exporting Company of Georgia and outfitted several ships to run the northern blockade of southern ports. Using contacts that he had in London, Paris, and New York, he hoped to make significant profits through cotton speculation. Assuming that cotton prices would grow increasingly higher as the war progressed, he started purchasing and hoarding large supplies of the commodity in hopes of selling it overseas as demand increased. Although he pledged to import "nothing but useful articles—and to take government freights when desired inward," Lamar was willing to trade in anything that would make a dollar. Among his business partners were Columbus, Georgia, businessman L. G. Bowers and William H. Guion, owner of a New York shipping firm. During the summer of 1863, Lamar sent his son, Charles Augustus "Charlie" Lamar, to Europe to act as an agent for his company, and it was the younger Lamar with whom Foote dealt.

Charlie Lamar had the confidence of a man who had never had to worry about money, and he liked to come and go as he pleased, without considering the long-term consequences of his actions. He had become somewhat infamous before the war by illegally importing slaves from Africa in direct violation of laws that restricted international slave trading. Charlie Lamar had many grand financial schemes, but in the end most never reached fruition. He was a popular member of Savannah, Georgia's, social elite, but he was also a loose cannon, and his judgment as a businessman was questionable. While the evidence is sketchy, Lamar apparently hoped to make significant profits by speculating in gold and silver, using his father's ships to ferry commodities between New York and Europe.

Evidence of Foote's involvement with Lamar came from a letter that Lamar wrote to his father from Paris, in 1863. The letter never made its way into Gazaway Lamar's hands. Instead, it was confiscated by authorities and leaked to northern newspapers. In the correspondence, the younger Lamar informed his father of his plans and named Foote as a partner, writing "I have made $5,000 on cotton; am arranging to purchase $200,000 of gold in New York;

Gov. Foote, Bowers and self. Guion is to borrow the greenbacks in New York, buy the gold, and ship it to England; we then draw sterling, which is sold in New York for greenbacks, pay up what we owe, and the balance is profit." The plan probably never got off the ground, due to the deteriorating state of the Confederacy at the time and the fact that Charlie Lamar routinely had trouble following through on commitments. Foote never mentioned Charlie Lamar in any of his voluminous postwar writings, but the fact that Foote's name came up in the correspondence seemed to indicate that service to the Confederate Congress did not monopolize all of his attention during the period.[28]

As time wore on, it became apparent that Foote's act was wearing thin with many of his House colleagues. Other congressmen were tired of his bluster, and many agreed with a North Carolina editor who called him "an impetuous and troublesome man who often makes great noise about nothing." In a committee meeting, Foote disrespectfully laughed at a presentation being made by Arkansas congressman Thomas B. Handley, leading to harsh words between the two men and, finally, a fistfight. The incident created quite a ruckus in the committee room, although, according to reports, "more ink than blood was shed" before others pulled the men apart. On the floor of the House, Foote got into a heated exchange with Representative Edmund S. Dargan, during which he called the Alabaman "a damned rascal." Dargen rushed toward Foote with what some people later reported was a Bowie knife but was intercepted before he could do any damage. Always one for theatrical flair, Foote puffed out his chest as others wrestled Dargen to the ground, and shouted, "I defy the steel of the assassin!"[29]

Another fracas involving Foote took place in November of 1864, after he made derogatory remarks on the floor of the House about John Mitchell, a rough-and-tumble Irish correspondent from the *Richmond Examiner*. When Mitchell heard about Foote's tirade, he was furious and decided to challenge the congressman to a duel. He asked his friend William Swan, who represented East Tennessee in the House and did not care for Foote, to deliver the challenge. Swan, in turn, asked Foote's acquaintance and the editor of the *Examiner*, H. Rives Pollard, to take him to Foote's apartment in Richmond, at the Ballard House on Franklin Street. Pollard, who was apparently unaware of Swan's mission, agreed, and the two men went to the Ballard House and knocked on Foote's door. Mrs. Foote opened the door and Pollard introduced himself, at which point Foote appeared. Pollard told him that Swan wanted a word, and Foote said that he would not receive his fellow Tennessean because the man was "no gentleman." Angered, Swan immediately moved toward Foote and struck him with a heavy umbrella that he was carrying, causing a deep gash on Foote's bald head. Foote pulled a revolver from a drawer and threatened to shoot Swan, but Pollard stepped between the two men before any more blows were struck, and he and Swan left the building.[30]

Foote changed political course, yet again, in the summer of 1864, casting himself in the role of peacemaker as the Confederacy crumbled. In a long, emotionally charged letter published in newspapers across the South, he stated that the Confederate government, "without compromising its dignity in any way, or sacrificing the honor of our cause," should actively seek an end to the war. He was impressed by the work of the Peace Democrats in the North and claimed that the South would be able to negotiate an honorable peace with the United States government if George McClellan, the Democratic nominee, defeated Lincoln in the upcoming U.S. presidential election. He praised northern Democrats, particularly George H. Pendleton, a staunch peace advocate and the vice presidential nominee, for their "willingness to run on a pure peace platform," and he condemned the Lincoln administration as "the traitors and murderers who are responsible before God and man for all the crimes and mischiefs which this unpardonable war has produced." In the letter, he also advocated the call for a southern peace convention to deliberate on options related to ending the war.

On the surface, Foote's calls for peace could be interpreted as a noble effort to prevent further bloodshed, but he also was thinking of himself and his postwar political life. While he feigned hope that the Confederacy would survive as a nation, Foote believed that it was finished and that Jefferson Davis and his administration would be blamed for the defeat. He also knew that many Confederate citizens were war weary. Finally, he believed that McClellan would likely defeat Lincoln in the election, giving the Democrats control of the government and the Reconstruction process.[31]

His effusive praise of northern Democrats in his public letter, along with his brutal condemnation of Lincoln and the northern Republicans, was designed to curry favor with the national Democratic Party in hopes of reviving his national political career once the war ended. He wanted to position himself as a man who had opposed secession in the beginning and advocated peace in the end. He wanted to make sure that he separated himself from Davis and other southern Democrats, who he believed might be punished for their role in the secession process. Even Foote's suggestion that the South should hold a peace convention was self-serving in that he hoped to lead the gathering and thereby position himself as a southerner that the federal government could work with. Of course, to Foote, a resurrection of his national political career in postwar America would also serve as a final revenge against Jefferson Davis, whose political career would be terminated by the results of the conflict.

Foote's assumption that McClellan would win the election proved false, and Lincoln's victory upset the Tennessee representative's plans to ingratiate himself with northern Democrats by leading a southern peace initiative. As a result, he began formulating a new plan for himself, which would ultimately end his career as an elected official and lead some to question his sanity. He continued preaching peace in the House, but even those members who looked favorably on some type of peace settlement did not want to listen to him. He offered up two resolutions to "secure as early a cessation of hostilities and restoration of peace as would be compatible with the honor, the safety, and the permanent happiness of the people of the Confederate States," but both were tabled.

Foote fumed as fellow House members ignored his ramblings, finally letting off a huge blast of steam in the Confederate Congress of December 17, 1864. It would be his last official speech on policy in the Confederate Congress, and he knew it. "I beseech honorable gentleman," he began, with his usual dramatic flair, "on this last occasion perhaps that I shall have the honor of addressing this House, to look with me on the present condition of the country." He went on to state in great detail the misfortunes that had befallen the Confederacy over the previous year, laying the blame squarely at the feet of Jefferson Davis and, to an extent, the Confederate Congress. He accused fellow House members of poisoning the body by silencing dissent in favor of creating "an irresponsible military despotism, the like of which has never been seen before on this earth." He accused the Congress of abandoning traditional states' rights principles and trampling on the liberties of Confederate citizens. Saving his most pointed criticism for Davis himself, Foote bellowed that the Confederacy was on the "verge of ruin" because of "unjust, unwise, and criminal" policies dictated by the Confederate president.

While the southern press took little notice of Foote's tirade, northern newspapers that had always used the congressman's public insults toward Davis as propaganda had a field day. "We can ill afford to lose Foote," one Philadelphia editor wrote, after reading Foote's speech. "He has been a very useful man to lovers of the Union. His eccentricity and irascibility have kept him in constant quarrels with his associates. He has a habit of 'speaking out in meetings' and he has revealed more of the secret distresses of the Rebel cause than any other Confederate orator."[32]

A few days after giving his final policy speech to the House, Henry Foote made his first attempt to flee the Confederacy, setting in motion a bizarre chain of events that led some to question his mental stability. Foote left Richmond with his wife in hopes of crossing Union lines and making his way to Washington, DC, as a self-appointed peace emissary. In a great, typical manifestation of his ego, Foote assumed that, once he made it to the capital, federal officials would be eager to meet with him and he could then try to broker a peace settlement that would end the war. "Should I succeed in my present undertaking," he wrote at the time, to Confederate Speaker of the House Thomas S. Bocock, "my country and the cause of freedom will be materially benefitted."

In a way, Foote became a man without a country after he left Richmond. Confederate officials would shun him when they found out his plan, while federal officials were certainly not inclined to accept him as a statesman or to seek his counsel on weighty issues. Regardless, Foote left the Confederate capital with his wife, Rachel, and made his way north toward Washington, wandering around northern Virginia for several days. On the night of January 7, 1865, the Footes spent the night at the home of Joseph B. Ficklen, a prominent businessman, in Falmouth, Virginia, about sixty miles north of Richmond and seventy miles from Washington. Confederate authorities in the area were tipped off that Foote was close by and that he planned to cross into the United States. The local provost marshal sent two men to trail the congressman as he moved on toward Washington, and once the soldiers were confident that Foote was intent on crossing enemy lines, they arrested him at Occoquan, Virginia, on January 10. Confederate authorities released Mrs. Foote and she was allowed to continue her trip, but they held her husband in custody at Fredericksburg.

Many southern newspapers condemned Foote for abandoning the Confederacy, while the northern press continued to relish the chaos that he seemed to be causing in the Confederate government. Foote's comings and goings also caught the attention of President Lincoln. "You may have seen in the papers that ex-senator Foote, with his family, attempted to escape from Richmond to Washington," he wrote to Ulysses S. Grant on January 14. "Please give me the earliest information you may receive concerning him." Unsure what might happen to Foote, Grant replied to Lincoln the next day, speculating that Confederate authorities would "at furthest do nothing more than imprison him."[33]

Foote was released several days later, and he immediately returned to Richmond to explain himself to his congressional colleagues, who were already considering his expulsion from the House. Congressman Ethelbert Barksdale of Mississippi, a veteran Democratic politician who knew Foote well, introduced a resolution to censure and remove Foote from the Confederate Congress on the grounds that he was "unworthy to occupy a seat on the floor of this House." Foote defended himself by making a states' rights argument that only the voters of his district had the right to remove him from office. He argued that Tennessee "was proud of her sovereignty" and that he still "enjoyed the confidence of his people and constituency." Furthermore, he said that the proceedings to have him expelled from the House were unconstitutional and part of a vindictive conspiracy carried out by his "bitter and personal enemies of long standing." Foote then left the House floor before any vote was taken. After some debate, new resolutions for censure and expulsion were advanced separately. The vote to censure Foote passed overwhelmingly, by a count of 64 to 6, but the resolution to expel, which required a two-thirds vote of the entire House, failed, most likely due to the fact that many congressmen were absent at the time the vote was taken.[34]

Oddly enough, Foote seemed energized by the censure. Rather than reflecting on his downfall as a Confederate congressman, he instead became even more committed to his original plan of traveling to Washington to promote peace. On January 28, he left Richmond again and this time made his way successfully across Federal lines to Lovettsville, Virginia, where he reported to the headquarters of Union general Charles Devens. Devens, in turn, sent a message to his superior, General Philip Sheridan, who immediately contacted U.S. officials about Foote's arrival. Orders came from Washington that the Confederate congressman should be detained, but he was allowed to send a message to Secretary of State William Seward.

Despite the fact that Foote had absolutely no authority to speak for the Confederate government, he seemed to believe that Seward would be interested in what he had to say and would be sympathetic to his cause. Foote also seemed to forget that, when the two men served in the Senate together, he had been intensely critical of Seward on multiple occasions. That said, if Foote considered himself a representative from a foreign government, then he would naturally want to communicate with the U.S. State Department. In addition, when Mrs. Foote was allowed into Washington, several weeks earlier, Seward had personally secured her a room at the Willard Hotel and had issued orders that she should be well cared for. Foote may have believed that Seward would be willing to treat him with the same modicum of respect.

Foote ended up producing two letters to Seward, both of which were long, rambling treatises designed to promote a peace settlement and curry favor with U.S. government officials, not necessarily in that order. Foote went to great lengths to distance himself from the Confederacy, reminding Seward of Foote's role in the 1850 compromise debates and his defeat of Jefferson Davis in the 1851 Mississippi gubernatorial election. Hedging a bit, he claimed that he had remained a unionist up to the point that the war began in earnest, and he went on to echo in his correspondence the same criticism of Davis that he had made again and again on the floor of the Confederate House. "I became thoroughly satisfied that Mr. Davis and his associates were bent on establishing a despotism," he wrote, "[and] I resolved in the most open manner, to denounce the conspirators against the freedom of my fellow citizens of the South." Foote said that the Davis administration had no intention of forging an honorable peace and that the government had lost the confidence of "a large number of the most weighty and influential statesmen of the South" as well as "a large majority of the sovereign people of the Southern states." Finally, he pledged that he and his fellow "conservatives of the South" were ready to reunite with the federal government and that he felt it was his own "solemn duty to make one more manly and earnest effort for an early and honorable peace." Among the details of the "honorable peace" he promoted was a full amnesty for all Confederates and a plan to abandon the Emancipation Proclamation in favor of a plan for the gradual emancipation of all slaves in the South by January 1, 1900. Having little patience for Foote's seemingly endless rhetoric, Seward responded by giving the prodigal congressman two choices. Calling him simply "an insurgent who has voluntarily come within the military lines," Seward allowed that Foote could either return to the Confederacy or leave the United States.[35]

Not wanting to return to the Confederacy, where he might be arrested for treason, Foote traveled under guard to New York, where he reported to Major General John Adams Dix, who was under orders to help the congressman leave the country. While Foote's energies and abilities related to political correspondence and agitation seemed limitless, some contemporary reports indicated that by the time the sixty-year-old arrived in New York, his activities were beginning to take a physical toll. According to some reports, he had abandoned the hairpiece that he sometimes wore and appeared uncharacteristically scruffy and disheveled. Of Foote's arrival in New York, one newspaper reported:

> Rebel Senator Henry S. Foote came down by train last night under guard. . . . He looks much worn physically since he was in the United States Senate, and he has discarded his wig, and wears the greyest hair and whiskers. Of course he looks much older than at that time. In dress, etc. there was a marked change from his natty appearance of olden times. He has apparently discarded the use of the razor, and from the surplus of rough looking clothing upon his person, it would seem that he had taken this mode of conveying his wardrobe. He had on him at the [train] station three coats and two vests, all the worse for wear and tear, and also an old soldier's cap of the Confederate style of shabbiness, the band of which had slipped to the back of his head.[36]

Foote took a room at the Saint Nicholas Hotel on Broadway but did not remain in New York for very long. On February 11, he boarded the *City of Cork*, a mail steamer that was bound for Liverpool. Still under the delusion that U.S. authorities valued his counsel on a sectional reunion, he spent some of his time during the voyage penning a letter to President Lincoln. As with his correspondence to Seward, the letter was self-serving, self-aggrandizing, and filled with flowery language. "I write to you from mid-ocean," he began, "while the stormy billows of the surrounding sea are every moment painfully reminding me of that fearful scene of commotion and turmoil which I have left behind." He went on to school Lincoln on American constitutional history, to opine on the founding fathers' dedication to "the moral ascendancy as well as the physical domination of the Anglo-Saxon race," and to give the president meticulous instruction on how to reunite the nation and resolve the problems related to the slavery issue. Ignoring the fact that, within the past few months, he had on the floor of the Confederate House likened Lincoln to Satan, Foote referred to him as "not only the restorer of your country's happiness, but the vindicator also of the principles of civil and religious freedom."

Once in England, Foote also penned a wordy, thirty-seven-page pamphlet for his constituents back in Tennessee, explaining his actions and urging them to rejoin the Union. The pamphlet enraged the southern press, which now viewed him as a full-blown traitor. "Mr. Foote has hurt himself more than anyone else," one southern editor wrote. "We were all aware of his eccentricities, bordering on madness, but most of us thought him a man of truth and believed him when he proclaimed himself an honest patriot. He now entreats his constituents to lose no time returning to the bosom of the Federal Union. Let Mr. Foote remain sequestered [in England] for the rest of his existence." On February 27, 1865, the Confederate House of Representatives voted overwhelmingly to expel him from that body.[37]

Foote traveled through Europe for several weeks but eventually decided to return to the United States, even though he knew that he would probably be arrested. He secured a ticket on the *Etna*, a British passenger liner, and arrived in New York during the first week of April. He turned himself in to Major General Dix, who, as expected, had him secured in a local jail. Foote's arrival set off a flurry of communication between Dix and Secretary of War Edwin Stanton, who thought that Foote should be sent back to England. In the meantime, Foote proved that he had not lost his ability to produce self-absorbed written correspondence. He penned a letter to Stanton stating that he wanted to return to his home in Nashville, where he pledged to "engage to perform, in all respects, the duty of a good citizen and supporter of the Federal Union." Stanton was not impressed and refused to intervene.

Not long after the Lincoln assassination, Foote imposed on his son-in-law, William Morris Stewart, to get a message to new president Andrew Johnson. Stewart, who would later be credited with guiding the Fifteenth Amendment through Congress, had recently been elected to represent Nevada in the United States Senate. The senator lobbied Johnson to order the release of Foote and to allow him to relocate to the far West, where he had family. "If you will consent [to release Foote,] I will be responsible for his conduct," Stewart told Johnson. "I am sure he will do no harm in that country." He also sent the president a letter from Foote that was filled with effusive praise and his own request to move west.

Johnson was unmoved, ordering Foote to leave the country or face indictment for treason against the United States. What was left of the Confederate press had already written Foote off as a traitor; now, northern newspapers, too, were in no mood to give the "rebel congressman" the benefit of the doubt. In New York, the *Daily Herald* called Foote "as unstable as the wind," and, in

Cleveland, the *Daily Leader* was even more pointed, stating that "Foote is a traitor and should be dealt with as such. His sneaking desertion of his own cause simply because it is growing weak, is pitiful and contemptible."[38]

Johnson gave Foote only forty-eight hours to leave the United States, so he quickly relocated to Montreal, where, not certain whether he would ever be able to return to the United States, he began "to make arrangements for a permanent residence in Canada." According to one account, he set up housekeeping in a boardinghouse and pledged to "live in the greatest seclusion," devoting his time "exclusively to meditation and literary pursuits." It was in Montreal that he began writing a massive history of the Civil War era that would appear in print in 1866.

Foote's "literary pursuits" also included nonstop lobbying to return home. In an effort to ingratiate himself with northern officials and the northern public, he wrote letters blaming the Jefferson Davis administration for the harsh treatment of Union prisoners and postured himself as one of the only Confederate officials sympathetic to their plight. His claims that the Davis administration intentionally starved Union prisoners received considerable attention across the North. He also wrote letters to newspapers, claiming that his joining the Confederate Congress was simply a matter of honor and that he had vigorously opposed secession until "Tennessee had concluded to assume a warlike attitude." Only then, he said, did he consider joining the Confederate cause, and he likely would not have done so had he known how corrupt the Davis administration would become.[39]

Foote continued to produce correspondence at a furious pace, and as time passed, the U.S. government's view of him softened. In late June, the former Confederate congressman went to the office of John F. Potter, United States consul general for British-controlled Canada, and took an oath of allegiance to the United States, swearing to support "all laws and proclamations which have been made during the existing rebellion with reference to the emancipation of the slaves." Then, in early August, Foote wrote a letter to his friend, Tennessee lawyer Alfred O. P. Nicholson, that was published in a number of American newspapers. In the correspondence, Foote said he believed that the South should ratify the Thirteenth Amendment to the Constitution, officially ending slavery, and that the newly freed slaves should be given the right to vote "no matter what cherished notions we may entertain in regard to the mental inferiority of those whom some of us have heretofore regarded as the doomed posterity of Ham." Foote concluded his remarks by telling his friend that the South really had no choice but to comply with Republican Reconstruction policies. "We may regret this state of things as much as it is possible for us to do," he said, "we may bewail it as eloquently as we choose. . . . but we must consent." The tone of Foote's letter was designed to appeal politically to northern Republicans who might help him get back into the country. The fact that Foote personally leaked the letter to the press was also evidence that he was promoting an agenda for himself.[40]

Newspapers across the country were mixed in their evaluation of Foote's stance. In Cleveland, the *Daily Leader*, which had always been critical of Foote, called his position "sensible," while a Pennsylvania editor wrote similarly that "Mr. Foote is a sensible man, and like the prodigal son has returned to the proper mind." Of course, southern newspapers were not nearly as kind, expressing opinions similar to those of a Democratic editor in North Carolina who wrote, "Foote, as all well know, has been considered a crazy man for several years, and charity requires that we tribute his many delinquencies to this cause." In Virginia, Foote's native state, the Petersburg *Progress-Index* said that Foote's letter, as it related to suffrage for the freedmen, was nothing more than a political stunt and that "nobody believes that Mr. Foote thinks this policy is just or expedient."[41]

Around the middle of August an incident took place in Montreal that gave Foote some much needed positive publicity in Washington. At the time, the U.S. relationship with Canada was at a low ebb. Long-standing rumors that U.S. officials hoped to one day annex Canada angered many Canadians, as did a number of U.S.–Canadian trade agreements that seemed to favor the Americans at the expense of their northern neighbors. Many Canadians viewed the United States with suspicion, even as an enemy, and from time to time in Montreal they took their frustrations out on United States Consul General Potter. After attending a commercial convention in Detroit, the already unpopular Potter returned to find his Montreal office threatened by "an excited mob" that apparently included a number of Confederate sympathizers and refugees. The crowd was intent on removing the American flag from the roof of the consulate building, but before they could act, Foote, who was nearby, sprang into action. After reportedly telling his southern friends, "We've had our fight over [the flag], but by God damned foreigners shall not tear it down unless over my dead body," he was able to talk the group out of rash action. Several American newspapers picked up the story, and Foote's defense of the flag apparently was a factor in the government finally allowing him back in the country. "It might possibly be worthwhile to try to punish [Foote], though we think not," one sympathetic Wisconsin editor opined, "but what good can be secured, what evil averted, by compelling him to live in Canada?"[42]

On August 26, 1865, President Andrew Johnson issued orders allowing Henry Foote back into the United States. Many believed that Foote's defense of the American flag in Montreal had thawed some of the opposition against him, and some thought that his "letter in favor of negro suffrage" was his ticket back into the country. Even after all of the twists and turns of his political career, he still had a number of friends in high places who likely exercised influence on his behalf. These included son-in-law William Stewart in the Senate and old friend Noah Swayne, associate justice of the Supreme Court. Some reports stated that Foote had also corresponded about his status with William G. "Parson" Brownlow, the outspoken pro-Union governor of Tennessee, and in his memoirs Foote credited Consul General Potter in Montreal with helping his cause.

Many newspapers, North and South, took notice of Foote's return to the United States, but most did not bother to editorialize a great deal about the circumstances. Some newspapers poked fun at him. "[Foote] was pardoned, it is said, on condition that he keep his mouth closed on politics," the Shreveport *South-Western* reported sarcastically. "The condition is the most cruel punishment for that garrulous gentleman." Most observers assumed that, now back home, Foote would simply fade from public view and never be heard from again.

Of course, such prognostications underestimated Foote's resolve. His time as an elected official had passed, but his voice was still loud and his pen was still sharp. He would indeed fade away, but he would not go quickly or quietly. During the summer of 1865, an editor for the *New York Times* gave perhaps the best summary of Henry Foote's career up to that point, when he wrote, "The trouble in his case, as in plenty of others, is not in the world but in himself; and the old man, in his woes, need go to no higher authority than Satan to learn the profoundly wise philosophy that 'The mind is its own place, and in itself can make a hell of heaven or heaven of hell.'"[43]

9

The Final Years

I have lived a good while, and I sometimes flatter myself
that I have not lived altogether in vain.
—Henry Stuart Foote

ONCE HE RECEIVED PERMISSION to leave Canada, Foote wasted little time in returning to his home in Nashville, arriving there during the first week of September 1865. "Henry Foote is active and as bustling as ever," one newspaper reported, "and says that he will hereafter eschew politics and devote himself to the law." Despite reports to the contrary, Foote could not help himself as far as politics was concerned, and he was soon promoting Republican Reconstruction policies in the state capital. He later claimed that he became a Republican after the war because the party was dedicated to the "principles of progress," but coincidentally he also had nowhere else to hang his political hat. The Democratic Party would not take him in, and he had burned many bridges with his pro-Union friends after abandoning them for secession in 1861. The Republican Party was also the party of the winners, and Foote sought to ingratiate himself with Republican leaders in hopes of keeping his political career afloat. In short, his new affiliation with the Republicans, of whom he had been highly critical before the war, was motivated for the most part by self-preservation. Foote's ego would not let him retire, and he craved a political party to call his own, even if his motives were transparent. For their part, Tennessee Republicans seemed happy to welcome Foote into their ranks, with Republican governor Brownlow praising him as "a brave, generous man thoroughly attached to the Union."[1]

On September 23, Foote spoke at a public meeting in Nashville, where resolutions expressing an attachment to the Union and approving of the president's policies were unanimously adopted. The chaos and uncertainty produced by the war's end again seemed to work in Foote's favor, at least in the Tennessee capital. Some in the city still sought out his opinions on the day's issues, and in the early stages of Reconstruction he suddenly found himself far from irrelevant, at least locally. "Henry S. Foote is again with his family and friends," one Nashville correspondent wrote during the period, "and may be seen not infrequently in the center of an inquisitive group, at a street corner or in some public place, who have flanked or surrounded him, no doubt for the purpose of asking the question uppermost in the minds of all—'What is the political prospect?'" In October, Foote wrote a letter to a Nashville newspaper, again promoting the idea of the white South accepting African American suffrage as a means of ending Reconstruction. "I prefer to end our troubles at once by granting the right of suffrage," he wrote. "I prefer it to the longer continuance of the present distressing situation."[2]

During the latter months of 1865, Foote was also hard at work finishing a massive history of the Civil War era. In doing so, he became one of the first participants in the "the battle of the books" among Civil War participants, which would rage for years in postwar America. In the decades following the conflict, southern leaders—being the losing side—were particularly quick to produce tomes that told their version of the story and minimized any blame that they might deserve for the Confederate debacle.

In his history, Foote attempted to explain the southern cause, but he also used the book to settle old scores with other politicians. Though he told one newspaperman that he hoped the work would be "free of extreme—taking a medium ground," most who read the book recognized its self-serving agenda. Even before the completion of the book, word was out that it "will take a strong ground against Jeff Davis." Already suspicious, one hostile Tennessee editor wrote that the book "will doubtless prove to be a tirade against Jefferson Davis, rather than a history of the war; and an excuse for his own conduct, rather than an impartial narrative."

Foote had started work while in Montreal, and by late November he was in New York finishing the effort and finalizing his publishing contract with Harper and Brothers. The book, titled *War of the Rebellion; or, Scylla and Charybdis: Consisting of Observations upon the Causes, Course, and Consequences of the Late Civil War in the United States,* was published in early 1866. While it provided a good firsthand chronology of events, including copies of important correspondence, anyone reading the book would find it hard to deny its agenda. The work's main themes revolved around harsh criticism of Jefferson Davis and his administration and Foote's obvious attempt to align himself with the current Republican government. He held back nothing against Davis, criticizing both his political and military leadership in the harshest terms. He described Davis as a "shameful, hypocritical and tyrannical chief executive" and condemned "that compound of weakness, and corruption, and servility in the form of a cabinet which Mr. Davis so stupidly called around him." Foote devoted page after page to criticizing virtual every decision, military and civil, that Davis made as president of the Confederacy, and anyone sympathetic to Davis was also fair game. Conversely, he wrote that Lincoln's presidency was "singularly marked with moderation, elevated patriotism and true practical wisdom." He compared Lincoln to Davis on several levels and always concluded that Davis was by far the inferior leader.

Northern newspapers generally gave the book positive attention and gleefully reprinted sections that were critical of Davis and the Confederate hierarchy. The *Cleveland Daily Leader* said that Foote "accepts the logic of events, accepts the issues of the war [and] does justice to his former political opponents," while the *Detroit Free Press* seemed to disregard completely the self-aggrandizing tone of the work. "We must pay the author the rare compliment of saying that we have read few works of this kind which are so free of egotism," their correspondent wrote. "Indeed, in many instances the narrator hardly does justice to his own deserts. . . . Such rare modesty deserves some acknowledgment."

In the South, many former Confederates saw Foote as a traitor for criticizing the cause and aligning himself with the Republican Party. Southern newspapers moved quickly to discredit him through scathing reviews. The *New Orleans Crescent* claimed that his book was "a gross and malignant representation of the civil policy of the war on the part of the South," while the *Wilmington Daily Dispatch* called the book "a compilation of conceit mixed up with a general political history of the Government of the United States—falsehoods in relation to Confederate officials and heaps of abuse on the head of [Jefferson Davis]," adding that "we hope Mr. Foote's book will not be honored with a place in southern libraries." Jefferson Davis chose to ignore the work and withhold comment, but this was not the case for Davis ally Thomas C. Hindman Jr. Hindman, the former Confederate general, responded to Foote's literary attacks by calling him a "factionist, traitor and sycophant" whose book was nothing more than a weak attempt "to win credence from the public or pass his base lies for truth."[3]

Completely ignoring his past humiliations and controversial behavior, Henry Foote carried on after the war in much the same manner as he had before the war. He held firm in the belief that his opinions mattered and that others took them seriously, which apparently was still true to an extent, because his pronouncements on various subjects, for better or worse, continued to draw attention from newspapers around the country. That was always Foote's ace in the hole. Despite the fact that he had lost much of his credibility within the American political community, he could still draw attention to himself and could still draw crowds to hear him speak, if only because people were curious about what he would say next. He produced a string of letters for publication, urging the South to accept federal Reconstruction policies, and at one point unsuccessfully promoted the idea of a national convention for the purpose of ironing out all of the problems related to the Reconstruction process.

In March of 1866, he traveled to Washington, DC, in hopes of muscling his way into the national Reconstruction discussion. Accused by the local press of "loitering around Washington City," he met a number of times with his son-in-law Senator Stewart of Nevada, one of the few national politicians who would still take his counsel. His visit with the senator generated controversy when Stewart later introduced a resolution in the Senate suggesting an "even swap proposal" giving former Confederates a "universal amnesty" in exchange for "universal suffrage" for former slaves. Newspapers accused Foote, who was already on record as favoring suffrage for the freedmen, of writing the resolution himself. Foote denied the charge, although he did admit that he had discussed the proposition with his son-in-law beforehand. "I am, in no sense, the author of this wise and patriotic measure," he stated at the time. "It is true that I warmly approve it, and had the honor of being consulted by its author in regard to the probability of the South accepting it." He returned home still touting the proposal but also ecstatic that the controversy had led to his name being mentioned in newspapers around the country. As for Stewart, he went on to be one of the primary authors of the Fifteenth Amendment to the Constitution, which protects voters from discrimination based on "race, color, or previous condition of servitude."[4]

Leaving his family in Nashville during the summer of 1866, Foote took up residence in Louisville, Kentucky, where he opened a law firm in partnership with local attorney Boyd Winchester. He made a number of friends in the city and served as a defense attorney in several high-profile local cases. "Mr. Foote is a man of extraordinary information, of great talent," the editor of the *Louisville Daily Courier* gushed, "of exceeding talent as a speaker and writer, of courage that shrinks from nothing, and of great ability to express graphically whatever he knows or thinks." After such high praise, it is little wonder that, for a short time, Foote considered relocating permanently to the city. On January 18, 1867, he gave a well-received lecture at the University of Louisville law school on "the philosophy of evidence," uncharacteristically limiting his talk to only an hour.

The following April, the Saint Louis Public School Library invited him to the city to give a speech on pressing political issues of the day. He began that talk with self-deprecating humor, describing himself as nothing more than "a poor, unpardoned rebel, humbled in spirit, paralyzed in all my energies, reviled and disregarded by thousands who once professed to love and regard me, a forlorn Pariah in my native land." He went on to talk about the current state of affairs in the country and then surprised his audience by advocating women's suffrage. "I am in favor of allowing the ballot to women of mature years," he stated, "and I venture to predict that the time will be not far distant when this will be permitted in every state in the Union."

As he knew they would, his remarks on giving women the right to vote made the newspapers. "Henry S. Foote is determined to start the next political speculation," one southern editor wrote, half joking. "It would be interesting to see these [Republican] radicals wooing the votes of our ladies." Another editor, from West Virginia, was more critical, stating that "[Foote] is advocating the bestowment of the elective franchise upon women, with a good deal of zeal. It is hardly necessary to say that the genial old gentleman's views meet no very ready reception." Many people thought that Foote had suddenly advocated women's suffrage just to create a stir and, as a result, more publicity for himself. It seemed consistent with his past patterns of behavior. "There has been no vagary started in this country for fifty years," a correspondent from the *Daily Picayune* in New Orleans wrote, "that [Foote] didn't get into sooner or later."[5]

By the summer of 1867, Foote was back in Nashville, practicing law and giving political speeches. Though he had previously commented favorably on Republican Reconstruction policies, he was invited in November to speak at a great rally in Nashville to help reorganize the Democratic Party in Tennessee.

The crowd promised to be large, and Foote accepted the invitation, playing both sides of the fence during a fluid period when political uncertainty was the order of the day. Should the Democratic Party become dominant again in his adopted state, Foote certainly wanted to be in a position to have his voice heard. Of course, by speaking at the rally, he once again opened himself up to charges that he was a reckless political buccaneer with no real ideological base. Foote's speech went over well, as he had crafted it around the unassailable concepts of states' rights and personal liberty, and he continued flirting with state Democrats over the course of the next few months. He even attended the state Democratic convention in 1868, leading a group that unsuccessfully attempted to convince the delegates to back George H. Pendleton over Horatio Seymour, the eventual Democratic presidential nominee.

While some Tennessee Democrats seemed comfortable trying to recruit the politically vacillating Foote back over to their side, others despised him and would never forgive his past actions, particularly his letters related to giving the vote to former slaves. One Democratic editor disparaged Foote as a washed-up demagogue, joking to his readers that "after betraying every side and everybody, [Foote] is now betraying himself!" In December, the *Memphis Daily Appeal* reprinted a scathing rebuke of the former Confederate congressman that had earlier appeared in a New Orleans newspaper. "Mr. Foote has, in his long career, espoused all principles and attacked all men, independent of party and position," the paper told its readers. "Being destitute of common sense, he has almost always been in error. . . . Is there no way to put an end to his frothy twaddle?"[6]

Foote's flirtation with Tennessee's Democratic Party was short-lived, as it became apparent that much of the leadership and many of the party's members did not want him. He appeared at more and more Republican gatherings as the 1860s came to an end and the Democrats began reasserting political control in the state. After Republican Ulysses S. Grant's successful campaign for the presidency, in 1868, Foote spoke frequently at rallies, praising the new president's "honesty, patriotism, and capacity" while labeling his opposition "shallow and selfish." In direct contradiction to his prewar stance as a zealous proslavery man, Foote the Republican sympathizer promoted "the universal equality before the law of all men and all classes of men" and embraced the party's platform. He tried to brush aside claims by his detractors that he was merely pandering and had only turned to the Republicans because he had nowhere else to go. "If there are those who choose to repeat against me the oft-reiterated charge of vacillation and tergiversation," Foote said in one speech, with his usual sense of drama, "I have to say to them that I have never aspired to any consistency save that which is evidenced by the support of principle."

By 1872, Foote's "fair and patriotic purpose" was to cleave to the liberal elements within the Republican Party and to support their candidate, Horace Greeley, for president. While his own chances to win elected office again were slim, Foote was still in demand on the speaking circuit and in the courtroom. He formed a law partnership with Arthur S. Colyar to "practice in all the Courts of Nashville and attend special cases in other counties." Like Foote, Colyar had been a unionist before the war and had served in the Confederate Congress. He was also a proven businessman who brought to the partnership a number of high-profile corporate clients.[7]

Despite the twists and turns of Foote's life and career, one thing remained constant: he hated Jefferson Davis. During the summer of 1871, Davis gave a pair of speeches in Georgia during which he defended the Confederate cause and urged white southerners to persevere during the Reconstruction era. "He who reigns above and lives always will see that justice is done," Davis told a crowd in Augusta. "He will not allow the wicked to always remain in power or the righteous to be oppressed."

Reports that the former Confederate president was well received at the gatherings irritated Foote to the point that he could not help but respond. He penned a letter, reprinted in a number of southern newspapers, that was highly critical of Davis. He called his rival's speeches "fumy and seditious harangues" and, with obvious bitterness, referred to Davis as a "criminal" with designs to "rekindle among a generous and merciful people the flames of domestic conflict." In Tennessee, Foote's letter touched off a minor firestorm in the press; some newspapers applauded it while others came to Davis's defense. In Memphis, the *Daily Appeal* disparaged Foote as "an old political fossil and turncoat," while in Knoxville, a Republican stronghold, the *Weekly Chronicle* called Davis's speeches incendiary and urged its readers to "ponder and reflect" on what Foote had said.[8]

In addition to maintaining his speaking schedule, Foote continued to write at a furious pace. He contracted with the *Daily Morning Chronicle* in Washington to produce a series of reflections about his life and public career that became the basis for a personal memoir titled *Casket of Reminiscences*, published in 1874. Like his history of the Civil War era, Foote's memoir was designed to promote the views of the author, but it also made for interesting reading. Regardless of his biases, Foote was an eyewitness to many significant historical events during his lifetime, and his travels had taken him all over the country, from Virginia to Alabama, Mississippi, Texas, California, and Tennessee. He had rubbed elbows with many of the important men of his era and was willing to write about them all. "Reminiscences of this kind are always attractive," one reviewer wrote in the Washington *Evening Star*, "when the persons written about are of prominence, and the writer has good descriptive powers, and personal knowledge of what he writes."

Like his other works, the book received a mixed response in the press. Some viewed it as an important historical record while others dismissed it, like one editor who stated simply that "life is too short to grapple with Foote's books or listen to his speeches." The loose consensus seemed to be that the memoir had historical significance in that it chronicled an important period of American history but that readers should also take it with a grain of salt because of the work's volatile author. Foote's agenda was transparent, and his usual diatribes against Jefferson Davis and others he disliked were prominent in the five hundred–page volume. An editor of the *Baltimore Sun* summed up the attitude of most reviewers when he stated, "Mr. Foote is evidently a man of strong personal prejudices, and his pen is dipped in gall when he refers to Jefferson Davis and others. The undying animosity thus betrayed is a great drawback to these bright, racy reminiscences." It was also obvious to most who knew Foote that the former Confederate produced the work in part to rehabilitate himself in the eyes of his new Republican friends. In the work, he expressed regret over finally promoting secession in 1861 and also made flattering comments about national officials who might now be able to help him.[9]

For Foote, writing a memoir was also about preserving his legacy on his own terms, and it was certainly a significant extension of his ego. The act of producing a lengthy autobiographical record itself was a clear sign that Foote believed his story was worth telling. Putting pen to paper to permanently document their recollections was something that great men did. Foote considered himself a national figure who had taken part in important national events. He had witnessed history, and he believed that his memories needed to be captured and held for future generations. As a controversial figure, he had also been attacked in the press and by his enemies, which naturally led him to the conclusion that only Henry Foote could tell the story of Henry Foote. He wanted none of his personal history filtered through a biographer because he did not want to relinquish control of the narrative. He wanted the luxury of judging others while not being judged himself.

Foote's reminiscences were in large part honest evaluations of the past. There were many sincere moments of self-reflection in the book, where at times he was self-effacing and even apologetic for some of his past deeds and opinions. In other places, the manuscript was peppered with carefully calculated rhetoric. Throughout the work, he heaped effusive praise on his friends and belittled his enemies with either open criticism or by omitting facts that would have portrayed them in a more positive light. Through it all, one theme of the book remained constant: Foote hoped to elevate his status as a prominent man of his era and to create a record that would, in the future—years after his generation had passed—elevate his status as a historical figure of note.[10]

One person who certainly did not care for Foote's book was Jefferson Davis. From the time he lost the 1851 gubernatorial election in Mississippi, the former Confederate president had dealt with Foote's criticism by ignoring it. Though he considered Foote a man of "depraved taste" and a "constitutional liar," Davis usually chose not to take the bait and engage Foote to any great degree. Davis knew that his rival craved headlines for himself, and a protracted public feud between the two men would certainly generate press attention. Davis had never wanted to give Foote the satisfaction of a response, but apparently the criticisms included in the memoir were finally too much for Davis to take lying down.

Davis wrote a letter for publication, claiming that he had no desire to read anything that Foote wrote about him, that he had thought Foote was a liar since the 1851 election, and that "his subsequent career only served to confirm me in that judgment." He called Foote "faithless to his trust as a representative in the Congress of the Confederate States" and reminded southern readers of his rival's "subsequent desertion to their enemies." Foote could not have been more pleased that he had finally goaded Davis into a rare display of emotion, and Davis's rebuke likely sold more copies of the book. Foote responded publicly and with typical sarcasm. "I rejoice to know that the blighting curse of Mr. Davis's commendation it never can now be my ill fortune to incur!"[11]

While Foote's *Casket of Reminiscences* caused controversy, his fourth and final book did not. In 1876, he published *The Bench and the Bar of the South and Southwest*, a 261-page history of the legal community in the states where he had spent a considerable amount of his career. As with *Reminiscences,* much of the new book had already been published. It was the product of a series of articles that originally appeared in the *Southern Law Review* and other bits and pieces that Foote added in tribute to lawyers he had known and admired. He was especially charitable to men with whom he had crossed paths in the courtroom, such as Seargent S. Prentiss.

Reviews were favorable, particularly because *The Bench and the Bar* was more positive in tone, free of bitterness and the usual transparent political agendas that marked his previous work. One reviewer called it "a valuable contribution to national literature," while, in Washington, the *Evening Star* commented that "Mr. Foote's remarkable memory enables him to depict with graphic power and accuracy the men who figured most prominently at the bar in the Southwest, including orators and pleaders of great fame." The book was a somewhat nostalgic tribute to the legal profession as seen through Foote's eyes. There were no long ravings about Jefferson Davis or excuses for the author's past political behavior. Instead, there was effusive praise for lawyers he had known. "I found my brethren of the bar," he wrote, "with few exceptions, intelligent, astute, laborious, upright, and manly in their conduct, cherishing a high and delicate sense of personal honor."[12]

By the time the 1876 Tennessee Republican convention rolled around, Foote was firmly attached to the state party. He played a prominent role at the gathering, giving an important address and serving on the Resolutions Committee. Though he was in his seventies, his voice was still resolute and he was still long-winded. Democrats had already "redeemed" the state, giving Foote little choice but to try to carve out a place among the Republicans if he wanted to remain relevant. Shunned by the Democrats, he hoped that he could maintain some degree of political leverage if the Republicans could keep control of the national government.

His ace in the hole related to maintaining influence was his son-in-law, Nevada's Republican senator William M. Stewart. Foote visited Stewart frequently in the nation's capital and even opened a law office there. Another relative, Foote's nephew Francis Henry Hereford, had recently been elected to the House of Representatives as a Democrat, representing West Virginia's Third District. He was the son of Foote's sister Sarah. These family connections did not open every political door for Foote, but they kept a few from closing and allowed him to maintain informal contact with a number of national figures. Never hesitant to make his voice heard, and still in demand as a result of his longevity and unpredictability on stage, Foote had a full schedule of speaking engagements in Washington and Northern Virginia, whenever he was in the region.[13]

Recognizing that he was still a tough campaigner, Tennessee Republicans chose Foote as a presidential elector for the state at large in August of 1876, and he quickly went on tour, promoting Republican candidate Rutherford B. Hayes. Despite his age, Foote was still a force to be reckoned with on the stump, giving speech after speech across Tennessee. "He is seventy-two years old," a correspondent from a Memphis newspaper wrote at the time, "but yet retains no little of the fires of youth which thirty years ago made him so formidable an opponent." In late September, the editor of the Cleveland, Tennessee, *Weekly Herald* wrote, "We are not a particular admirer of Mr. Foote, but it is a fact that he is doing great work for the Republican ticket."

He kept up a grueling schedule, averaging five or six appearances a week. Most of his speeches followed a similar pattern. He began by explaining away his role in Tennessee's secession movement and his involvement in the Confederate government as if they were some sort of youthful indiscretions. Some of his detractors marveled at the ease with which he "regarded his course then as the great error and political sin of his life, for which he had long since repented." He would then, in typical Foote fashion, savage the Democratic presidential nominee, Samuel J. Tilden, as if he were the devil himself. He called Tilden a swindler and a gambler, describing the Democratic Party as massively corrupt and calling the candidate's closest political allies "the greatest thieves unhung." Forgetting his own involvement in the process, he attacked the Democrats in Tennessee as the reckless party of secession that had needlessly made the South suffer. The "present crisis," he said, was the result of "the wicked machinations of unscrupulous men called Democrats." He would then, in contrast, praise the sterling character of Hayes and the current president, U. S. Grant, whom he sometimes compared to George Washington. The Republican Party, Foote argued, was the only party capable of steering the nation on a productive course. "He made Democrats sit restlessly in their seats while he skinned them alive," one sympathetic newspaper reported. "Mr. Foote is doing good work for the cause of truth and justice."[14]

At most of his campaign stops, Foote shared the stage with Democrats who were arguing for Tilden and were more than willing to try to tear the former Confederate congressman down. Foote's rivals at speaking engage-

ments and their allies in the press gleefully quoted some of his past pronouncements against the Republican Party and, in general, tried to pass him off as a
washed-up former secessionist and an old fool. One newspaper claimed that
Foote was "venerable only in years," while another stated that his "abusive epi-
thets and slang applied to Mr. Tilden and the Democratic Party" were nothing
more than "the garrulous gibbering of old age." After a stop in Bolivar, the
local *Bulletin* savaged Foote. "He is in his dotage, and like a child must have
something to amuse his freakishness," the editorial began. "He is a good talker,
but back of his oily speech there is so much contradiction and self-stultification
that his arguments fall. . . . We opine that gall-bitterness of venom is the ruling
basis in his blood."

Unfortunately for Foote, his controversial career made him an easy target for Democrats. He had been a fully committed unionist during the 1850s,
and despite what anyone thought of him, that commitment was sound and, at
the time, respected by many. However, since the outbreak of the war, he had
twisted and turned politically to such a great degree that his allegiances were
suspect. Since 1860 he had gone from being a staunch unionist, to a secessionist, to a Confederate congressman, to a Confederate turncoat (in the eyes of
many), and had finally become a Republican only after testing the waters one
more time to see if he could find a place for himself among Tennessee Democrats. Though he outwardly exuded confidence, he seemed desperately adrift,
from a political standpoint, and willing to say anything to find safe harbor.[15]

The 1876 presidential election was one of the most controversial in history,
with neither major candidate immediately receiving an electoral majority. Initial results had Tilden with 184 electoral votes and a majority of the popular
vote, while Hayes trailed with 165. What complicated the situation were twenty
electoral votes that were in dispute, primarily from Florida, Louisiana, and
South Carolina, where violence and voter fraud were rampant on election day.
Congress created an electoral commission to decide the issue, and it eventually
voted to give the disputed votes to Hayes, giving the Republican a one-vote
majority and the presidency.

Foote was ecstatic, stating in a published letter that the ascension of Hayes
to the presidency was "an abundant reason for congratulations and rejoicing
among all who cherish a sincere regard for Republican institutions and prefer
the repose and happiness of the whole nation." Foote also saw it as a personal
victory. Although Tilden carried Tennessee, Foote's candidate won the elec-

tion, and the former senator had worked for Hayes as hard as anyone during the campaign. According to the Nashville *Tennessean,* "[Foote's] vigorous and hard canvas did much toward running up the Hayes vote, which reached nearly 100,000, the largest Republican vote ever cast in this state." Foote had maintained a high profile, and although the Republican Party was declining in Tennessee, many viewed him as one of state party's leaders. As Foote had hoped, this raised his profile with the national administration and within the Republican Party in general. While Democrats in Tennessee continued to disparage Foote as a doddering old man and "common slanderer," the Republican press in Washington lauded his "reputation as a jurist and statesman of extended experience." In August of 1877, when the new president visited Nashville, Foote played a prominent role in the proceedings, riding in the procession to the capitol building in a carriage with Mrs. Hayes and William Evarts, the incoming secretary of state. It was quite a political resurrection for someone whose career had seemed over in 1865.[16]

After Hayes became president, Foote continued to split his time between Nashville and Washington, DC, where he hoped to receive some sort of federal appointment. He corresponded with former secretary of state Hamilton Fish about the prospect, and also tried unsuccessfully to have one of his sons appointed to a judicial position.[17] He continued to give speeches in support of the Republican Party, and on one occasion a Memphis newspaper published a description of Foote, who in his old age was sporting long whiskers: "At present he is an aged-looking gentleman, with hair and beard of milky whiteness. A bald head rose up above the fringe of white hair like a mountain to above a line of verdure. He was dressed in the customary suit of solemn black. He is a voluble and impressive speaker, but his voice has the jingle of age, and shows that voices, like other things, lose their attractions as time goes by."[18]

In December of 1878, the president finally rewarded Foote for his support by nominating him to be superintendent of the United States mint in New Orleans, at a salary of $3,500 annually. The appointment drew some fire from Democrats around the country, who reveled in making fun of Foote's age and past associations, describing him as "white-haired and feeble" and calling Hayes a "body snatcher" for making the selection. Despite the criticisms, the Senate confirmed Foote with little rancor, and he even received considerable Democratic support "on personal or social grounds." At the time, most observers believed that the easy confirmation was a courtesy to Foote's son-in-law in the Senate and his nephew in the House of Representatives. Justice Noah Swayne, whose friendship with Foote went back decades, also threw his full support behind the nomination. The selection of someone from outside the state also raised eyebrows in Louisiana, seeming to be a sign that the current Republican leadership there was losing its influence in Washington.[19]

After his confirmation, Foote left Washington, DC, for New Orleans, stopping along the way in Nashville to spend Christmas with his family. He arrived in the Crescent City in time to welcome in the New Year of 1879, and he immediately began mingling with the city's Republican gentry. On January 4, 1879, he spoke at a lavish Republican dinner held in one of the large dining rooms at Antoine's Restaurant. He praised the party as "the party of law and order, the party of progress and the party of internal improvements," restating his firm belief in the Union and the U.S. Constitution. Afterwards, Foote made an effort to smooth any ruffled feathers that his appointment may have caused. He sent back to Washington positive reports of his reception in Louisiana and tried to cultivate good press locally by giving correspondents unfettered access for interviews. He praised the facilities and the "competent and skillful work-men" that the mint employed. He also tried to convince those with whom he spoke that, despite being a political appointee, he had no political agenda with regard to the mint's operation. "He states that he comes here as an officer of the United States," one reporter wrote, after an audience with Foote, "without any partisan feeling. . . . His endeavor will be to do his duty to the commonwealth as a public servant." Nothing could be further from the truth, of course. Foote remained a politician, and even though he was now on a much smaller stage than at previous points in his career, he still had his own agenda. Some believed that, even at his advanced age, he still had dreams of one day returning to the United States Senate.[20]

Although his strength was beginning to ebb, Foote still made the rounds as a public speaker. He dutifully lauded the Republican Party and, with regard to his job at the mint, always joked that he thought New Orleans was "a good place to make money." Foote apparently liked his new job and felt supported by officials in Washington. In March of 1879, he reported that "the government encourages the New Orleans Mint in every way. . . . So far everything has worked well here."[21]

He stirred little controversy in his new position, but in early May he created headlines after being named as a delegate to the Mississippi Valley Labor Convention. The meeting was held in Vicksburg, Mississippi, Foote's old stomping grounds, and the former governor made the most of his appearance there. In what amounted to a civil rights speech, he defended the rights of former slaves, demanding that the spirit and intent of the Thirteenth, Fourteenth, and Fifteenth Amendments be respected. He introduced resolutions calling for the formation of local committees charged with protecting the rights of the freedmen and their families "in each of the counties and parishes belonging to the states now represented at this convention." To emphasize his point, he peppered his remarks with references to lynchings and other crimes against former slaves that had recently been committed by "southern ruffians and murderers."

Because the convention had been called by Mississippi's Democratic governor, John M. Stone, and a group of affluent local planters, who were in the process of politically and socially subjugating the former slaves and their progeny, Foote's remarks met with a good deal of hostility from other delegates, and the speakers that followed Foote denounced the former governor and his provocative remarks. Democratic newspapers also attacked Foote as "an old fossil politician" and a "broken down hack." It was as if Foote knew that he was making his last significant public appearance in Mississippi and, regardless of whether anyone liked what he said, he wanted to make sure that he was remembered. His resolutions were voted down, as he knew they would be, but he also knew that his remarks would play well nationally among Republicans.[22]

Not long after his appearance at the Mississippi Valley Labor Convention, Foote's health began to decline, and he also received bad news from out West. His son Romilly Erskine Foote had died suddenly in Aurora, Nevada, on May 22, 1879, at the age of thirty-six. The cause of death was listed as "brain paralysis." Like his father, the younger Foote had been an attorney, practicing in California, Idaho, and Nevada.

The news was obviously a shock to Henry Foote and may have contributed to his overall physical deterioration.[23] He made fewer public appearances throughout the summer but continued to give interviews in New Orleans, most of which dealt with updates on how the mint was functioning. He also produced what would be his last significant piece of writing, a thirty-seven-page autobiography for Mississippi historian John Francis Hamtramck Claiborne, who was busy working on a history of the state. Foote visited his home in Nashville for several weeks in August and September and then returned to New Orleans.

On January 8, 1880, the first press reports began to appear stating that Foote was "very ill" with "cancer of the scalp," from which he had apparently been suffering for some time. One report claimed that the condition stemmed from a cancerous growth that had appeared on Foote's head after he gashed it on a low-hanging chandelier. He was in great pain, several weeks later, when New Orleans doctors performed surgery in an unsuccessful attempt to give him some relief.

On March 25, Foote asked for a leave of absence from his job at the mint, and a little less than a month later he left New Orleans for the final time to spend his last few weeks at home in Nashville. On May 7, he resigned his office, writing a letter to President Hayes stating that he could no longer perform his duties because of "the continued pressure of disease." Foote died at his home on May 20, 1880, at the age of seventy-six.[24]

Henry Stuart Foote's funeral was held in Nashville, at the First Presbyterian Church, and he received numerous tributes after his passing. The Nashville Bar Association called a special meeting to lament his death, and members of the city's legal community served as his pallbearers. As word circulated that Foote was gone, newspapers all over the country printed obituaries. In death, most of his overblown political antics were forgiven, at least to an extent, and many newspapers treated his earthly departure like the passing of an eccentric relative whose presence, for better or worse, had made life more interesting. "Take him all and all," the Memphis *Public Ledger* wrote of Foote, "as a public man, as a scholar, as a senator, and as a citizen, he was the most extraordinary character the South has produced since the death of John Randolph of Roanoke." The Nashville *Republican* called him "one of the last of an old school," while Mississippi newspapers were also generous. In the state capital, the *Clarion* said he was "talented, brilliant, and in some respects, as genius often is, eccentric. . . . He was impulsive and never counted the cost or consequences of the steps he deemed proper to take." In Natchez, the *Democrat* declared that "few men filled a larger place in the public eye in this state, than did this talented but erratic gentleman." Newspapers in larger cities around the country ran full obituaries that included many of the details of his "long and strangely varied career in active political warfare." Most highlighted his commitment to the Union, his role in the Compromise of 1850, his decades-long feud with Jefferson Davis, and his many disputes with other politicians. His confrontation with Thomas Hart Benton on the Senate floor and his duels with Seargent S. Prentiss were also recounted, as was the strange peace mission that he had assigned himself as a Confederate congressman near the end of the Civil War.

Of course, not all of his obituaries were flattering. He had made too many enemies to escape unscathed, even in death. The *Indianapolis News* remembered him as "a short, pompous old man, full of vanity and words, and boastful of his somewhat romantic career," while in Saint Louis, the *Post-Dispatch* summed him up by stating, "He was a droll personage, an odd mixture of virtues and defects. . . . He went through his life exuberant with vanity and full of self-delusion. A man of words rather than ideas, all his speeches and writings were remarkable for verbiage and bombast."[25]

In the end, Henry Foote's legacy as a political figure is mixed. On the one hand, before the Civil War, as the political tide in the South began to shift toward more radical action in the defense of slavery, Henry Foote stood firm. While he defended the institution of slavery, he never believed that its protection should come at the expense of the Union itself, and he was outspoken on that point. Against enormous political pressure as a governor and as a United States senator from the Deep South in the decade following the Mexican War, Henry Foote did not waver. His stance on the preservation of the Union effectively ended his political career in Mississippi during the 1850s, but it also garnered him a reputation strong enough to later forge political alliances in California and, later still, to win election to the Confederate Congress in Tennessee. On the other hand, once he abandoned the cause of the Union, on the eve of the Civil War, he played into the hands of his critics, who had always accused him of being nothing more than a loud, obnoxious demagogue.

In the end, though, no one could say that Henry Foote did not live a remarkable life. It was a life full of fistfights, duels, earnest deliberations, rhetorical brilliance, self-serving showmanship, aggressive bullying, embarrassing tantrums, and a talent for placing himself in the center of every controversy that he came in contact with, or at times created himself. "I have lived a good while," Foote said, just a few years before his death, "and I sometimes flatter myself that I have not lived altogether in vain."[26]

⟳⟳⟳ APPENDIX ⟳⟳⟳
Henry Stuart Foote Chronology

1804	(February 28) Henry Stuart Foote is born in Fauquier County, Virginia.
1825	Foote moves from Virginia to Tuscumbia, Alabama.
1826	Foote marries Elizabeth Winter.
1827	Foote is slightly wounded in a duel with Edmund Winston.
1828	Foote's daughter Jane is born.
1831	Foote leaves northern Alabama and eventually settles in Mississippi.
1832	Foote runs unsuccessfully for a seat at the Mississippi constitutional convention.
1833	Foote participates in two duels against Seargent Smith Prentiss.
1834	Foote canvasses Mississippi in support of Robert J. Walker for U.S. senator.
	Foote's daughter Annie Elizabeth is born.
	Foote runs unsuccessfully for state chancellor.
1835	Foote witnesses the great Mississippi slave insurrection scare.
	Foote's daughter Virginia Cecilia is born.
1836	Foote is appointed surveyor general of the lands south of Tennessee.
1837	Foote's daughter Arabella is born.
1838	Foote resigns his federal post and runs successfully for a seat in the Mississippi House of Representatives, as a Whig.
1839	Foote makes his first extended trip to Texas and considers relocating there.
1840	Foote's son Henry Stuart Jr. is born.
1841	Foote's Texas history, *Texas and the Texans,* is published.

1842   Foote abandons Texas and returns to Mississippi.

1843   Foote's son Romilly Erskine is born.

1844   Foote is selected as a delegate from Mississippi to the Democratic National Convention.

    In a Louisiana murder trial, Foote successfully defends John T. Mason, who was accused of killing Jefferson Davis's brother-in-law David Bradford.

    Foote campaigns heavily for Democratic presidential candidate James K. Polk.

1846   The Mississippi legislature selects Foote to represent the state in the United States Senate for the term beginning in 1847.

1847   Henry Foote takes office as United States Senator from Mississippi.

    Foote engages in a physical altercation with Jefferson Davis in a Washington, DC, boardinghouse.

1848   Foote's son William Winter is born.

1849–1850 Foote takes part in debates leading to the Compromise of 1850.

1850   Foote is involved in a physical altercation with Arkansas senator Solon Borland on the streets of Washington, DC.

    The Mississippi legislature votes to censure Foote for his role in the proceeding that led to the Compromise of 1850.

1851   Foote is elected governor of Mississippi, as a Union Democrat.

1852   Foote resigns his Senate seat to take office as Mississippi's governor.

1854   Foote unsuccessfully seeks to return to the U.S. Senate, but loses out to Albert Gallatin Brown.

    Foote resigns as Mississippi's governor.

    Foote relocates to California, where he quickly gets involved in state politics.

1855   Foote announces his official support for the American Party (the Know-Nothings) in California.

    Foote's wife, Elizabeth, dies in California.

1857   Foote is nominated as the Know-Nothing candidate for the United States Senate but fails to secure the seat.

    Foote moves back east, first to Mississippi and then (in 1859) to Nashville, Tennessee.

1859   Foote marries Rachel Smiley, widow of Robert G. Smiley, a Nashville attorney.

1860   Foote campaigns for presidential candidate Stephen Douglas.

1861   Foote abandons the union principles that had been the hallmark of his public career and backs secession in Tennessee.

Campaigning as a secessionist, Foote wins election to the Confederate Congress, representing Tennessee's Fifth District.

1861–1865 Foote serves in the Confederate Congress, where he is one of the most vocal critics of Jefferson Davis and the Confederate national government.

1865   Foote leaves the Confederacy for Washington, DC, as a self-appointed peace emissary. He is arrested and detained by federal authorities.

Given the choice of returning to the Confederacy or leaving the country, Foote chooses to go to England for several weeks.

Returning from Europe, Foote relocates for a time in Montreal, Canada, but is eventually allowed to return to the United States.

1866   Foote's history of the Civil War era, *War of the Rebellion; or, Scylla and Charybdis,* is published.

1868   Foote begins attending events sponsored by the Republican Party in Tennessee.

1872   Foote supports Horace Greeley for president.

1874   Foote's memoir, *Casket of Reminiscences,* is published.

1876   Foote's *The Bench and the Bar of the South and Southwest* is published. Foote attends the Tennessee Republican convention, where he serves on the Resolutions Committee.

Foote campaigns for Republican presidential candidate Rutherford B. Hayes.

1878   Foote is appointed superintendent of the United States mint in New Orleans.

1879   Foote's son Romilly Erskine Foote dies suddenly in Aurora, Nevada, at age thirty-six.

1880   Foote resigns as superintendent of the United States mint in New Orleans.

(May 20) Foote dies at his home in Nashville, Tennessee.

～～ NOTES ～～

INTRODUCTION

Note to epigraph: William C. Carter, ed., *Conversations with Shelby Foote* (Jackson: University Press of Mississippi, 1989), 154. Author Shelby Foote was distantly related to Henry Stuart Foote.

1. William C. Davis, *Jefferson Davis: The Man and His Honor* (Baton Rouge: Louisiana State University Press, 1991), 171–172; A. C. Venable to Jefferson Davis, August 8, 1874, in Dunbar Roland, *Jefferson Davis: His Letters, Papers and Speeches,* vol. 7 (Jackson: Mississippi Department of Archives and History, 1923), 393–395.

2. Reuben Davis, *Recollections of Mississippi and Mississippians* (New York: Houghton, Mifflin, 1889), 101.

3. Davis, *Recollections,* 120.

4. George Baber, "Personal Recollections of Senator H. S. Foote: The Character and Career of a Brilliant Southern Lawyer, Orator, and Statesman," *Overland Monthly,* 26, no. 152, second series (August 1895), 163. Some sources say Foote was born in 1800. For biographical information on Foote, see John Edmond Gonzales, "The Public Career of Henry Stuart Foote" (PhD diss., University of North Carolina, 1957).

5. John Hallum, *The Diary of an Old Lawyer: Scenes Behind the Curtain* (Nashville, TN: Southwestern Publishing House, 1895), 239; *Alexandria (VA) Gazette,* October 18, 1836; Mary Boykin Chesnut and C. Vann Woodward, eds., *Mary Chesnut's Civil War* (New Haven, CT: Yale University Press, 1993), 304; Edmund Ruffin and William Kauffman Scarborough, eds., *The Diary of Edmund Ruffin: Toward Independence, October 1856–April 1861* (Baton Rouge: Louisiana State University Press, 1972), 687.

6. James D. Lynch, *The Bench and Bar of Mississippi* (New York: E. J. Hale and Sons, 1881), 286–287.

7. Henry S. Foote, *Casket of Reminiscences* (Washington, DC: Chronicle, 1874), 181.

CHAPTER ONE

Note to epigraph: *New York Times,* May 24, 1878.

1. Kathi Ann Brown, Walter Nicklin, and John T. Toler, *250 Years in Fauquier County: A Virginia Story* (Charlottesville: University of Virginia Press, 2009), 12, 25.

2. Abram William Foote, *Foote Family: Comprising the Genealogy and History of Nathaniel Foote of Wethersfield, CT and His Descendants* (Rutland VT: Marble City Press, 1907), 552–555; Arnold Harris Hord, *Genealogy of the Hord Family* (Philadelphia: J. R. Lippincott, 1898), 82–83; T. Triplett Russell and John K. Gott, *Fauquier County in the Revolution* (Westminster, MD: Heritage Books, 1977), 33; Stella Pickett, *Colonial Families of the Southern States of America: A History and Genealogy of Colonial Families Who Settled in the Colonies Prior to the Revolution* (New York: Tobias A. Wright, 1911), 492–493.

3. Henry S. Foote, *Casket of Reminiscences* (Washington, DC: Chronicle, 1874), 357–360; Donald A. Ritchie, *Press Gallery: Congress and the Washington Correspondents* (Cambridge, MA: Harvard University Press, 1991), 58; Washington, DC, *Evening Star,* February 1, 1883, February 6, 1883; James Woodrow Parkerson, "Senator Henry Stuart Foote of Mississippi: A Rhetorical Analysis of His Speeches" (PhD diss., Louisiana State University, 1971), 29.

4. Foote, *Casket of Reminiscences,* 2.

5. *New York Times,* May 24, 1878; Lyon Gardiner Tyler, *Encyclopedia of Virginia Biography,* vol. 2 (New York: Lewis Historical Publishing, 1915), 275; Henry Stuart Foote, *War of the Rebellion; or, Scylla and Charybdis: Consisting of Observations upon the Causes, Course, and Consequences of the Late Civil War in the United States* (New York: Harper and Brothers, 1866), i; David Mayer Silver, *Lincoln's Supreme Court* (Urbana: University of Illinois Press, 1957), 62.

6. Joshua D. Rothman, *Flush Times and Fever Dreams: A Story of Capitalism and Slavery in the Age of Jackson* (Athens: University of Georgia Press, 2014), 9–10; Joseph G. Baldwin, *Flush Times in Mississippi and Alabama: A Series of Sketches* (New York: D. Appleton, 1853), 237–239.

7. Tuscumbia (AL) *Tuscumbian,* November 12, 1824; United States Census, 1820, Franklin County, Alabama; Census, 1830, Franklin County.

8. Baldwin, *Flush Times,* 83.

9. Tuscumbia (AL) *Tuscumbian,* April 17, 1826; Noah Smithwick, *The Evolution of a State, or Recollections of Old Texas Days* (Austin: University of Texas Press, 1983), 201; United States Census, 1900, Alameda County, California; *San Francisco* (CA) *Call,* April 29, 1905; Ruth Hermann, *Gold and Silver Colossus: William Morris Stewart and His Southern Bride* (Sparks, NV: Dave's Printing and Publishing, 1975), 329–330.

10. Cullen Tuller Carter, *Methodism in the Wilderness* (Nashville, TN: Parthenon Press, 1959), 50–52. For information on presidential elections, see Hanes Walton, Donald Deskins Jr., and Sherman Puckett, *Presidential Elections 1798–2008: County, State and National Mapping of Election Data* (Ann Arbor: University of Michigan Press, 2010).

11. *Tuscumbia* (AL) *Patriot,* April 7, 1827; Kenneth Coleman, *A History of Georgia* (Athens: University of Georgia Press, 1991), 131; Greg Russell, "John Quincy Adams," in *The American Presidents*:

Critical Essays, ed. Melvin I. Urofsky (New York: Garland, 2010), 93; Alan Pell Crawford, *Twilight at Monticello: The Final Years of Thomas Jefferson* (New York: Random House, 2009), 216–218.

12. For information on Anthony Winston and the Winston family, see Mrs. Patrick Hues Mell, *Revolutionary Soldiers Buried in Alabama,* reprint no. 26 (Montgomery: Alabama Historical Society, 1904), 569–572; and Thomas McAdory Owen, *Dictionary of Alabama Biography,* vol. 4 (Chicago, IL: S. J. Clarke, 1921), 1790–1791.

13. *New York Spectator,* August 21, 1827; Boston *Massachusetts Spy,* November 21, 1827.

14. Reuben Davis, *Recollections of Mississippi and Mississippians* (New York: Houghton, Mifflin, 1889),121; Bertram Wyatt-Brown, *Honor and Violence in the Old South* (New York: Oxford University Press, 1986), 147; *Overland Monthly* 26, no. 144, second series (December 1894): 338; Joseph G. Baldwin, *Flush Times,* 72; Foote, *Casket of Reminiscences,* 184.

15. John G. Aikin, ed., *A Digest of the Laws of the State of Alabama Containing All the Statutes of a Public and General Nature in Force at the Close of the Session of the General Assembly in 1833* (Philadelphia, PA: Alexander Tower, 1833), 134; Foote, *Casket of Reminiscences,* 187. Some sources claim that the Foote–Winston duel was actually fought in Tuscaloosa, Alabama, which at the time served as the state capital. However, scheduling the encounter in the state capital would have drawn a good bit of attention to the fact that both men were doing something illegal, whereas having the duel take place in the small village of Hamilton, Mississippi, outside the state, would draw less attention.

16. Foote, *Casket of Reminiscences,* 427; Henry S. Foote, *The Bench and the Bar of the South and Southwest* (Saint Louis, MO: Soule, Thomas and Wentworth, 1876), 203.

17. Byrle A. Kynerd, "British West Florida," in *A History of Mississippi,* vol. 1, ed. Richard A. McLemore (Hattiesburg: University and College Press of Mississippi, 1973), 145; Julie Sass, "Chronology of Natchez," in *Natchez Before 1830,* ed. Noel Polk (Jackson: University Press of Mississippi, 1989).

18. Porter L. Fortune Jr., "The Formative Period," in *History of Mississippi,* 1:251; Foote, *Casket of Reminiscences,* 427–428.

19. Dunbar Rowland, *Encyclopedia of Mississippi History; Comprising Sketches of Counties, Towns, Events, Institutions and Persons,* vol. 2 (Madison, WI: Selwyn A. Brant, 1907), 858. For information on the origins and history of Vicksburg, see Christopher Morris, *Becoming Southern: The Evolution of a Way of Life, Warren County and Vicksburg, Mississippi, 1770–1860* (New York: Oxford University Press, 1995).

20. James D. Lynch, *The Bench and Bar of Mississippi* (New York: E. J. Hale and Sons, 1881), 287; Guy Carleton Lee, *The World's Great Orators, Comprising the Great Orations of the World's History* (New York: G. P. Putnam and Sons, 1905), 57; Foote, *Casket of Reminiscences,* 429; Anthony E. Kaye, *Joining Places: Slave Neighborhoods in the Old South* (Chapel Hill: University of North Carolina Press, 2007), 170; J. F. H. Claiborne, "Henry Stuart Foote," in J. F. H. Claiborne Papers, folder 27, Southern Historical Collection, Louis Round Wilson Library, University of North Carolina, Chapel Hill.

21. Lee Sandlin, *Wicked River: When the Mississippi Last Ran Wild* (New York: Vintage, 2010), 92; Foote, *Casket of Reminiscences,* 188; George Lewis Prentiss, ed., *A Memoir of S. S. Prentiss,* vol.

1 (New York: Charles Scribner's Sons, 1899), 132–133; Ben C. Truman, *The Field of Honor: Being a Complete and Comprehensive History of Dueling in All Countries* (New York: Fords, Howard, and Hulbert, 1884), 384.

22. Joseph D. Shields, *Life and Times of Seargent Smith Prentiss* (Philadelphia: J. P. Lippincott, 1884), 72; Foote, *Casket of Reminiscences*, 188; Prentiss, *A Memoir of S. S. Prentiss*, 133.

23. Rowland, *Encyclopedia of Mississippi History*, 2:421; Julian Alvin Carroll Chandler et al., eds., *The South in the Building of the Nation* (Richmond, VA: Southern Publication Society, 1909), 120; Bertram Wyatt-Brown, *Southern Honor: Ethics and Behavior in the Old South* (New York: Oxford University Press, 1982), 397–399: Foote, *Casket of Reminiscences*, 433.

24. Mississippi Historical Society, *Publications of the Mississippi Historical Society*, vol. 8 (Oxford: Mississippi Historical Society, 1904), 438; Foote, *Casket of Reminiscences*, 434; Jackson *Mississippian*, November 21, 1834.

25. David J. Libby, *Slavery and Frontier Mississippi, 1720–1835* (Jackson: University Press of Mississippi, 2004), 96; Morris, *Becoming Southern*, 77; *Vicksburg* (MS) *Whig*, May 10, 1832.

26. Foote, *Casket of Reminiscences*, 201; Frederick Anderson, Lin Salamo, and Bernard L. Stein, eds., *Mark Twain's Notebooks and Journals*, vol. 2, *1877–1883* (Berkeley: University of California Press, 1976), 137–139.

27. Foote, *Casket of Reminiscences*, 201–206, 436; Volney E. Howard, *Cases Argued and Decided in the High Court of Errors and Appeals of the State of Mississippi*, vol. 1 (Philadelphia, PA: T. K. and P. G. Collins, 1839), 247–255; Rowland, *Encyclopedia of Mississippi History, vol. 2*, 348–349; Jackson *Mississippian*, September 29, 1837; *Natchez* (MS) *Courier*, September 29, 1837; Natchez (MS) *Free Trader*, October 5, 1837.

28. Boston (MA) *Liberator*, January 1, 1831; Junius P. Rodriguez, ed., *Slavery in the United States: A Social, Political, and Historical Encyclopedia*, vol. 1 (Santa Barbara, CA: ABC-CLIO, 2007), 89; Foote, *Casket of Reminiscences*, 252. For a good treatment of the Nat Turner uprising, see Kenneth S. Greenberg, *Nat Turner: A Slave Rebellion in History and Memory* (New York: Oxford University Press, 2003).

29. United States Census, 1840, Madison County, Mississippi; Edwin A. Miles, "The Mississippi Slave Insurrection Scare of 1835," *Journal of Negro History* 42, no. 1 (January 1957): 47–49.

30. Foote, *Casket of Reminiscences*, 251.

31. Robert M. Coates, *The Outlaw Years: The History of the Land Pirates of the Natchez Trace* (New York: Literary Guild of America, 1930), 273; *Columbus* (MS) *Democrat*, reprinted in *Niles' Weekly Register*, August 8, 1835; Foote, *Casket of Reminiscences*, 251; *Vicksburg* (MS) *Whig*, July 16, 1835.

32. Saint Louis (MO) *Daily Commercial Bulletin*, July 27, 1835; Davidson Burns McKibben, "Negro Slave Insurrections in Mississippi, 1800–1865," *Journal of Negro History* 34, no. 1 (January 1949), 76–77; Miles, "Mississippi Slave Insurrection Scare," 48–60; Rothman, *Flush Times*, 140–145; *Vicksburg* (MS) *Whig*, July 16, 1835.

33. David Grimstead, *American Mobbing, 1828–1861: Toward the Civil War* (New York: Oxford University Press, 1998), 146–147; Harry Sinclair Drago, *The Great Range Wars: Violence on the Grasslands* (Lincoln, NE: Bison Books, 1985), 291–292; Foote, *Casket of Reminiscences*, 253–255; *Vicksburg* (MS) *Whig*, September 10, 1835.

34. Foote, *Casket of Reminiscences*, 255.

35. Foote, *Casket of Reminiscences*, 253; Rothman, *Flush Times*, 150–152, 215; Grimstead, *American Mobbing*, 146–148; Drago, *The Great Range Wars*, 292–294; Boston (MA) *Liberator*, August 15, 1835.

36. Grimstead, *American Mobbing*, 319; Miles, "Mississippi Slave Insurrection Scare," 52–54.; Jackson *Mississippian*, July 24, 1835; Foote, *Casket of Reminiscences*, 259.

37. Foote, *War of the Rebellion*, 13.

38. Clement Eaton, *The Freedom of Thought Struggles in the Old South* (New York: Harper and Row, 1964), 97–100; Rothman, *Flush Times*, 227–229; Herbert Aptheker, *American Negro Slave Revolts*, 6th ed. (New York: Columbia University Press, 1993), 326–327; Foote, *Casket of Reminiscences*, 258–261; William W. Freehling, *The Road to Disunion*, vol. 1, *Secessionists at Bay, 1776–1854* (New York: Oxford University Press, 1990), 111–113.

39. Rowland, *Encyclopedia of Mississippi History*, 1:27, 1:830: Jackson (MS) *Southron*, June 14, 1843; *Vicksburg* (MS) *Sentinel*, June 28, 1844, July 2, 1844, July 9, 1844.

40. Jackson (MS) *Southern Reformer*, June 29, 1844; Foote, *Casket of Reminiscences*, 382–383.

41. *Overland Monthly* 26, no. 144, second series (December 1894), 645.

CHAPTER TWO

Note to epigraph: Reuben Davis, *Recollections of Mississippi and Mississippians* (New York: Houghton, Mifflin, 1889), 197.

1. Mississippi's free white population increased from 43,228 in 1820 to 70,443 in 1830 to 179,083 in 1840.

2. Westley F. Busbee Jr., *Mississippi: A History* (Wheeling, IL: Harlan Davidson, 2005), 84–88; Joseph L. Blau, ed., *Social Theories of Jacksonian Democracy: Representative Writings of the Period, 1825–1850* (Indianapolis, IN: Hackett Publishing Company, 1954), ix–x; John Ray Skates, *Mississippi: A Bicentennial History* (New York: W. W. Norton, 1979), 18–20; John W. Winkle III, *The Mississippi State Constitution* (New York: Oxford University Press, 2014), 7–9; Porter L. Fortune Jr., "The Formative Period," in *A History of Mississippi*, vol. 1, ed. Richard A. McLemore (Hattiesburg: University and College Press of Mississippi, 1973), 273–276.

3. Fortune, "The Formative Period," 274–275; D. Clayton James, *Antebellum Natchez* (Baton Rouge: Louisiana State University Press, 1968), 113–115; John H. Aldrich, *Why Parties?: The Origin and Transformation of Political Parties in America* (Chicago: University of Chicago Press, 1995), 97–104.

4. Fortune, "The Formative Period," 252; Christopher J. Olsen, *Political Culture and Secession in Mississippi: Masculinity, Honor and the Anti-Party Tradition, 1830–1860* (New York: Oxford University Press, 2000), 17; *Vicksburg* (MS) *Eagle*, July 27, 1826. For a treatment of Mississippi politics during the 1820s, see M. Philip Lucas, "Beyond McCormick and Miles: The Pre-Partisan Political Culture of Mississippi," *Journal of Mississippi History* 44, no. 4 (November 1982).

5. Bertram Wyatt-Brown, *Honor and Violence in the Old South* (New York: Oxford University Press, 1986), 30–35.

6. Benjamin Ray Wynne, "Politics and Pragmatism: Unionism in Antebellum Mississippi, 1832 to 1860" (PhD diss., University of Mississippi, 2000), 38–42; Fortune, "The Formative Period," 273–276.

7. Edwin Arthur Miles, *Jacksonian Democracy in Mississippi* (Chapel Hill: University of North Carolina Press, 1960), 168; Fortune, "The Formative Period," 275–276.

8. *Overland Monthly* 26, no. 152, second series (August 1895), 164.

9. James O'Meara, *Broderick and Gwin: The Most Extraordinary Contest for a Seat in the Senate of the United States Ever Known* (San Francisco, CA: Bacon and Company, 1881), 125; Davis, *Recollections*, 198–199; James Woodrow Parkerson, "Senator Henry Stuart Foote of Mississippi: A Rhetorical Analysis of His Speeches" (PhD diss., University of North Carolina, 1957), 65–67, 73–74; J. J. Peatfield, "Famous Californians of Other Days," *Overland Monthly* 24, no. 153, second series (September 1895), 645; Henry S. Foote, *The Bench and the Bar of the South and Southwest* (Saint Louis, MO: Soule, Thomas and Wentworth, 1876), 157–158 (Foote's emphasis).

10. Henry S. Foote, *Casket of Reminiscences* (Washington, DC: Chronicle, 1874), 286.

11. Foote, *Casket of Reminiscences,* 347; James D. Lynch, *The Bench and Bar of Mississippi* (New York: E. J. Hale and Sons, 1881), 137; Vicksburg *Mississippian,* January 9, 1832; *Vicksburg* (MS) *Whig,* January 12, 1832.

12. Richard E. Ellis, *The Union at Risk: Jacksonian Democracy, States' Rights and the Nullification Crisis* (New York: Oxford University Press, 1987), 1–2.

13. For more information on the nullification controversy, a number of sources are available, including Ellis, *The Union at Risk*; William W. Freehling, *Prelude to Civil War: The Nullification Controversy in South Carolina, 1816–1836* (New York: Oxford University Press, 1992); and Merrill D. Peterson, *Olive Branch and Sword: The Compromise of 1833* (Baton Rouge: Louisiana State University Press, 1982).

14. Frank Moore, ed., *The Rebellion Record: A Diary of American Events, with Documents, Narratives, Illustrative Incidents, Poetry, etc.* (New York: G. P. Putnam, 1861), 139, 179; Henry Stuart Foote, *War of the Rebellion; or, Scylla and Charybdis: Consisting of Observations upon the Causes, Course, and Consequences of the Late Civil War in the United States* (New York: Harper and Brothers, 1866), 61.

15. "The United States Magazine and Democratic Review" 14 (New York: Henry G. Langley's Astor House, 1845): 159. For information on Walker's life and career, see James P. Shenton, *Robert John Walker: A Politician from Jackson to Lincoln* (New York: Columbia University Press, 1961).

16. Foote, *Casket of Reminiscences,* 217; *Alexandria* (VA) *Gazette,* September 18, 1833; Asbury Dickens and John W. Forney, eds., *American State Papers: Documents of the Congress of the United States in Relation to the Public Lands, from the First Session of the Twenty-Fourth Congress to the Second Session of the Twenty-Fourth Congress,* vol. 8 (Washington, DC: Gales and Seaton, 1861), 761.

17. Shenton, *Robert John Walker,* 13–14; David Alan Johnson, *Founding the Far West: California, Oregon and Nevada, 1840–1890* (Berkeley: University of California Press, 1992), 118–119.

18. John Francis Hamtramck Claiborne, *Mississippi as a Province, Territory, and State, with*

Biographical Notices of Eminent Citizens, vol. 1 (Jackson, MS: Powers and Barksdale, 1880), 417; Herbert Weaver, ed., *Correspondence of James K. Polk,* vol. 3, *1835–1836* (Nashville, TN: Vanderbilt University Press, 1975), 449–450.

19. Miles, *Jacksonian Democracy in Mississippi,* 112; *Alexandria* (VA) *Gazette,* February 2, 1836; Tallahassee *Floridian and Journal,* February 20, 1836; Foote, *Casket of Reminiscences,* 443; Olsen, *Political Culture and Secession,* 170–173; Jackson *Mississippian,* January 22, 1836; Raleigh (NC) *Standard,* February 11, 1836; *Boston* (MA) *Post,* February 6, 1836.

20. J. F. H. Claiborne, "Henry Stuart Foote," in J. F. H. Claiborne Papers, folder 27, Southern Historical Collection, Louis Round Wilson Library, University of North Carolina, Chapel Hill; Lynch, *The Bench and Bar of Mississippi,* 287.

21. C. Albert White, *A History of the Rectangular Survey System,* vol. 2 (Washington, DC: Bureau of Land Management, 1987), 94, 96; United States Senate, *Journal of the Executive Proceedings of the Senate of the United States of America from March 4, 1829 to March 3, 1837, Inclusive,* vol. 4 (Washington DC: Government Printing Office, 1837), 530; Jackson *Mississippian,* June 24, 1838.

22. M. Philip Lucas, "'To Carry Out Great Political Principles': The Antebellum Southern Political Culture," *Journal of Mississippi History* 52, no. 1 (February 1990): 7.

23. Lucas, "'To Carry Out Great Political Principles,'" 1–9; Kenneth H. Greenberg, *Masters and Statesmen: The Political Culture of American Slavery* (Baltimore, MD: Johns Hopkins University Press, 1985), 45–64; William N. Chambers and Philip C. Davis, "Party, Competition, and Mass Participation: The Case of the Democratizing Party System, 1824–1852," in *A History of American Electoral Behavior,* ed. Joel H. Silbey, Allan G. Bogue, and William H. Flanigan (Princeton, NJ: Princeton University Press, 1978), 174–179; Michael F. Holt, *Political Parties and American Political Development from the Age of Jackson to the Age of Lincoln* (Baton Rouge: Louisiana State University Press, 1992), 119.

24. Foote, *Casket of Reminiscences,* 54–55; William G. Shade, "'The Most Delicate and Exciting Topics': Martin Van Buren, Slavery, and the Election of 1836," *Journal of the Early Republic* 18, no. 3 (Autumn 1998): 476–478.

25. Foote, *Casket of Reminiscences,* 53–59.

26. Foote, *Casket of Reminiscences,* 54–60; Jackson *Mississippian,* December 30, 1836.

27. Matthew A. Byron, "Crime and Punishment: The Impotency of Dueling Laws in the United States (PhD diss., University of Arkansas, 2008), 105–108; Christopher G. Kingston and Robert E. Wright, "Deadliest of Games: The Institution of Dueling, *Southern Economic Journal* 76, no. 4 (April 2010): 1094–1099; C. A. Harwell Wells, "The End of the Affair?: Anti-Dueling Laws and Social Norms in Antebellum America," *Vanderbilt Law Review* 54 (2001): 1817–1819; Ben C. Truman, *The Field of Honor: Being a Complete and Comprehensive History of Dueling in All Countries* (New York: Fords, Howard, and Hulbert, 1884), 385; Foote, *Casket of Reminiscences,* 187–188; New Orleans (LA) *Daily Picayune,* July 21, 1895; *Natchez* (MS) *Democrat,* May 26, 1880.

28. State of Mississippi, *Laws of the State of Mississippi Embracing All Acts of a Public Nature from January Session, 1824, to January Session, 1838, Inclusive* (Jackson: State of Mississippi, 1838), 883.

29. T. J. Fox Alden and J. A. Van Hobson, *Digest of the Laws of Mississippi Comprising all the Laws of a General Nature Including the Acts of the Session of 1839* (New York: Alexander S. Gould,

1839), 933; Miles, *Jacksonian Democracy in Mississippi,* 164–165; Foote, *Casket of Reminiscences,* 271; *Journal of the American Temperance Union* 1, no. 1 (March 1839), 38.

30. Jackson *Mississippian,* January 12, 1839, May 20, 1845; *Richmond* (VA) *Inquirer,* September 25, 1840.

CHAPTER THREE

Note to epigraph: Henry S. Foote, *Casket of Reminiscences* (Washington, DC: Chronicle, 1874), 44–45.

1. Tom Chaffin, *Met His Every Goal?: James K. Polk and the Legends of Manifest Destiny* (Knoxville: University of Tennessee Press, 2014), 60; Lynn Hudson Parson, *John Quincy Adams* (Lanham, MD: Rowman and Littlefield, 2001), 111–112; Robert W. Johannsen, "The Meaning of Manifest Destiny," in *Manifest Destiny and Empire: American Antebellum Expansion,* ed. Sam W. Haynes and Christopher Morris (College Station: Texas A&M University Press, 1997); Andrew J. Torgett, *Seeds of Empire: Cotton, Slavery and the Transformation of the Texas Borderlands, 1800–1850* (Chapel Hill: University of North Carolina Press, 2015), 17–30; H. W. Brands, *Andrew Jackson, His Life and Times* (New York: Anchor, 2006), 509. Journalist John L. O'Sullivan is credited with coining the phrase *Manifest Destiny* in an article that appeared in the July–August 1845 issue of the *Democratic Review.*

2. *Natchez* (MS) *Courier,* April 29, 1836.

3. Randolph B. Campbell, *Gone to Texas: A History of the Lone Star State* (New York: Oxford University Press, 2003), 100–118; David J. Weber, *The Mexican Frontier, 1821–1846* (Albuquerque: University of New Mexico Press, 1982), 160–167.

4. James P. Shenton, *Robert John Walker: A Politician from Jackson to Lincoln* (New York: Columbia University Press, 1961), 22–40; William W. Freehling, *The Road to Disunion,* vol. 1, *Secessionists at Bay, 1776–1854* (New York: Oxford University Press, 1990), 22–25, 419.

5. Houston *Telegraph and Texas Register,* June 3, 1837; George J. Leftwich, "Robert J. Walker," in *Publications of the Mississippi Historical Society,* vol. 6 (Jackson: Mississippi Historical Society, 1902), 365–366.

6. Henry Stuart Foote, *Texas and the Texans: or, Advance of the Anglo-Americans to the South-West; Including a History of Leading Events in Mexico, from the Conquest by Hernando Cortes to the Termination of the Texan Revolution* (Philadelphia, PA: Thomas, Cowperthwait, 1841), 336; James E. Winston, "Mississippi and the Independence of Texas," *Southwestern Historical Quarterly* 21, no. 1 (July 1917), 38.

7. Foote, *Casket of Reminiscences,* 45.

8. American Historical Society, *Publications of the American Historical Association,* vol. 2, part 2, *Diplomatic Correspondence of the Republic of Texas* (Washington, DC: Government Printing Office, 1911), 187.

9. Foote, *Texas and the Texans,* 337–338.

10. Foote, *Casket of Reminiscences,* 45; Marion Jessel Parr, "Henry Stuart Foote: The Little Pacificator, An Account of His Political Career" (master's thesis, University of Texas, 1947), 38–39; *Vicksburg* (MS) *Sentinel,* April 4, 1839; Houston *Telegraph and Texas Register,* May 15, 1839.

11. Laura Lyons McLemore, *Inventing Texas: Early Historians of the Lone Star State* (College Station: Texas A&M University Press, 2004), 46; T. J. Green to M. B. Lamar, August 14, 1839, in *The Papers of Mirabeau Lamar,* vol. 3, ed. Charles Adams Gulick Jr. and Katherine Elliott (Austin, TX: Von Boeckmann-Jones Company, 1922), 66; Houston *Telegraph and Texas Register,* March 20, 1839; Foote, *Texas and the Texans,* 198.

12. McLemore, *Inventing Texas,* 46–49; Foote, *Texas and the Texans,* 23–27; Gregg Cantrell and Elizabeth Hayes Turner, *Lone Star Pasts: Memory and History in Texas* (College Station: Texas A&M University Press), 21–24.

13. Parr, "Henry Stuart Foote: The Little Pacificator," 44–45; Foote, *Texas and the Texans,* 442–459.

14. Henry S. Foote to M. B. Lamar, November 20, 1839, in *The Papers of Mirabeau Lamar,* vol. 5, ed. Harriet Smither (Austin, TX: Von Boeckmann-Jones Company, 1922), 327.

15. Henry S. Foote to M. B. Lamar, November 20, 1839, 327; Parr, "Henry Stuart Foote: The Little Pacificator," 38–40; Houston *Telegraph and Texas Register,* March 24, 1841; Ruth Hermann, *Gold and Silver Colossus: William Morris Stewart and His Southern Bride* (Sparks, NV: Dave's Printing and Publishing, 1975), 347.

16. Foote, *Casket of Reminiscences,* 46.

17. Sam Houston to "My Dear Love," December 23, 1851, in *The Personal Correspondence of Sam Houston,* vol. 3, *1848–1852,* ed. Madge Thornall Roberts (Denton: University of North Texas Press, 1999), 355; Alfred Mason Williams, *Sam Houston and the War of Independence in Texas* (New York: Houghton and Mifflin, 1893), v; Amelia W. Williams and Eugene C. Barker, eds., *The Writings of Sam Houston, 1813–1863* (Austin, TX: Jenkins Publishing Company, 1970), 395; McLemore, *Inventing Texas,* 49; Jackson *Mississippian,* April 23, 1841; New Orleans (LA) *Daily Picayune,* June 1, 1842.

18. Robert W. Merry, *A Country of Vast Designs: James K. Polk, the Mexican War, and the Conquest of the American Continent* (New York: Simon and Schuster, 2009), 67–73.

19. Foote, *Casket of Reminiscences,* 46–49.

20. John Hallum, *The Diary of an Old Lawyer: Scenes Behind the Curtain* (Nashville, TN: Southwestern Publishing House, 1895), 239; Jackson (MS) *Southern Reformer,* September 14, 1844.

CHAPTER FOUR

Note to epigraph: Jackson (MS) *Old Soldier,* August 25, 1840.

1. *Overland Monthly* 26, no. 152, second series (August 1895): 164; Dunbar Rowland, *The Official and Statistical Register of the State of Mississippi* (Madison, WI: Democrat Printing Company, 1908), 301; Jackson (MS) *Old Soldier,* August 11, 1840, August 25, 1840; Jackson (MS) *Southern Sun,* May 19, 1840.

2. Henry S. Foote, *Casket of Reminiscences* (Washington, DC: Chronicle, 1874), 194.

3. Department of the Interior, Bureau of Land Management, General Land Office Records: State of Mississippi (Washington, DC).

4. *San Francisco* (CA) *Call,* October 23, 1896, September 15, 1902; San Jose (CA) *Sunday Mercury and Herald,* February 14, 1902; United States Census, 1850, Georgetown, Washington, DC; United States Census, 1860, Sierra County, California; United States Census, 1880, San Francisco, California; United States Census, 1900, San Francisco, California; United States Census, 1870, Buchanan County, Missouri; Ruth Hermann, *Gold and Silver Colossus: William Morris Stewart and his Southern Bride* (Sparks, NV: Dave's Printing and Publishing, 1975), 359–360, 365; William Winter Foote headstone, Mountain View Cemetery, Oakland, California; Arabella Foote Wood headstone, Presbyterian Cemetery, Alexandria, Virginia. There are some slight discrepancies regarding the exact birth year of some of the Foote children. For the purposes of this book, I record those years that seem most likely, based on available evidence.

5. Springfield *Illinois State Register,* February 2, 1844.

6. Natchez (MS) *Free Trader* May 1, 1844, June 22, 1844, June 26, 1844; *Vicksburg* (MS) *Whig* June 17, 1844, Jackson (MS) *Southern Reformer,* June 22, 1844.

7. Michael F. Holt, *Political Parties and American Political Development from the Age of Jackson to the Age of Lincoln* (Baton Rouge, Louisiana State University Press, 1992), 59–64; James E. Winston, "Texas Annexation Sentiment in Mississippi, 1835–1844," *Southwestern Historical Quarterly* 23, no. 1 (July 1919), 12; William J. Cooper, *The South and the Politics of Slavery, 1828–1856* (Baton Rouge: Louisiana State University Press, 1978), 199.

8. *Pontotoc* (MS) *Southern Tribune and Spirit of the Times,* July 31, 1844; Reuben Davis, *Recollections of Mississippi and Mississippians* (New York: Houghton, Mifflin, 1889), 101.

9. *Pontotoc* (MS) *Southern Tribune and Spirit of the Times,* August 7, 1844, August 21, 1844.

10. *Port Gibson* (MS) *Herald,* July 4, 1844.

11. Stephanie McCurry, *Masters of Small Worlds: Yeomen Households, Gender Relations, and Political Culture of the South Carolina Low Country* (New York: Oxford University Press, 1995), 12–27; William L. Barney, *The Road to Secession* (New York: Praeger Publishers, 1972), 105.

12. McCurry, *Masters of Small Worlds,* 12–27; Barney, *The Road to Secession,* 104–106; John C. Calhoun, "Speech on the Oregon Bill, Delivered in the Senate, June 27, 1848," in *Speeches of John C. Calhoun, Delivered in the House of Representatives and Delivered in the Senate of the United States,* ed. Richard K. Crallé (New York: D. Appleton, 1883), 505; Ben Wynne, *A Hard Trip: A History of the 15th Mississippi Infantry, C.S.A.* (Macon, GA: Mercer University Press, 2003), 21.

13. Fergus M. Bordewich, *America's Great Debate: Henry Clay, Stephen Douglas and the Compromise that Preserved the Union* (New York: Simon and Schuster, 2012), 229.

14. John Francis Hamtramck Claiborne, *Life and Correspondence of John A. Quitman, Major-General, U.S.A., and Governor of the State of Mississippi,* vol. 1 (New York: Harper and Brothers, 1860), 219.

15. Richmond (LA) *Compiler,* March 15, 1844; Jackson (MS) *Southern Reformer,* April 6, 1844; Merritt M. Robinson, ed., *Reports of Cases Argued and Determined in the Supreme Court of the State of Louisiana,* vol. 9, *From 1 September 1844 to 28 February 1845* (New Orleans: Samuel M. Stewart,

1845), 104–109; Jefferson Davis to Varina Howell, March 15, 1844, in *Jefferson Davis: Private Letters, 1823–1889*, ed. Hudson Strode (New York: Da Capo, 1966), 20–21. Another version of the story, possibly promoted by Bradford's family, claimed that Bradford was shot from ambush. However, contemporary accounts seem to indicate that the two men met in the street in what amounted to some type of duel.

16. Richmond (LA) *Compiler*, May 24, 1844; Jackson (MS) *Southern Reformer*, May 25, 1844.

17. Davis, *Recollections*, 196–197; Clement Eaton, *Jefferson Davis* (New York: The Free Press, 1977), 49.

18. James T. McIntosh, ed., *The Papers of Jefferson Davis*, vol. 2, *June 1841–July 1846* (Baton Rouge: Louisiana State University Press, 1974), 38–39, 233; Jackson *Southern* (MS) *Reformer*, December 6, 1844; Henry S. Foote, *The Bench and the Bar of the South and Southwest* (Saint Louis, MO: Soule, Thomas and Wentworth, 1876), 251–253; Robert W. Winston, *High Stakes and Hair Trigger: The Life of Jefferson Davis* (New York: Henry Holt, 1930), 37.

19. Macon (MS) *Jeffersonian*, August 8, 1844.

20. Dunbar Rowland, *Encyclopedia of Mississippi History; Comprising Sketches of Counties, Towns, Events, Institutions and Persons*, vol. 2 (Madison, WI: Selwyn A. Brant, 1907), 192–201; Davis, *Recollections*, 84; Robert Lowry and William H. McCardle, *A History of Mississippi, from the Discovery of the Great River by Hernando DeSoto, Including the Earliest Settlement Made by the French Under Iberville to the Death of Jefferson Davis* (Jackson, MS: R. H. Henry, 1891), 298; Foote, *Casket of Reminiscences*, 198; J. F. H. Claiborne, "Henry Stuart Foote," in J. F. H. Claiborne Papers, folder 27, Southern Historical Collection, Louis Round Wilson Library, University of North Carolina, Chapel Hill.

21. Foote, *Casket of Reminiscences*, 210, 340.

22. John Francis Hamtramck Claiborne, *Mississippi as a Province, Territory and State, with Biographical Notices of Eminent Citizens*, vol. 1 (Jackson, MS: Powers and Barksdale, 1880), 439; Claiborne, *Life and Correspondence of John A. Quitman*, 1:210.

23. J. A. Orr, "A Trip from Houston to Jackson, Miss. in 1845," in *Publications of the Mississippi Historical Society*, vol. 9 (Oxford: Mississippi Historical Society, 1906), 178; Henry S. Foote to John A. Quitman, August 9, 1845, in *Life and Correspondence of John A. Quitman*, 1:220–221.

24. Robert E. May, *John A. Quitman: Old South Crusader* (Baton Rouge: Louisiana State University Press, 1985), 127–129; Kosciusko (MS) *Chronicle*, January 17, 1846; Grenada (MS) *Dollar Democrat*, January 23, 1846; Jackson (MS) *Southern Reformer*, January 12, 1846.

25. Foote, *Casket of Reminiscences*, 212.

26. John I. Guion to Jefferson Davis, January 16, 1846, in *The Papers of Jefferson Davis*, 2:412; Rowland, *Encyclopedia of Mississippi History*, 2:488–489.

27. For more information on Jefferson Davis's service in the Mexican War, see Joseph E. Chance, *Jefferson Davis's Mexican War Regiment* (Jackson: University Press of Mississippi, 1991).

28. John A. Quitman to Eliza Quitman, February 20, 1847, in Quitman Family Papers, Southern Historical Collection, Louis Round Wilson Library, University of North Carolina, Chapel Hill; Eric H. Walther, *The Fire-Eaters* (Baton Rouge: Louisiana State University Press, 1992), 96.

29. *Washington*, DC, *Globe*, November 8, 1838; Washington, DC, *National Intelligencer*, August

10, 1844. For a complete list of the members of the 30th Congress as well as a list of their accommodations, see Robert Mills, *Guide to the Capitol and National Executive Offices of the United States* (Washington, DC: William Greer, 1847–1848); and William J. Cooper, *Jefferson Davis, American* (New York: Vintage, 2000), 175.

30. For information on the altercation between Foote and Davis, see Mills, *Guide to the Capitol*, 85–92; A. W. Venable to Jefferson Davis, August 8, 1874, in *Jefferson Davis, Constitutionalist: His Letters, Papers and Speeches*, vol. 7, ed. Dunbar Rowland (Jackson: Mississippi Department of Archives and History, 1923), 393–395; Jefferson Davis to Howell Hinds, September 30, 1856, in *The Papers of Jefferson Davis*, vol. 6, *1856–1860*, ed. Lynda Lasswell Crist and Mary Seaton Dix (Baton Rouge: Louisiana State University Press, 1989), 50–53; William C. Davis, *Jefferson Davis: The Man and His Honor* (Baton Rouge: Louisiana State University Press, 1991), 171–172; William Edward Dodd, *Jefferson Davis* (Philadelphia: George W. Jacobs, 1907), 124–125; Felicity Allen, *Jefferson Davis: Unconquerable Heart* (Columbia: University of Missouri Press, 1999), 163–164; and *Atlanta Constitution*, January 29, 1874. Some sources state that the altercation took place at Gadsby's Hotel in Washington. However, everyone present except Foote was living at Owner's boardinghouse at the time, and A. W. Venable's 1874 letter to Davis states that the fight took place at Owner's, which seems to indicate that the incident took place at the boardinghouse. In his 1856 letter to Howell Hinds, Davis also makes reference to his room at Owner's in the context of the fight.

31. Mills, *Guide to the Capitol*, 1–7, 82–92.

32. Thelma Jennings, *The Nashville Convention: Southern Movement for Unity, 1848–1851* (Memphis: Memphis State University Press, 1980), 5–7; Henry S. Foote to John C. Calhoun, October 28, 1849, in Clyde N. Wilson and Shirley Bright Cook, eds. *The Papers of John C. Calhoun*, vol. 27, *1849–1850* (Columbia: University of South Carolina Press, 2003), 93–94; Henry Stuart Foote, *War of the Rebellion; or, Scylla and Charybdis: Consisting of Observations upon the Causes, Course, and Consequences of the Late Civil War in the United States* (New York: Harper and Brothers, 1866), 71–76; Jefferson Davis to Charles J. Searles, September 19, 1847, in James T. McIntosh, ed., *The Papers of Jefferson Davis*, vol. 3, *July 1846–December 1848* (Baton Rouge: Louisiana State University Press, 1981), 225–226.

33. Francis P. Blair and John C. Rives, appendix to *The Congressional Globe for the First Session of the Thirtieth Congress Containing Speeches and Important State Papers*, vol. 17, *Series 1847–1848* (Washington, DC: Blair and Rives, 1848), 122.

34. Clyde N. Wilson and Shirley Bright Cook, eds., *The Papers of John C. Calhoun*, vol. 25, *1847–1848* (Columbia: University of South Carolina Press, 1999), 64.

35. *Congressional Globe*, January 19, 1847.

36. *Natchez* (MS) *Courier*, November 22, 1850; *Charleston* (SC) *Mercury*, quoted in the *Columbus* (MS) *Democrat*, February 9, 1850; Dunbar Rowland, *Political and Parliamentary Orators in Mississippi* (Harrisburg Publishing Company, 1901), 369.

37. May, *John A. Quitman: Old South Crusader*, 209–210; Foote, *Casket of Reminiscences*, 350–352.

38. Edwin Williams, ed., *The Statesman's Manual, Containing the President's Messages, Inaugural, Annual, and Special, from 1789 to 1849*, vol. IV (New York: Edward Walker, 1849), 1699; *Congressional Globe*, 30th Congress, House of Representatives, 441.

39. *Congressional Globe*, 30th Congress, First Session, Senate, 511.

40. *Congressional Globe*, 30th Congress, First Session, Senate, 511.

41. *Congressional Globe*, 30th Congress, First Session, Senate, 456.

42. *Congressional Globe*, 30th Congress, First Session, Senate, 461–465.

43. *Congressional Globe*, 30th Congress, First Session, Senate, 461–465.

44. Portsmouth *New Hampshire Gazette and Republican Union,* April 18, 1848; Brattleboro (VT) *Semi-Weekly Eagle,* April 17, 1848; Debby Applegate, *The Most Famous Man in America: The Biography of Henry Ward Beecher* (New York: Doubleday), 224–225. During the period, many American newspapers called "La Marseillaise," the French national anthem, "Marseilles Hymn," in reference to its connection with the city of Marseille.

45. *Baltimore* (MD) *Sun,* July 31, 1848; Harriet Beecher Stowe, *A Key to Uncle Tom's Cabin: Presenting the General Facts and Documents upon Which the Story Is Founded, Together with Corroborative Statements Verifying the Truth of the Work* (Boston, MA: John P. Jewett, 1853), 157–158.

46. *Congressional Globe*, 31st Congress, Second Session, Senate, 580.

47. *Baltimore* (MD) *Sun,* December 6, 1851.

48. *Congressional Globe*, 32nd Congress, Second Session, Senate, 21.

49. *Congressional Globe*, 32nd Congress, Second Session, Senate, 22; Elizabeth Fox-Genovese and Eugene D. Genovese, *The Mind of the Master Class: History and Faith in the Southern Slaveholders' World* (New York: Cambridge University Press, 2005), 57–59.

50. *Salem* (MA) *Register,* December 8, 1851; *Congressional Globe,* 32nd Congress, Second Session, Senate, 22; *Congressional Globe,* 31st Congress, First Session, Senate, 1849–1850; Timothy Mason Roberts, *Distant Revolutions: 1848 and the Challenge of American Exceptionalism* (Charlottesville: University of Virginia Press, 2009), 161–162.

51. James Woodrow Parkinson, "Senator Henry Stuart Foote of Mississippi: A Rhetorical Analysis of his Speeches on Behalf of the Union, 1849–1852" (PhD diss., Louisiana State University, 1971), 341.

52. *Cincinnati* (OH) *Gazette,* as published in the *Boston* (MA) *Daily Atlas,* January 31, 1848; Richard Davis, *Justices and Journalists: The U.S. Supreme Court in the Media Age* (New York: Cambridge University Press, 2011), 76–78.

53. *Congressional Globe*, 30th Congress, Second Session, Senate 276–279, 324–325; Davis, *Justices and Journalists,* 77.

54. Philadelphia (PA) *North American,* January 19, 1849; Washington, DC, *National Era,* January 25, 1849; *Alexandria* (VA) *Gazette,* January 22, 1849.

55. *Congressional Globe*, 30th Congress, First Session, Senate, 364–368.

56. *Congressional Globe*, 30th Congress, First Session, Senate, 656; Stanley C. Harrold Jr., "The Pearl Affair: The Washington Riot of 1848," *Records of the Columbia Historical Society* 50 (1980): 155–156.

57. Henry G. Wheeler, *History of Congress, Biographical and Political, Comprising Memoirs of Members of the Congress of the United States* (New York: Harper and Brothers, 1848), 309–311.

58. *Congressional Globe*, 30th Congress, First Session, Senate, 502.

59. *Congressional Globe*, 30th Congress, First Session, Senate, 502–506; Brattleboro (VT) *Semi-Weekly Eagle,* May 22, 1848.

60. *Milwaukee* (WI) *Sentinel and Gazette,* October 9, 1848; *Boston* (MA) *Courier,* as quoted in the Brattleboro (VT) *Semi-Weekly Eagle,* February 5, 1849; *Semi-Weekly Eagle,* April 28, 1848; Thomas Prentice Kettell, ed., *The United States Democratic Review* 22, no. 119 (May 1848), 471–472.

61. Foote, *Casket of Reminiscences,* 76.

62. James D. Lynch, *The Bench and Bar of Mississippi* (New York: E. J. Hale and Sons, 1881), 286; Grace Greenwood, *Greenwood Leaves: A Collection of Sketches and Letters by Grace Greenwood* (Boston, MA: Ticknor, Reed and Fields, 1852), 302–303; correspondent from the *Detroit* (MI) *Advertiser,* quoted in the Boston (MA) *Emancipator & Republican,* September 12, 1850.

63. *Niles' Weekly Register,* December 27, 1848; *Congressional Globe,* December 19, 1848; American and Foreign Anti-Slavery Society, *Facts for the People of the Free States* 1, no. 12 (April 1, 1858), 181.

64. Merrill D. Peterson, *The Great Triumvirate: Webster, Clay, and Calhoun* (New York: Oxford University Press, 1987), 447–448.

65. John H. Lumpkin to Howell Cobb, December 25, 1848, in *Annual Report of the American Historical Association for 1911,* vol. 2, ed. Ulrich B. Phillips (Washington, DC: American Historical Association, 1913), 138.

66. *Charleston* (SC) *Courier,* February 1, 1849; Milo Milton Quaife, ed., *The Diary of James K. Polk During His Presidency, 1845–1849,* vol. 4 (Chicago, IL: A. C. McClurg, 1910), 252–253.

67. *Baltimore* (MD) *Sun,* March 5, 1849; *Boston* (MA) *Evening Transcript,* March 5, 1849; *Harrisburg* (PA) *Telegraph,* September 4, 1890; Oliver Dyer, *Great Senators of the United States Forty Years Ago, (1848 and 1849): With Personal Recollections and Delineations of Calhoun, Benton, Clay, Webster, General Houston, Jefferson Davis, and Other Distinguished Statesmen of the Period* (New York: Robert Bonner's Sons, 1889), 139–140; Bordewich, *America's Great Debate,* 44–46.

CHAPTER FIVE

Note to epigraph: Jackson (MS) *Old Soldier,* August 25, 1840.

1. United States Congress, *Reports of Committees: 30th Congress, First Session* (Washington, DC: Government Printing Office 1850), 93.

2. *Portland* (ME) *Weekly Advertiser,* January 8, 1850; John Francis Maguire, *Father Mathew: A Biography* (London: Longman, Green, Longman, Roberts, and Green, 1863), 417–418, 484.

3. *Congressional Globe,* 31st Congress, First Session, Senate, 51–55.

4. *Congressional Globe,* 31st Congress, First Session, Senate, 51–55.

5. Lawrence M. Denton, *William Henry Seward and the Secession Crisis: The Effort to Prevent the Civil War* (Jefferson, NC: McFarland, 2009), 59; Frederic Bancroft, *The Life of William H. Seward,* vol. 2 (New York: Harper and Brothers, 1900), 81; Rachel A. Shelden, *Washington Brotherhood: Politics, Social Life and the Coming of the Civil War* (Chapel Hill: University of North Carolina Press, 2013), 34.

6. Hamilton Holman, *Prologue to Conflict: The Crisis and Compromise of 1850* (Lexington: University of Kentucky Press, 2005), 45–46; Henry Stuart Foote, *War of the Rebellion; or, Scylla and*

Charybdis: Consisting of Observations upon the Causes, Course, and Consequences of the Late Civil War in the United States (New York: Harper and Brothers, 1866), 129.

7. Holman, *Prologue to Conflict*, 50–51; Franklin Benjamin Hough, *American Constitutions,* vol. 2 (Albany, NY: Weed, Parsons, 1872), 540; and *Congressional Globe,* 31st Congress, First Session, Senate, 210–212. For a complete outline of Foote's bill, see H. S. Foote, *Speech of Hon. H. S. Foote, of Mississippi, on Establishing Governments for California, Deseret, New Mexico, and Jacinto: Delivered in Senate of the United States, January 8, 1850* (Washington, DC: Congressional Globe, 1850).

8. *Congressional Globe,* 31st Congress, First Session, Senate, 244; *Baltimore* (MD) *Sun,* January 30, 1850.

9. Foote, *War of the Rebellion,* 119.

10. Holman, *Prologue to Conflict,* 32–34.

11. *Congressional Globe,* 31st Congress, First Session, 366.

12. Cleo Hearon, "Mississippi and the Compromise of 1850," in *Publications of the Mississippi Historical Society,* vol. 14, ed. Frank L. Ridley (University: Mississippi Historical Society, 1914), 83–84; *Congressional Globe,* 31st Congress, First Session, vol. 2, 1792.

13. *Congressional Globe,* 31st Congress, First Session, 368; Albert Bushnell Hart, *American Patriots and Statesmen from Washington to Lincoln,* vol. 5 (New York: P. F. Collier and Sons, 1916), 105–106; Marion Jessel Parr, "Henry Stuart Foote: The Little Pacificator, An Account of His Political Career" (master's thesis, University of Texas, 1947), 157–163.

14. Holman, *Prologue to Conflict,* 32–34; *United States Congress, Abridgement of the Debates of Congress, 1789–1856,* vol. 16 (New York: D. Appleton, 1861), 414.

15. *Sumter* (SC) *Banner,* July 11, 1849; Henry Stuart Foote, *Casket of Reminiscences* (Washington, DC: Chronicle, 1874), 80–81.

16. *Natchez* (MS) *Courier,* March 12, 1850; Parr, "Henry Stuart Foote: The Little Pacificator," 163.

17. *Journal of the House of Representatives of the State of Mississippi, at a Regular Session Thereof Held in the City of Jackson* (Jackson, MS: Fall and Marshall, 1850), 278; "William Lewis Sharkey," biographical subject file, Mississippi Department of Archives and History, Jackson; William L. Sharkey to Henry Stuart Foote, in *Natchez* (MS) *Courier,* June 18, 1850.

18. *Congressional Globe,* 31st Congress, First Session, 461–464; Clyde N. Wilson and Shirley Bright Cook, eds., *The Papers of John C. Calhoun,* vol. 27, 1849–1850 (Columbia: University of South Carolina Press, 2003), 268.

19. Worcester *Massachusetts Spy,* March 13, 1850; *Appendix to the Congressional Globe,* 31st Congress, First Session, 591.

20. William C. Davis, *Jefferson Davis: The Man and His Honor* (Baton Rouge: Louisiana State University Press, 1991), 171–172; Fredrika Bremer, *The Homes of the New World: Impressions of America,* vol. 1 (New York: Harper and Brothers, 1853), 467–468.

21. Montgomery *Alabama Journal,* March 25, 1850; *Trenton* (NJ) *State Gazette,* March 18, 1850; *Washington* (PA) *Reporter,* March 20, 1850; *Albany* (NY) *Journal,* March 18, 1850.

22. Charles Henry Ambler, *Thomas Ritchie: A Study of Virginia Politics* (Richmond, VA: Bell Book and Stationery Company, 1913), 281; Holman, *Prologue to Conflict,* 62.

23. Parr, "Henry Stuart Foote: The Little Pacificator," 180–181; Natchez (MS) *Free Trader,* May 11, 1850.

24. William M. Meigs, *The Life of Thomas Hart Benton* (Philadelphia, PA: J. P. Lippincott, 1904), 337–338, 396–397; Fergus M. Bordewich, *America's Great Debate: Henry Clay, Stephen A. Douglas, and the Compromise that Preserved the Union* (New York: Simon and Schuster, 2012), 192–193.

25. *Congressional Globe,* 31st Congress, First Session, 762; *Cleveland* (OH) *Plain Dealer,* April 18, 1850; *Milwaukee* (WI) *Sentinel and Gazette,* April 19, 1850; *Albany* (NY) *Journal,* April 19, 1850; Cayuga (NY) *Chief,* April 23, 1850; Robert J. Scarry, *Millard Fillmore* (Jefferson, NC: McFarland, 2010), 150; Holman, *Prologue to Conflict,* 93–94; William Nisbet Chambers, *Old Bullion Benton, Senator from the West: Thomas Hart Benton, 1782–1858* (New York: Russell and Russell, 1979), 361; Mark Scroggins, *Hannibal: The Life of Lincoln's First Vice President* (Lanham, MD: University Press of America 1994), 77; *Richmond* (VA) *Enquirer,* April 23, 1850; *Vicksburg* (MS) *Whig,* May 1, 1850; Natchez (MS) *Free Trader,* April 24, 1850.

26. James Woodrow Parkerson, "Senator Henry Stuart Foote of Mississippi: A Rhetorical Analysis of his Speeches on Behalf of the Union, 1849–1852" (PhD diss., Louisiana State University, 1971), 205–207; Jackson *Mississippian,* May 31, 1850.

27. Parkerson, "Senator Henry Stuart Foote of Mississippi," 212–216; Washington, DC, *National Era,* August 8, 1850; Parr, "Henry Stuart Foote: The Little Pacificator," 218.

28. Congressional Globe, 31st Congress, First Session, 532; Parkerson, "Senator Henry Stuart Foote of Mississippi," 211–218; Parr, "Henry Stuart Foote: The Little Pacificator," 182–186.

29. William L. Sharkey to Henry Stuart Foote, in *Natchez* (MS) *Courier,* June 18, 1850. For more information on the Nashville Convention, see Thelma Jennings, *The Nashville Convention: Southern Movement for Unity, 1848–1851* (Memphis: Memphis State University Press, 1980).

30. *Congressional Globe,* 31st Congress, First Session, Senate, 990, 1504; John J. McRae, *Reply of Hon. John J. McRae, to the Speech of Senator Foote* (1851; London: Forgotten Books, 2013), 14–18.; Parr, "Henry Stuart Foote: The Little Pacificator," 194.

31. *Appendix to the Congressional Globe,* 31st Congress, First Session, 1521.

32. *Appendix to the Congressional Globe,* 31st Congress, First Session, 1492, 1644.

33. *Congressional Globe,* 31st Congress, First Session, 1830.

34. Melba Porter Hay, ed., *The Papers of Henry Clay,* vol. 10 (Lexington: University of Kentucky Press, 1991), 794, 801; Washington, DC, *National Era,* August 8, 1850; *Alexandria* (VA) *Gazette,* September 13, 1850; Portsmouth *New Hampshire Gazette and Republican Union,* September 12, 1850.

35. *South Carolina Journal,* as reported in the Natchez (MS) *Free Trader,* September 28, 1850; Jackson *Mississippian,* as reported in the *Macon* (GA) *Telegraph,* September 24, 1850; *Tallahassee* (FL) *Floridian and Journal,* September 28, 1850; *Milwaukee* (WI) *Sentinel and Gazette,* November 19, 1850; Foote, *War of the Rebellion,* 172.

36. *Mining and Scientific Press* 104, no. 1 (1901), 528; Middletown (CT) *Constitution,* October 2, 1850; *Charleston* (SC) *Courier,* October 1, 1850; *Albany* (NY) *Evening Journal,* September 30, 1850.

37. New Orleans (LA) *Daily Picayune,* November 27, 1850.

CHAPTER SIX

Note to epigraph: Natchez (MS) *Free Trader,* January 10, 1854.

1. Reuben Davis, *Recollections of Mississippi and Mississippians* (New York: Houghton, Mifflin, 1889), 317.

2. Robert E. May, *John A. Quitman: Old South Crusader* (Baton Rouge: Louisiana State University Press, 1985), 216–225; J. F. H. Claiborne, *Life and Correspondence of John A. Quitman, Major General, USA, and Governor of the State of Mississippi,* vol. 2 (New York: Harper and Brothers, 1860), 23.

3. William L. Sharkey to Henry Stuart Foote, in *Natchez* (MS) *Courier,* June 18, 1850.

4. Boston (MA) *Evening Transcript,* November 25, 1850.

5. Joseph B. Cobb, "The True Issue Between the Parties in the South: Union or Disunion," *American Whig Review* 36, no. 72 (December 1850): 587, 602.

6. Jefferson Davis to the Citizens of Lowndes County, November 22, 1850, in James T. McIntosh, ed., *The Papers of Jefferson Davis,* vol. 3, *July 1846–December 1848* (Baton Rouge: Louisiana State University Press, 1981), 138; Jefferson Davis to B. D. Nabors and Others, in Natchez (MS) *Free Trader,* November 30, 1850; Dunbar Rowland, ed., *Jefferson Davis, Constitutionalist: His Letters, Papers and Speeches,* vol. 1 (New York: J. J. Little & Ives, 1923), 599; James Byrne Ranck, *Albert Gallatin Brown, Radical Southern Nationalist* (Philadelphia, PA: Porcupine Press, 1974), 77; Jackson *Mississippian,* October 11, 1850; *Woodville* (MS) *Republican,* September 17, 1850.

7. Natchez (MS) *Free Trader,* October 16, 1850, November 5, 1850; *Albany* (NY) *Journal,* November 12, 1850.

8. Jackson *Mississippian,* November 1, 1950; John McCardell, "John A. Quitman and the Compromise of 1850," *Journal of Mississippi History* 37, no. 3 (August 1975): 248–250.

9. Cleo Hearon, "Mississippi and the Compromise of 1850," in *Publications of the Mississippi Historical Society,* vol. 14, ed. Frank L. Ridley (University: Mississippi Historical Society, 1914), 157–158.

10. Rowland, *Jefferson Davis, Constitutionalist,* 1:599; *New York Herald,* November 30, 1850; *Charleston* (SC) *Courier,* December 9, 1850; Natchez (MS) *Free Trader,* November 27, 1850; Jackson (MS) *Flag of the Union,* November 29, 1850.

11. *Richmond* (VA) *Enquirer,* November 26, 1850.

12. *Vicksburg* (MS) *Whig,* September 4, 1850; *Natchez* (MS) *Courier,* November 22, 1850.

13. Hearon, "Mississippi and the Compromise of 1850," 187.

14. New Orleans (LA) *Daily Picayune,* November 28, 1850; *Baltimore* (MD) *Sun,* December 11, 1850.

15. For Foote's entire address in Philadelphia, see Henry S. Foote, Sam Houston, and Henry W. Hilliard, *Lectures on Popular Subjects, Delivered in the Musical Fund Hall, to Aid in Rebuilding the Southwark Church* (Philadelphia, PA: T. K. Collins Jr., 1851), 9–18.

16. Hearon, "Mississippi and the Compromise of 1850," 188–195.

17. Ray F. Broussard, "Governor John A. Quitman and the Lopez Expedition of 1851–1852," *Journal of Mississippi History* 28 (May 1966): 103–120; Robert E. May, *Manifest Destiny's Under-*

world: Filibustering in Antebellum America (Chapel Hill: University of North Carolina Press, 2002), 138. For a general treatment of filibustering during the period, see Tom Chaffin, *Fatal Glory: Narciso López and the First Clandestine U.S. War Against Cuba* (Baton Rouge: Louisiana State University Press, 2002).

18. Jackson (MS) *Flag of the Union*, February 21, 1851, May 9, 1851; *Flag of the Union*, quoted in the *Columbus* (MS) *Democrat*, April 4, 1851.

19. *Natchez* (MS) *Courier*, April 7, 1851.

20. Jackson (MS) *Flag of the Union*, May 9, 1851, May 30, 1851; *Vicksburg* (MS) *Whig*, May 7, 1851; Raymond (MS) *Hinds County Gazette*, May 22, 1851.

21. Hearon, "Mississippi and the Compromise of 1850," 205; Jefferson Davis, *The Rise and Fall of the Confederate Government*, vol. 1 (New York: D. Appleton, 1881), 1920; Horatio J. Harris to Jefferson Davis, April 17, 1851, in Lynda Lasswell Crist, ed., *The Papers of Jefferson Davis*, vol. 4, *1849–1852* (Baton Rouge: Louisiana State University Press, 1983), 178–179, 181; William C. Davis, *Jefferson Davis: The Man and His Honor* (Baton Rouge: Louisiana State University Press, 1991), 212; "The Correspondence of Robert Toombs, Alexander H. Stephens, and Howell Cobb," in *Annual Report of the American Historical Association for the Year 1911*, vol. 2, ed. Ulrich B. Phillips (Washington, DC: American Historical Association, 1913), 310–311.

22. Jackson *Mississippian*, June 20, 1851; Davis, *Recollections*, 317; May, *John A. Quitman*, 261–262.

23. May, *John A. Quitman*, 262; Davis, *Recollections*, 318; *Natchez* (MS) *Courier*, July 29, 1851; *Vicksburg* (MS) *Whig*, July 30, 1851.

24. John Edmond Gonzales, "The Public Career of Henry Stuart Foote" (PhD diss., University of North Carolina, 1957), 102; Jackson *Mississippian*, September 5, 1851, September 6, 1851; Jackson (MS) *Flag of the Union*, August 5, 1851; *Woodville* (MS) *Republican*, September 16, 1851.

25. Davis, *Jefferson Davis*, 214–215.

26. Ethelbert Barksdale to Jefferson Davis, September 19, 1851, in Crist, *The Papers of Jefferson Davis*, 4:222–223.

27. Natchez (MS) *Free Trader*, October 8, 1851.

28. Davis, *Recollections*, 320; Hearon, "Mississippi and the Compromise of 1850," 215, note 14.

29. Reuben Davis to Jefferson Davis, November 1851, in Crist, *The Papers of Jefferson Davis*, 4:232–233.

30. Hearon, "Mississippi and the Compromise of 1850," 216; Jackson (MS) *Flag of the Union*, November 14, 1851.

31. New Orleans (LA) *Daily Picayune*, November 17, 1851; *Alexandria* (VA) *Gazette*, December 17, 1851; Boston (MA) *Daily Atlas*, December 19, 1851.

32. *Congressional Globe*, 32nd Congress, First Session, 5; James Ford Rhodes, *History of the United States from the Compromise of 1850 to the McKinley-Bryan Campaign of 1896*, vol. 1 (New York: Macmillan, 1920), 236–238, 243–244; John Bassett Moore, "Kossuth: Sketch of a Revolutionary. II," *Political Science Quarterly* 10, no. 2 (June 1895), 279–280; Jackson (MI) *American Citizen*, December 17, 1851.

33. *Alexandria* (VA) *Gazette,* December 29, 1851.

34. New Orleans (LA) *Daily Picayune,* December 20, 1851, January 24, 1852; Boston (MA) *Evening Transcript,* December 19, 1851; *Albany* (NY) *Journal,* December 19, 1851.

35. Dunbar Rowland, *Encyclopedia of Mississippi History; Comprising Sketches of Counties, Towns, Events, Institutions and Persons,* vol. 2 (Madison, WI: Selwyn A. Brant, 1907), 720–722; Holly Springs *Mississippi Palladium,* January 22, 1852; *Vicksburg* (MS) *Whig,* January 13, 1852; Marion Jessel Parr, "Henry Stuart Foote: The Little Pacificator, An Account of His Political Career" (master's thesis, University of Texas, 1947), 276–278.

36. Benjamin Ray Wynne, "Politics and Pragmatism: Unionism in Antebellum Mississippi, 1832 to 1860" (PhD diss., University of Mississippi, 2000), 209–212.

37. Donald M. Rawson, "Party Politics in Mississippi, 1850–1860" (PhD diss., Vanderbilt University, 1964), 103–106; John Edmond Gonzales, "Flush Times, Depression, War, and Compromise," in *A History of Mississippi,* vol. 1, ed. Richard Aubrey McLemore (Hattiesburg: University and College Press of Mississippi, 1973), 306–309; Jackson *Mississippian,* October 22, 1852; *Natchez* (MS) *Courier,* October 14, 1852.

38. Holly Springs *Mississippi Palladium,* February 12, 1852.

39. Jackson *Mississippian,* November 21, 1851; Natchez (MS) *Free Trader,* February 4, 1852.

40. William J. Cooper Jr., *Liberty and Slavery: Southern Politics to 1860* (New York: McGraw-Hill, 1983), 233–239; William W. Freehling, *The Road to Disunion,* vol. 1, *Secessionists at Bay, 1776–1854* (New York: Oxford University Press, 1990), 553–554.

41. Henry Stuart Foote, *War of the Rebellion; or, Scylla and Charybdis: Consisting of Observations upon the Causes, Course, and Consequences of the Late Civil War in the United States* (New York: Harper and Brothers, 1866), 76.

42. Gonzales, "Flush Times," 307.

43. Jackson *Mississippian,* December 15, 1854.

44. Henry S. Foote, *Casket of Reminiscences* (Washington, DC: Chronicle, 1874), 88–92; Washington, DC, *National Era,* January 5, 1854.

45. New Orleans (LA) *Daily Picayune,* March 23, 1852; Natchez (MS) *Free Trader,* March 24, 1852; *Natchez* (MS) *Courier,* March 31, 1852; Louis Kossuth and Francis William Newman, *Select Speeches of Kossuth* (New York: C. S. Francis, 1854), 287–292; Robert Lowry and William H. McCardle, *A History of Mississippi from the Discovery of the Great River by Hernando DeSoto, Including the Earliest Settlements Made by the French Under Iberville to the Death of Jefferson Davis* (Jackson, MS: R. H. Henry, 1891), 338.

46. Natchez (MS) *Free Trader,* December 29, 1852, January 12, 1853; Parr, "Henry Stuart Foote: The Little Pacificator," 285–287.

47. Natchez (MS) *Free Trader,* November 11, 1852, November 24, 1852; *Vicksburg* (MS) *Sentinel,* as reported in the New Orleans (LA) *Daily Picayune,* November 18, 1852; United States Census, 1850, Washington County, Mississippi; United States Census, 1850 Slave Schedule, Washington County, Mississippi; Marion Bragg, *Historic Names and Places of the Lower Mississippi Valley* (Vicksburg: Mississippi River Commission, 1977), 136.

48. Gayle Thornbrough, ed., *A Friendly Mission: John Candler's Letters from America, 1853–1854* (Indianapolis: Indiana Historical Society, 1951), 75–76.

49. Jackson *Mississippi State Gazette,* November 3, 1852; Parr, "Henry Stuart Foote: The Little Pacificator," 292–294.

50. *Kosciusko* (MS) *Chronicle,* July 20, 1853; *Natchez* (MS) *Courier,* June 1, 1853, August 3, 1853; Natchez (MS) *Free Trader,* August 3, 1853; *Holly Springs* (MS) *Guard,* as quoted in the Natchez (MS) *Free Trader,* July 13, 1853

51. Jackson *Mississippian,* February 6, 1852; Natchez (MS) *Free Trader,* October 25, 1853.

52. *Memphis* (TN) *Daily Appeal,* December 2, 1853; John Ezell, "Jefferson Davis Seeks Political Vindication, 1851–1857," *Journal of Mississippi History* 26, no. 4 (November 1964), 312–315.

53. *Memphis* (TN) *Daily Appeal,* December 2, 1853.

54. *Baltimore* (MD) *Sun,* January 18, 1854: Raymond (MS) *Hinds County Gazette,* January 11, 1854.

55. Henry S. Foote, *Message of the Governor of the State of Mississippi, Delivered in Jackson, January 2, 1854* (Jackson, MS: Barksdale and Jones State Printers, 1854), 1–4, 7–8, 13, 19–20, 23–24; Jackson *Mississippian,* January 27, 1854.

CHAPTER SEVEN

1. Washington, DC, *Sentinel,* January 24, 1854.

2. *Alexandria* (VA) *Gazette,* January 20, 1854; *Salem* (MA) *Register,* January 23, 1854; Washington, DC, *National Intelligencer,* January 18, 1854.

3. *Baltimore* (MD) *Sun,* January 23, 1854; *Alexandria* (VA) *Gazette,* January 24, 1854; Dennis W. Nixon, *Marine and Coastal Law: Cases and Materials* (Westport, CT: Praeger, 1994), 291.

4. *Baltimore* (MD) *Sun,* January 23, 1854; *Alexandria* (VA) *Gazette,* January 24, 1854; Felicity Allen, *Jefferson Davis: Unconquerable Heart* (Columbia: University of Missouri Press, 1999), 218; *New York Tribune,* as reported in the *Clarksville* (TX) *Standard,* February 11, 1854; Sacramento (CA) *Daily Democratic State Journal,* February 17, 1854; San Francisco (CA) *Daily Placer Times and Transcript,* February 16, 1854; San Francisco *Alta California,* March 1, 1854.

5. San Francisco (CA) *Daily Placer Times and Transcript,* February 17, 1854, February 28, 1854.

6. Arthur Quinn, *The Rivals: William Gwin, David Broderick, and the Birth of California* (Lincoln: University of Nebraska Press, 1994), 149–150; San Francisco (CA) *Daily Placer Times and Transcript,* February 27, 1854.

7. San Francisco *Alta California,* March 1, 1854; Sacramento (CA) *Daily Democratic State Journal,* March 2, 1854.

8. Robert Glass Cleland, *A History of California: The American Period* (New York: MacMillan, 1922), 334–335; William Oscar Scroggs, *Filibusters and Financiers: The Story of William Walker and His Associates* (New York: MacMillan, 1916), 53–54.

9. W. O. Scroggs, "William Walker's Designs on Cuba," *Mississippi Valley Historical Review* 1

(June 1914–March 1915): 202–204; Scroggs, *Filibusters and Financiers,* 53–55; Sacramento (CA) *Daily Democratic State Journal,* March 24, 1854; Sacramento *California Farmer and Journal of Useful Sciences,* May 18, 1854; San Francisco *Alta California,* March 1, 1854. For a treatment of the career of Guillaume Patrice Dillon, see A. P. Nasatir, "Guillaume Patrice Dillon," *California Historical Society Quarterly* 35, no. 4 (December 1956): 309–324.

10. San Francisco (CA) *Daily Placer Times and Transcript,* May 8, 1854, May 22, 1854, May 26, 1854, May 30, 1854, June 13, 1854; John D. Carter, "Henry Stuart Foote in California Politics," *Journal of Southern History* 9, no. 2 (May 1943), 226, note 5; William Morris Stewart and George Rothwell Brown, *Reminiscences of Senator William M. Stewart of Nevada* (New York: Neale, 1908), 103.

11. San Francisco *Daily Placer Times and Transcript,* July 6, 1854, July 27, 1854, December 15, 1854; Ruth Hermann, *Gold and Silver Colossus: William Morris Stewart and his Southern Bride* (Sparks, NV: Dave's Printing and Publishing, 1975), 360–370. What was the town of Clinton is now part of Oakland, California.

12. San Francisco *Alta California,* September 16, 1854; Michael F. Holt, *The Rise and Fall of the Whig Party: Jacksonian Politics and the Onset of the Civil War* (New York: Oxford University Press, 1999), 858. For a treatment of the Know-Nothing movement and the American Party in California, see Peyton Hurt, "The Rise and Fall of the 'Know Nothings' in California," *California Historical Society Quarterly* 9, no. 1 (March 1930), 16–49.

13. *Sacramento* (CA) *Union,* June 25, 1855; Carter, "Henry Stuart Foote in California Politics," 227–229.

14. San Francisco (CA) *Daily Placer Times and Transcript,* July 4, 1855, July 9, 1855.

15. Sacramento (CA) *Daily Democratic State Journal,* July 9, 1855, September 6, 1855; Carter, "Henry Stuart Foote in California Politics," 228.

16. San Francisco (CA) *Daily Placer Times and Transcript,* September 10, 1855.

17. Carter, "Henry Stuart Foote in California Politics," 228; Quinn, *The Rivals,* 172–173; Sacramento (CA) *Union,* December 21, 1855, December 22, 1855, December 24, 1855.

18. Stockton (CA) *Weekly San Joaquin Republican,* February 2, 1856; Sacramento (CA) *Daily Democratic State Journal,* January 31, 1856, February 25, 1856.

19. Hubert Howe Bancroft, *The Works of Hubert Howe Bancroft: A History of California,* vol. 6, 1848–1859 (San Francisco, CA: History Company, 1888), 697–699; Carter, "Henry Stuart Foote in California Politics," 229–230; Quinn, *The Rivals,* 173–174; Marysville (CA) *Express,* as reported in the Sacramento (CA) *Daily Democratic State Journal,* January 25, 1856.

20. San Francisco *Alta California,* August 8, 1856; Sacramento (CA) *Daily Democratic State Journal,* September 17, 1856; Stockton (CA) *Weekly San Joaquin Republican,* October 18, 1856.

21. Winfield J. Davis, "History of Political Conventions in California, 1849–1852," *Publications of the California State Library,* vol. 1 (Sacramento: California State Library, 1893), 79–80; Carter, "Henry Stuart Foote in California Politics," 234–235; San Francisco (CA) *Daily Globe,* April 3, 1857; Sacramento (CA) *Union,* April 4, 1857; San Francisco (CA) *Daily Evening Bulletin,* July 29, 1857; September 25, 1857; San Francisco (CA) *Daily Globe,* October 8, 1857.

CHAPTER EIGHT

Note to epigraph: New Orleans (LA) *Daily Picayune,* December 2, 1864.

1. Washington, DC, *National Intelligencer,* October 10, 1857; *New York Herald,* October 10, 1857; *Alexandria* (VA) *Gazette,* October 28, 1857; Henry S. Foote, *Casket of Reminiscences* (Washington, DC: Chronicle, 1874), 116–117.

2. Nancy D. Baird, "A Kentucky Physician Examines Memphis," *Tennessee Historical Quarterly* 7, no. 2 (Summer 1978): 192.

3. New Orleans (LA) *Daily Picayune,* June 12, 1859, June 23, 1859, July 31, 1859. John D. Wright, ed., *The Routledge Encyclopedia of Civil War Era Biographies* (New York: Routledge, 2013), 197; United States Census, 1860, Davidson County, Tennessee; United States Census, 1860, Slave Schedule, Davidson County, Tennessee.

4. New Orleans (LA) *Daily Picayune,* July 6, 1859; *San Francisco* (CA) *Bulletin,* December 31, 1859.

5. *Alexandria* (VA) *Gazette,* September 29, 1859; *New York Herald,* as reported in the *San Francisco* (CA) *Bulletin,* November 30, 1859.

6. *Charleston* (SC) *Mercury,* September 20, 1859; *Mobile* (AL) *Register,* November 17, 1859; *Alexandria* (VA) *Gazette,* April 12, 1860.

7. *Alexandria* (VA) *Gazette,* August 21, 1860, August 24, 1860.

8. Henry Stuart Foote, *War of the Rebellion; or, Scylla and Charybdis: Consisting of Observations upon the Causes, Course, and Consequences of the Late Civil War in the United States* (New York: Harper and Brothers, 1866), 276–290; *Richmond* (VA) *Whig,* July 17, 1860.

9. *Staunton* (VA) *Spectator,* as reported in the *Alexandria* (VA) *Gazette,* August 24, 1860; *Alexandria* (VA) *Gazette,* November 11, 1860, November 13, 1860; *Augusta* (GA) *Chronicle,* March 9, 1860; *Richmond* (VA) *Whig,* October 19, 1860; Rome (GA) *Tri-Weekly Courier,* March 17, 1860.

10. Daniel W. Crofts, *Reluctant Confederates: Upper South Unionists in the Secession Crisis* (Chapel Hill: University of North Carolina Press, 1989), 325; *New York Daily Tribune,* January 30, 1861.

11. Nashville *Tennessean,* December 2, 1860, February 5, 1861; *Richmond* (VA) *Whig,* February 5, 1861; Crofts, *Reluctant Confederates,* 325.

12. James Alex Baggett, *The Scalawags: Southern Dissenters in the Civil War and Reconstruction* (Baton Rouge: Louisiana State University Press, 2003), 43; United States War Department, *The War of the Rebellion: A Compilation of the Official Records of the Union and Confederate Armies,* series 1, vol. 52, part 2 (Washington, DC: Government Printing Office, 1898), 58.

13. *Daily Nashville* (TN) *Patriot,* June 10, 1861.

14. *Daily Nashville* (TN) *Patriot,* November 6, 1861; Nashville *Tennessean,* September 27, 1861; Henry S. Foote, *The Bench and the Bar of the South and Southwest* (Saint Louis: Soule, Thomas and Wentworth, 1876), 167.

15. John E. Gonzales, "Henry Stuart Foote: Confederate Congressman in Exile," *Civil War History* (December 1, 1965): 384; Foote, *Casket of Reminiscences,* 293.

16. Nashville *Tennessean*, May 24, 1861; *Nashville* (TN) *Union and American*, May 24, 1861.

17. *Journal of the Senate of the Second Congress of the Confederate States of America*, vol. 4 (Washington, DC: Government Printing Office, 1904), 531, 532, 536, 714, 715, 719; *San Francisco* (CA) *Call*, February 14, 1904.

18. *Journal of the Senate of the Second Congress of the Confederate States of America*, vol. 5 (Washington, DC: Government Printing Office, 1904), 11, 18.

19. *Journal of the Senate of the Second Congress of the Confederate States of America*, 5:76, 5:404; United States War Department, *The War of the Rebellion: A Compilation of the Official Records of the Union and Confederate Armies*, series 1, vol. 7 (Washington, DC: Government Printing Office, 1882), 403–405.

20. Eli N. Evans, *Judah Benjamin: The Jewish Confederate* (New York: Free Press, 1988), 149, 200–202; Robert N. Rosen, *The Jewish Confederates* (Columbia: University of South Carolina Press, 2000), 72–73; Foote, *Casket of Reminiscences*, 236–237; Foote, *War of the Rebellion*, 357; Herbert Tobias Ezekiel and Gaston Lichtenstein, *The History of the Jews in Richmond, 1769–1917* (Richmond, VA: Herbert T. Ezekiel, 1917), 167.

21. *Journal of the Senate of the Second Congress of the Confederate States of America*, 5:153–155.

22. *Journal of the Senate of the Second Congress of the Confederate States of America*, 5:154–155.

23. *Journal of the Senate of the Second Congress of the Confederate States of America*, 5:321; George M. Brooke Jr., ed., *Ironclads and Big Guns of the Confederacy: The Journal and Letters of John M. Brooke* (Columbia: University of South Carolina Press, 2002), 86; *Charlotte* (NC) *Democrat*, September 1, 1863.

24. *Journal of the Senate of the Second Congress of the Confederate States of America*, 5:321; Harold S. Wilson, *Confederate Industry: Manufacturers and Quartermasters in the Civil War* (Jackson: University of Mississippi Press, 2002), 76; David J. Eicher, *Dixie Betrayed: How the South Really Lost the Civil War* (Lincoln: University of Nebraska Press, 2003), 177.

25. Eicher, *Dixie Betrayed*, 160–161; *Richmond* (VA) *Whig*, August 26, 1863.

26. Diane Neal, *The Lion of the South: General Thomas C. Hindman* (Macon, GA: Mercer University Press, 1993), 15–17, 159–160; Foote, *Casket of Reminiscences*, 396.

27. Raleigh (NC) *Standard*, January 6, 1854; *Salisbury* (NC) *Watchman*, reported in the *Charlotte* (NC) *Democrat*, January 12, 1864; Indianapolis *Indiana Herald*, December 30, 1863; Howard Swiggett, ed., *A Rebel War Clerk's Diary at the Confederate States Capital by J. B. Jones*, vol. 2 (New York: Old Hickory Bookshop, 1935), 113.

28. *Philadelphia* (PA) *Enquirer*, January 18, 1864. For information on Gazaway B. Lamar and his son Charles Augustus Lafayette Lamar, see Edwin B. Cottington, "The Activities and Attitudes of a Confederate Business Man: Gazaway B. Lamar," *Journal of Southern History* 9 (February–November 1943): 3–36; and Jim Jordan, "Charles Augustus Lafayette Lamar and the Movement to Reopen the African Slave Trade," *Georgia Historical Quarterly* 93, no. 3 (Fall 2009), 247–290.

29. Raleigh (NC) *Daily State Journal*, January 11, 1864; *Charlotte* (NC) *Democrat*, September 27, 1864; Wilfred Buck Yearns, *The Confederate Congress* (Athens: University of Georgia Press, 1960), 15–16; Milwaukee *Semi-Weekly Wisconsin*, April 14, 1863; *Cleveland* (OH) *Plain Dealer*, April 9,

1863. An alternate version of the Foote–Dargen incident also circulated that had Dargan armed not with a Bowie knife but with an ink pen.

30. *Cincinnati* (OH) *Enquirer,* December 1, 1864; *Sacramento* (CA) *Union,* December 27, 1864; *Nashville* (TN) *Daily Union,* December 2, 1864; *Pittsburgh* (PA) *Daily Post,* December 3, 1864.

31. Raleigh (NC) *Weekly Conservative,* September 14, 1864.

32. *Nashville* (TN) *Daily Union,* December, 23, 1864; *Journal of the Senate of the Second Congress of the Confederate States of America,* vol. 7 (Washington, DC: Government Printing Office, 1904), 312–315; Gonzales, "Henry Stuart Foote: Confederate Congressman in Exile," 391–392; *Philadelphia* (PA) *Enquirer,* December 24, 1864.

33. Foote, *Casket of Reminiscences,* 155; United States War Department, *The War of the Rebellion: A Compilation of the Official Records of the Union and Confederate Armies,* series 2, vol. 8 (Washington, DC: Government Printing Office, 1899), 68–69; Roy P. Basler, ed., *The Collected Works of Abraham Lincoln,* vol. 8 (New Brunswick, NJ: Rutgers University Press, 1953), 216.

34. *Greensboro* (NC) *Patriot,* December 26, 1864; *New York Times,* January 28, 1865; *Wheeling* (WV) *Daily Intelligencer,* January 26, 1865.

35. For complete copies of both letters that Foote wrote to Seward, as well as Seward's response, see Foote, *War of the Rebellion,* 388–404.

36. *Richmond* (VA) *Dispatch,* February 11, 1865; *Wheeling* (WV) *Daily Intelligencer,* February 11, 1865.

37. *Baltimore* (MD) *Sun,* February 13, 1865; Fayetteville (NC) *Daily Telegraph,* March 1, 1865; *Cleveland* (OH) *Daily Leader,* February 13, 1865; *Wilmington* (NC) *Herald,* April 4, 1865; Foote, *War of the Rebellion,* 405–413; Gonzales, "Henry Stuart Foote: Confederate Congressman in Exile," 392.

38. United States War Department, *War of the Rebellion,* series 2, 8:471–472, 8:526; *New York Daily News,* quoted in the New Orleans (LA) *Daily Picayune,* April 4, 1865; *Cleveland* (OH) *Daily Leader,* April 8, 1865.

39. *Pomeroy* (OH) *Weekly Telegraph,* May 25, 1865; *Ottawa* (IL) *Free Trader,* May 20, 1865; *Pittsburgh* (PA) *Daily Commercial,* May 20, 1865; *New York Times,* May 22, 1865; *Detroit* (MI) *Free Press,* May 19, 1865.

40. *Nashville* (TN) *Daily Union,* August 6, 1865.

41. *Cleveland* (OH) *Daily Leader,* August 9, 1865; Butler (PA) *American Citizen,* August 9, 1865; *Charlotte* (NC) *Democrat,* August 22, 1865; Petersburg (VA) *Progress-Index,* August 8, 1865.

42. *Daily Milwaukee* (WI) *News,* May 27, 1865; *White Cloud Kansas Chief,* August 24, 1865; Salisbury (NC) *Weekly Union Banner,* August 23, 1865; Gonzales, "Henry Stuart Foote: Confederate Congressman in Exile," 395. For more information on U.S. Consul General to Canada John F. Potter, see J. G. Snell, "John F. Potter, Consul General to British North America," *Wisconsin Magazine of History* 55, no. 2 (Winter 1971–1972), 107–119.

43. Gonzales, "Henry Stuart Foote: Confederate Congressman in Exile," 395; Foote, *Casket of Reminiscences,* 245–246; Columbus *Daily Ohio Statesman,* September 8, 1865; Shreveport (LA) *South-Western,* September 27, 1865; *Pittsburgh* (PA) *Gazette,* September 8, 1865; *Indianapolis* (IN) *Star,* September 8, 1865; Raleigh (NC) *Standard,* September 11, 1865; Jackson *Mississippian,* September 16, 1865; *New York Times,* June 2, 1865.

CHAPTER NINE

Note to epigraph: Henry S. Foote, *Casket of Reminiscences* (Washington, DC: Chronicle, 1874), 463.

1. Foote, *Casket of Reminiscences*, 402; Pittsburgh (PA) *Daily Commercial*, September 17, 1865; Baltimore (MD) *Sun*, September 30, 1865; John Edmond Gonzales, "Henry Stuart Foote: A Republican Appointee in Louisiana," *Louisiana History: The Journal of the Louisiana Historical Association* 1, no. 2 (Spring 1960): 138.

2. *Reading* (PA) *Times*, September 29, 1865; *Baltimore* (MD) *Sun*, September 30, 1865; Wilmington (NC) *Daily Journal*, October 17, 1865; *Chicago* (IL) *Tribune*, October 11, 1865; *Coshocton* (OH) *Democrat*, October 3, 1865.

3. *Fort Wayne* (IN) *Daily Gazette*, October 9, 1865; Pittsburgh (PA) *Daily Commercial*, November 3, 1865. *Pulaski* (TN) *Citizen*, February 23, 1866; Henry Stuart Foote, *War of the Rebellion; or, Scylla and Charybdis: Consisting of Observations upon the Causes, Course, and Consequences of the Late Civil War in the United States* (New York: Harper and Brothers, 1866), 196, 324–325; *Cleveland* (OH) *Daily Leader*, February 19, 1866; *Detroit* (MI) *Free Press*, February 25, 1866; *New Orleans* (LA) *Crescent*, April 18, 1866; *Wilmington* (NC) *Daily Dispatch*, March 14, 1866; *Fayetteville* (TN) *Observer*, September 6, 1866.

4. Raleigh (NC) *Standard*, April 10, 1866; *Cleveland* (OH) *Daily Leader*, March 27, 1866; *Cincinnati* (OH) *Enquirer*, March 24, 1866; Washington, DC, *Evening Star*, March 23, 1866; *Louisville* (KY) *Daily Courier*, March 23, 1866.

5. Louisville (KY) *Daily Courier*, February 20, 1866; Edwardsville (IL) *Madison County Courier*, April 5, 1866; Raleigh (NC) *Weekly Progress*, June 13, 1867; Wheeling (WV) *Intelligencer*, June 29, 1867; New Orleans (LA) *Daily Picayune*, June 20, 1867.

6. *Memphis* (TN) *Daily Appeal*, Tuesday, December 15, 1868; *Nashville* (TN) *Union and American*, January 27, 1869; *Atlanta* (GA) *Constitution*, April 17, 1869.

7. *Nashville* (TN) *Union and American*, March 14, 1869.

8. *Knoxville* (TN) *Weekly Chronicle*, June 14, 1871; Memphis (TN) *Public Record*, June 6, 1871; *Memphis* (TN) *Daily Appeal*, June 15, 1871; *Charlotte* (NC) *Democrat*, June 27, 1871.

9. *Chicago* (IL) *Tribune*, July 26, 1874; Nashville *Tennessean*, July 14, 1874; Elizabeth City *North Carolinian*, September 2, 1874; Washington, DC, *Evening Star*, July 18, 1874; *Galveston* (TX) *Daily News*, August 1, 1874; New Orleans (LA) *Daily Picayune*, July 25, 1874; *Nashville* (TN) *Union and American*, December 18, 1874. For a full treatment of Foote's memoir, see John Gonzales, "Reminiscences of a Mississippian," *Journal of Mississippi History* 22 (January–October 1960): 101–108.

10. For an interesting treatment of how prominent figures of Foote's era thought of biography and memoir, see Scott E. Casper, *Constructing American Lives: Biography and Culture in Nineteenth-Century America* (Chapel Hill: University of North Carolina Press, 1999).

11. Minneapolis (MN) *Star Tribune*, January 28, 1874; Chicago (IL) *Tribune*, January 28, 1874; Harrisburg (PA) *Telegraph*, January 27, 1874; *New York Times*, January 27, 1874, January 29, 1874.

12. *Boston* (MA) *Post*, June 7, 1876; Washington, DC, *Evening Star*, August 10, 1876; Henry S.

Foote, *The Bench and the Bar of the South and Southwest* (Saint Louis, MO: Soule, Thomas and Wentworth, 1876), 5.

13. Nashville *Tennessean,* March 19, 1875, July 27, 1876, November 3, 1876; Gonzales, "Henry Stuart Foote: A Republican Appointee in Louisiana," 138.

14. Cleveland (TN) *Weekly Herald,* September 15, 1876, September 22, 1876; Nashville *Tennessean,* August 25, 1876, October 6, 1876; Memphis (TN) *Public Ledger,* October 5, 1876; *Milan* (TN) *Exchange,* October 5, 1876; Gonzales, "Henry Stuart Foote: A Republican Appointee in Louisiana," 139–140.

15. *Morristown* (TN) *Gazette,* September 13, 1876; Columbia (TN) *Herald and Mail,* September 1, 1876; *Bolivar* (TN) *Bulletin,* August 31, 1976.

16. Washington, DC, *National Republican,* January 2, 1877, February 25, 1877; *Memphis* (TN) *Daily Appeal,* October 10, 1877; Nashville *Tennessean,* September 13, 1877, September 20, 1877, December 18, 1878. In the presidential election of 1876, Tilden received 133,177 votes in Tennessee and Hayes received 89,566. Support for Hayes was strongest in the eastern part of the state.

17. Gonzales, "Reminiscences of a Mississippian," 108–109.

18. Memphis (TN) *Public Ledger,* October 20, 1876.

19. Washington, DC, *Evening Star,* December 3, 1878; *New Orleans* (LA) *Daily Democrat,* December 4, 1878, November 29, 1879; New Orleans (LA) *Daily Picayune,* December 4, 1878, December 6, 1878; *Colifax* (LA) *Chronicle,* January 4, 1879.

20. *New Orleans* (LA) *Daily Democrat,* January 2, 1879, March 7, 1879; Monroe (LA) *Ouachita Telegraph,* January 10, 1879; New Orleans (LA) *Daily Picayune,* January 5, 1879; Gonzales, "Henry Stuart Foote: A Republican Appointee in Louisiana," 142–144.

21. New Orleans (LA) *Daily Picayune,* February 6, 1879

22. *New Orleans* (LA) *Daily Democrat,* May 7, 1879, May 8, 1879; Jackson (MS) *Clarion Ledger* May 14, 1879; New Orleans (LA) *Daily Picayune,* May 22, 1879; Natchitoches (LA) *People's Vindicator,* June 7, 1879; *Opelousas* (LA) *Courier,* May 31, 1879.

23. Nashville *Tennessean,* June 5, 1879; *Oakland* (CA) *Tribune,* May 27, 1879; *Yazoo* (MS) *Herald,* May 27, 1879.

24. Gonzales, "Henry Stuart Foote: A Republican Appointee in Louisiana," 144–146; *Shreveport* (LA) *Times,* May 14, 1880; New Orleans (LA) *Daily Picayune,* May 15, 1880; Memphis (TN) *Public Ledger,* May 21, 1880; Nashville *Tennessean,* May 21, 1880; *Memphis* (TN) *Daily Appeal,* May 20, 1880.

25. Nashville *Tennessean,* May 21, 1880; Nashville (TN) *Republican,* May 20, 1880; Memphis (TN) *Public Ledger,* May 20, 1880; *Indianapolis* (IN) *News,* May 20 1880; *Saint Louis* (MO) *Post-Dispatch,* May 20, 1880; Jackson (MS) *Clarion,* May 26, 1880; *New York Times,* May 20, 1880; *Natchez* (MS) *Democrat,* May 26, 1880; *Philadelphia* (PA) *Times,* May 20, 1880.

26. Foote, *Casket of Reminiscences,* 463; William C. Carter, ed., *Conversations with Shelby Foote* (Jackson: University Press of Mississippi, 1989), 154.

✐✐✐✐ BIBLIOGRAPHY ✐✐✐✐

PRIMARY SOURCES

Manuscript Collections

Claiborne, J. F. H. Papers. Southern Historical Collection. Louis Round Wilson Library, University of North Carolina, Chapel Hill.

Foote, Henry Stuart. Papers, 1836, 1852. Briscoe Center for American History, University of Texas, Austin.

Governors Papers. Mississippi Department of Archives and History, Jackson.

Natchez Trace Collection. Briscoe Center for American History, University of Texas, Austin.

Quitman Family Papers. Southern Historical Collection. Louis Round Wilson Library, University of North Carolina, Chapel Hill.

Western Americana Collection. Beinecke Rare Book and Manuscript Library, Yale University.

Published Primary Sources

American and Foreign Anti-Slavery Society. *Facts for the People of the Free States* 1, no. 12 (April 1, 1858).

Anderson, Frederick, Lin Salamo, and Bernard L. Stein, eds. *Mark Twain's Notebooks and Journals.* Vol. 2, *1877–1883.* Berkeley: University of California Press, 1976.

Baber, George. "Personal Recollections of Senator H. S. Foote: The Character and Career of a Brilliant Southern Lawyer, Orator, and Statesman." *Overland Monthly,* 26, no. 152, second series (August 1895).

Baldwin, Joseph G. *Flush Times in Mississippi and Alabama: A Series of Sketches.* New York: D. Appleton, 1853.

Basler, Roy P., ed. *The Collected Works of Abraham Lincoln,* vol. 8. New Brunswick, NJ: Rutgers University Press, 1953.

Bremer, Fredrika. *The Homes of the New World: Impressions of America,* vol. 1. New York: Harper and Brothers, 1853.

Chesnut, Mary Boykin C., and Vann Woodward, eds. *Mary Chesnut's Civil War.* New Haven, CT: Yale University Press, 1993.

Claiborne, John Francis Hamtramck. *Life and Correspondence of John A. Quitman, Major-General, U.S.A., and Governor of the State of Mississippi,* vol. 1. New York: Harper and Brothers, 1860.

Cobb, Joseph B. "The True Issue Between the Parties in the South: Union or Disunion." *American Whig Review,* 36, no. 72 (December, 1850).

Crallé, Richard K., ed. *Speeches of John C. Calhoun, Delivered in the House of Representatives and Delivered in the Senate of the United States.* New York: D. Appleton, 1883.

Crist, Lynda Lasswell, ed. *The Papers of Jefferson Davis.* Vol. 4, *1849–1852.* Baton Rouge: Louisiana State University Press, 1983.

Crist, Lynda Lasswell, and Mary Seaton Dix, eds. *The Papers of Jefferson Davis.* Vol. 6, *1856–1860.* Baton Rouge: Louisiana State University Press, 1989.

Davis, Jefferson. *The Rise and Fall of the Confederate Government,* vol. 1. New York: D. Appleton, 1881.

Davis, Reuben. *Recollections of Mississippi and Mississippians.* New York: Houghton, Mifflin, 1889.

Dyer, Oliver, ed. *Great Senators of the United States Forty Years Ago, (1848 and 1849): With Personal Recollections and Delineations of Calhoun, Benton, Clay, Webster, General Houston, Jefferson Davis, and Other Distinguished Statesmen of the Period.* New York: Robert Bonner's Sons, 1889.

Foote, Henry S. *The Bench and the Bar of the South and Southwest.* Saint Louis, MO: Soule, Thomas and Wentworth, 1876.

Foote, Henry S. *Casket of Reminiscences.* Washington, DC: Chronicle, 1874.

Foote, Henry S. *Message of the Governor of the State of Mississippi, Delivered in Jackson, January 2, 1854.* Jackson, MS: Barksdale and Jones State Printers, 1854.

Foote, Henry S. *Texas and the Texans: or, Advance of the Anglo-Americans to the South-West; Including a History of Leading Events in Mexico, from the Conquest by Hernando Cortes to the Termination of the Texan Revolution.* Philadelphia, PA: Thomas, Cowperthwait, 1841.

Foote, Henry S. *War of the Rebellion; or, Scylla and Charybdis: Consisting of Observations upon the Causes, Course, and Consequences of the Late Civil War in the United States.* New York: Harper and Brothers, 1866.

Foote, Henry S., Sam Houston, and Henry W. Hilliard. *Lectures on Popular Subjects, Delivered in the Musical Fund Hall, to Aid in Rebuilding the Southwark Church.* Philadelphia, PA: T. K. Collins Jr., 1851.

Greenwood, Grace. *Greenwood Leaves: A Collection of Sketches and Letters by Grace Greenwood.* Boston, MA: Ticknor, Reed and Fields, 1852.

Gulick, Charles Adams, Jr., and Katherine Elliott, eds. *The Papers of Mirabeau Lamar,* vol. 3. Austin, TX: Von Boeckmann-Jones, 1922.

Hallum, John. *The Diary of an Old Lawyer: Scenes Behind the Curtain.* Nashville, TN: Southwestern Publishing House, 1895.

Hay, Melba Porter, ed. *The Papers of Henry Clay,* vol. 10. Lexington: University of Kentucky Press, 1991.

Howard, Volney E. *Cases Argued and Decided in the High Court of Errors and Appeals of the State of Mississippi,* vol. 1. Philadelphia, PA: T. K. and P. G. Collins, 1839.

Kettell, Thomas Prentice, ed. *The United States Democratic Review* 22, no. 119 (May 1848).

Kossuth, Louis, and Francis William Newman. *Select Speeches of Kossuth.* New York: C. S. Francis, 1854.

McIntosh, James T., ed. *The Papers of Jefferson Davis.* Vol. 2, *June 1841–July 1846.* Baton Rouge: Louisiana State University Press, 1974.

McIntosh, James T., ed. *The Papers of Jefferson Davis.* Vol. 3, *July 1846–December 1848.* Baton Rouge: Louisiana State University Press, 1981.

McRae, John J. *Reply of Hon. John J. McRae, to the Speech of Senator Foote.* 1851. London: Forgotten Books, 2013.

Mills, Robert. *Guide to the Capitol and National Executive Offices of the United States.* Washington, DC: William Greer, 1848.

Orr, J. A. "A Trip from Houston to Jackson, Miss. in 1845." In *Publications of the Mississippi Historical Society,* vol. 9 (Oxford: Mississippi Historical Society, 1906).

Prentiss, Lewis, ed. *A Memoir of S. S. Prentiss,* vol. 1. New York: Charles Scribner's Sons, 1899.

Quaife, Milo Milton, ed. *The Diary of James K. Polk During His Presidency, 1845–1849,* vol. 4. Chicago, IL: A. C. McClurg, 1910.

Roberts, Madge Thornall, ed. *The Personal Correspondence of Sam Houston.* Vol. 3, *1848–1852.* Denton: University of North Texas Press, 1999.

Robinson, Merritt M., ed. *Reports of Cases Argued and Determined in the Supreme Court of the State of Louisiana.* Vol. 9, *From 1 September 1844 to 28 February 1845.* New Orleans, LA: Samuel M. Stewart, 1845.

Rowland, Dunbar. *Jefferson Davis: His Letters, Papers and Speeches.* 10 vols. Jackson: Mississippi Department of Archives and History, 1923.

Ruffin, Edmund, and William Kauffman Scarborough, eds. *The Diary of Edmund Ruf-fin: Toward Independence, October 1856–April 1861.* Baton Rouge: Louisiana State University Press, 1972.

Smither, Harriet, ed. *The Papers of Mirabeau Lamar,* vol. 5. Austin, TX: Von Boeckmann-Jones, 1922.

Sparks, W. H. *The Memories of Fifty Years: Containing Brief Biographical Notices of Dis-tinguished Americans, and Anecdotes of Remarkable Men; Interspersed With Scenes and Incidents Occurring During a Long Life of Observation Chiefly Spent in the Southwest.* Philadelphia, PA: Claxton, Remsen, and Haffelfinger, 1872.

Stewart, William Morris, and George Rothwell Brown. *Reminiscences of Senator Wil-liam M. Stewart of Nevada.* New York: Neale, 1908.

Stowe, Harriet Beecher. *A Key to Uncle Tom's Cabin: Presenting the General Facts and Documents upon Which the Story Is Founded, Together with Corroborative Statements Verifying the Truth of the Work.* Boston, MA: John P. Jewett, 1853.

Strode, Hudson, ed. *Jefferson Davis: Private Letters, 1823–1889.* New York: Da Capo, 1966.

Swiggett, Howard, ed. *A Rebel War Clerk's Diary at the Confederate States Capital by J. B. Jones,* vol. 2. New York: Old Hickory Bookshop, 1935.

Thornbrough, Gayle, ed. *A Friendly Mission: John Candler's Letters from America, 1853–1854.* Indianapolis: Indiana Historical Society, 1951.

Williams, Amelia W., and Eugene C. Barker, eds. *The Writings of Sam Houston, 1813–1863.* Austin, TX: Jenkins, 1970.

Wilson Clyde N., and Shirley Bright Cook, eds. *The Papers of John C. Calhoun.* Vol. 25, *1847–1848.* Columbia: University of South Carolina Press, 1999.

Wilson, Clyde N., and Shirley Bright Cook, eds. *The Papers of John C. Calhoun.* Vol. 27, *1849–1850.* Columbia: University of South Carolina Press, 2003.

Government Sources

Aikin, John G., ed. *A Digest of the Laws of the State of Alabama Containing All the Stat-utes of a Public and General Nature in Force at the Close of the Session of the General Assembly in 1833.* Philadelphia: Alexander Tower, 1833.

Department of the Interior, Bureau of Land Management. General Land Office Re-cords: State of Mississippi. Washington, DC.

Journal of the Senate of the Second Congress of the Confederate States of America, vol. 4. Washington, DC: Government Printing Office, 1904.

Journal of the Senate of the Second Congress of the Confederate States of America, vol. 5. Washington, DC: Government Printing Office, 1904.

Journal of the Senate of the Second Congress of the Confederate States of America, vol. 7. Washington, DC: Government Printing Office, 1904.

Mississippi House of Representatives. *Journal of the House of Representatives of the State of Mississippi, at a Regular Session Thereof Held in the City of Jackson.* Jackson, MS: Fall and Marshall, 1850.

United States Census, 1820, Franklin County, Alabama.

United States Census, 1840, Madison County, Mississippi

United States Census, 1850, Georgetown, Washington, DC.

United States Census, 1850, Slave Schedule, Washington County, Mississippi.

United States Census, 1850, Washington County, Mississippi.

United States Census, 1860, Davidson County, Tennessee.

United States Census, 1860, Sierra County, California.

United States Census, 1860, Slave Schedule, Davidson County, Tennessee.

United States Census, 1870, Buchanan County, Missouri.

United States Census, 1880, San Francisco, California.

United States Census, 1900, Alameda County, California.

United States Census, 1900, San Francisco, California.

United States Congress, Abridgement of the Debates of Congress, 1789–1856, vol. 16. New York: D. Appleton, 1861.

United States War Department. *The War of the Rebellion: A Compilation of the Official Records of the Union and Confederate Armies.* Washington, DC: Government Printing Office, 1880–1902.

United States Congress. *Congressional Globe,* 30th Congress.

United States Congress. *Congressional Globe,* 31st Congress.

United States Congress. *Congressional Globe,* 32nd Congress.

Newspapers

Albany (NY) *Journal.*

Alexandria (VA) *Gazette.*

Atlanta (GA) *Constitution.*

Baltimore (MD) *Sun.*

Bolivar (TN) *Bulletin.*

Boston (MA) *Courier.*

Boston (MA) *Daily Atlas.*

Boston (MA) *Emancipator & Republican.*

Boston (MA) *Evening Transcript.*

Boston (MA) *The Liberator.*
Boston *Massachusetts Spy.*
Boston (MA) *Post.*
Brattleboro (VT) *Semi-Weekly Eagle.*
Butler (PA) *American Citizen.*
Cayuga (NY) *Chief.*
Charleston (SC) *Courier.*
Charleston (SC) *Mercury.*
Charlotte (NC) *Democrat.*
Chicago (IL) *Tribune.*
Cincinnati (OH) *Enquirer.*
Cincinnati (OH) *Gazette.*
Clarksville (TX) *Standard.*
Cleveland (OH) *Daily Leader.*
Cleveland (OH) *Plain Dealer.*
Coshocton (OH) *Democrat.*
Colifax (LA) *Chronicle.*
Columbia (TN) *Herald and Mail.*
Columbus (MS) *Democrat.*
Columbus *Daily Ohio Statesman.*
Concord *New Hampshire Patriot and State Gazette.*
Daily Milwaukee (WI) *News.*
Daily Nashville (TN) *Patriot*
Detroit (MI) *Advertiser.*
Edwardsville (IL) *Madison County Courier.*
Elizabeth City *North Carolinian.*
Fayetteville (NC) *Daily Telegraph.*
Fayetteville (TN) *Observer.*
Fort Wayne (IN) *Daily Gazette.*
Galveston (TX) *Daily News.*
Grenada (MS) *Dollar Democrat.*
Greensboro (NC) *Patriot.*
Harrisburg (PA) *Telegraph.*
Holly Springs (MS) *Guard.*
Holly Springs *Mississippi Palladium.*
Houston *Telegraph and Texas Register.*
Indianapolis *Indiana Herald.*

Indianapolis (IN) *News.*

Indianapolis (IN) *Star.*

Jackson (MI) *American Citizen.*

Jackson (MS) *Clarion Ledger.*

Jackson (MS) *Flag of the Union.*

Jackson *Mississippi State Gazette.*

Jackson *Mississippian.*

Jackson (MS) *Old Soldier.*

Jackson (MS) *Southern Reformer.*

Jackson (MS) *Southron.*

Knoxville (TN) *Weekly Chronicle.*

Kosciusko (MS) *Chronicle.*

Louisville (KY) *Daily Courier.*

Macon (GA) *Telegraph.*

Macon (MS) *Jeffersonian.*

Marysville (CA) *Express.*

Memphis (TN) *Daily Appeal.*

Memphis (TN) *Public Ledger.*

Memphis (TN) *Public Record.*

Middletown (CT) *Constitution.*

Milan (TN) *Exchange.*

Milwaukee *Semi-Weekly Wisconsin.*

Milwaukee (WI) *Sentinel.*

Milwaukee (WI) *Sentinel and Gazette.*

Minneapolis (MN) *Star Tribune.*

Mobile (AL) *Register.*

Montgomery *Alabama Journal.*

Monroe (LA) *Ouachita Telegraph.*

Morristown (TN) *Gazette.*

Nashville (TN) *Daily Union.*

Nashville (TN) *Republican.*

Nashville *Tennessean.*

Nashville (TN) *Union and American.*

Natchitoches (LA) *People's Vindicator.*

Natchez (MS) *Courier.*

Natchez (MS) *Democrat.*

Natchez (MS) *Free Trader.*

New Orleans (LA) *Crescent.*
New Orleans (LA) *Daily Democrat.*
New Orleans (LA) *Daily Picayune.*
New York Daily Tribune.
New York Evening Express.
New York Herald.
New York Spectator.
New York Times.
Niles' Weekly Register.
Oakland (CA) *Tribune.*
Opelousas (LA) *Courier.*
Ottawa (IL) *Free Trader.*
Petersburg (VA) *Progress-Index.*
Philadelphia (PA) *Enquirer.*
Philadelphia (PA) *North American.*
Philadelphia (PA) *Times.*
Pittsburgh (PA) *Daily Commercial.*
Pittsburgh (PA) *Daily Post.*
Pittsburgh (PA) *Gazette.*
Pomeroy (OH) *Weekly Telegraph.*
Pontotoc (MS) *Southern Tribune and Spirit of the Times.*
Port Gibson (MS) *Herald.*
Portland (ME) *Weekly Advertiser.*
Portsmouth *New Hampshire Gazette and Republican Union.*
Pulaski (TN) *Citizen.*
Raleigh (NC) *Daily State Journal.*
Raleigh (NC) *Standard.*
Raleigh (NC) *Weekly Conservative.*
Raleigh (NC) *Weekly Progress.*
Raymond (MS) *Hinds County Gazette.*
Reading (PA) *Times.*
Richmond (LA) *Compiler.*
Richmond (VA) *Enquirer.*
Richmond (VA) *Whig*
Rome (GA) *Tri-Weekly Courier.*
Sacramento *California Farmer and Journal of Useful Sciences.*
Sacramento (CA) *Daily Democratic State Journal.*
Sacramento (CA) *Union.*

Saint Louis (MO) *Daily Commercial Bulletin.*
Saint Louis (MO) *Post-Dispatch.*
Salem (MA) *Register.*
Salisbury (NC) *Watchman.*
Salisbury (NC) *Weekly Union Banner.*
San Francisco *Alta California.*
San Francisco (CA) *Bulletin.*
San Francisco (CA) *Call.*
San Francisco (CA) *Daily Evening Bulletin.*
San Francisco (CA) *Daily Globe.*
San Francisco (CA) *Daily Placer Times and Transcript.*
San Jose (CA) *Sunday Mercury and Herald.*
Shreveport (LA) *South-Western.*
Shreveport (LA) *Times*
Springfield *Illinois State Register.*
Staunton (VA) *Spectator.*
Stockton (CA) *Weekly San Joaquin Republican.*
Sumter (SC) *Banner.*
Tallahassee Floridian and Journal.
Trenton (NJ) *State Gazette.*
Tuscumbia (AL) *Tuscumbian.*
Tuscumbia (AL) *Patriot.*
Vicksburg (MS) *Sentinel.*
Vicksburg (MS) *Whig.*
Washington, DC, *Evening Star.*
Washington, DC, *Globe.*
Washington, DC, *National Era.*
Washington, DC, *National Intelligencer.*
Washington (PA) *Reporter.*
Wheeling (WV) *Daily Intelligencer.*
White Cloud Kansas Chief.
Wilmington (NC) *Daily Dispatch.*
Wilmington (NC) *Daily Journal.*
Wilmington (NC) *Herald.*
Woodville (MS) *Republican.*
Worcester *Massachusetts Spy.*
Yazoo (MS) *Herald.*

SECONDARY SOURCES

Books

Aldrich, John H. *Why Parties?: The Origin and Transformation of Political Parties in America.* Chicago, IL: University of Chicago Press, 1995.

Allen, Felicity. *Jefferson Davis: Unconquerable Heart.* Columbia: University of Missouri Press, 1999.

Ambler, Charles Henry. *Thomas Ritchie: A Study of Virginia Politics.* Richmond, VA: Bell Book and Stationery Company, 1913.

American Historical Society. *Publications of the American Historical Association.* Vol. 2, part 2, *Diplomatic Correspondence of the Republic of Texas.* Washington, DC: Government Printing Office, 1911.

Applegate, Debby. *The Most Famous Man in America: The Biography of Henry Ward Beecher.* New York: Doubleday, 2006.

Apthcker, Herbert. *American Negro Slave Revolts.* 6th ed. New York: Columbia University Press, 1993.

Baggett, James Alex. *The Scalawags: Southern Dissenters in the Civil War and Reconstruction.* Baton Rouge: Louisiana State University Press, 2003.

Bancroft, Frederic. *The Life of William H. Seward,* vol. 2. New York: Harper and Brothers, 1900.

Bancroft, Hubert Howe. *The Works of Hubert Howe Bancroft: A History of California.* Vol. 6, *1848–1859.* San Francisco, CA: History Company, 1888.

Barney, William L. *The Road to Secession.* New York: Praeger, 1972.

Blau, Joseph L., ed. *Social Theories of Jacksonian Democracy: Representative Writings of the Period, 1825–1850.* Indianapolis, IN: Hackett, 1954.

Bordewich, Fergus M. *America's Great Debate: Henry Clay, Stephen Douglas, and the Compromise that Preserved the Union.* New York: Simon and Schuster, 2012.

Bragg, Marion. *Historic Names and Places of the Lower Mississippi Valley.* Vicksburg: The Mississippi River Commission, 1977.

Brands, H. W. *Andrew Jackson, His Life and Times.* New York: Anchor, 2006.

Brooke, George M., Jr., ed. *Ironclads and Big Guns of the Confederacy: The Journal and Letters of John M. Brooke.* Columbia: University of South Carolina Press, 2002.

Brown, Kathi Ann, Walter Nicklin, and John T. Toler. *250 Years in Fauquier County: A Virginia Story.* Charlottesville: University of Virginia Press, 2009.

Campbell, Randolph B. *Gone to Texas: A History of the Lone Star State.* New York: Oxford University Press, 2003.

Cantrell, Gregg, and Elizabeth Hayes Turner. *Lone Star Pasts: Memory and History in Texas.* College Station: Texas A&M University Press.

Carter, Cullen Tuller. *Methodism in the Wilderness.* Nashville, TN: Parthenon Press, 1959.

Carter, William C., ed. *Conversations with Shelby Foote.* Jackson: University Press of Mississippi, 1989.

Casper, Scott E. *Constructing American Lives: Biography and Culture in Nineteenth-Century America.* Chapel Hill: University of North Carolina Press, 1999.

Chaffin, Tom. *Fatal Glory: Narciso López and the First Clandestine U.S. War against Cuba.* Baton Rouge: Louisiana State University Press, 2002.

Chambers, William Nisbet. *Old Bullion Benton, Senator from the West: Thomas Hart Benton, 1782–1858.* New York: Russell and Russell, 1979.

Chance, Joseph E. *Jefferson Davis's Mexican War Regiment.* Jackson: University Press of Mississippi, 1991.

Chandler, Julian Alvin Carroll et al., eds. *The South in the Building of the Nation.* Richmond, VA: Southern Publication Society, 1909.

Cleland, Robert Glass. *A History of California: The American Period.* New York: Macmillan Company, 1922.

Coates, Robert M. *The Outlaw Years: The History of the Land Pirates of the Natchez Trace.* New York: Literary Guild of America, 1930.

Coleman, Kenneth. *A History of Georgia.* Athens: University of Georgia Press, 1991.

Cooper, William J. *Jefferson Davis, American.* New York: Vintage, 2000.

Cooper, William J. *Liberty and Slavery: Southern Politics to 1860.* New York: McGraw-Hill, 1983.

Cooper, William J. *The South and the Politics of Slavery, 1828–1856.* Baton Rouge: Louisiana State University Press, 1978.

Crawford, Alan Pell. *Twilight at Monticello: The Final Years of Thomas Jefferson.* New York: Random House, 2009.

Crofts, Daniel W. *Reluctant Confederates: Upper South Unionists in the Secession Crisis.* Chapel Hill: University of North Carolina Press, 1989.

Davis, Richard. *Justices and Journalists: The U.S. Supreme Court in the Media Age.* New York: Cambridge University Press, 2011.

Davis, William C. *Jefferson Davis: The Man and His Honor.* Baton Rouge: Louisiana State University Press, 1991.

Denton, Lawrence M. *William Henry Seward and the Secession Crisis: The Effort to Prevent the Civil War.* Jefferson, NC: McFarland, 2009.

Dodd, William Edward. *Jefferson Davis.* Philadelphia, PA: George W. Jacobs, 1907.

Drago, Harry Sinclair. *The Great Range Wars: Violence on the Grasslands*. Lincoln, NE: Bison Books, 1985.

Eaton, Clement. *The Freedom of Thought Struggles in the Old South*. New York: Harper and Row, 1964.

Eaton, Clement. *Jefferson Davis*. New York: The Free Press, 1977.

Eicher, David J. *Dixie Betrayed: How the South Really Lost the Civil War*. Lincoln: University of Nebraska Press, 2003.

Evans, Eli N. *Judah Benjamin: The Jewish Confederate*. New York: The Free Press, 1988.

Ezekiel, Herbert Tobias, and Gaston Lichtenstein. *The History of the Jews in Richmond, 1769–1917*. Richmond, VA: Herbert T. Ezekiel, 1917.

Foote, Abram William. *Foote Family: Comprising the Genealogy and History of Nathaniel Foote of Wethersfield, Conn. and His Descendants*. Rutland VT: Marble City Press, 1907.

Fox-Genovese, Elizabeth, and Eugene D. Genovese. *The Mind of the Master Class: History and Faith in the Southern Slaveholders' World*. New York: Cambridge University Press, 2005.

Freehling, William W. *The Road to Disunion*. Vol. I, *Secessionists at Bay, 1776–1854*. New York: Oxford University Press, 1990.

Greenberg, Kenneth S. *Nat Turner: A Slave Rebellion in History and Memory*. New York: Oxford University Press, 2003.

Grimstead, David. *American Mobbing, 1828–1861: Toward the Civil War*. New York: Oxford University Press, 1998.

Hart, Albert Bushnell. *American Patriots and Statesmen from Washington to Lincoln*, vol. 5. New York: P. F. Collier and Sons, 1916.

Haynes, Sam W., and Christopher Morris, eds. *Manifest Destiny and Empire: American Antebellum Expansion*. College Station: Texas A&M University Press, 1997.

Henry G. Wheeler. *History of Congress, Biographical and Political, Comprising Memoirs of Members of the Congress of the United States*. New York: Harper and Brothers, 1848.

Hermann, Ruth. *Gold and Silver Colossus: William Morris Stewart and his Southern Bride*. Sparks, NV: Dave's Printing and Publishing, 1975.

Holman, Hamilton. *Prologue to Conflict: The Crisis and Compromise of 1850*. Lexington: University of Kentucky Press, 2005.

Holt, Michael F. *Political Parties and American Political Development from the Age of Jackson to the Age of Lincoln*. Baton Rouge: Louisiana State University Press, 1992.

Holt, Michael F. *The Rise and Fall of the Whig Party: Jacksonian Politics and the Onset of the Civil War*. New York: Oxford University Press, 1999.

Hord, Arnold Harris. *Genealogy of the Hord Family*. Philadelphia, PA: J. R. Lippincott, 1898.

Hough, Franklin Benjamin. *American Constitutions,* vol. 2. Albany, NY: Weed, Parsons, 1872.

James, D. Clayton. *Antebellum Natchez.* Baton Rouge: Louisiana State University Press, 1968.

Jennings, Thelma. *The Nashville Convention: Southern Movement for Unity, 1848–1851.* Memphis, TN: Memphis State University Press, 1980.

Kaye, Anthony E. *Joining Places: Slave Neighborhoods in the Old South.* Chapel Hill: University of North Carolina Press, 2007.

Lee, Guy Carleton. *The World's Great Orators, Comprising the Great Orations of the World's History.* New York: G. P. Putnam and Sons, 1905.

Libby, David J. *Slavery and Frontier Mississippi, 1720–1835.* Jackson: University Press of Mississippi, 2004.

Lowry, Robert, and William H. McCardle. *A History of Mississippi from the Discovery of the Great River by Hernando DeSoto, Including the Earliest Settlements Made by the French Under Iberville to the Death of Jefferson Davis.* Jackson, MS: R. H. Henry, 1891.

Lynch, James D. *The Bench and Bar of Mississippi.* New York: E. J. Hale and Sons, 1881.

Maguire, John Francis. *Father Mathew: A Biography.* London: Longman, Green, Longman, Roberts, and Green, 1863.

May, Robert E. *John A. Quitman: Old South Crusader.* Baton Rouge: Louisiana State University Press, 1985.

May, Robert E. *Manifest Destiny's Underworld: Filibustering in Antebellum America.* Chapel Hill: University of North Carolina Press, 2002.

McCurry, Stephanie. *Masters of Small Worlds: Yeomen Households, Gender Relations, and Political Culture of the South Carolina Low Country.* New York: Oxford University Press, 1995.

McLemore, Laura Lyons. *Inventing Texas: Early Historians of the Lone Star State.* College Station: Texas A&M University Press, 2004.

McLemore, Richard A., ed. *A History of Mississippi.* 2 vols. Hattiesburg: University and College Press of Mississippi, 1973.

Meigs, William M. *The Life of Thomas Hart Benton.* Philadelphia, PA: J. P. Lippincott, 1904.

Mell, Mrs. Patrick Hues. *Revolutionary Soldiers Buried in Alabama.* Reprint no. 26. Montgomery: Alabama Historical Society, 1904.

Merry, Robert W. *A Country of Vast Designs: James K. Polk, the Mexican War, and the Conquest of the American Continent.* New York: Simon and Schuster, 2009.

Mining and Scientific Press 104, no. 1 (1912).

Mississippi Historical Society. *Publications of the Mississippi Historical Society,* vol. 8. Oxford: Mississippi Historical Society, 1904.

Morris, Christopher. *Becoming Southern: The Evolution of a Way of Life, Warren County and Vicksburg, Mississippi, 1770–1860.* New York: Oxford University Press, 1995.

Neal, Diane. *The Lion of the South: General Thomas C. Hindman.* Macon, GA: Mercer University Press, 1993.

Nixon, Dennis W. *Marine and Coastal Law: Cases and Materials.* Westport, CT: Praeger, 1994.

Overland Monthly 26, no. 144, second series (December 1894).

Owen, Thomas McAdory. *Dictionary of Alabama Biography,* vol. 4. Chicago, IL: S. J. Clarke, 1921.

Parson, Lynn Hudson. *John Quincy Adams.* Lanham, MD: Rowman and Littlefield, 2001.

Peterson, Merrill D. *The Great Triumvirate: Webster, Clay, and Calhoun.* New York: Oxford University Press, 1987.

Phillips, Ulrich B., ed. *Annual Report of the American Historical Association for 1911,* vol. 2. Washington, DC: American Historical Association, 1913.

Pickett, Stella. *Colonial Families of the Southern States of America: A History and Genealogy of Colonial Families Who Settled in the Colonies Prior to the Revolution.* New York: Tobias A. Wright, 1911.

Quinn, Arthur. *The Rivals: William Gwin, David Broderick, and the Birth of California.* Lincoln: University of Nebraska Press, 1994.

Ranck, James Byrne. *Albert Gallatin Brown, Radical Southern Nationalist.* Philadelphia, PA: Porcupine Press, 1974.

Rhodes, James Ford. *History of the United States from the Compromise of 1850 to the McKinley-Bryan Campaign of 1896,* vol. 1. New York: Macmillan, 1920.

Ridley, Frank L., ed. *Publications of the Mississippi Historical Society,* vol. 14. University: Mississippi Historical Society, 1914.

Ritchie, Donald A. *Press Gallery: Congress and the Washington Correspondents.* Cambridge, MA: Harvard University Press, 1991.

Roberts, Timothy Mason. *Distant Revolutions: 1848 and the Challenge of American Exceptionalism.* Charlottesville: University of Virginia Press, 2009.

Rodriguez, Junius P., ed. *Slavery in the United States: A Social, Political, and Historical Encyclopedia,* vol. 1. Santa Barbara, CA: ABC-CLIO, 2007.

Rosen, Robert N. *The Jewish Confederates.* Columbia: University of South Carolina Press, 2000.

Rothman, Joshua D. *Flush Times and Fever Dreams: A Story of Capitalism and Slavery in the Age of Jackson.* Athens: University of Georgia Press, 2014.

Rowland, Dunbar. *Encyclopedia of Mississippi History; Comprising Sketches of Counties, Towns, Events, Institutions and Persons.* 2 vols. Madison, WI: Selwyn A. Brant, 1907.

Rowland, Dunbar. *The Official and Statistical Register of the State of Mississippi.* Madison, WI: Democrat Printing Company, 1908.

Rowland, Dunbar. *Political and Parliamentary Orators in Mississippi.* Harrisburg Publishing Company, 1901.

Russell, Greg. "John Quincy Adams." In *The American Presidents: Critical Essays,* ed. Melvin I. Urofsky. New York: Garland, 2010.

Russell, T. Triplett, and John K. Gott. *Fauquier County in the Revolution.* Westminster, MD: Heritage Books, 1977.

Sandlin, Lee. *Wicked River: When the Mississippi Last Ran Wild.* New York: Vintage, 2010.

Sass, Julie. "Chronology of Natchez." In *Natchez Before 1830,* ed. Noel Polk. Jackson: University Press of Mississippi, 1989.

Scarry, Robert J. *Millard Fillmore.* Jefferson, NC: McFarland, 2010.

Scroggins, Mark. *Hannibal: The Life of Lincoln's First Vice President.* Lanham, MD: University Press of America 1994.

Scroggs, William Oscar. *Filibusters and Financiers: The Story of William Walker and His Associates.* New York: Macmillan Company, 1916.

Shelden, Rachel A. *Washington Brotherhood: Politics, Social Life, and the Coming of the Civil War.* Chapel Hill: University of North Carolina Press, 2013.

Shenton, James P. *Robert John Walker: A Politician from Jackson to Lincoln.* New York: Columbia University Press, 1961.

Shields, Joseph D. *Life and Times of Seargent Smith Prentiss.* Philadelphia, PA: J. P. Lippincott, 1884.

Silver, David Mayer. *Lincoln's Supreme Court.* Urbana: University of Illinois Press, 1957.

Smithwick, Noah. *The Evolution of a State, or Recollections of Old Texas Days.* Austin: University of Texas Press, 1983.

Torgett, Andrew J. *Seeds of Empire: Cotton, Slavery, and the Transformation of the Texas Borderlands, 1800–1850.* Chapel Hill: University of North Carolina Press, 2015.

Truman, Ben C. *The Field of Honor: Being a Complete and Comprehensive History of Dueling in All Countries.* New York: Fords, Howard, and Hulbert, 1884.

Tyler, Lyon Gardiner. *Encyclopedia of Virginia Biography,* vol. 2. New York: Lewis Historical Publishing, 1915.

Walther, Eric H. *The Fire-Eaters.* Baton Rouge: Louisiana State University Press, 1992.

Walton, Hanes, Donald Deskins, Jr., and Sherman Puckett. *Presidential Elections 1798–2008: County, State and National Mapping of Election Data.* Ann Arbor: University of Michigan Press, 2010.

Weber, David J. *The Mexican Frontier, 1821–1846.* Albuquerque: University of New Mexico Press, 1982.

Williams, Alfred Mason. *Sam Houston and the War of Independence in Texas.* New York: Houghton and Mifflin, 1893.

Williams, Edwin, ed. *The Statesman's Manual, Containing the President's Messages, Inaugural, Annual, and Special, from 1789 to 1849,* vol. 4. New York: Edward Walker, 1849.

Wilson, Harold S. *Confederate Industry: Manufacturers and Quartermasters in the Civil War.* Jackson: University of Mississippi Press, 2002.

Winston, Robert W. *High Stakes and Hair Trigger: The Life of Jefferson Davis.* New York: Henry Holt, 1930.

Wright, John D., ed. *The Routledge Encyclopedia of Civil War Era Biographies.* New York: Routledge, 2013.

Wyatt-Brown, Bertram. *Honor and Violence in the Old South.* New York: Oxford University Press, 1986.

Wyatt-Brown, Bertram. *Southern Honor: Ethics and Behavior in the Old South.* New York: Oxford University Press, 1982.

Wynne, Ben. *A Hard Trip: A History of the 15th Mississippi Infantry, C.S.A.* Macon, GA: Mercer University Press, 2003.

Yearns, Wilfred Buck. *The Confederate Congress.* Athens: University of Georgia Press, 1960.

Articles

Baird, Nancy D. "A Kentucky Physician Examines Memphis." *Tennessee Historical Quarterly* 7, no. 2 (Summer 1978): 190–202.

Broussard, Ray F. "Governor John A. Quitman and the Lopez Expedition of 1851–1852." *Journal of Mississippi History* 28 (May 1966): 103–120.

Carter, John D. "Henry Stuart Foote in California Politics." *The Journal of Southern History* 9 no. 2 (May 1943): 224–237.

Cottington, Edwin B. "The Activities and Attitudes of a Confederate Business Man: Gazaway B. Lamar." *Journal of Southern History* 9 (February–November 1943): 3–36.

Davis, Winfield J. "History of Political Conventions in California, 1849–1852." *Publications of the California State Library,* vol. 1. Sacramento: California State Library, 1893.

Ezell, John. "Jefferson Davis Seeks Political Vindication, 1851–1857." *The Journal of Mississippi History* 26, no. 4 (November 1964): 307–321.

Gonzales, John. "Reminiscences of a Mississippian." *Journal of Mississippi History* 22 (January–October 1960): 101–108.

Gonzales, John E. "Henry Stuart Foote: Confederate Congressman in Exile." *Civil War History* (December 1, 1965).

Gonzales, John Edmond. "Henry Stuart Foote: A Republican Appointee in Louisiana." *Louisiana History: The Journal of the Louisiana Historical Association* 1, no. 2 (Spring 1960): 137–146.

Harrold, Stanley C, Jr. "The Pearl Affair: The Washington Riot of 1848." *Records of the Columbia Historical Society* 50 (1980): 140–160.

Hurt, Peyton. "The Rise and Fall of the 'Know Nothings' in California." *California Historical Society Quarterly* 9, no. 1 (March 1930): 16–49.

Jordan, Jim. "Charles Augustus Lafayette Lamar and the Movement to Reopen the African Slave Trade." *Georgia Historical Quarterly* 93, no. 3 (Fall 2009): 247–290.

Kingston, Christopher G., and Robert E. Wright. "Deadliest of Games: The Institution of Dueling." *Southern Economic Journal* 76, no. 4 (April 2010): 1094–1106.

Leftwich, George J. "Robert J. Walker." In *Publications of the Mississippi Historical Society*, vol. 6. Jackson: Mississippi Historical Society, 1902): 359–371.

McCardell, John. "John A. Quitman and the Compromise of 1850." *Journal of Mississippi History* 37, no. 3 (August 1975): 239–266.

McKibben, Davidson Burns. "Negro Slave Insurrections in Mississippi, 1800–1865." *The Journal of Negro History* 34, no. 1 (January 1949): 73–90.

Miles, Edwin A. "The Mississippi Slave Insurrection Scare of 1835." *Journal of Negro History* 42, no. 1 (January 1957): 48–60.

Moore, John Bassett. "Kossuth: A Sketch of a Revolutionist. II." *Political Science Quarterly* 10, no. 2 (June 1895): 257–295.

Nasatir, A. P. "Guillaume Patrice Dillon." *California Historical Society Quarterly* 35, no. 4 (December 1956): 309–324.

Scroggs, W. O. "William Walker's Designs on Cuba." *The Mississippi Valley Historical Review* 1 (June 1914–March 1915): 198–211.

Snell, J. G. "John F. Potter, Consul General to British North America." *Wisconsin Magazine of History* 55, no. 2 (Winter 1971–1972): 107–119.

Wells, Harwell. "The End of the Affair?: Anti-Dueling Laws and Social Norms in Antebellum America." *Vanderbilt Law Review* 54 (2001): 1805–1847.

Winkle, John W., III. *The Mississippi State Constitution.* New York: Oxford University Press, 2014.

Winston, James E. "Mississippi and the Independence of Texas." *Southwestern Historical Quarterly* 21, no. 1 (July 1917): 36–60.

Winston, James E. "Texas Annexation Sentiment in Mississippi, 1835–1844." *Southwestern Historical Quarterly* 23, no. 1 (July 1919): 1–19.

Theses and Dissertations

Byron, Matthew A. "Crime and Punishment: The Impotency of Dueling Laws in the United States." PhD diss., University of Arkansas, 2008.

Gonzales, John Edmond. "The Public Career of Henry Stuart Foote." PhD diss., University of North Carolina, 1957.

Parkerson, James Woodrow. "Senator Henry Stuart Foote of Mississippi: A Rhetorical Analysis of his Speeches on Behalf of the Union, 1849–1852." PhD diss., Louisiana State University, 1971.

Parr, Marion Jessel. "Henry Stuart Foote: The Little Pacificator, An Account of His Political Career." Master's thesis, University of Texas, 1947.

Rawson, Donald M. "Party Politics in Mississippi, 1850–1860." PhD diss., Vanderbilt University, 1964.

Wynne, Benjamin Ray. "Politics and Pragmatism: Unionism in Antebellum Mississippi, 1832–1860." PhD diss., University of Mississippi, 2000.

Other

"Sharkey, William Lewis." Biographical subject file. Mississippi Department of Archives and History, Jackson.

◯⫘⫘⫘ **INDEX** ⫘⫘⫘◯

Battle of San Jacinto (1836), 57, 58, 60, 64
Battle of Yorktown, 41
Bayly, Thomas H., 114, 149
Bell, John, 150, 217
Bell, Robert, 29
The Bench and the Bar of the South and Southwest (HSF), 251–52
Benjamin, Judah P., 224–26
Benton, Thomas Hart: and Committee of Thirteen, 151; and John C. Fremont, 160; HSF's altercation with, 150–52, 207, 258; and Andrew Jackson, 150; photograph of, *126;* political cartoon depicting altercation between HSF and Benton, *127;* political cartoon on relationship between HSF and Benton, *128*
Berrien, John M., 140, 150
Biddle, Nicholas, 68
Bigler, John, 199
Bleeding Kansas, 212
Bocock, Thomas S., 235
Borden, Gail, 60
Borland, Solon, *125,* 148–49
Bowers, L. G., 231, 232
Bradford, Amanda, 79
Bradford, David, 79–80, 275n15
Brady, Matthew, photograph of HSF, *117*
Bragg, Braxton, 229
Breckinridge, John C., 216, 217–18
Bremer, Fredrika, 148
Bright, Jesse D., 150
Britain, 41, 67–68, 94, 238–39
Broderick, David, 199–201, 205, 209
Brooke, Walter, 183, 189
Brooks, Francis P., 9
Brooks, John Mercer, 227–28
Brown, Albert Gallatin, 83, 86, 88, 165, 192, 194
Brownlow, William G. "Parson," 242, 243
Buchanan, James, 99, 139, 210–11
Buckner, Simon Bolivar, 223
Burnett, David G., 66
Burr, Aaron, 59

Burton, Roger, 166
Butler, Andrew P., 140, 154
Byrd, Mercer, 22–23

Cabell, Edward C., 114
Caldwell, Isaac, 46
Caldwell, John, 12
Calhoun, John C.: "Address of the Southern Delegates in Congress to their Constituents," 93, 115; on annexation of Mexico, 94; and Compromise of 1850, 140, 143–44, 145, 146; Jefferson Davis's eulogy for, 147–48; death of, 147; in drawing depicting Compromise of 1850, *129;* and generational change in U.S. Congress, 92, 140, 147; and John Hale, 111; health of, 146–47; HSF's break with, 115, 144, 145, 146–47, 148, 153; HSF's former allegiance to, 208; justification of slavery, 78, 93, 114; and nullification, 40, 42, 43, 114; and secessionism, 114, 143–44; on slavery in Washington, DC, 114; speech on slavery question, 143–44, 146, 147; and states' rights, 49, 73, 93; and tariff issue, 40, 42
Calhoun, John C., Jr., 146
California: Democratic Party in, 198, 199–201, 205–6, 209, 210–11; John C. Fremont's bill on goldfields, 160; as frontier state, 204; HSF's family moving to, 203–4; HSF's law practice in, 200, 201–3, 210; HSF's political ambitions in, 3, 199, 200–201, 204, 205–10, 218; HSF's political contacts in, 193–94, 198–99, 259; HSF's speeches in, 206, 207, 210; HSF's travel to, 196–98; HSF's U.S. Senate nomination, 207–8; statehood and status of slavery, 138–39, 141–44, 151, 153, 156–58
Cameron, Joel, 22–23
Cameron, Simon, 115–16
Canada, 3, 240–42, 243
Candler, John, 190
Canton, Mississippi, 144, 165
Carneal, Thomas D., 189–90
Casket of Reminiscences (HSF): on abandon-

Crawford, William, 8–9
Crittenden, John J., 110
Cuba, 171

Dallas, George M., 68, 75
Danley, C. C., 229–30
Dargan, Edmund S., 232, 288n29
Davis, Jefferson: aloofness of, 1, 80, 156; and
   John C. Calhoun's eulogy, 147–48; and Sim-
   eon Cameron, 116; campaign for governor
   in 1851, 3, 176–77, 178, 181, 183, 195, 237, 251;
   and Compromise of 1850, 148, 156, 165, 200;
   as delegate to Democratic National Convention, 73; and Democratic Party, 73, 80–81,
   176–77, 178, 187, 201, 213; on expansion of
   slavery, 90; and Father Mathew debate, 137,
   138; and generational change in U.S. Congress, 92; and William Gwin, 200; and John
   Hale, 111; and Mexican War, 1, 88, 89, 177,
   178; photograph of, 122; and Franklin Pierce,
   186, 188, 193, 194, 216; possible campaign
   for governor, 173–74; and presidential election of 1844, 73, 75, 80–81, 88; as president
   of Confederacy, 223–26, 227, 228, 229, 230,
   233–35; promotion of coordinated action of
   slaveholding states, 165; and John Anthony
   Quitman, 89, 95, 96–97; self-control of, 2,
   80; speeches of, 249; and states' rights coalition, 169, 173; on Texas annexation, 73; on
   union of states, 139; as U.S. Representative,
   81, 88, 89; as U.S. Senator, 88, 89–90, 137, 138,
   176, 181; and John Ellis Wool, 197–98, 200.
   See also Foote–Davis relationship
Davis, Joseph, 44
Davis, Reuben, 15, 38, 76, 162, 174
Davis, Varina, 230
Dawson, William C., 104
del Valle, Luis, 202
Democratic National Convention, Baltimore
   (1844), 73, 74–75
Democratic Party: and American Party, 205,
   206, 213; Chivalry branch of, 199–200, 201;

and Compromise of 1850, 158, 159, 162, 165,
   166–67, 176, 186, 191, 193; and Jefferson Davis,
   73, 80–81, 176–77, 178, 187, 201, 213; HSF's
   involvement in, 39, 45, 47, 49–53, 54, 70–71,
   73, 75, 79, 80–81, 86, 99–100, 179, 191–92, 193,
   211, 212, 213–18, 233–34, 247–48; northern
   and southern factions of, 216–17, 218, 233–34;
   party doctrine of, 141; and politics of fear,
   77, 213; and presidential election of 1852, 184,
   185–87; pro-Union sentiment in Mississippi,
   145–46, 167, 179, 182, 183, 213; and secessionism, 213, 216–17, 253; and slavery question, 49,
   50, 77, 78; states' rights wing of, 145, 162, 166,
   167, 168–69, 170, 173–74, 176, 178, 183, 186, 187;
   and Texas annexation, 73–74, 75; and Union
   Party, 167, 168, 172–73, 177, 184–85, 188, 191, 213
Democratic States Rights Party: control of
   Mississippi House of Representatives, 192;
   control of Mississippi Senate, 181, 182, 183,
   192; convention of, 173–74; joint convention
   with Union Democrats, 184–85; opposition
   to Compromise of 1850, 167, 170, 173, 176,
   186; and secession, 168, 169, 173, 174, 177, 186;
   Union Party's arguments against, 171; weakness of, 173–76
Devens, Charles, 236
Dickinson, Daniel S., 150, 152, 159
Dillon, Guillaume Patrice, 202
Dix, John Adams, 237, 239
Dodge, Henry, 152
Donovan, Angus, 26–28, 29, 30
Douglas, Stephen: and Compromise of
   1850, 155–56, 158, 159; in drawing depicting
   Compromise of 1850, 129; and generational
   change in U.S. Congress, 92; and HSF's bill
   to organize western territories, 140; HSF's
   speeches for, 215, 216–18; and popular sover-
   eignty, 115, 215; and presidential election of
   1860, 215, 216–17; and John A. Quitman, 96
Downs, Solomon W., 114, 150
Drayton, Daniel, 102
Dred Scott v. Sanford (1857), 109

Hayes, Rutherford B., 253–55, 258, 290n16
Henry, Patrick, 14
Hereford, Francis Henry, 252–53
Hilliard, Henry W., 170
Hindman, Thomas C., Jr., 229, 245–46
Hinds, Howell, 276n30
Hinds County, Mississippi, 52–53
Holly Springs, Mississippi, 165
Houston, Sam: and Compromise of 1850, 159;
    HSF's relationship with, 63, 64, 66, 67, 116;
    and HSF's speaking tours, 170; and Mira-
    beau Lamar, 61, 63; as president of Texas, 61,
    65, 66, 68
Hungary, 102–5, 179–80
Hunt, Memucan, 59, 64
Huston, Felix, 59
Hutchinson, Anderson, 46, 65

immigration, 97–98, 204–5
Importing and Exporting Company of Geor-
    gia, 231
Ingersoll, Charles, 68
Ingersoll, Joseph, 68
Issaquena County, Mississippi, 171

Jackson, Andrew: and Bank War, 68; and
    Thomas Hart Benton, 150; and common
    man, 12, 34, 36, 42, 43; and Democratic Party
    in Mississippi, 48; and federal patronage, 48;
    and John McLean, 107; and military road
    project, 11; and Nullification Crisis, 42–43,
    48; personal popularity in Mississippi, 33–37;
    and George Poindexter, 45, 46; presidential
    election of 1824, 8–9, 12; presidential election
    of 1828, 12, 43; presidential election of 1832,
    12, 43; rivalry with John C. Calhoun, 40, 42,
    43; and Samuel Swartwout, 59; and Union
    Party in Mississippi, 171; and Martin Van
    Buren, 50; and Robert J. Walker, 43, 44,
    83; in Washington, DC, 89; and Edmund
    Winston, 16
Jackson, Mississippi, 18, 34, 47, 144, 153, 167–68

Jackson Association, 3
Jackson Democratic Association, 179
Jacksonian democracy: HSF's beliefs on, 39–
    40; in Mississippi, 33–34, 36, 37, 39, 47–48, 83;
    tenets of, 12, 33–35; and Martin Van Buren,
    51; and Robert J. Walker, 43
James, Peter, 189–90
Johnson, Andrew, 239–40, 242
Johnson, Bushrod, 224
Johnson, Henry, 92
Johnson, Herschel, 217
Johnson, J. Neely, 206–7
Johnston, Albert Sidney, 61, 225

Kentucky, 143, 214, 224, 246–47
King, William R. D., 108, 114, 140, 150
Kingman, Eliab, 7–8
Kinyon, Benjamin N., 189
Know-Nothing movement, 97–98, 99, 204–11,
    213, 214, 216–17
Kossuth, Louis, 103–6, 179–80, 188–89
Kossuth, Terézia, 188

Lafayette, Marquis de, 104, 136
Lamar, Charles Augustus "Charlie," 231–32
Lamar, Gazaway Bugg, 231
Lamar, L. Q. C., 231
Lamar, Mirabeau Buonaparte, 60–66, *121*, 231
Latin America, 201
Lea, Luke, 163
LeFleur, Louis, 18
Leigh, Watkins, 202–3
Levin, Lewis E., 98
Lincoln, Abraham: appointment of Noah
    Swayne to U.S. Supreme Court, 10; assassi-
    nation of, 239; election as president, 218, 219;
    and Fort Sumter, 219, 221; Grant's telegram
    concerning HSF's whereabouts, *131*, 236; on
    HSF's attempted escape from Confederacy,
    235–36; and HSF's Civil War history, 245;
    HSF's letters on, 233; HSF's speeches on,
    220, 222; and presidential election of 1860,

Whigs, 185, 186; and Texas annexation, 74; and Union Party, 167, 168, 171, 172–73, 175, 179, 182–83, 214; weakness of, 185; and western expansion, 94
Whiskey Rebellion, 79
White, Hugh Lawson, 49, 51
white southerners: fears of slave rebellions, 23–29; psychological impact of slavery debate on, 77–78; and race-based equality between planter elite and small farmers, 77, 78, 187; and slavery question, 93, 115, 138, 141, 162, 187
Wick, William W., 90
Williams, Alfred M., 67
Wilmot, David, 92–93

Wilmot Proviso, 92–93, 113
Winchester, George, 86
Winston, Anthony, 14
Winston, Edmund, 14, 15–16, 20, 53, 267n15
Winston, Robert W., 81
Winston family, 14–15, 16
Wise, Henry A., 135
women's suffrage, 247
Wood, Arabella Foote (daughter), 72, 204
Wood, Clement F., 204
Wood, D. H., 228
Wool, John Ellis, 197–98, 200, 201

Yandell, Lunsford Pitts, 214
Yerger, George S., 31, 70–71